Introduction to AutoCAD 2018 for Civil Engineering Applications

Nighat Yasmin
Clemson University

Publications

SDC Publications
P.O. Box 1334
Mission, KS 66222
913-262-2664
www.SDCpublications.com
Publisher: Stephen Schroff

Copyright 2017 Nighat Yasmin

All rights reserved. This document may not be copied, photocopied, reproduced, transmitted, or translated in any form or for any purpose without the express written consent of the publisher, SDC Publications.

It is a violation of United States copyright laws to make copies in any form or media of the contents of this book for commercial or educational purposes without written permission.

Examination Copies
Books received as examination copies are for review purposes only and may not be made available for student use. Resale of examination copies is prohibited.

Electronic Files
Any electronic files associated with this book are licensed to the original user only. These files may not be transferred to any other party.

Trademarks
Autodesk and AutoCAD are registered trademarks of Autodesk, Inc., in the U.S.A. and certain other countries.

The author and publisher of this book have used their best efforts in preparing this book. These efforts include the development, research and testing of the material presented. The author and publisher shall not be liable in any event for incidental or consequential damages with, or arising out of, the furnishing, performance, or use of the material.

ISBN-13: 978-1-63057-124-5
ISBN-10: 1-63057-124-5

Printed and bound in the United States of America.

Dedication

This book is dedicated to
my parents Shamim and Wajid
my Family and
my siblings and
my students.

Acknowledgment

I wish to acknowledge the patience and continuous support of my husband,

Abdul, and my children Nayel, Haaris, and Kirin during the countless hours I

spent in preparation of the manuscript.

I would greatly appreciate hearing your comments and suggestions to improve

the future editions, or any problem related to this edition.

Nighat Yasmin

yasmin@clemson.edu

Preface

A picture is worth a thousand words! This is an old saying that an engineer describes every idea with a drawing. With the advancement in computer technology and drawing software, academia is aware of the importance of teaching students computer aided design. The main purpose of this book is to provide civil engineering students with a clear presentation of the theory of engineering graphics and the use of AutoCAD 2018 (CAD software). The illustrations used in this book are created using *AutoCAD 2018* and the *Paint* software.

Several improvements are made to the current edition. The major contents of the book are based on the ribbon interface. The index is improved. In the dimensioning chapter, a detailed section is added to explain the usage of smart and quick dimensions. The chapter titled as *Suggested In-Class Activities* provides in-class activities (or ICA). For some of the initial ICAs, it explains the drawing with the help of step-by-step instruction. Also, new problems are added to the ICA's chapter. Furthermore, the contents and the drawings of every chapter are improved.

Each chapter starts with the chapter's learning objectives followed by the introduction. The bulleted objectives provide a general overview of the material covered. The contents of each chapter are organized into well-defined sections that contain detailed step-by-step instruction with graphical illustrations to carry out the AutoCAD commands.

This book has been categorized into 11 parts.

Part 1:	Chapters 1-7:	Introduction to AutoCAD2018 ribbon interface
Part 2:	Chapters 8-9:	Dimensions and tolerance using AutoCAD 2018
Part 3:	Chapters 10-11:	Use of AutoCAD in land survey data plotting
Part 4:	Chapters 12-13:	The use of AutoCAD in hydrology
Part 5:	Chapters 14-15:	Transportation engineering and AutoCAD
Part 6:	Chapters 16-18:	AutoCAD and architecture technology
Part 7:	Chapters 19:	Introduction to working drawing
Part 8:	Chapters 20:	Plotting from AutoCAD
Part 9:	Chapters 21-22:	Suggested drawing problems
Part 10:	Chapter 23:	Bibliography
Part 11:	Chapters 24:	Index

1. The 1st chapter, *Introduction to Engineering Graphics*, provides a relationship between an engineering problem and engineering graphics.

2. The 2nd chapter, *Getting started with AutoCAD 2018*, explains the basics of AutoCAD 2018. The emphasis is on the drawing area (save or delete), ribbons, tabs (add, remove, and relocate), panels (add, remove, and relocate), command line, and file operations (open, close, save, and plot). The chapter also explains the basic features of a new file and provides their default values. Furthermore, the

chapter explains how the grid and snap points in the x-y plane help a user during the drawing creation process.

3. The 3rd chapter, *Basics of 2-Dimensional Drawings*, begins with the details of the dynamic input capabilities. The major part of this chapter is devoted to the commands description for 2D objects, such as point, lines, circles, ellipse, rectangles, polygons, polylines, arcs, and appearance of object (color, line thickness, and line style). The remaining part of the chapter focuses on creating tables and multiline text objects. This chapter also explains the concept of hatching.

4. The 4th chapter, *Basics of 2-Dimensional Editing* begins with object selection and de-selection methodology. The chapter discusses object snap facility, a fast and easy access to the strategic points on a 2D object. The major emphasis of the chapter is the explanation of the commands (erase, delete duplicate objects, mirror, copy, move, rotate, offset, trim, extend, fillet, chamfer, scale, break, join, oops, and explode) to modify 2D objects. An alternate method, the use of grips points, to modify an object is discussed, too. This chapter also explains the process of creating rectangular, polar, and path arrays. Finally, the last topic of the chapter explains the use of the property sheet for object editing.

5. The 5th chapter, *Layers*, explains the art of creating, using, and modifying layers.

6. The 6th chapter, *Blocks*, explains how to create and insert different types of blocks.

7. The 7th chapter, *Layouts and Template files* explains how to manipulate layouts and how to create template files.

8. The 8th chapter, *Dimensioning Techniques*, explains the art of creating and reading a dimensioned drawing. The chapter provides the basics of dimensioning techniques, placement of dimensions, and choice of dimensions. This chapter also explains the concept of smart dimensions and quick dimensions.

9. The 9th chapter, *Tolerance*, explains the art of adding tolerance to the dimensions of a drawing. The chapter provides the basics of tolerance techniques, types of tolerance, and choice of tolerance.

10. The 10th chapter, *Land Survey*, describes parcel, deed, display angles (azimuth and bearing), open and close traverse, and different types of survey systems.

11. The 11th chapter, *Contours*, introduces the basic terminology used in contour maps. It also provides step-by-step instructions to draw and label contour maps.

12. The 12th chapter, *Drainage Basin*, explains the characteristics of a drainage basin. At the end, it provides step-by-step instructions to delineate channels and their drainage basins on a contour map.

13. The 13th chapter, *Floodplains*, explains characteristics of a channel and its floodplain. At the end, it provides step-by-step instructions to delineate a channel and its floodplain on a contour map.

14. The 14th chapter, *Road design*, explains how to draw PnP (plan and profile) and cross-sections drawing for a proposed road on a contour map.

15. The 15th chapter, *Earthwork*, explains how to use a PnP (plan and profile) drawing for the excavation and embankment delineation on the given contour map.

16. The 16th chapter, *Floor Plan*, explains how to create an architectural drawing of a residential building using simple commands such as point, polyline, circle, trim, extend, offset, and hatch. It also makes use of the blocks from the Design center.

17. The 17th chapter, *Elevation*, describes the techniques used to create basic elevation by projecting lines from a floor and roof plans. It also provides step-by-step instruction to create side elevation by projecting lines from a floor and roof plan and from front elevation using 45° miter lines. It provides step-by-step instruction to create hip and gable roofs used in the elevation, too.

18. The 18th chapter, *Site Plan*, provides step-by-step instructions to draw and label a site map of the residential building created in Chapter 16.

19. The 19th chapter, *Construction Drawings*, briefly describes a family of drawings.

20. The 20th chapter, *Plotting From AutoCAD 2018*, explains commands for paper printing and file PDF file creation.

21. The 21st chapter, *Suggested In-Class Activities*, provides a list of design problem for the in-class activities or labs.

22. The 22nd chapter, *Homework Drawings*, provides a list of design problem for the homework assignments.

23. The 23rd chapter, *Bibliography*, provides a list of the books and papers referenced in the preparation of the manuscript.

24. Finally, the 24th chapter, *Index*, provides an alphabetical list of the major topics discussed in the book.

TABLE OF CONTENTS

1. Introduction to Engineering Graphics

1.1. Learning Objectives

After completing this chapter, you will demonstrate competency in the following areas:

- What is a computer graphic?
- What is a technical drawing?
- How to enlarge or shrink a drawing?

1.2.   Engineering Problem

Extensive studies have shown that engineering problem solving techniques are complicated processes. A solution to most of the engineering problems requires a combination of organization, analysis, problem solving principles, communication skills, and graphical representations of the problem. The concept map shown in Figure 1-1 represents a simplified version of the interaction and complexities involved in the solution processes. The focus of this book is the graphical representations of the problem that can be used to find a solution.

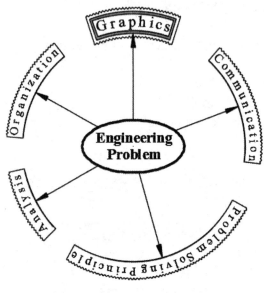

Figure 1-1

1.3.   Technical Drawing

A technical drawing process, also known as drafting, is a drawing technique that creates accurate representations (drawing) of object(s) in engineering and science. The drawing represents designs and specifications of the physical object and data relationships.

Graphical communication using technical drawings is a non-verbal method of communicating information. The technical drawing technique is a clear precise language with definite rules that must be followed. Consider a technical drawing of a door panel shown in Figure 1-2. The figure is self-explanatory. The designer has added the dimensions necessary to manufacture the door and the door can be manufactured without any confusion. In this figure, dimensions are added using dimension placement rules; and the plus and minus numbers indicate the maximum and minimum acceptable errors.

1.4.   Drawing Methods

A drawing can be made manually (that is freehand or by using mechanical tools) and/or on a computer screen using Computer Aided Design (CAD) software. For example, drawing a line between two points can be done by hand (freehand method), by using compass, protractor, rulers, etc. (mechanical method), or on a computer using a software

(CAD software). Figure 1-3a shows a freehand sketch and Figure 1-3b shows the mechanical drawing of the door panel, respectively. Figure 1-3c is the drawing of the same door created using CAD software.

Figure 1-2

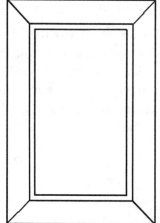

Figure 1-3a   **Figure 1-3b**   **Figure 1-3c**

The appearances of the three drawings shown in Figure 1-3 indicate that free hand sketches are good candidates for the brainstorming session. On the other hand, a CAD drawing should be delivered to the client on the completion of the project. One of the major advantages of a CAD drawing is that the editing process is fast compared to manual methods. The focus of this book is AutoCAD 2018, a Computer Aided Design software.

1.5.   Drawing Standards

The drawing standard or technical standards are set of rules that govern how technical drawings are represented. The standards for the appearance of technical drawings have been developed to ensure that they are easily interpreted across the nation and the world. Standards are periodically revised to reflect the changing needs of industry and technology. The commonly used standards are the ANSI and ISO.

- ANSI: American National Standard Institute
  - Y series of ANSI standards is for technical drawing
  - ANSI Y14.1-1980 (R1987): Drawing Sheet Size and Format
  - ANSI Y14.5M-1994: Dimensioning and Tolerancing
- ISO: International Standard Organization
  - Metric standard
  - System is called International System of Units or System Internationale, abbreviated SI

1.6.   Scale

The size of a drawing representing an object depends on the sizes of the object and the drawing paper. The ratio of the two sizes is known as the drawing's scale or simply the scale.

1.6.1.   Type of scale

The scale of a drawing can be represented as a mathematical relation (representative fraction or an equivalence relation) or a graphical representation of the drawing scale.

1.6.1.1.   Representative Fraction

The representative fraction method assumes that the unit of measurement is the same both on the drawing and the object. Let *a* equal the distance between two points on the drawing and *b* equal the corresponding distance on the actual object. The scale, representative fraction (RF), of a drawing is specified as *a:b* or *a/b*. The representative fraction can be calculated using the equation:

$$RF = a : b$$

Assume the scale of a drawing is given as a representative fraction, *a* / *b*. Let, L_d be the length on the drawing and L_o be the corresponding length on the object. The user of the drawing can find the size of the actual object as follows.

1. Measure the length of an object on the drawing (L_d): If the object is straight then ruler can be used to find its length (or distance between two points). If the object is not straight then take a string and place it on top of the drawing and then measure the length of the string.

2. Calculate the object length (L_o): Calculate the length of the object using the equation:

$$L_d/L_o = a/b \qquad \text{Implies} \qquad L_o = (b/a) * L_d$$

- Example #1: Let the scale equal 1:240 (that is $a = 1$ inch and $b = 240$ inches), and $L_d = 25$ inches then
$$L_o = (240/1) * 25 = 6000 \text{ inches}$$

- Example #2: Let the scale equal 50:1 (that is $a = 50$ inches and $b = 1$ inch), and $L_d = 250$ inches then
$$L_o = (1/50) * 250 = 5 \text{ inches}$$

1.6.1.2.   Equivalence relation

The equivalence relation method assumes that the units of measurement are different on the drawing and the object. The equivalence relation is also known as an engineer's scale. Assume, *a inches* is the distance between two points on the drawing and *b feet* is the corresponding distance on the actual object. The scale, equivalence relation (ER), of a drawing is specified as $a'' = b'$.

Assume the scale of a drawing is given as an equivalence relation. Let, L_d be the length on the drawing and L_o be the corresponding length on the object. The user of the drawing can find the size of the object as follows.

1. Measure the length on the drawing (L_d): If the object is straight then ruler can be used to find the distance between two points. If the object is not straight then take a string and place it on the top of the drawing and then measure the length of the string.
2. Calculate the object length (L_o): Calculate the length of the object using the equation:

$$a'' = b' \text{ and } L_d \text{ inches} = L_o \text{ feet}$$
$$\implies L_d/a = L_o/b$$
$$\implies L_o \text{ feet} = (b \text{ feet}) * [(L_d \text{ inches})/(a \text{ inches})]$$

- Example #1: Let the scale be 1" = 240' (that is $a = 1$ inch, $b = 240$ feet), and $L_d = 25$ inches; then
$$L_o = 240 * 25 = 6000 \text{ feet}$$

- Example #2: Let the scale is 50" = 1' (that is $a = 50$ inches, $b = 1$ foot), and $L_d = 250$ inches; then
$$L_o = (1/50) * 250 = 5 \text{ feet}$$

1.6.1.3.   Converting RF to ER

A representative fraction (RF) scale can be converted into an equivalence relation (ER) and vice versa. An RF scale can be converted into an ER using the methodology explained in the following example.

<u>Example #1</u>: The RF scale is 1:600 and the units of measurement are inches. Find the corresponding ER.

1. Convert the right side of the scale into feet. The conversion of inches of the scale into feet is shown here.

$$600 \text{ inches} = (600/12) \text{ feet} = 50 \text{ feet}$$

2. Hence, the RF scale of 1:600 can be written in ER format as 1" = 50'.

1.6.1.4.   Graphical representation

The graphical representation is known as graphical or bar scale. Generally, the graphical scales are used for large scale maps. In this representation, a ruler is drawn on the map as shown in Figure 1-4. In this representation, the bar is divided into two parts: the left and right part. In the left part (*Part 1* in Figure 1-4) the scale is divided into tenths and in the right part (*Part 2* in Figure 1-4) the scale is marked in full units. This representation assumes that the unit of measurement is the same both on the drawing and the object. For the current example, assume that the unit of measurement is inch.

Figure 1-4

<u>Example #1</u>: Assume the scale of a drawing is given as a ruler shown in Figure 1-4. Let, L_m be the distance between two points on the map and L_G be the corresponding distance on the ground. The user of the map can find the distance on the ground as follows.

1. <u>Measure the distance of an object on the drawing (L_m)</u>: If the path is straight then any straight edge object can be used to find the distance between two stations. If the path is not straight then take a string and place it on the top of the path and then measure the length of the string Assume the user of the map (Figure 1-5a) desired to measure the straight line distance between two points A and B. The user will use a piece of paper and will mark two points on the straight edge, one point at the starting station (A) and the second point at the destination station (B), Figure 1-5b. For the demonstration purpose, the marks at A and B are represented as small line segments; the segments are highlighted by displaying their grip points.
2. <u>Find the object distance of the drawing (L_G)</u>: Now place the straight edge on the graphical scale as shown in Figure 1-5c. The distance between the stations A and B is 11.3 inches.

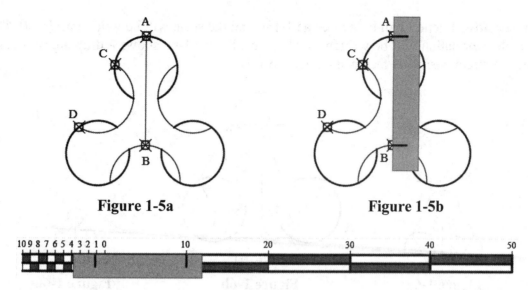

Figure 1-5a   **Figure 1-5b**

Figure 1-5c

1.7.   Scale of a Drawing

Generally, drawings are drawn to a scale, because either the object is too large or too small to draw on a drawing sheet. Hence, a drawing can be smaller or larger than the object itself.

1.7.1. Full scale

The scale of a drawing is full, if the drawing of an object is of the same size as of the object. That is, one unit on the drawing will represent one unit on the object. For example, a drawing of an average calculator (which is 6 inches long and 2.75 inches wide) can be a full scale drawing. For full scale drawings, $a = 1$ and $b = 1$. The representative fraction will be written as 1/1 and the scale will be written *1:1* or *FULL*. Figure 1-6a shows a drawing of a plate drawn at full scale.

1.7.2. Large scale

The scale of a drawing is large, if the drawing of an object is larger than the actual size of the object. That is, one unit on the drawing will represent a fraction of a unit on the object. For example, a printed circuit board of a computer chip may be 36 times the actual size; that is, 36 units on the drawing is actually 1 unit on the circuit board. For the enlarged drawing of the computer chip, $a = 36$ and $b = 1$. The representative fraction will be written as 36/1 and the scale will be written as *36:1*. The equivalence relation will be written as *3' = 1"*. Figure 1-6b shows a drawing of a plate drawn at a representative factor of 2 (Scale 2:1).

1.7.3. Small scale

The scale of a drawing is small, if the drawing of an object is smaller than the actual size of the object. That is, one unit of the object will be represented by a fraction of a unit on the drawing. Consider a drawing of a building. One unit of drawing may represent 180 units of the building. For the reduced drawing of the building, $a = 1$ and $b = 180$. The representative fraction will be written as 1/180 and the scale will be written as *1:180*. The equivalence relation will be written as *1" = 15'*. Figure 1-6c shows a drawing of a plate drawn at a representative factor of 0.5 (Scale 1:2).

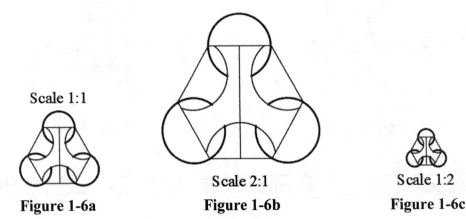

Scale 1:1

Figure 1-6a

Scale 2:1

Figure 1-6b

Scale 1:2

Figure 1-6c

1.8.   Computer Aided Graphics

A Computer Aided Design (commonly abbreviated as CAD) software provides the capability to create graphics, hence, the name computer graphics. The graphics created can be used to analyze, modify, and finalize a graphical solution for the problem being studied. The focus of this book is AutoCAD 2018.

1.8.1.   AutoCAD 2018

AutoCAD is a suite of popular CAD software products for 2- and 3-dimensional design and drafting. It is developed and sold by Autodesk.

1.8.2.   AutoCAD and drawing scale

A draftsman creating a drawing on a drawing sheet using mechanical equipment needs to decide about the drawing scale before starting the drawing. The selected scale will depend upon the size of the object and the paper, such that the drawing will fit on the drawing sheet. On the other hand, in AutoCAD, every drawing is drawn to full scale (that is 1:1). Generally, a draftsman starts a drawing in AutoCAD without thinking about the scale and chooses the scale when s/he decides to print the drawing. However, it is important to think about the plotting scale early in the drawing process because the text size, line thickness, and line style (linetype scale) will be affected by changing the drawing scale.

AutoCAD provides both the representative factors and the equivalence relation techniques. The software provides a long list of scale factors, Figure 1-7. Also, the user can make more entries in the list or can delete the existing scale factors. This dialog box is discussed in details in Chapter 7.

The user can create graphical scale using Line, Hatch, and Text commands. These commands are discussed in detail in Chapter 3.

Figure 1-7

Notes:

2.   Getting started with AutoCAD 2018

2.1.   Learning Objectives

After completing this chapter, you will demonstrate competency in the following areas:

- Features of AutoCAD 2018 interface
- The drawing area
- The ribbon
- Tabs and panels of ribbon
- Add and/or remove a tab and panel of ribbon
- The command line capabilities
- Save and/or delete a workspace
- Open a new file and/or pre-existing file
- Save a new file and/or previously saved file
- The basic features of a new file
- The grid and snap capabilities

2.2.   Introduction

Initially a general-purpose 2D drafting program, AutoCAD has evolved into a family of products that provides a platform for 2D and 3D computer aided design (CAD). Currently, it is used by civil engineers, land developers, architects, mechanical engineers, interior designers, and medical and other design professionals.

AutoCAD can be launched by either double clicking on the AutoCAD icon (Figure 2-1a) on the desktop or clicking *Start* → *All Programs* → *Autodesk* → *AutoCAD 2018*→ *AutoCAD 2018*. If the path of the software is different on your computer, then follow that path. Either of the two launching processes will result in opening a new drawing. For the first launch of the software, the AutoCAD interface appears as shown in Figure 2-1b.

Figure 2-1a

Figure 2-1b shows the *Autodesk Data collection* dialog box. Click the *OK* button and this closes the *Autodesk Data collection* dialog box, and opens the *Autodesk Licensing* dialog box as shown in Figure 2-1c.

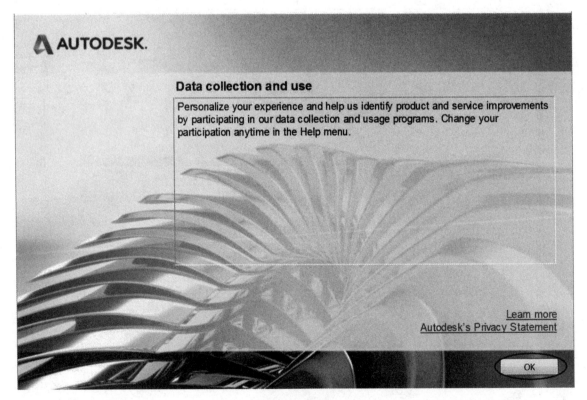

Figure 2-1b

Figure 2-1c shows the *Autodesk Licensing* dialog box. Click the *I Agree* button and this closes the *Autodesk Licensing* dialog box (based on the license status, the user may be asked to provide identification/authentication information) and opens *Autodesk AutoCAD 2018* interface as shown in Figure 2-2a.

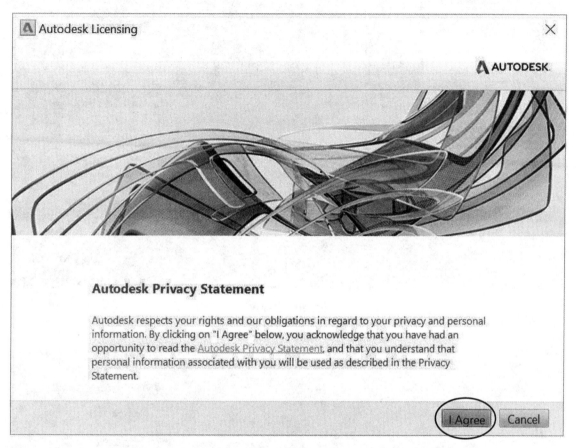

Figure 2-1c

Click the left arrow or *LEARN* label on the left side of the interface, Figure 2-2a. The screen shown in Figure 2-2b will appear. This screen provides access to video and online resources.

Click the right arrow or *CREATE* label on the right side of the interface, Figure 2-2b. The screen shown in Figure 2-2a will reappear.

Figure 2-2a

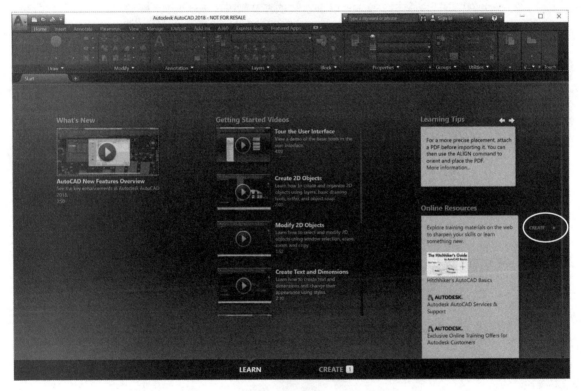

Figure 2-2b

Click the down arrow on the upper left corner of the interface (adjacent to the AutoCAD symbol) Figure 2-2a and Figure 2-2c. A dropdown list, Figure 2-2d, will appear on the screen. Click the *New* button, and the *Select Template* dialog box will open, Figure 2-2e.

Figure 2-2c

Figure 2-2d

Click the *acad* option on the *Select Template* dialog box, Figure 2-2e. Now click the *Open* button. This closes the dialog box and opens a new file, Figure 2-3a.

In AutoCAD, commands are executed by pressing the *Enter* key on the keyboard, left button of the mouse, and right button of the mouse. Hence, in this text, unless otherwise mentioned, the terms *click* or *clicking* mean press the left button of the mouse. Also, in this text "a → b" means click "a" followed by clicking at "b".

Figure 2-2e

Figure 2-3a

2.3.   Focus of the Book

The focus of this book is two dimensional drawings using *Drafting and Annotation* workspace. For the first time launch, AutoCAD is in the *Drafting & Annotation* mode, Figure 2-3a. However, a user can switch to the other environment using the following method.

- Click the small downward arrow on the *Workspace Switching* wheel in the lower right corner of the interface, Figure 2-3a. A small window displaying various options will appear on the screen, Figure 2-3b. The user can select one of the three options: *Drafting & Annotation*, *3D Basics*, and *3D Modeling*. A checkmark will appear beside the selected option. Figure 2-3b shows the selection of the *Drafting and Annotation* option.
- Click the desired option and the interface is switched to the selected format.

Figure 2-3b

2.4.   Initial setup

For the demonstration purpose, the ribbon color (*top portion of the interface with command buttons*) and the background color of the drawing area (*the big rectangular area*) is changed to a lighter color, Figure 2-4a; and the grid is turned off, Figure 2-4b. The drawing area, color change, ribbons, and grid are discussed in the later sections of this chapter.

Figure 2-4a

Figure 2-4b

2.5.   Typical Window Screen

Technically, the AutoCAD interface is called a workspace. A typical (*Drafting and Annotation*) window screen (Figure 2-5a and Figure 2-5b) is a display of the drawing area, cursor, World coordinate system, viewcube, navigation bar, drawing display format, scroll bars, command line, status bar, ribbon and its tabs and panels, and dockable windows (not shown in the figure), etc. These features are grouped and organized based on the drawing environment and the user requirements.

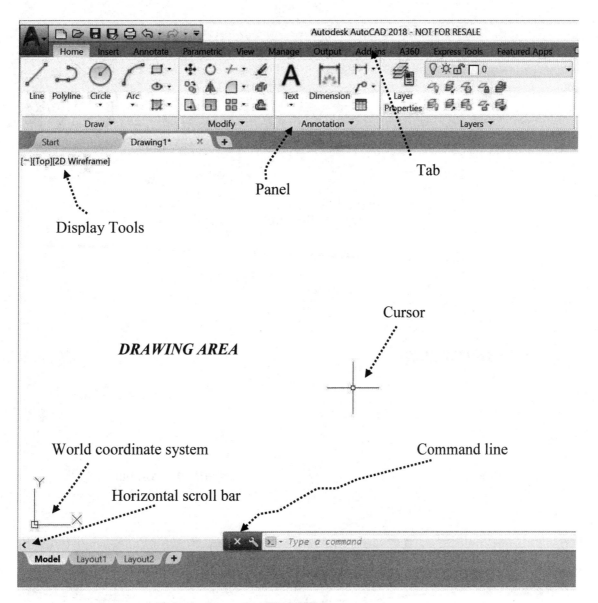

Figure 2-5a

2.6.   Drawing Area

The drawing area is the empty blank rectangular area in Figure 2-5a and Figure 2-5b that is used to create a new drawing or modify a previously created drawing. Although the drawing area is unlimited, the size of the drawing window depends on various factors such as the size of the computer screen, AutoCAD's window, and other elements displayed.

The drawing area is classified as a model space or layout. The user can switch to the model space or a layout by selecting the *Model* or *Layout* (*Layout1* or *Layout2*) tabs, respectively, from the lower left corner of the drawing area, Figure 2-5a and Figure 2-6.

Figure 2-5b

Figure 2-6

2.6.1.   Model space

Generally, the model (workspace) space is used to create two- or three-dimensional models. The default color of the model space can be changed as follows:

- Click with the right button in the *Drawing area* and select the *Options* option, Figure 2-7a or type *Options* on the command line and press the *Enter* key. The *Options* dialog box shown in Figure 2-7b appears on the screen.
- Click the *Display* tab of the *Options* dialog box.
- Press the *Color* button in the *Window Elements* panel to open the *Drawing Window Colors* (Figure 2-7c) dialog box.

Figure 2-7a

Figure 2-7b

- In the *Drawing Window Colors* dialog box, under the *Context* panel choose *2D model space*, under the *Interface element* panel choose *Uniform background*, and under the *Color* options panel select the desired color. The selection is highlighted. In the current example, *White* color is chosen. In the *Preview* window, the color of the model changes to the selected color.
- Click the *Apply & Close* button of the *Drawing Window Colors* dialog box.
- Finally, click the *OK* button of the *Options* dialog box.
- Both the dialog boxes will be closed and the background color will be updated to the selected color.
- *NOTE: The background color will not be printed during the plotting process of a drawing.*

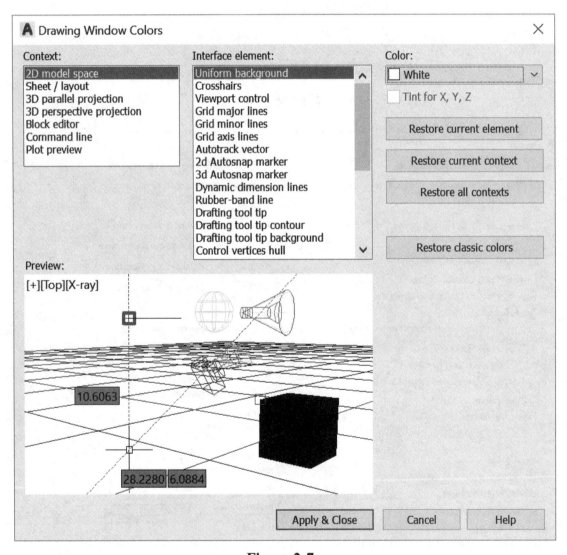

Figure 2-7c

2.6.2. Layout

The layouts are also known as paper space. When a user clicks on a layout tab, the drawing area appears as shown in Figure 2-8. Typically, layouts are not used for drafting or design work. Generally, layouts are used for printing or plotting the drawing. The self-explanatory options for a layout are shown in the *Layout elements* of Figure 2-9a (the lower left quarter of the Figure 2-7b). By default, AutoCAD creates two layouts; however, more layouts can be created for each drawing. Layouts are discussed in detail in Chapter 7.

Figure 2-8a

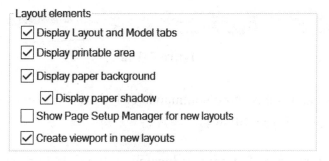

Figure 2-9a

2.6.3. Display/hide Model and Layout tabs
A user can display/ hide the *Model* and *Layout* tabs using one of the following methods.

Method #1
- Click with the right button of the mouse in the *Drawing area* and select the *Options* option or type *Options* on the command line and press the *Enter* key.
- The *Options* dialog box appears on the screen.

- Click the *Display* tab of the *Options* dialog box.
- Check or clear the *Display Layout and Model tabs* box in the *Layout elements* panel, Figure 2-9a, to display or hide the tabs, respectively.
- Click the *Apply* or *OK* button. The *Apply* button does NOT close the *Options* dialog box but hides the tabs and the *OK* button closes the *Options* dialog box and hides the tabs.

Method #2

- Click the *View* tab; on the *Interface* panel click the *Layout Tabs* ( ) icon. If the *Layout Tabs* are *On* then the *Layout Tabs* tool is highlighted, Figure 2-9b.

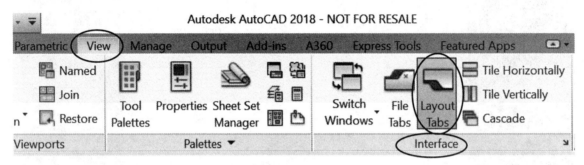

Figure 2-9b

2.7.   Status Bar

The set of commands on the lower right corner of the interface are collectively known as a status bar, Figure 2-10a. The figure shows the default set of commands.

Figure 2-10a

However, the user can display more commands or hide the existing commands using the customization button ( ) as follows.

- Click the customization button; it is located on the right hand side of the status bar, Figure 2-10a and Figure 2-10b.
- A list of commands opens as shown in Figure 2-10b. A check mark on the left side of a command indicates that the command is available on the status bar.
- To display/hide a command, click on its name.
- To exit the customization mode, click in the drawing area. This hides the commands list and the customization mode is turned off.

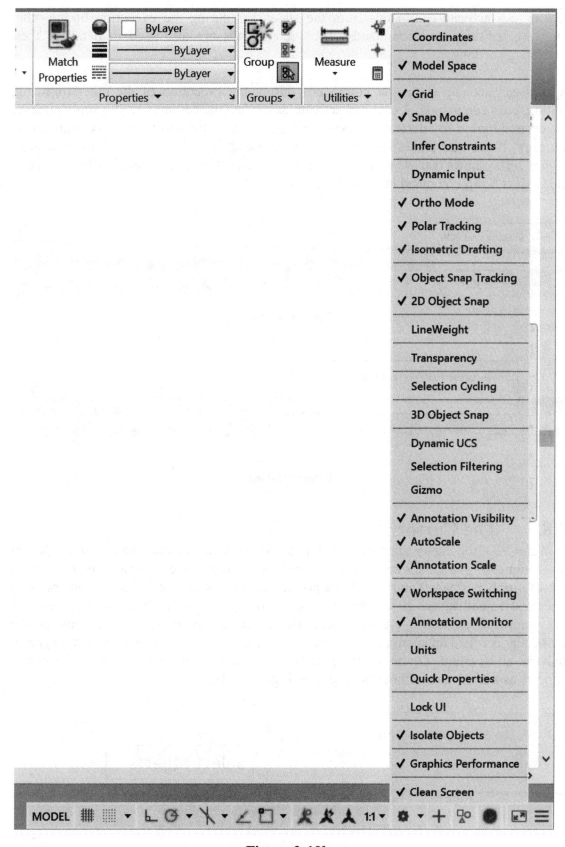

Figure 2-10b

A user can activate commands from the status bar during the execution of the other (drawing, editing, etc.) commands. These commands are discussed in detail in their respective sections.

A user can activate status bar commands during the execution of the other (drawing, editing, etc.) commands. A user can activate/deactivate the commands by simply clicking the desired button. By default, the active commands are blue and the inactive commands are grey. If the user places the cursor on a command icon, its name and status appear. Figure 2-10c shows that the **Grid** command is inactive (Off) and Figure 2-10d shows that the **Object Snap** command is active (On).

Figure 2-10c

Figure 2-10d

2.8. The Cursor

In AutoCAD, the cursor appears in different shapes based on the location and status of the command. The cursor appears as an arrowhead outside the drawing area (if it is on top of a ribbon's panel) and is called a pointer. It appears as crosshairs (two intersecting lines and a small square surrounding the intersection point) in the drawing area if none of the command is active, Figure 2-11a. The small square at the intersection of the crosshairs is called an aperture. If the cursor is waiting for object selection then it appears only as an aperture, Figure 2-11b. However, if a command is active then the cursor appears as a cross-hair without the aperture, Figure 2-11c.

Figure 2-11a   **Figure 2-11b**

Figure 2-11c

2.8.1. Location of the cursor

As the cursor moves in the drawing area its position coordinates (x, y, z) change; for two dimensional drawings, the z-coordinate is always zero. By default the position of the cursor (that is, the coordinates) is not displayed on the workspace. However, it is good drawing practice to display the coordinates of the cursor location in the drawing area. The user can display the coordinates as follows.

- Click the *Customization* button; it is located on the lower right corner of the workspace, Figure 2-10b.
- A selection list will appear on the screen. The Figure 2-10b shows the list.
- Select the *Coordinates* option; it is on the top of the list.
- This will close the list and the coordinates of the cursor will appear on the status bar, Figure 2-12. In the figure, note that the z-coordinate is zero.

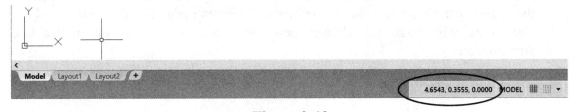

Figure 2-12

2.8.2. Size of the intersecting lines

The size of the intersecting lines of the cursor's crosshairs can be changed from the *Options* dialog box as follows.

- Click with the right button of the mouse in the *Drawing area* and select the *Options* option or type *Options* on the command line and press the *Enter* key.
- The *Options* dialog box will appear on the screen.
- Click the *Display* tab of the *Options* dialog box.
- Change the size of the intersecting lines using one of the following methods.
  1. Move the slider of the *Crosshair size* to the right or left (to increase or decrease), Figure 2-13. The slider is in the lower right quarter of the dialog box.
  2. Enter the desired value (1 - 100) in the small box; this value represents the size of the crosshairs as a percentage of the drawing screen.
- Press the *Apply* or *OK* button or press the *Enter* key. The *Apply* button makes the change permanent and the dialog box remains open. The *OK* button or the *Enter* key makes the changes permanent and closes the dialog box, too.

- The size of the crosshair does not influence the accuracy of the drawing. However, it is not a good practice to keep the crosshair's size larger than 10.

Figure 2-13

2.8.3. Size of the aperture

The size of the aperture of the crosshairs of the cursor can be changed from the *Options* dialog box as follows.

- Click with the right button of the mouse in the *Drawing area* and select the *Options* option or type *Options* on the command line and press the *Enter* key.
- The *Options* dialog box will appear on the screen.
- Click the *Drafting* tab of the *Options* dialog box.
- To increase the size of the aperture, move the slider of the *Aperture Size* to the right, Figure 2-14. The slider is in the right side of the dialog box.
- The aperture size does not influence the accuracy of the drawing. However, it is not a good practice to keep the aperture's size too large or too small.
- Press the *Apply* or *OK* button or press the *Enter* key. The *Apply* button will make the change permanent and the dialog box will remain open. The *OK* button and the *Enter* key will make the change permanent and will close the dialog box simultaneously.

Figure 2-14

2.8.4. Color of the cursor

The color of the crosshairs of the cursor in model space or layout can be changed from the *Options* dialog box as follows.

- Click with the right button of the mouse in the *Drawing area* and select the *Options* option or type *Options* on the command line and press the *Enter* key.
- The *Options* dialog box will appear on the screen.
- Click the *Display* tab of the *Options* dialog box.
- Press the *Color* button in the *Window Elements* panel to open the *Drawing Window Colors* dialog box, Figure 2-15.
- In the *Drawing Window Colors* dialog box, under the *Context* choose *2D model space* under the *Interface element* choose *Crosshairs*, and under the *Color* option

choose the desired color. The selection will be highlighted. In the current example, the *Magenta* color is selected. In the *Preview* window, the color of the cursor will change to the selected color.

- Finally, click the *Apply & Close* button to close the dialog box.
- In the 2D model space, the color of the cursor will change to the selected color.

Figure 2-15

2.9.   World Coordinate System (WCS)

In AutoCAD, there are two types of coordinate systems. The first is a fixed Cartesian system known as the *World Coordinate System* (WCS). The WCS is used as the basis for defining the drawing object. The second is a movable Cartesian coordinate system and is called the *User Coordinate System* (UCS). A UCS is defined relative to the WCS. In both the WCS and UCS, the Z-axis is always perpendicular to the XY-plane. In the default setting for 2D drawings, the WCS's X-axis is horizontal, the Y-axis is vertical, and the origin is located at the intersection of the X- and Y-axes (Figures 2-16). **Note the box at the origin; this box indicates that the coordinate system is WCS.**

Figure 2-16

2.10.   Scroll Bars

The scroll bar can be added or removed from the workspace as follows.

- Open the *Options* dialog box. The *Options* dialog box (Figure 2-17) can be opened by clicking with the right button of the mouse in the *Drawing area* and selecting the *Options* option.
- Click the *Display* tab of the *Options* dialog box by clicking on it.
- In the *Window Elements* panel (Figure 2-17), check (or clear) the first box (*Display scroll bars in drawing window*) to display (or hide) the scroll bar, respectively.

Figure 2-17

2.11.   ViewCube

The *ViewCube* is a navigational tool. It is displayed in 2D or 3D visual style, both in model space and layouts. By default, the tool is on, inactive, and semi-transparent. The *ViewCube* tool contains coordinate system (WCS) and compass (NSWE), Figure 2-18a. By default, it is located in the upper right corner of the drawing area. In 2D model space, the default view is the top view as shown in Figure 2-18a. A sample cube with its sides labeled is shown in Figure 2-18b.

The *ViewCube* can be turned *On/Off* by using one of the following procedures.

1. Panel method: From the *View* tab and *Viewport Tools* panel click the *ViewCube* tool. If the tool was *off* then it turns *on* or vice versa.
2. Command line method: Type "navvcube", "Navvcube", or "NAVVCUBE" in the command line and press the *Enter* key; the option list shown in Figure 2-18c appears. Click the desired option.

Figure 2-18a

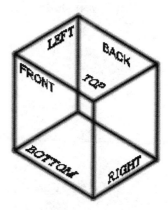

Figure 2-18b

2.11.1. ViewCube settings

The various features of the ViewCube can be changed from the *ViewCube Settings* dialog box. The self-explanatory dialog box is shown in Figure 2-18e. The dialog box can be opened using one of the two methods.

- Type "navvcube", "Navvcube", or "NAVVCUBE" in the command line and press the *Enter* key. The option list shown in Figure 2-18c appears. Click on the *Settings* option.
- (i) Bring the cursor on the NESW circle of the *ViewCube*, (ii) press the right button of the mouse, and (iii) select the *ViewCube Settings* option, Figure 2-18d.

Figure 2-18c

Figure 2-18d

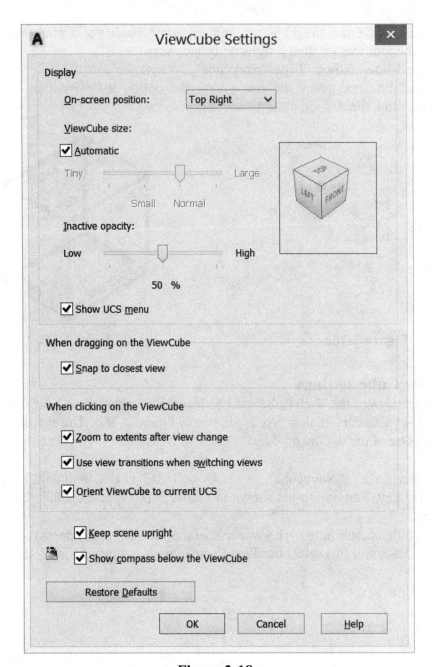

Figure 2-18e

2.11.2. View switching

In 2D model space, by default the *ViewCube* is in the top view. However, this tool allows the user to switch between standard 2D view (top, bottom, left, right, front, and back), and 3D isometric view (south-east, north-east, south-west, and north- west). The user can also switch between any combinations of the six 2D standard views.

The *ViewCube* can be activated by placing the cursor on any part of the tool. The coordinate system can be changed by pressing the down arrow to the right of WCS and selecting the desired option. The other features are discussed in the remainder of this section. The user can switch from one view to the other as follows.

- Click on a quadrant of the compass (W is selected in Figure 2-19a) or a face of the square and the view changes to the corresponding standard view, Figure 2-19b.
- Click an edge of the square (Figure 2-19c) and the view changes to the corresponding standard view, Figure 2-19d.

Figure 2-19a   **Figure 2-19b**

Figure 2-19c   **Figure 2-19d**

- Click a corner of the square (Figure 2-19e) and the view changes to the corresponding 3D view, Figure 2-19f.

Figure 2-19e   **Figure 2-19f**

2.12. Drawing Display Format

The three items (*[-] [Top] [2D Wireframe]*) in the upper left corner of the drawing area represent the format of the drawing appearance, Figure 2-20a: [-] represents viewport control, [Top] represents view control, and [2D Wireframe] represents the visual style control. These controls are discussed briefly.

Figure 2-20a

- Viewport control: The *Viewport control* allows the user to manipulate the viewports in model space and layouts, Figure 2-20b. The user can use single (the default option) or multiple viewports; and how to arrange multiple viewports. The viewports are discussed in detail in Chapter 7.

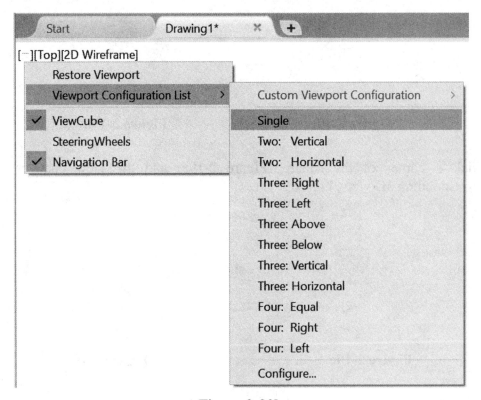

Figure 2-20b

- View control: The *View control* allows the user to switch between standard 2D view (top, bottom, left, right, front, and back), and 3D isometric view SW, SE, NE, and NW, Figure 2-20c. In this figure, N, S, E, and W represents north, south, east, and west, respectively. Generally, 2D drawings are looked at from the top and other styles are used to display the 3D models.

- Visual style control: The *Visual style control* allows the user to switch between various visual styles, Figure 2-20d. Generally, 2D drawings are in *2D Wireframe* style and the other styles are used to display 3D models.

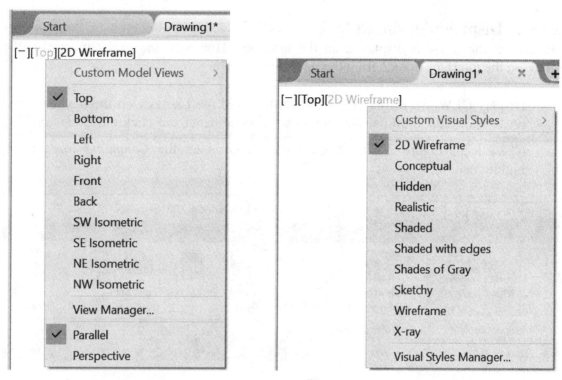

Figure 2-20c   **Figure 2-20d**

2.13.   Command Line Window

The command line window (CLW) is a text area reserved for the prompts, keyboard input, and error messages, Figure 2-21. By default, the CLW is *On*, located at the bottom of the AutoCAD's window.

Figure 2-21

2.13.1. Move the CLW

The user can move the command line window on the interface.

- Bring the cursor on the left gray end of the CLW, Figure 2-21.

- Press the left button of the mouse.
- Keep pressing the left button and move the cursor.
- The CLW will appear as a light gray box.
- Keep holding down the left button and move the cursor to the new location.
- Release the left button; and the CLW moves to new location.

2.13.2. Display/hide the CLW

By default the CLW is displayed on the interface. However, the user can display the CLW on the interface or hide from the interface.

- Display CLW: To display the CLW, either hold the *Ctrl* key on the keyboard and press 9; or click the *View* tab and on the *Palette* panel and click the *Command line* ( ) icon, Figure 2-22a. If the CLW is *On* then the *Command line* tool is highlighted.

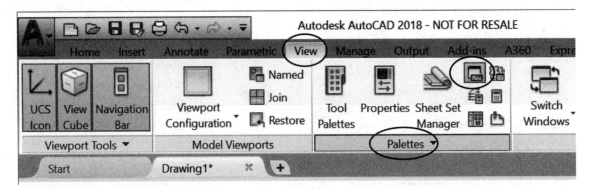

Figure 2-22a

- Hide CLW:
  a) To hide the CLW, either click on the small cross (Figure 2-21); or click the *View* tab, on the Palette panel, and click the *Command line* ( ) icon, Figure 2-22a. If the CLW is *Off* then the *Command line* tool is not highlighted.
  b) (i) The dialog box shown in Figure 2-22b appears. (ii) Click the *Yes* button. This closes the dialog box and hides the CLW.

Figure 2-22b

2.13.3. Resize the CLW

By default, only one command can be written in the CLW and three commands are displayed above the CLW, Figure 2-23a. However, the user can resize the CLW as follows.

- Bring the cursor on the top edge of the CLW and a double-headed arrow appears.
- Press and hold the left button of the mouse, and move the cursor. The CLW expands as the cursor moves upward or contracts as the cursor moves downward. In the current example, the cursor is move upward, Figure 2-23b.
- Release the left button of the mouse to resize the CLW.
- Similarly, the width can be increased or decreased. In the current example, the width is reduced, Figure 2-23b.

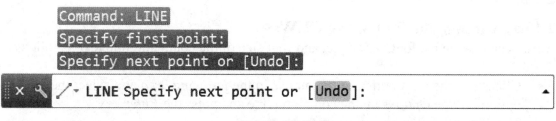

Figure 2-23a

Figure 2-23b

2.13.4. Change the color of the CLW

A user can change the background and the text color of the command line window as follows.

- Click with the right button of the mouse in the *Drawing area* and select the *Options* option or type *Options* on the command line and press the *Enter* key.
- The *Options* dialog box appears on the screen.
- Click the *Display* tab of the *Options* dialog box.
- Press the *Color* button in the *Window Elements* panel to open the *Drawing Window Colors* dialog box.
- In the *Drawing Window Colors* dialog box, Figure 2-24, under the *Context* choose the *Command line*, under the *Interface elements* choose the *Command history background* to change the color of the background, and under the *Color* option choose the desired color. The selection is highlighted. In the current example, the *Yellow* color is selected. In the *Preview* window, the color of the CLW changes to the selected color.

- Finally, click the *Apply & Close* button to close the dialog box.
- The color of the CLW changes to the selected color.
- Similarly, change the color of the text of the CLW.

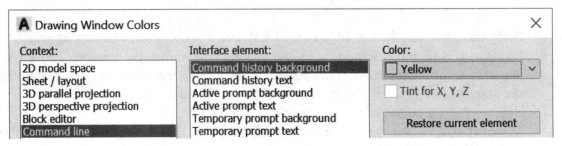

Figure 2-24

2.13.5. Change the font of the CLW
A user can change the font, font style, and font size of the command line text as follows.

- Click with the right button of the mouse in the *Drawing area* and select the *Options* option or type *Options* on the command line and press the *Enter* key.
- The *Options* dialog box appears on the screen.
- Click the *Display* tab of the *Options* dialog box.
- Press the *Font* button in the *Window Elements* panel (Figure 2-25a) to open the *Command Line Window Font* dialog box, Figure 2-25b.

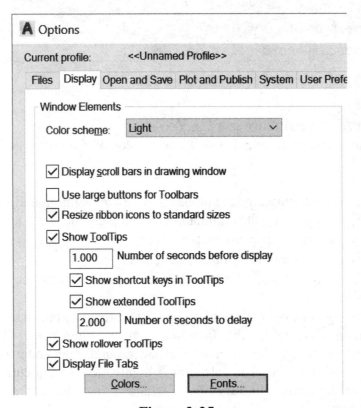

Figure 2-25a

- Select the desired *Font*, *Font Style*, and *Size*. In the current example, the *Courier New*, *Regular*, and *10* are selected. In the *Preview* panel, the selected font appears.

Figure 2-25b

- Click the *Apply & Close* button. This updates the font of the CLW and closes the *Command Line Window Font* dialog box.
- Finally, click the *OK* button of the *Options* dialog box to close it.
- This changes the CLW font. Figure 2-25c shows the newly selected font and color.

```
Command: LINE
Specify first point:
Specify next point or [Undo]:
Specify next point or [Undo]:
LINE Specify next point or [Close Undo]:
```

Figure 2-25c

2.14.   Ribbon

The Ribbon is an important part of AutoCAD's interface. It is a collection of tabs, panels, and tools. Figure 2-26 shows the selection of the *Home* tab, *Modify* panel, and the *Offset* command tool. A tab is a collection of panels. A panel is collection of tools. A tool is a pictured icon that represents an AutoCAD command; that is, a tool is a graphical representation of a command.

In this text "Tab → Panel → Command tool" means first select the "Tab" then on the "Panel", and then click the "Command tool" icon.

Tab (*Home*)   Panel (*Modify*)   Tool (*Offset*)

Figure 2-26

2.14.1. Color scheme

The background color scheme of ribbons has two options: *Dark* and *Light*, Figure 2-27. The default option is *Dark*. The user can change the color scheme as follows.

- Click with the right button of the mouse in the *Drawing area* and select the *Options* option or type *Options* on the command line and press the *Enter* key.
- The *Options* dialog box will appear on the screen.
- Click the *Display* tab of the *Options* dialog box.
- In the *Window Elements* panel, in the *Color scheme*, click on *Dark*, or the down arrow, Figure 2-27.
- This opens a drop down list.
- Select the *desired* option. In the current example, the *Light*, option is selected.
- Finally, click the *OK* button on the *Options* dialog box to close it.
- The *Option* dialog box is closed and the ribbon colors are reduced to lighter color.

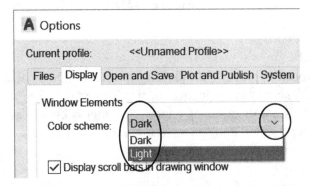

Figure 2-27

2.14.2. Relocate

By default, the ribbon is docked above the drawing area, Figure 2-26. However, the user can move the ribbon to the left or right side of the interface as follows.

- Undock the ribbon: (i) Bring the cursor in the tabs area and click with the right button of the mouse, Figure 2-28a. (ii) The selection list shown in Figure 2-28a appears. Select the *Undock* option. (iii) This closes the option list and undocks the ribbon, Figure 2-28b.

Figure 2-28a

- Select the ribbon by placing the cursor on the left gray side of the ribbon, Figure 2-28b.
- Press and hold down the left button of the mouse.
- Keep pressing the left button, and move the cursor to the left or right side of the interface. In the current example, the ribbon is moved to the left.
- Move the cursor to the left of the AutoCAD window; the ribbon will appear as a light gray box.

Figure 2-28b

- Release the left button of the mouse and the gray box will be replaced by the ribbon, Figure 2-28c. The ribbon is docked on the left side of the interface.

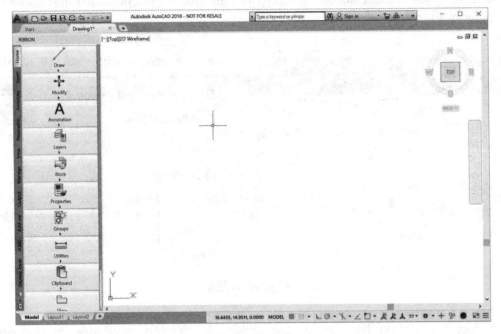

Figure 2-28c

2.14.3. Hide/Display a ribbon

By default the ribbon is *On*. However, the user can hide (turn *off*) the ribbon from the interface or display (turn *on*) on the interface.

- Hide ribbon: (i) Bring the cursor in the tabs area and click with the right button of the mouse, Figure 2-29a. (ii) A selection list appears, Figure 2-29a. Select the *Close* option. (iii) This closes the option list and hides the ribbon from the interface, Figure 2-29b.

Figure 2-29a

Figure 2-29b

- Display ribbon: The ribbon is displayed in a three step process.
  a) <u>Display the menu bar:</u> Click on the small triangular arrow on the upper left corner of the interface, Figure 2-30a. (ii) A selection list appears. (ii) Select the *Show Menu Bar* option. (iii) This closes the option list and displays the menu bar, Figure 2-30b.

Figure 2-30a

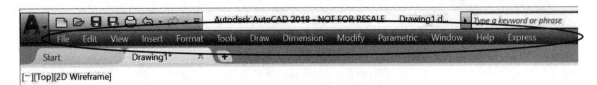

Figure 2-30b

b) <u>Display the ribbon:</u> Refer to Figure 2-30c. (i) On the menu bar, select the *Tool* menu and a selection list appears. (ii) Select the *Palettes* option and another selection list appears. (iii) Finally, select the *Ribbon* option. (iv) This closes the two selection lists and displays the ribbon on the interface.

Figure 2-30c

Figure 2-30d

c) <u>Hide the menu bar:</u> (i) Bring the cursor on the menu bar and click with the right button of the mouse. The *Show Menu Bar* option appears on the screen, Figure 2-30e. (ii) Clear the check box; this closes the option list and hides the menu bar.

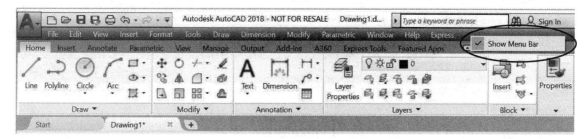

Figure 2-30e

2.14.4. States

By default, the ribbon is *On* and the tabs, the panels, and the panel names are displayed, Figure 2-31a. However, the user can display/hide any of the tabs, panels, and/or panel names using the two arrows on the right end of the tab bar.

- Hide option: Click on the arrow at the right end of the tab bar (Figure 2-31a) and select the desired option. Figure 2-31b shows only the tabs; Figure 2-31c shows the tabs and the panel names; and Figure 2-31d shows the tabs and the panel buttons.

- Display option: The user can display the full ribbon using one of the two methods. (i) Click on the second arrow from the right end of the tab bar to display the full ribbon. (ii) Click on *Cycle through All* option in Figure 2-31a and the full ribbon will be displayed.

Figure 2-31a

Figure 2-31b

Figure 2-31c

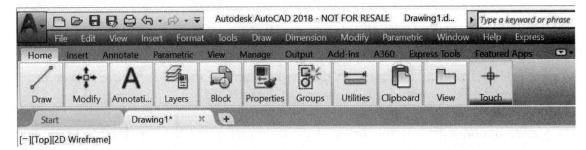

Figure 2-31d

2.14.5. Ribbon's Tab

The ribbon tabs are not used for command execution; these tabs are used to display the panel. A user can display or hide and relocate the default tabs, and can create new tabs.

2.14.5.1. Display/Hide Tabs

By default the tabs of the ribbon are *On*. However, the user can hide (turn *off*) the tabs from the ribbon or display (turn *on*) on the ribbon.

- Display a tab: Refer to Figure 2-32. (i) Bring the cursor in the tab area and click with the right button of the mouse. (ii) The selection list will appear. Select the *Show Tabs* option. (iii) This opens a tab's list. If a tab is displayed on the ribbon, then it has a check mark on the left side of its name. (iv) To display a tab, click on a tab without a check mark, *3D Tools* in the current example. (iv) This closes both the option lists and displays the selected tab and associated panels on the ribbon.

- Hide a tab: Refer to Figure 2-32. (i) Bring the cursor in the tab area and click with the right button of the mouse. (ii) The selection list will appear. Select the *Show Tabs* option. (iii) This will open a tab's list. If a tab is displayed on the ribbon then it has a check mark on the left side its name, Figure 2-32. (iv) To hide a tab, click on a tab with a check mark, *Express Tools* in the current example. (v) This closes both the option lists and hides the selected tab.

Figure 2-32

2.14.5.2. Tab relocation

A user can relocate a tab of the ribbon using a drag and drop method. By default the *Home* tab is on the left end of the tab bar, Figure 2-32. This example will move the *Home* tab to the right end.

- (i) Click on the *Home* tab with the left button of the mouse, (ii) keep pressing the left button, and (iii) move the cursor to the desired location. A grayed tab appears at the new location, Figure 2-33, the right end of the tab bar in the current example.
- Release the left button of the mouse and the tab is moved to the new location. Figure 2-33 shows the new location of *Home* tab, the right end of the tab bar in the current example.

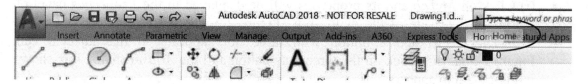

Figure 2-33

2.14.5.3. New tab

The user can create a new tab for the ribbon using the method discussed in this section. This example creates a tab; and the panels will be added in the panel's section.

- (i) From the tab bar, select the *Manage* tab, Figure 2-34a. (ii) From the *Customization* panel click on the *User Interface* command, the *CUI* icon. (iii) This opens the *Customize User Interface* dialog box shown in Figure 2-34b.

Figure 2-34a

- From the *Customize User Interface* dialog box, Figure 2-34b, select the *Customize* tab. The tab is located on the upper left corner of the dialog box. The figure also shows that the *Drafting & Annotation* is the current workspace.
- In the upper left quadrant, Figure 2-34b, click on the '+' adjacent to the *Ribbon* label. This displays an option list, Figure 2-35a.
- (i) Select the *Tab* option, Figure 2-35a. (ii) Click with the right button of the mouse on the *Tab* option. (iii) This displays an option list. (iv) Select the *New Tab* option.
- This closes the option list and creates a new tab labeled as *New Tab* at the lower end of the *Tab* options list. Move the scroll bar downward to display the *New Tab*, Figure 2-35b.
- (i) Select the *New Tab*, (ii) Press the right button of the mouse and options list will appear, Figure 2-35c, (iii) select the *Rename* option from the list, (iv) rename *New Tab* to *MyTab*, Figure 2-35d.

- (i) Click on *MyTab* and its properties will be displayed in the *Properties* panel on the upper right side of the dialog box, Figure 2-36a. (ii) Click on *Aliases* in the *Properties* panel and a button with three dots appears in the adjacent cell, Figure 2-36a. (iii) Click on the three dots button and the *Aliases* dialog box shown in Figure 2-36b appears.
- Enter the aliases name, Figure 2-36b, and press the *OK* button. This closes the *Aliases* dialog box and the aliases appears in the *Properties* panel, Figure 2-36c.
- Under *General* and for the *Display Text*, enter *MyTab*, Figure 2-36c.

Figure 2-34b

Figure 2-35a   Figure 2-35a

Figure 2-35b   **Figure 2-35c**

Figure 2-35d

Figure 2-36a

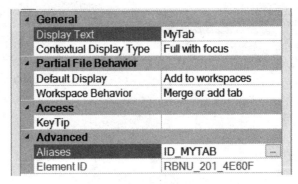

Figure 2-36b   **Figure 2-36c**

- Double click on *Drafting & Annotation* under the *Workspaces*, Figure 2-36d, and the list of workspace content will appear on the right side of the dialog box.
- On the right side of the dialog box, click on the '+' adjacent to the *Ribbon Tabs* label. This displays an option list shown in Figure 2-36d.

Figure 2-36d

- Click on *MyTab* and keep pressing the left button of the mouse; the selected tab will be highlighted, Figure 2-37a.
- (i) Keep pressing the left button of the mouse, (ii) move the cursor to the right side of the dialog box under the *Ribbon Tabs*, Figure 2-37a. (iii) Click anywhere below the *Ribbon Tabs* and above the *Performance* (the last tab) and release the left button of the mouse. The figure shows the cursor below the *Home* tab.

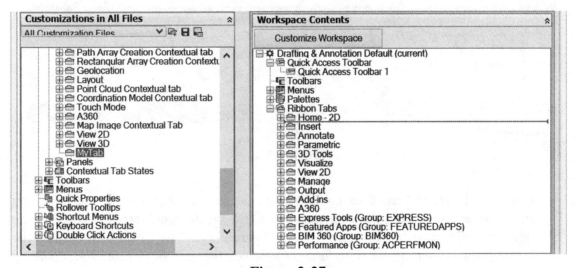

Figure 2-37a

- The new tab is added to the *Ribbon Tabs* list, Figure 2-37b. By default, the tab is always added at the end of the list (independent of the location selected). If necessary, move the new tab to the desired location.

- Click the *OK* button of the dialog box. This closes the dialog box and creates the new tab (*MyTab*) in the tab bar of the workspace, Figure 2-37c. The new tab is at the end of the tab bar. If the newly created tab does not appear in the tab list, then complete the next step.

Figure 2-37b

Figure 2-37c

- If the newly created tab does not appear in the tab list then refresh the modeling environment using the following steps: (i) Click on the small arrow located at the right side of *Workspace Switching* wheel, Figure 2-37d. The wheel is located on the lower right corner of the interface. (ii) Select the *3D Basics* or *3D Modeling* environment. This closes the list and changes the drawing environment to the selected option. (iii) Repeat step (i) and (ii). However, select the *Drafting & Annotation* option in step (ii). The new tab appears at the end of the tab bar.

Figure 2-37d

2.14.6. Ribbon's panel

The ribbon panels are used to display the commands. Some of the panels also provide access to related dialog box. A user can display or hide and relocate the default panel, and can create new panels.

2.14.6.1. Panel components

Every panel shows three rows of commands icons, Figure 2-38a. If a panel's commands cannot be accommodated in three rows, then those commands can be accessed through the panel expander, Figure 2-38a. If a command has several options available through a dropdown menu, then those options can be accessed through the command expander; and the command icon displays the most recently used option.

- Panel expander: (i) Bring the cursor on the tiny arrow near the panel label, Figure 2-38a and (ii) click with the left button of the mouse and the panel expands, Figure 2-38b. However, if the user moves the cursor, then the panel collapses to the original size. However, the user can pin the panel expansion using the *Pin* command

Figure 2-38a

- Pin the panel: The user can pin the panel expansion using the *Pin* command. The pin command is located in the lower left corner of the expanded panel, Figure 2-38b. (i) The pin command is executed by clicking on the pin icon, Figure 2-38b. (ii) Figure 2-38c shows that the panel is pinned. Note carefully the difference in the appearance of the pin in the two figures.

Figure 2-38b

Figure 2-38c

- Dialog box launcher: (i) Bring the cursor on the tiny arrow near the lower right corner of the panel, Figure 2-38a and (ii) click the arrow and the *Dimension Style Manager* dialog box will appear, Figure 2-38d. This dialog box is discussed in detail in *Dimensions* chapter. Click the *Close* button to close the dialog box.
- Command expander: (i) Bring the cursor on the tiny arrow below the command label, Figure 2-38a and Figure 2-38e and (ii) click with the left button of the mouse and the panel will expand, Figure 2-38e. (iii) The user can click on any command; this will close the list and execute the selected command. The figure shows the selection of the *Radius* dimension command. (iv) The user can cycle through the list using the down arrow key of the keyboard; and can close the list by clicking the same arrow again.

Figure 2-38d   **Figure 2-38e**

2.14.6.2. Display/Hide panel

By default the panels of the ribbon are *On*. However, the user can hide (turn *off*) the panel from the ribbon or display (turn *on*) on the ribbon.

- Display a panel: (i) Bring the cursor in the tab area and click with the right button of the mouse, Figure 2-39a. (ii) The selection list shown in Figure 2-39a appears. Select the *Show Panels* option. (iii) This opens a panel's list for the selected tab. In the current example the panels under the *Home* tab are displayed. If a panel is displayed on the ribbon then it shows a check mark on the left side of its name, Figure 2-39a. (iv) To display a panel, click on a panel without a check mark, *Properties* in the current example. (iv) This closes both the option lists and displays the selected panel on the ribbon and check mark appears on the left side its name, Figure 2-39b.

Figure 2-39a

Figure 2-39b

2.14.6.3. Panel relocation

A user can relocate a panel of the ribbon using a drag and drop method. In the *Home* tab, by default the *Draw* panel is on the left end of the ribbon, Figure 2-40a. This example moves the *Draw* panel on the right side of the *Modify* panel using the following steps.

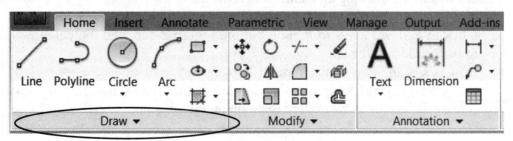

Figure 2-40a

- Select the *Home* tab.
- Click on the *Draw* panel's name area with the left button of the mouse.
- Keep pressing the left button and move the cursor to the desired location. A grayed panel appears at the new location and rectangular space is created; in the current example, it is on the right end of the *Modify* panel, Figure 2-40.
- Release the left button of the mouse, and the panel is moved to the new location. Figure 2-40c shows the new location of the *Draw* panel.

Figure 2-40b

Figure 2-40c

2.14.6.4.   Floating panel

If a user drags and drops a panel in the drawing area then it is called a floating panel. A panel can be converted to a floating panel using the following steps.

- (i) Bring the cursor on the panel's name, Figure 2-41a. (ii) Select the panel's label bar by pressing the left button. (iii) Keep pressing the left button and move the cursor to the drawing area. For the current example, *Text* panel under the *Express Tools* tab is selected.
- Release the left button of the mouse and the panel becomes the floating panel. The panel stays in the drawing area until it is returned to the ribbon. The user can return the panel back to the ribbon using one of the two methods.
    o Click at *Return Panels to Ribbon* button, Figure 2-41b, and the panel is moved to its location on the tab.
    o (a) Click at the two dotted parallel lines on the left side of the panel. (b) Press the left button. (c) Keep pressing the left button of the mouse. (d) Move and release the cursor at the desired location on the ribbon.

Figure 2-41a

Figure 2-41b

2.14.6.5.   Create new panel

A user can create a new panel for the ribbon using the method discussed in this section. This example will create a new panel.

- (i) From the tab bar, select the *Manage* tab, Figure 2-42a. (ii) From the *Customization* panel click on the *User Interface* command, the *CUI* icon 📄. (iii) This opens the *Customize User Interface* dialog box shown in Figure 2-42b.

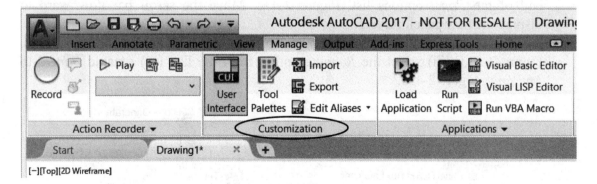

Figure 2-42a

- From the *Customize User Interface* dialog box, Figure 2-42b, select the *Customize* tab. The tab is located on the upper left corner of the dialog box. The figure also shows the selection of *Drafting & Annotation* under the Workspace.

Figure 2-42b

- In the upper left quadrant, Figure 2-42b, click on the '+' adjacent to the *Ribbon* label. This displays an option list, Figure 2-43a.
- (i) Select the *Panel* option, Figure 2-43b. (ii) Click with the right button of the mouse on the *Panel* option, this displays an option list, Figure 2-43b. (iv) Select the *New Panel* option.

Figure 2-43a   **Figure 2-43b**

- This closes the option list and creates a new panel labeled as *Panel1* at the lower end of the *Panel* options list, Figure 2-43c. Move the scroll bar downward to display the new panel, *Panel1*.
- (i) Select *Panel1*, (ii) Press the right button of the mouse and an options list appears, Figure 2-43d, (iii) select the *Rename* option from the list, (iv) rename *Panel1* to *MyPanel*, Figure 2-43e.

Figure 2-43c   **Figure 2-43d**

Figure 2-43e

- Click on *MyPanel* and its appearance is displayed in the *Panel Preview* and its properties are displayed in the *Properties* panel on the upper right side of the dialog box, Figure 2-44a. Nothing is displayed in the *Panel Preview* because the commands are not added to the panel.
- Click on *Aliases* in the *Properties* section (lower right end of the dialog box) and a button with three dots appears in the adjacent cell, Figure 2-44a.

Figure 2-44a

- Click on the three dots button and the *Aliases* dialog box, Figure 2-44b, appears.
- Type the aliases name, Figure 2-44b, and press the *OK* button. This closes the *Aliases* dialog box and the aliases name appears in the *Properties* section, Figure 2-44c.

Figure 2-44b   **Figure 2-44c**

2.14.6.6.   Add panel to a tab

A user can add a panel to a tab using the method discussed in this section. This example adds the newly created panel, *MyPanel* to *MyTab* (this tab is created in the section *New Tab*).

- (i) From the tab bar, select the *Manage* tab. (ii) From the *Customization* panel click on the *User Interface* command, the *CUI* icon ![CUI]. (iii) This opens the *Customize User Interface* dialog box.
- In the upper left quadrant, click on the '+' adjacent to the *Ribbon* label. This displays an option list.
- The move process described in this step is not necessary; however, it makes the process discussed in the next step easier to understand. (i) Click on the '+' adjacent to the *Panel* label. This displays the list of panels with *MyPanel* at the lower end of the panel list (the newly created panel). (ii) Click on *MyPanel*. (ii) Press the left button of the mouse and keep pressing. (iii) Move the cursor upward. (iv) Release the cursor when it is on the top of the panel list, Figure 2-45a.
- Click on the '+' adjacent to the *Tab* label. This displays the list of tabs with *MyTab* at the lower end of the tab list (the previously created tab), Figure 2-45a.
- (i) Select *MyPanel* again. (ii) Press the left button of the mouse and keep pressing. A light grey rectangle appears at the tail of the pointer and is not shown in the figure. (iii) Move the cursor upward to *MyTab*; a small blue arrowhead appears beside *MyTab*, Figure 2-45b. (iv) Release the cursor when it is on *MyTab*.
- The newly created panel is added to the previously created tab, Figure 2-45c.

Figure 2-45a   **Figure 2-45b**   **Figure 2-45c**

2.14.6.7.   Add commands to a panel

A user can add commands to a panel arranged in rows, sub-panel, and drop-down menus. A row can be further subdivided into rows, sub-panel, and drop-down menus.

This section creates two rows in *MyPanel*, Figure 2-46 and Figure 2-52. The *Row 1* contains two commands and a sub-panel. The sub-panel is further subdivided into three rows; the *Row 1-1* contains three commands and the *Row 1-2* and *Row 1-3* contains one command each. The *Row 2* contains one drop-down menu and is named as *Array*; and the menu contains three commands. The remainder of this section describes the step-by-step process to add commands to a panel.

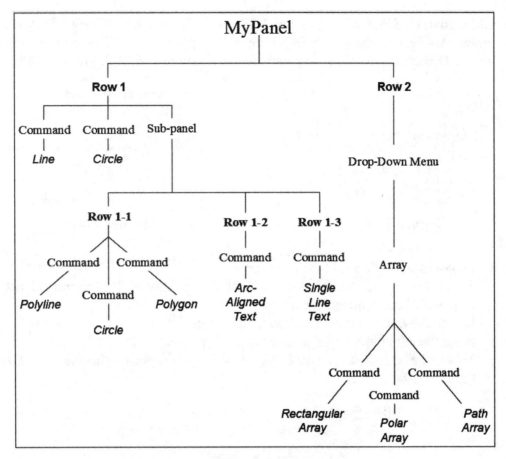

Figure 2-46

- (i) From the tab bar, select the *Manage* tab. (ii) From the *Customization* panel click on the *User Interface* command, the *CUI* icon ▨. (iii) This opens the *Customize User Interface* dialog box.
- In the upper left quadrant, click on the '+' adjacent to the *Ribbon* label. This displays an option list, Figure 2-47a.
- In the upper left quadrant, click on the '+' adjacent to the *Panel* label. This displays an option list, Figure 2-47a.
- In the upper left quadrant, click on the '+' adjacent to the *MyPanel* label. This displays an option list. The newly created panel has three components as shown in Figure 2-47.

Figure 2-47

- **Add a row:** (i) Select *Row 1*, Figure 2-48a, and (ii) click with the right button of the mouse. A selection list shown in Figure 2-48a appears. (iii) Click on the *New Row* option. This closes the option list and creates a new row, *Row 2*, Figure 2-48b.

Figure 2-48a

Figure 2-48b

- **Add a command:** Now add the *Line* command to *Row 1*.
  - Type *Line* in the search command list, Figure 2-49a. The command list box displays all the commands containing the word "Line".
  - Locate the *Line* command and select it, Figure 2-49a.
  - Press the left button of the mouse and keep pressing.
  - Move the cursor to *Row 1*. A small arrow appears beside the *Row 1*, Figure 2-49a.

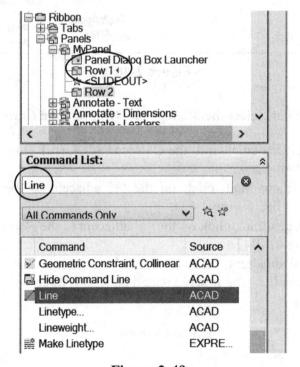

Figure 2-49a

- Release the left button and the *Line* command is added to the *Row 1*, Figure 2-49b.
- Click on the *Line* under *Row 1* and its properties are displayed on the right side of the dialog box, Figure 2-49b.

o In the *Properties* group, under the *Appearance*, click on the *Button Style* and a dropdown arrow appears in the right cell.

o Press the down arrow and select *SmallWithText* option, Figure 2-49b. The command picture and label is displayed in the *Panel Preview* window; it is on the upper right corner of the dialog box, Figure 2-49b.

Figure 2-49b

- Similarly, add the circle command, Figure 2-49c.

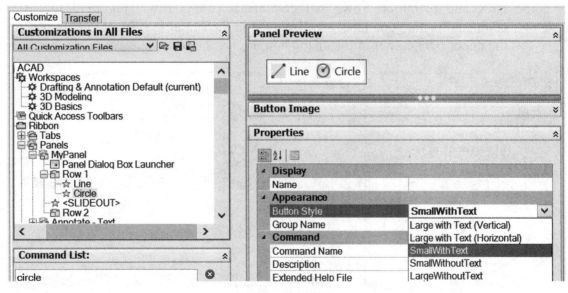

Figure 2-49c

- **Add a sub-panel:**
  - Select *Row 1*, Figure 2-50a.
  - Click with the right button of the mouse. A selection list shown in Figure 2-50a appears.
  - Click on the *New Sub-Panel* option. This closes the option list and a new sub-panel, *Sub-Panel 1*, is created, Figure 2-50b. The sub-panel is created with one unnamed row.

Figure 2-50a

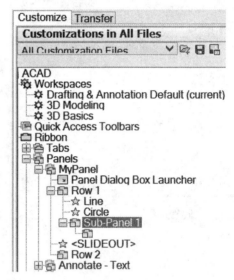

Figure 2-50b

  - Now add two more rows and commands to the rows, Figure 2-50c. The command picture and label are displayed in the *Panel Preview* window; it is on the upper right corner of the dialog box, Figure 2-50c.

Figure 2-50c

- **Add a drop-down:**
  - Select *Row 2*, Figure 2-51a.
  - Click with the right button of the mouse. A selection list shown in Figure 2-51a appears.
  - Click on the *New Drop-Down* option. This closes the option list and a new drop-down menu, *Drop-Down 1*, is created, Figure 2-51b.

Figure 2-51a   **Figure 2-51b**

  - Select the New Drop-Down and press the right button of the mouse. A selection list appears. Select the Rename option, Figure 2-51c.
  - Rename the drop-down to Array, Figure 2-51d.
  - Now add three commands to the drop-down as shown in Figure 2-51e and discussed in the corresponding steps. The command picture and label is displayed in the *Panel Preview* window; it is on the upper right corner of the dialog box, Figure 2-51e.
- The Figure 2-52 shows the selection of *MyTab* and *MyPanel*. The figure also shows the expanded *Array* drop-down menu.

Figure 2-51c   **Figure 2-51d**

Figure 2-51e

Figure 2-52

2.15.   Workspace

The collection of the drawing area, cursor, World coordinate system, viewcube, drawing display format, scroll bars, ribbon, pull down menus, command line, status bar, toolbars, and dockable windows is known as workspace, but the ribbon panels, set of toolbars, and menus used in 2D and 3D drawings are different. Hence, to increase efficiency and productivity, a user can customize and save the workspace according to the project.

2.15.1. Save a workspace

A workspace can be saved as follows.

- Press the down arrow (⊡) on the *Workspace Switching* wheel, Figure 2-53a; it is located on the lower right side of the workspace. An option list appears; click on the *Save Current As* option, Figure 2-53b, to open the *Save Workspace* dialog box, Figure 2-50c.

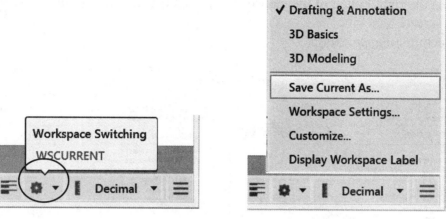

Figure 2-53a   **Figure 2-53b**

- Specify the name for the workspace, *Sample*, and press the *Save* button. The example workspace is saved as *Sample*, Figure 2-53c.
- If a workspace exists with the specified name, then the *AutoCAD* warning dialog box appears. Select *Replace* or *Cancel* as desired. The new workspace appears in the list of the workspaces, Figure 2-53d.

Figure 2-53c   **Figure 2-53d**

2.15.2. Rename a workspace

A workspace can be renamed as follows.

- (i) From the tab bar, select the *Manage* tab. (ii) From the *Customization* panel click on the *User Interface* command, the *CUI* icon ![CUI]. (iii) This opens the *Customize User Interface* dialog box.
- Click on the *Customize* tab of the *Customize User Interface* dialog box, Figure 2-54.
- Click on the workspace to be renamed, *Sample* in our example.

- Press the right button of the mouse; an options list shown in Figure 2-54 appears on the screen.
- Select the *rename* option.

Figure 2-54

- This closes the options list and the name (to be changed) is highlighted.
- Enter the new name and click anywhere on the screen. This activates the *Apply* button of the dialog box.
- Click the *Apply* or *OK* button.
- The *Apply* button does NOT close the *Customize User Interface* dialog box but makes the rename operation effective.
- The *OK* button closes the *Customize User Interface* dialog box as well as makes the rename operation permanent.

2.15.3. Switch a workspace

A workspace can be switched as follows. In this example, the current workspace, *Drafting & Annotation*, is switched to the *3D Basics* workspace.

- Press the down arrow (▾) on *Workspace Switching* wheel, Figure 2-55a; it is located on the lower right side of the workspace. An option list appears; click on the desired workspace, *3D Basics*, Figure 2-55b.
- The list is closed and the workspace is switched.

Figure 2-55a   **Figure 2-55b**

2.15.4. Delete a workspace

A workspace can be deleted as follows.

- (i) From the tab bar, select the *Manage* tab. (ii) From the *Customization* panel click on the *User Interface* command, the *CUI* icon ▦. (iii) This opens the *Customize User Interface* dialog box.
- Click on the *Customize* tab of the *Customize User Interface* dialog box.
- Click on the workspace to be deleted, 'Sample' in our example, Figure 2-56a.
- Press the right button of the mouse, the option box shown in Figure 2-56a appears on the screen.
- Select the *Delete* option.
- Press the *Enter* key or left or right button of the mouse.
- This closes the option box and opens the *AutoCAD* error message box, Figure 2-56b.
- Click the *Yes* button, Figure 2-56b. This closes the *AutoCAD* error message box and activates the *Apply* button of the *Customize User Interface* dialog box.
- Click the *Apply* or *OK* button of the *Customize User Interface* dialog box.
- The *Apply* button does NOT close the *Customize User Interface* dialog box but makes the delete operation permanent.

- The *OK* button closes the *Customize User Interface* dialog box as well as makes the delete operation permanent.

Figure 2-56a

Figure 2-56b

2.16.   Basics of a Drawing File

The basic features of any drawing are its name, input units format, drawing limits and grid and snap spacing. The user can select the default values when a new file is opened or reset as needed.

AutoCAD's native/standard file format is DWG; that is, files are saved with the extension '.dwg'. For example, a file named *My_First_Drawing* will be saved as *My_First_Drawing.dwg*. AutoCAD allows file interchange to (and/or from) other CAD applications. The commonly used formats are DXF (Drawing Exchange Format), DWF (Design Web Format), and WMF (Window Metafile Format). DXF is an ASCII or binary file for exporting/importing drawings to/from other applications. DWF is a compressed file created from a DWG file for faster publishing and viewing on the web. WMF files are commonly used to produce clip art.

2.17.   New Drawing

In AutoCAD, a new drawing can be opened using one of the following methods.

1. Menu method: Click on the down arrow from the *Application* pull-down menu, Figure 2-57a, and select the *New* option.

2. Toolbar method: Select the new drawing tool (⬚), Figure 2-57b, in the quick access toolbar. It is located on the upper left corner of the dialog box.

3. Command line method: Type "new", "New", or "NEW" in the command line, Figure 2-57c, and press the *Enter* key.

4. From the interface: Click with the **right** button of the mouse on the "+" sign as shown in Figure 2-57d, and select the *New* option.

5. Keyboard method: Hold down the control "Ctrl" key and type "N".

6. From the interface: Click with the **left** button of the mouse on the "+" sign as shown in Figure 2-57e, and select the *New Drawing* option.

Methods 1 - 5 discussed above open the *Select template* dialog box shown in Figure 2-58a and Figure 2-58b. Whereas, method 6 opens the default file.

Figure 2-57a

Figure 2-57b

Figure 2-57c

Figure 2-57d

Figure 2-57e

The *Select template* dialog box shown in Figure 2-58a shows the selection of the "acad" template, giving the drawing imperial (inch) units and ANSI style dimensions. Figure 2-58b shows the "acadiso" template, giving the drawing metric (millimeters) units and ISO style dimensions. To create a new drawing file, use the following steps: (i) select an appropriate template file based on the dimension's style; and (ii) click the *Open* button of the dialog box. This closes the dialog box and creates a new file.

The basic features of a drawing file are its name, drawing units, drawing limits, and grid and snap size. The *name* represents the unique identification of the file. As the name suggests, *drawing units* is used to set the input format of the sizes of the objects to create the drawing. The *drawing limit* is the metaphor for the size of the paper on which the drawing will be printed. The grid (a visible dotted or lined grid background) and snap (an invisible grid background) are used to improve the drawing process. These features are discussed in the next few sections of this chapter.

Figure 2-58a shows the selection of the "acad" template, giving the drawing imperial (inch) units and ANSI style dimensions. The drawing uses internal default values. In AutoCAD, a new drawing file is opened with the default values. For example, its name is

Drawing1, Drawing2, etc.; its units are decimal; the drawing limits are 12 x 9 inches; and the default values for both the grid and snap are 0.5 inches.

Figure 2-58a

Figure 2-58b shows the "acadiso" template, giving the drawing metric (millimeters) units and ISO style dimensions. The drawing uses internal default values. In AutoCAD, a new drawing file is opened with the default values. For example, its name is Drawing1, Drawing2, etc.; its units are decimal; the drawing limits are 420 x 290 millimeters; and the default values for both the grid and snap are 10 millimeters.

Figure 2-58b

In AutoCAD 2018, the open files (new or previously created) appear as tabs in the workspace, Figure 2-58c. In the figure, a tab (*Start*) and two files (*Drawing1* and *PanelCommands*) are open. A file can be made current by clicking its tab. The current file (*PanelCommands*) is highlighted and the other file (*Drawing1*) and the *Start* are grayed. The asterisk symbol indicates that the file contents are changed and the changes are not saved. File renaming and saving are discussed in later sections of this chapter.

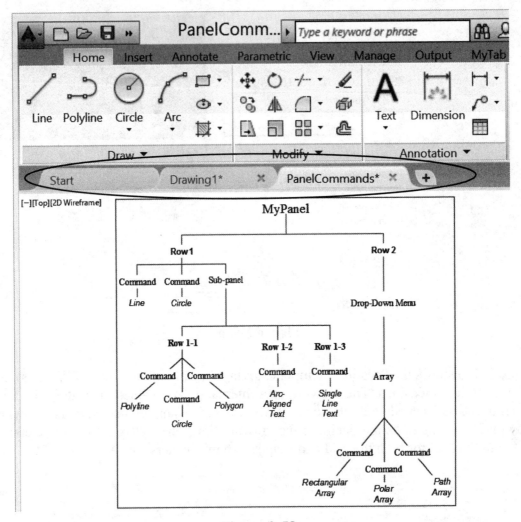

Figure 2-58c

2.18.   Drawing's Name
A drawing should always be assigned a short and meaningful name. For example, the file *Angles and NS* contains angles and north-south direction representation. A drawing name can be 256 characters long; and it can be any combination of letters (both upper and lower case), numbers, and symbols. Although, the user is allowed to use the characters $, %, and *, these characters should not be used. For example, YourName_1.dwg and ENGR2100_1.dwg are legitimate names but not 1_%.dwg or *.*.dwg.

2.19.   Drawing Units

As the name suggests, the drawing units is used to set the input format of the dimensions of the objects to create the drawing, that is, the style of the input values. For example, in ANSI style dimensions, the efficiency of the drafter can be increased if the lengths could be specified in architectural units (feet and inches) for drawing a floor plan. The *Units* command is used to set the input units. *A user must remember that the Units command is used to set the input format; the type of the units ANSI or ISO is set when a new file is open as "acad" or "acadiso" template file, respectively.*

1. Activate the *Units* command using command line method.
    a. Command line method: Type "units", "Units", or "UNITS" on the command line and press the *Enter* key.

The *Units* command opens the *Drawing Units* dialog box shown in Figure 2-59. Using the *Length* and *Angle* panels, the dialog box allows for setting the type and precision of the linear and angular measurements.

Figure 2-59

By default, AutoCAD sets the length in decimal format with precision of four decimal places; that is, length appears in the form 0.0000. The angular unit precision is set to whole degrees, that is, an angle appears in the form 0°. The dialog box also provides the capability to change the units of measurement for blocks and drawings that are inserted into the current drawing under *Insertion scale* panel.

2.19.1. Length

The *Length* panel specifies the format and the precision for the linear measurement of the current drawing. The linear measurements can be in five different formats, Figure 2-60a. The various options for length units (Figures 2-60a) can be visualized by clicking on the downward arrowhead (▾) for *Type* window in the *Length* panel of the *Drawing Units* dialog box, Figures 2-60a.

- To change the format, click on the desired format. This updates the format and closes the dropdown list. The example figure shows the selection of *Architectural* units.
- To close the dropdown list without changing the format, either press the *Esc* key or click outside the length panel.
- Similarly, the precision can be modified, Figures 2-60b. The example figure shows the precision for the *Architectural* units.

Figure 2-60a

Figure 2-60b

Each of the linear measurement's formats can be specified to nine degrees of precision, Table #1. The *Engineering* and *Architectural* formats produce feet-and-inches displays, and assume that each drawing unit represents one inch. The other three can be used for both the SI and ANSI systems to represent any real-world units. The *Decimal* formats produce a scale broken down into 10s. This is the default unit system in AutoCAD. The *Fractional* formats produce a scale in a mixed number format. The *Scientific* format uses exponential notation to display very large or small numbers.

Table #1: Linear measurements

Format	Precision
Architectural	0′-0″ to 0′-1/256″
Decimal	0 to 0.00000000
Fractional	0′-0″ to 0′-1/256″
Engineering	0′-0″ to 0′-0.00000000″
Scientific	0E+01 to 0.00000000E+01

2.19.2. Angle

The *Angle* panel specifies the format and the precision for the current angular measurement of the current drawing. The angular measurement can be in five different formats, Figure 2-61a. The various options for an angle shown in Figure 2-61a, can be visualized by clicking on the down arrowhead (▼) for *Type* window in the *Angle* panel of the *Drawing Units* dialog box, Figures 2-59.

- To change the angle format, click on the desired format. This will update the format and close the dropdown list. Figure 2-61a shows the selection of the *Decimal Degree.*
- To close the dropdown list without changing the format, either press the *Esc* key or click outside the *Angle* panel.
- Similarly, the precision can be modified, Figures 2-61b. The figure shows the precision for the *Decimal Degree.*

Each of the angular measurements can be specified to seven degrees of precision, Table #2. **Remember** the conversion! 400 grads are equal to 360 degrees and 2 Pi radians are equal to 360 degrees (2 π = 360° = 400 grad).

Figure 2-61a

Figure 2-61b

Table #2: Angular measurements

Format	Precision
Decimal degree	0 to 0.00000000
Deg/Min/Sec	0d to 0d00′00.0000″
Grads	0g to 0.00000000g
Radian	0r to 0.00000000r
Surveyor's Units	N 0d E to N 0d00′00.0000″ E

- An angle appears as a decimal number in the *Decimal* format.
- The *Deg/Min/Sec* format is represented with suffixes "d", "'", and "''" for degrees, minutes, and seconds, respectively.
- A lowercase "g" suffix is used for the *Grads* formats.
- A lowercase "r" suffix is used for the *Radians* formats.
- The *Surveyor's Units* show angles as bearings (angle always less than 90 degrees) measured from north or south towards east or west, Figure 2-61c. This representation has three parts: (i) N or S for north or south, (ii) angle's numerical value in degrees/minutes/seconds for how far from east or west, and (iii) E or W for east or west, for example N 35° 24′ 19″ W. If the angle is precisely north, south, east, or west, then only the single letter representing the compass point is displayed.

By default, AutoCAD starts with the zero angles at the 3 o'clock position (East) with angles increasing in the counterclockwise direction, Figure 2-61c and Figure 2-61d. To change the direction of angular measurement, check the *Clockwise* check box in the *Angle* panel of the *Drawing Units* dialogue box, Figure 2-59. When this box is checked, positive angles are measured in a clockwise direction.

To change the start angle, click on the "Direction…" button (Figure 2-59) in the *Drawing Units* dialogue box. The *Direction Control* dialogue box appears. The user can set the *Base Angle* to any one of the four major directions by clicking on the appropriate radio button or can set it to a specific angle with the "Other" option, Figures 2-61e. The user can enter a specific angle into the edit box. To change the directions of angular measurement (to E, N, S, or W) simply click on the appropriate radio button.

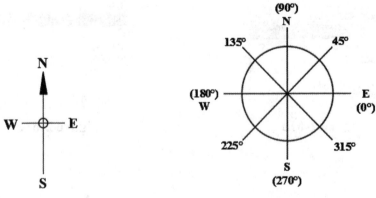

Figure 2-61c   Figure 2-61d

2.19.3. Insertion scale

The insertion scale is the ratio of the units used in the source drawing and the units used in the target drawing. That is, it controls the units of measurement for a drawing (source) that is inserted into the current drawing (target). If no scaling is desired then choose the *Unitless* option, Figure 2-62. The various options for insertion scale are shown in Figure 2-59; and can be visualized by clicking on the down arrowhead (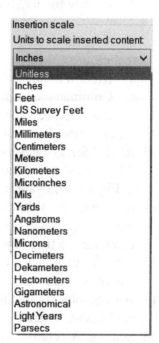) in the *Insertion scale* panel of the *Drawing Units* dialog box, Figure 2-62.

Figure 2-61e

Figure 2-62

2.19.4. Convert measurements from ISO to ANSI (and vice versa)

Every object in AutoCAD is measured in the drawing units. Before starting the drawing, the user must decide on the type and format of the input unit. The input type can be ANSI (inches, feet, miles, etc.) or ISO (milli-, centi-, kilo-, meters, etc.); and the input format can be decimal, architectural, engineering, fractional, and scientific. Based on the type, a user should open the correct type of template file (acad for ANSI or acadiso for ISO). However, if a user opens an incorrect file type and realizes the mistake after drawing a part (or complete) drawing, then the user can fix the mistake using *Copy* and *Scale* command. The *Copy* and *Scale* commands are discussed in Chapter 4.

If a drawing is started in one system of measurement (ANSI or ISO), then it can be switched to the other system by scaling the model geometry with the appropriate scaling factor. For example, if a drawing is created in centimeters and needs to be converted to inches, then scale the model geometry by a factor of 0.3937 (1 cm = 1/2.54 inch). To convert from inches to centimeters, the scale factor of 1/0.3937 or 2.54 must be used (1 inch = 2.54 cm).

Convert a drawing from centimeters to inches

1. *Note: Mac users should use the Command key instead of the Ctrl key.*
2. Select every object from the source file (hold the *Ctrl* key and press the '*A*' key).
3. Copy the content of the source drawing, (hold the *Ctrl* key and press the '*C*' key).
4. Open a new acad file (target file).
5. Click in the drawing area of the target file.
6. Paste the contents in the target drawing, (hold the *Ctrl* key and press the '*V*' key).
7. Now, scale the target drawing.

8. Scale command: Activate the *Scale* (⬚) command using one of the following techniques
   a. Ribbon method: From the *Home* tab and the *Modify* panel select the *Scale* tool.
   b. Command line method: Type "scale", "Scale", or "SCALE" in the command line and press the *Enter* key.
9. The prompt shown in Figure 2-63a appears on the screen.
10. At the *Select Objects* prompt, click on every object and then press the *Enter* key. All objects in the drawing are selected for scaling, Figure 2-63b. The prompt shown in Figure 2-63b appears.
11. A base point is the point which does not change its location after the completion of the scaling process. In this example, the tip of the nose is selected as the base point. Click on the tip of the nose. The prompt shown in Figure 2-63c appears.
12. Enter a scale factor of 0.3937, Figure 2-63c, (1 inch = 2.54 cm or 1/2.54 = 0.3937) and press the *Enter* key.
13. All the objects in the drawing are now 2.54 times smaller, corresponding to the equivalent distance in inches, Figure 2-63d.
14. Scaling is relative to the world coordinate system origin and the location of the drawing origin remains at the WCS origin.

Select objects:

Figure 2-63a

Figure 2-63b

Figure 2-63c

Figure 2-63d

2.20. Drawing Limits

Generally, the *drawing limits* is the metaphor for the size of the paper on which the drawing will be printed. The *Limits* command is used to set the boundaries of the drawing or grid display in the current *Model* or *Layout* tab. Generally, limits are set to match the size of the paper (on which the drawing will be printed). Figure 2-64a shows the standard size drawing papers for the engineering and architectural applications.

Standard Drawing Sheet Sizes – Millimeters
A4 = 210 * 297
A3 = 297 * 420
A2 = 420 * 594
A1 = 594 * 841
A0 = 841 * 1189

Standard Drawing Sheet Sizes – Inches
A = 8.5 * 11.0
B = 11.0 * 17.0
C = 17.0 * 22.0
D = 22.0 * 34.0
E = 34.0 * 44.0

Figure 2-64a

The default drawing limits are 12 x 9 inches in ANSI system and 420 x 290 millimeters in the ISO system. The following section provides step by step instructions for setting the drawing limits.

1. Activate the drawing limits command *Limits* using command line method.
   a. Command line method: Type "limits", "Limits", or "LIMITS" in the command line and press the *Enter* key.
2. This displays the prompt for the lower left corner shown in Figure 2-64b. The user can select any value for the lower limits. However, the *Limits* specification process can be simplified if the origin of the WCS (0, 0, 0) is selected as the lower limits.
3. Press the down arrow key on the keyboard to reveal the various options. The *ON* option restricts entering points outside the drawing limits. However, portions of objects such as circles can extend outside the drawing limits because limits check only test points that are entered. The default is *Off* (no limits checking).
4. Press the up arrow key on the keyboard to hide the various options.
5. To choose the default values (for either of the lower left and upper right corners) just press the *Enter* key on the keyboard.
6. Specify the coordinates of the lower left corner using one of the following methods. This example uses (0, 0) for the lower left corner.
   a. (i) Type '0' at the prompt, (ii) press the 'TAB' key on the keyboard, the cursor moves to the second cell, (iii) type '0', and (iv) press the *Enter* key.
   b. (i) Specify the x,y (no space) coordinates in the command line and (ii) press the *Enter* key.
   c. Click with the left button of the mouse at the desired location.
7. The prompt for the upper right corner appears, Figure 2-64c. Specify (10, 12) the coordinates for this point as follows. (i) Type '10' at the prompt, (ii) press the 'TAB' key on the keyboard, the cursor moves to the second cell, (iii) type '12', and (iv) press the *Enter* key.

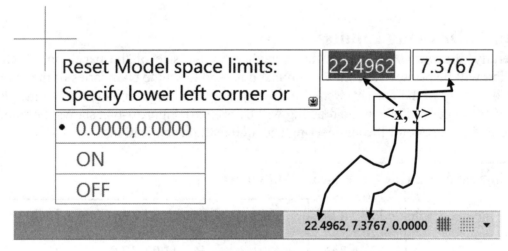

Figure 2-64b

Specify upper right corner < 10.0000,12.0000 >: ‖ 10 ▣ ‖ 12 ‖

Figure 2-64c

8. Turn on the *Grid* to check the drawing limits; the *Grid* command is discussed in next section. Figure 2-64d and Figure 2-64e shows the lower left corner   (0, 0, 0) and upper right corner (10, 12, 0) of the drawing limits, respectively.

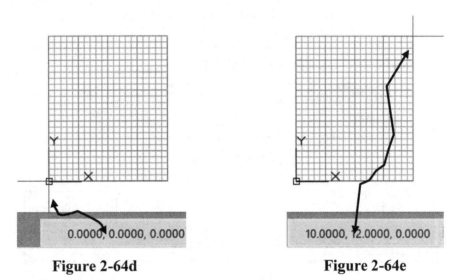

Figure 2-64d   **Figure 2-64e**

2.21.   Grid ( ) and Snap ( ) Commands

The *Grid* command is used to display a visible grid (similar to graph or engineering paper) background on the drawing screen. The *Snap* command is used to set an invisible grid background on the drawing screen; and to limit the movement of the cursor to the snap grid's points only. The snap grid is completely independent of the visible grid. However, the grid spacing and snap spacing are usually set to the same value to avoid confusion. The default *Grid* and *Snap* setting for an acad template is 0.50 inch and for an acadiso template is 10 millimeters. By default, the *Grid* (Figure 2-65a) and *Snap* (Figure 2-65b) command icons are located on the status bar. Notice the difference in appearance of the *On* and *Off* commands. However, if the command icons are not available from the status bar, Figure 2-65c, then the user must add the icon using *Customization* command.

A user can add the *Grid* and *Snap* commands icons on the status bar using the following techniques.
- Click the *Customize* button on the lower right corner of the status bar, Figure 2-65c. This opens a selection list, Figure 2-65d.
- Select the *Grid* option. A check mark appears on the left side of the *Grid* option, Figure 2-65e; and the *Grid* icon appears in the status bar.
- Repeat the process with *Snap Mode* option, Figure 2-65e.

By default, the grid appears both in the drawing area of the model space and in the layouts. However, the user can set the grid and snap properties independently in the model space and layouts. In addition, every layout can be set to its own style.

Figure 2-65a

Figure 2-65b

Figure 2-65c

Figure 2-65d

Figure 2-65e

2.21.1. Toggle Grid and Snap in the model space

A user can toggle the *Grid* and *Snap* options in the model space using one of the techniques listed below.

- Click the *Grid* and/or *Snap* buttons on the status bar (Figure 2-65a, Figure 2-65b).
- Press *F7* (for the *Grid*) and *F9* (for the *Snap*) keys of the keyboard.
- A user can toggle the *Grid* and *Snap* options using the *Drafting Setting* dialog box, Figure 2-66b, using the following methods.

o Open the *Drafting Setting* dialog box using one of the following methods.
- Bring the cursor on the *Grid* button on the status bar and click with the **right** button of the mouse, Figure 2-66a.
- Bring the cursor on the *Snap* button on the status bar and click with the **right** button of the mouse, Figure 2-66b.
- Bring the cursor on the small arrow on the *Snap* button on the status bar and click with the **left** button of the mouse, Figure 2-66b.
o On the dialog box, click the *Snap and Grid* tab.
o Finally, check or clear the boxes to the left of *Snap On* and *Grid On* to turn *On* or *Off* the corresponding option, Figure 2-66c.

Figure 2-66a   **Figure 2-66b**

Figure 2-66c

2.21.2. Toggle the Grid and Snap in the layout

In order to toggle the *Grid* and *Snap* buttons in a layout, first double click in the viewport (the solid rectangle), this makes the solid rectangle bold and the WCS appears in the viewport. Now toggle the grid and snap following the options discussed for the model space.

2.21.3. Grid properties

The grid properties (style, spacing, behavior, and color) can be set using the *Drafting Setting* dialog box, Figure 2-66c.

2.21.3.1. Grid style

A user can convert the solid grid lines (Figure 2-67a) into the dotted line (Figure 2-67b) and vice versa as follows. (i) In the *Drafting Setting* dialog box, Figure 2-66c, (ii) under the *Grid style* panel, the top panel on the left side of the dialog box, (iii) check the box beside the *2D model space*. The grid in the model space will change its appearance as shown in Figure 2-67b; however, the grid in the layout will not be changed.

Figure 2-67a

Figure 2-67b

2.21.3.2. Grid spacing

In the *Drafting Settings* dialog box, Figure 2-66c, the *Grid spacing* panel controls the spacing between the grid lines. It is on the left side of the dialog box.

- *Grid X-* and *Grid Y-Spacing*: The *Grid X-* and *Grid Y-Spacing* specifies the grid spacing in the X- and Y-direction, respectively. If the value is 0, then the grid assumes the value set for the Snap X- and Snap Y-spacing, respectively. **Important point**: To enhance the drawing speed, choose the grid spacing such that it is multiple of the minimum dimension. For example in Figure 2-68a the X- and Y-spacing should be 0.5.

- Major Line Every: This option is used to specify the frequency of major grid lines compared to minor grid lines. If the grid is displayed as lines then the bold lines are called major grid lines, and the lighter lines are called minor lines. In Figure 2-68b, the frequency is set to 5. When working in decimal units, the major grid lines are especially useful for measuring distances quickly. In order to turn *Off* the display of major grid lines, set the frequency of the major grid lines to be 1.

Figure 2-68a

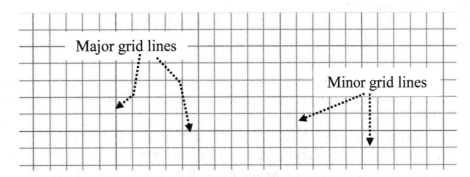

Figure 2-68b

2.21.3.3.   Grid behavior

In the *Drafting Settings* dialog box, Figure 2-66c, the *Grid behavior* panel controls the appearance of the grid lines. It is the bottom panel on the left side of the dialog box. In case of the dotted grid, the grid dots are displayed only for the major grid lines.

- Adaptive grid: If the *Adaptive Grid* box is checked, then the density of the grid lines is updated when zooming options are used.
- *Allow subdivision below grid spacing*: This option generates additional, grid lines when zoomed in. The frequency of these additional lines is determined by the frequency of the major grid lines.
- Display grid beyond limits: This option displays the grid beyond the area specified by the drawing limits.
- Follow Dynamic UCS: This option changes the grid plane to follow the XY plane of the dynamic UCS.

2.21.3.4. Grid color
The dotted grid's color is the same as the cursor color. The grid color can be changed as follows:

- Click with the right button in the *Drawing area* and select the *Options* option or type *Options* on the command line and press the *Enter* key.
- The *Options* dialog box will appear on the screen.
- Click the *Display* tab of the *Options* dialog box by clicking on it.
- Press the *Color* button in the *Window Elements* panel to open the *Drawing Window Colors* dialog box.
- In the *Drawing Window Colors* dialog box, under *Context* panel choose *2D model space*, under *Interface element* panel choose *Grid major line*, and under the *Color* options panel select the desired color. The selection is highlighted. In the *Preview* window, the color of the grid will change to the selected color.
- Similarly, change the colors of the *Grid minor line* and *Grid axes line*.

2.21.4. Snap properties

2.21.4.1. Snap spacing
In the *Drafting Setting* dialog box, Figure 2-66c, the *Snap spacing* panel controls the spacing of the invisible, rectangular snap's grid.

- *Snap X- and Snap Y-Spacing*: This option specifies the invisible grid spacing in the X- and Y-directions, respectively. The value must be a positive real number (that is 0.5, 1.0, etc.).
- *Equal X-and Y-Spacing*: The snap and grid spacing intervals can be different from each other. If this box is checked, then both the *Grid X-* and *Y-spacing* are the same; and both the *Snap X-* and *Y-spacing* are of the same values. However, if this box is not checked, then *Snap X-*, *Snap Y-*, *Grid X-*, and *Grid Y-spacing* can be different from each other. In Figure 2-69, the *Grid* and *Snap's* *X-* and *Y-spacing* are all different.

2.21.4.2. Polar spacing
In the *Drafting Setting* dialog box, Figure 2-69, the *Polar spacing* panel controls the polar snap's increment distance.

- *Polar Distance*: Sets the snap increment distance when *PolarSnap* is selected under the *Snap Type*. If this value is 0, then the *PolarSnap* distance assumes the value for the *Snap X spacing*.

2.21.4.3. Snap type
In the *Drafting Settings* dialog box, Figure 2-69, the *Snap type* panel controls the type of the snap.

- *Grid snap*: This option sets the snap type to the *Grid*. In this case, the cursor snaps along vertical or horizontal grid points. This type is further subdivided into two groups.

- o Rectangular snap: This radio button sets the snap style to a rectangular snap mode. Now, the cursor snaps to the rectangular snap grid, Figure 2-70a.
- o Isometric snap: This radio button sets the snap style to the isometric snap mode. Now, the cursor snaps to an isometric snap grid, Figure 2-70b.
- *PolarSnap*: Sets the snap type to *Polar*. When *Snap* mode is *On* and the user specify points with polar tracking turned *On*, the cursor snaps along polar alignment angles set on the *Polar Tracking* tab relative to the starting polar tracking point.

Figure 2-69

Figure 2-70a   **Figure 2-70b**

2.22. Save a File

In AutoCAD, a file can be saved using the *Save As* or *Save* command.

2.22.1. Save As

A newly created file can be saved using the *Save As* command. The same technique is used to save a copy of a previously saved file with a different name. The *Save As* command is activated using one of the following procedures.

1. Menu method: Select the *Application* pull-down menu, Figure 2-71a, and select the *Save As* option.
2. Toolbar method: Select the save as drawing tool (), Figure 2-71b, in the quick access toolbar. It is located on the upper left corner of the dialog box.
3. Command line method: Type "Saveas", "SaveAs", or "SAVEAS" in the command line and press the *Enter* key.
4. Keyboard method: Hold down the control "Ctrl" key and type "s".

Figure 2-71a

Figure 2-71b

Any of the four methods discussed above opens the *Save Drawing As* dialog box, Figure 2-71c. The dialog box shows the default name, *Drawing1*. To save a file, specify the name in the *File Name* box using the naming convention and press the *Save* button. The AutoCAD files are automatically saved with the *dwg* extension. For example, if the user specifies the name Ex_2_1, it is saved as Ex_2_1.dwg.

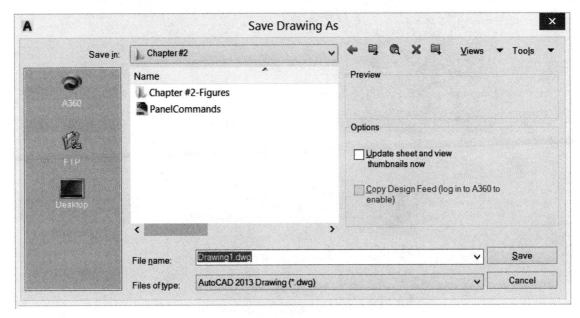

Figure 2-71c

2.22.2. Save

The *Save* command is also called a quick save. It is mainly used to save previously saved files with the same name. The *Save* command is activated using one of the following procedures.

1. Menu method: Select the *Application* pull-down menu, Figure 2-72a, and select the *Save* option.
2. Toolbar method: Select the save as drawing tool (), Figure 2-72b, in the quick access toolbar. It is located on the upper left corner of the dialog box.
3. Command line method: Type "Save", "Save", or "SAVE" in the command line and press the *Enter* key.
4. Keyboard method: Hold down the control "Ctrl" key and type "s".

Figure 2-72a

Figure 2-72b

2.23.   Open a Pre-existing File

In AutoCAD, a pre-existing file can be opened in four different ways using the open command. The *Open* command is activated using one of the following methods.

1. Menu method: Select the *Application* pull-down menu, Figure 2-73a, and select the *Open* option.

2. Toolbar method: Select the open drawing tool ( ), Figure 2-73b, in the quick access toolbar. It is located on the upper left corner of the dialog box.

3. Command line method: Type "open", "Open", or "OPEN" in the command line and press the *Enter* key.

4. Keyboard method: Hold down the control "Ctrl" key and type 'o' or 'O'

Any of the four methods discussed above will open the *Select File* dialog box shown in Figure 2-73c.

The dialog box lists all of the drawing files in the folder. If the *Thumbnail* option under the *View* menu is selected, then thumbnails are displayed. If the *Preview* option under the *View* menu is selected, then a bitmap of the selected file is displayed in the *Preview* window. The *Preview* window is blank if none of the files are selected. The preview option is the default method and is shown in Figure 2-73c.

Figure 2-73a

Figure 2-73b

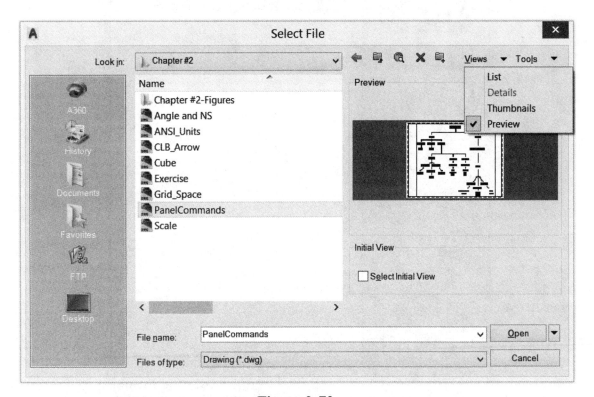

Figure 2-73c

2.24.   Close a File

In AutoCAD, an open file can be closed via *Close* command. The command is activated using one of the following procedures.

1. Menu method: Select the *Application* pull-down menu, Figure 2-74a, and select the *Close* option.
2. Interface method: Click on the "x" sign on the right side of the file name as shown in Figure 2-74b.
3. From the file: Click on the "x" sign on the upper right corner of the file as shown in Figure 2-74c.
4. Command line method: Type "close", "Close", or "CLOSE" in the command line and press the *Enter* key.

Figure 2-74a

Figure 2-74b **Figure 2-74c**

The above methods either close the file (if it was saved after the last modification) or the file save error message (Figure 2-74d) appears. In case of an error message, click the appropriate button and follow the prompts.

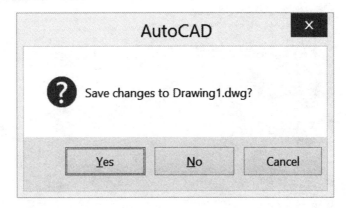

Figure 2-74d

2.25. Exit AutoCAD

The *Exit* command is used to close AutoCAD; it can be activated using one of the following techniques.

1. Menu method: Select the *Application* pull-down menu, Figure 2-75a, and select the *Exit Autodesk AutoCAD 2018* option.
2. Interface method: Click on the "X" at the upper right corner of the AutoCAD window, Figure 2-75b.
3. Command line method: Type "exit", "Exit", "EXIT", "quit", "Quit", or "QUIT" on the command line and press the *Enter* key.
4. Keyboard method: Hold the *Ctrl* key and press the 'q' or 'Q' key.

The activation of this command quits the program! However, if the drawing has been modified after the last save, the prompt to save or discard the changes appears. If there has been no change since the drawing was last saved, then both the file and AutoCAD are closed.

Figure 2-75a

Figure 2-75b

3.   Basics of 2-Dimensional Drawings

3.1.   Learning Objectives

After completing this chapter, you will demonstrate competency in the following areas:

- The dynamic input capabilities
- Draw commands (Point, Line, Circle, Polygon, Polyline, Ellipse, Arc, Rectangle)
- Appearance of an object: color, line thickness, and pattern (dotted, dashed, phantom, etc.)
- Hatch
- Multiline text
- Tables

3.2.   Introduction

A drafter can create unlimited designs by creating new drawings and editing existing drawings. The focus of this chapter is the AutoCAD capabilities to draw two-dimensional drawing objects. To achieve these functionalities, AutoCAD provides the *Draw* panel from the *Home* tab, Figure 3-1. The figure shows the expanded and pinned (check the pin at the lower left corner) panel.

Figure 3-1

Before discussing the commands, it is important to know about the appearance of the prompt, data input, and the coordinates systems necessary to complete the commands.

3.3.   Dynamic Input ⁺▬

The draftsman can keep focus in the drawing area if the prompt to a command appears near the cursor, Figure 3-2a. The software provides this capability through the usage of *Dynamic Input*. The dynamic input is the command interface near the cursor.

Figure 3-2a

The *Dynamic Input* icon (⁺▬) is located on the status bar, Figure 3-2b. By default, the icon is not displayed on the status bar. Therefore, the user can display the icon as follows: (i) Press the *Customization* option with the left button of the mouse, Figure 3-2b. This displays an option list Figure 3-2c. (ii) Click on the *Dynamic Input* option. This closes the options list and displays the icon in the status bar.

Figure 3-2b

Figure 3-2c

Figure 3-2d

3.3.1. Toggle dynamic input

The dynamic input option can be activated by clicking the *Dynamic Input* button on the status bar or by pressing the *F12* key. However, the dynamic input option can be deactivated by clicking the *Dynamic Input* button on the status bar.

3.3.2. Components of a dynamic input

A user can set the dynamic input properties from the *Drafting Settings* dialog box, Figure 3-3b. The *Drafting Settings* dialog box can be opened as follows.

- (i) Bring the cursor on the *Dynamic Input* button. (ii) Right click and select the *Dynamic Input Settings* option, Figure 3-3a. This opens the *Drafting Settings* dialog box. (ii) Select the *Dynamic Input* tab of the dialog box, Figure 3-3b.

Figure 3-3a

The *Dynamic Input* tab, Figure 3-3b, of the *Drafting Settings* dialog box contains three major components: *Pointer Input*, *Dimension Input*, and *Dynamic Prompts*. The dialog box also contains four check boxes, and all of the boxes should be checked as shown in Figure 3-3b. The details of these boxes are provided in their respective sections.

Figure 3-3b

3.3.2.1.   Pointer input

To check the capabilities of the pointer input, click the *Settings* button in the *Pointer Input* panel (Figure 3-3b); this opens the *Pointer Input Settings* dialog box (Figure 3-4a). The *Pointer Input Settings* dialog box is used to change the coordinates' format: polar or Cartesian and relative or absolute; the coordinates are discussed in the next section. This dialog box also controls the pointer input tooltips display.

If the *Enable Pointer Input* box (Figure 3-3b) is checked and in Figure 3-4a under the *Visibility* panel the last option (*Always*) is selected then the location of the crosshairs is displayed as coordinates in the tooltip near the cursor, Figure 3-4b. To avoid confusion, it is a good drawing practice to use the *When a command asks for a point* option, Figure 3-4a under the *Visibility* panel. The coordinate values can be entered in the tooltip, too.

Note: The user must check the *Enable Pointer Input* box in Figure 3-3b. Otherwise, the capabilities discussed in this section are NOT effective!

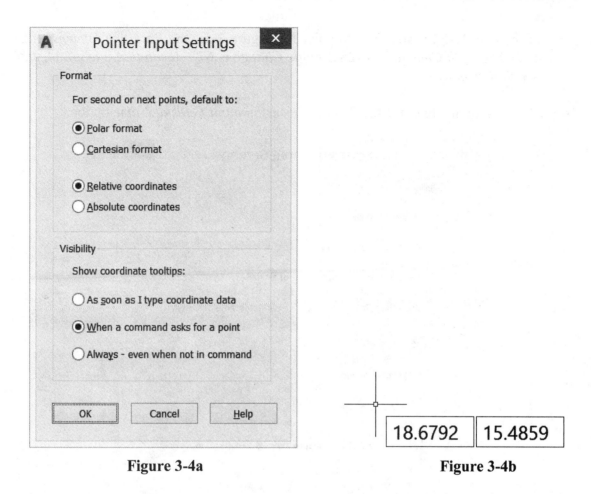

Figure 3-4a   **Figure 3-4b**

3.3.2.2.   Dimension input

To check the capabilities of the dimension input, click the *Enable Dimensional Input where possible* box (Figure 3-3b). This option is used to display the dimensions' values when a command demands for a second point. The value in the dimensional tooltip changes as the cursor moves.

The user can set the dimensional input characteristics from the *Dimension Input Settings* dialog box, Figure 3-5a. The dialog box can be opened by clicking the *Settings* button in the *Dimension Input* panel, Figure 3-3b. The line P1-P2 of length 4.39 at an angle of 64° with the x-axis and point P3 shown in Figure 3-5b are used to explain the behavior of the options of the dialog box. The remainder of this section discusses the *Dimension Input Settings* dialog box.

- *Show only 1 dimension input field at a time*: If this option is selected then only the change in length (0.1282) is displayed when point P2 of the line P1-P2 is stretched to point P3, Figure 3-5c.
- *Show 2 dimension input fields at a time*: If this option is selected then the change in length (0.1282) and the new length (4.2569) are displayed when point P2 of the line P1-P2 is stretched to point P3, Figure 3-5d.
- *Show the following dimension input fields simultaneously*: This option displays a combination of the dimensions by checking the appropriate boxes. When point P2

of the line P1-P2 is stretched to point P3, Figure 3-5e, the *Resulting Dimension* is 4.2569, *Length Change* is 0.1282, *Angle Change* is 67°, *Absolute Angle* is 21°, and *Arc Radius* is 43°.

Note: The best option to use is the *Show 2 dimension input fields at a time* option.

Figure 3-5a

Figure 3-5b   **Figure 3-5c**

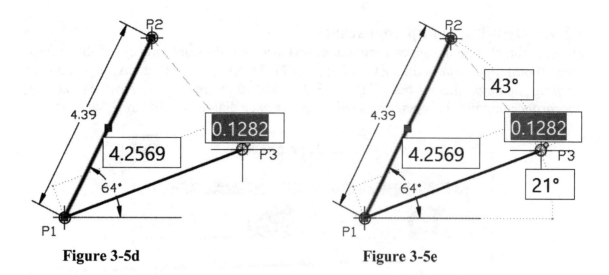

Figure 3-5d   **Figure 3-5e**

3.3.2.3.   Dynamic prompts

To display the dynamic prompt, in the *Dynamic Prompts* panel, click the check box in the *Show command prompting and command input near the crosshairs* (Figure 3-3b). If the box is checked then the prompts are displayed in a tooltip near the cursor. Figure 3-6a shows a command's prompt near the cursor.

Figure 3-6a

On some of the prompts, the down arrow (⬇) indicates that the current prompt has multiple options. To display the options list, press the down arrow key of the keyboard. The Figure 3-6b shows the commands to hatch an area after pressing the down arrow key. The down arrow key of the keyboard and/or the left button of the mouse can be used to select the options. The figure shows the selection of the *Undo* option.

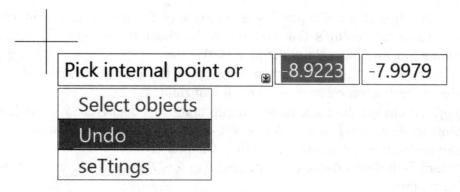

Figure 3-6b

3.3.3. Drafting tooltip appearance

The user can change the appearance (color, text size, and the transparency) of the prompt using *Tooltip Appearance* dialog box, Figure 3-7a. To open this dialog box, first open the *Drafting Settings* dialog box (Figure 3-3b) and then press the *Drafting Tooltip Appearance* button. This opens the *Tooltip Appearance* dialog box, Figure 3-7a.

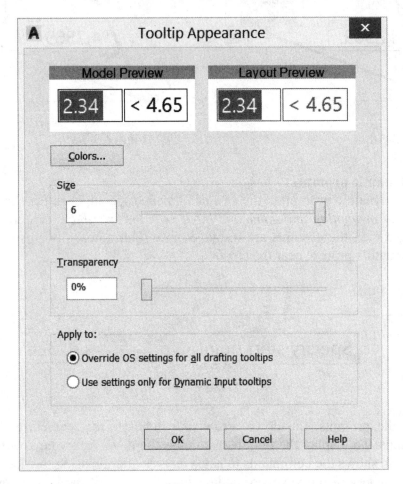

Figure 3-7a

- Size: The slider in the *Size* panel is used to change the size of the text in the tool tip. To increase the tooltip's font size move the slider to the right. To decrease the tooltip's font size move the slider to the left.
- Transparency: To change the transparency of the tooltip background, move the slider in the *Transparency* panel to the left or right.
- Color: To change the color of the tooltip and/or its background, press the *Colors* button to open the *Drawing Window Colors* dialog box. The *Drawing Window Color* dialog box is discussed in detail in Chapter 2.
  o Figure 3-7b shows the color of the *Drafting tool tip* that is, the color of the text of the prompt.
  o Figure 3-7c shows the color of the *Drafting tool tip contour* that is, the rectangular outline of the prompt.
  o Figure 3-7d shows the color of the *Drafting tool tip background* used in the text.

Figure 3-7b

Figure 3-7c

Figure 3-7d

3.4. Input Data

The input prompt of the Figure 3.6a contains 2 input fields. The cursor can be moved from one input field to the other using the *Tab*, ",", or "<" keys of the keyboard. Type a value in an input field and press one of the three keys. However, if a value is typed followed by pressing the *Enter* key, then the second and subsequent input fields will be ignored.

3.4.1.1. Tab key

The tab key is used for entering the polar (length, angle) coordinates.

1. Type a value in an input field and press the tab key; the field will display a lock icon (Figure 3-8a) and the cursor is constrained by the value just entered. The cursor also moves to the second input field. Finally, type in the value in the second field and press the *Enter* key.

Figure 3-8a

2. If the user wants to move to the second field without changing the value of the first field then press the tab key and the cursor moves to the second input field, Figure 3-8b. Note that the lock did not appear in the first field. Type in the value in the second field and press the *Enter* key.

Figure 3-8b

3.4.1.2.   Comma key

The comma "," key is used for entering the Cartesian coordinates, 2D (x, y) or 3D (x, y, z).

1. Type a value in an input field and press the comma key; the field displays a lock icon (Figure 3-8c) and the cursor is constrained by the value just entered. The cursor, also moves to the second input field. Finally, type in the value in the second field and press the *Enter* key. For the Three-dimensional values, repeat the process of the second input field with the third input field.
2. If the user wants to move to the second field without changing the value of the first field then first move the cursor to the right end of the input field and then just press the comma key and the cursor moves to the second input field, Figure 3-8c. Type in the value in the second field and press the *Enter* key.

Figure 3-8c

3.4.1.3.   Less than key

The less than (<) key is used for entering the polar (length, angle) coordinates.

1. Type a value in an input field and press the "<" key; the field displays a lock icon (Figure 3-8d) and the cursor is constrained by the value just entered. The cursor also moves to the second input field. Finally, type in the value in the second field and press the *Enter* key.

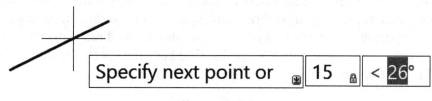

Figure 3-8d

2. If the user wants to move to the second field without changing the value of the first field then first move the cursor to the right end of the input field and then press the "<" key and the cursor moves to the second input field, Figure 3-8e. Note the difference in the prompts of Figure 3-8d and Figure 3-8e. In Figure 3-8e, the length of the line is not displayed. Type in the value in the second field and press the *Enter* key.

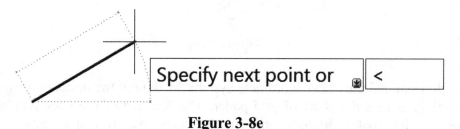

Figure 3-8e

3.4.1.4.   Remove typing errors from the dynamic input tooltips

If there is an error in the dynamic input then the tooltip displays the red outline, Figure 3-8f. To remove the error, type over the selected text to replace it and continue the command.

Figure 3-8f

3.5.   Reference System

For the two-dimensional drawing, AutoCAD provides two reference systems: Cartesian coordinates and polar coordinates systems.

3.5.1. Cartesian coordinates

A Cartesian (also known as a rectangular) coordinate system has three mutually perpendicular and intersecting axes, X, Y, and Z. The origin (0, 0, 0) is the location where the three axes intersect. The x-coordinate value indicates a point's distance in units and its direction, positive or negative, along the X-axis with respect to the origin. This principle also applies to the Y- and Z axes.

In AutoCAD, the three-dimensional Cartesian coordinates values are specified as a comma separated tuple (x,y,z) without any space. The coordinate's values can be a positive or a negative number. Figure 3-9a shows a three-dimensional Cartesian coordinate system with the origin at point P1. The coordinates for P1 and P2 are (0, 0, 0) and (4.0, 5.0, 3.0), respectively.

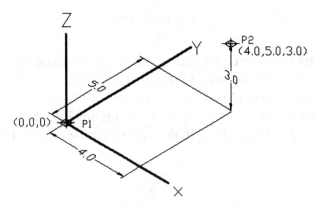

Figure 3-9a

In a two-dimensional Cartesian coordinate system, by default the drawing area is the XY plane, analogous to a flat sheet of grid paper. The X value of the Cartesian coordinate specifies the horizontal distance and the Y value specifies the vertical distance. Figure 3-9b shows a two-dimensional Cartesian coordinate system with the origin at point P1. The coordinates for P1 and P2 are (0, 0) and (3.4, 2.9), respectively.

Figure 3-9b

3.5.2. Polar coordinates

A polar system uses a distance and an angle to locate a point. Figure 3-9c shows a polar coordinate system with its origin at point P1. The angle is measured with respect to a reference axis. For polar coordinates, the coordinate values are specified as an ordered pair (distance, angle). The coordinates for P1 and P2 are (0,0) and (6.6,34°), respectively.

In AutoCAD, the coordinate values are specified as an ordered pair separated by an angle bracket (Length<Angle). By default, the angle increases in the counterclockwise direction and decreases in the clockwise direction. To specify a clockwise direction, enter a negative value for the angle. For example, (5<300) and (5<-60) locates the same point.

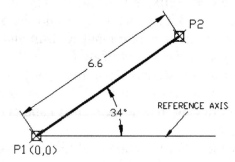

Figure 3-9c

3.5.3.   AutoCAD and the coordinate systems

Distance is always measured from a benchmark or a reference point. Based on the benchmark, there are two types of coordinate system, absolute and relative. The absolute coordinates are always measured from the benchmark, whereas, the relative coordinates are measured with respect to the previous point. Both the Cartesian and polar coordinates can be measured either as absolute coordinates or relative coordinates.

In Figure 3-10, point P1 (0, 0) is the benchmark. The figure shows the absolute coordinates of the points P2 (4.5,3.2) and P3 (8.1,1.2). The figure also shows the relative coordinates of point P3 (3.5,-2.0) with respect to point P2.

Figure 3-10

In AutoCAD, both the absolute and relative coordinates can be specified on the command line or on the tooltip of the dynamic input.

3.5.3.1.   Absolute Cartesian coordinates

In AutoCAD, the origin of the WCS is used as the benchmark for the absolute coordinates. The absolute Cartesian coordinates are used when the precise location of x-

and y-coordinates of a point are known. In the dynamic input, the absolute coordinates are specified using the # prefix. However, for the command line the prefix is not used.

- **_Example:_** Using absolute coordinate (AC) draw a line from point P2 to point P3 of Figure 3-10 using one of the following two methods.

  1. Dynamic input method: In the case of the dynamic input, specify the absolute coordinates with the # prefix, Figure 3-11a. (i) Activate the *Line* command. (ii) Click at point P2. (iii) Type the # sign (hold the *Shift* key and press # key). The # sign appears in the dynamic input tool tip and cursor moves to the first input field. (iv) Type in the x-coordinate (that is 8). (v) Press the comma key. The cursor moves to the second input field. (vi) Now, type the y-coordinate (that is 1.2). (vii) For a two-dimensional drawing, press the *Enter* key. For the three-dimensional drawing, repeat the step (v) and (vi) for the z-coordinate and then press the *Enter* key.
  2. Command line method: For the command line the # is not used. Type 8,1.2 (no space) and press the *Enter* key.

Figure 3-11a

3.5.3.2. Relative Cartesian coordinates

For the relative coordinates, the last point is used as the benchmark for the relative coordinates of the next point. The relative coordinates are used when the location of the next point is known with respect to the previous point.

- **_Example:_** Using relative coordinates (RC) draw a line from point P2 to point P3 of Figure 3-10 using one of the following two methods.

  1. Dynamic input method: In the case of the dynamic input, specify the relative coordinates with the @ prefix, Figure 3-11b. (i) Activate the *Line* command. (ii) Click at point P2. (iii) Type the @ sign (hold the *Shift* key and press @ key). The @ sign appears in the dynamic input tool tip and the cursor will move to the first input field. (iv) Type in the x-coordinate (that is 3.5). (v) Press the comma key. The cursor moves to the second input field. (vi) Now, type the y-coordinate (that is -2.0). (vii) For the two-dimensional drawing, press the *Enter* key. For the three-dimensional drawing, repeat the steps (v) and (vi) for the z-coordinate and then press the *Enter* key.

2. Command line method: For the command line the @ is used. Type @1.5,-2.5 (no space) and press the *Enter* key.

Figure 3-11b

3.5.3.3.   Absolute Polar coordinates

In AutoCAD, the origin of the WCS is used as the benchmark for the absolute coordinates. The absolute polar coordinates are used when the precise distance and angle coordinates of a point are known.

*   ***Example:*** Draw a line from point P2 to point P3. The absolute polar coordinates of point P3 are (8.09,9°) using one of the following two methods.

    1. Dynamic input method: In case of the dynamic input, specify the absolute coordinates with the # prefix, Figure 3-12a. (i) Activate the line Command. (ii) Click at point P2. (iii) Type the # sign (hold the *Shift* key and press # key). The # sign appears in the dynamic input tool tip and cursor moves to the first input field. (iv) Type in the distance (that is 8.09). (v) Press the Less than (<) key. The cursor moves to the second input field. (vi) Now, type the angle (that is 9). (vii) Finally, press the *Enter* key.
    2. Command line method: For the command line, the # is not used. Type 8.09<9 (no space) and press the *Enter* key.

Figure 3-12a

3.5.3.4.   Relative Polar coordinates

For the relative coordinates, the last point is used as the benchmark for the relative coordinates of the next point. The relative coordinates are used when the location of the next point is known with respect to the previous point.

- **_Example:_** Draw a line from point P2 to point P3. The relative polar coordinates of point P3 with respect to P2 are (4.03, -30°) using one of the following two methods.

  1. Dynamic input method: In the case of the dynamic input, specify the relative coordinates with the @ prefix, Figure 3-12b. (i) Click at point P2. (ii) Type the @ sign (hold the *Shift* key and press @ key). The @ sign appears in the dynamic input tool tip and cursor moves to the first input field. (iii) Type in the distance (that is 4.03). (iv) Press the Less than (<) key. The cursor moves to the second input field. (v) Now, type the angle (that is -30). (vi) Finally, press the *Enter* key.
  2. Command line method: For the command line the @ is used. Type @4.03<-30 (no space) and press the *Enter* key.

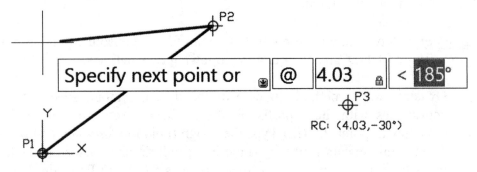

Figure 3-12b

3.6.   Point

Figure 3-13a shows an electric circuit with bulbs; in this circuit, bulbs are represented by points. In AutoCAD, points are drawn using the *Point* command. AutoCAD's *Point* command makes a distinction between drawing a single point and multiple points. The multiple points command can be used to draw a single point; however, the single point command cannot be used to draw multiple points.

- The *Point* command is activated using one of the following methods.
  1. Panel method: From the *Home* tab and *Draw* panel, select the *Point* tool to activate the option to draw multiple points, Figure 3-13b.
  2. Command line method: Type "point", "Point", or "POINT" in the command line and press the *Enter* key to activate an option to draw a single point.

Figure 3-13a

Figure 3-13b

- The activation of the command results in the prompt to specify a point, Figure 3-13c. A point can be drawn using one of the following procedures.

Figure 3-13c

1. Click at a random point on the screen.
2. Specify the coordinates on the command line: (i) type in the values of the point as x,y (no space); and (ii) press the *Enter* key.
3. Specify the coordinates as a dynamic input.
   a. To specify the (x, y) coordinates (i) type the value of the x-coordinate in the first field; (ii) press the "," key; (iii) type the y-coordinate; and (iv) finally press the *Enter* key.
   b. To specify the (x, y, z) coordinates (i) type the value of the x-coordinate in the first field; (ii) press the "," key; (iii) type the y-coordinate; (iv) press the "," key; (v) type the z-coordinate; (vi) and finally press the *Enter* key.
   c. To specify the polar coordinates (length and angle), (i) type the value of length in the first field; (ii) press "<" or "tab" key; (iii) type the angle in the second field; and (iv) finally press the *Enter* key.

- **Note**: To change a locked value, Figure 3-13c, cycle through the input field using the *Tab* key to reach to the desired field, and then follow the procedure discussed above.
- To **Exit** the command, press the *Esc* key from the keyboard. Do **NOT** press the *Enter* key on the keyboard.

3.6.1. Change style and size of a point

To change the appearance and size of a point, from the *Home* tab and *Utilities* panel select the *Point Style* option, Figure 3-13d. This openes the *Point Style* dialog box, Figure 3-13e. This dialog box is used to change the style and size of a point.

3.6.1.1.   Style

Changing the style makes the points more visible and easier to differentiate from the grid dots. To change the style, click on the desired shape and press the *OK* button. This will close the dialog box and changes the appearance of every point in the current drawing to the selected shape.

3.6.1.2.   Point size

This option allows for changing the size of the points. The *Set Size Relative to Screen* option sets the point display size as a percentage of the screen size. The *Set Size in Absolute Units* option sets the point display size as the actual units. In order to keep the point size independent of the zooming effect, choose the second option.

| Figure 3-13d | Figure 3-13e |

3.7.   Line

The *Line* command is used to draw a straight line between two points.

- The *Line* command is activated using one of the following methods.
  1. Panel method: From the *Home* tab and *Draw* panel, select the *Line* tool, Figure 3-14a.
  2. Command line method: Type "line", "Line", or "LINE" on the command line and press the *Enter* key.

In order to visualize the prompts near the cursor, turn on the dynamic input option by clicking the dynamic input button ( ) on the status bar. In AutoCAD, based on the available information, a line segment can be drawn using one of the following techniques.

Figure 3-14a

3.7.1. Points selection

In point selection method, lines are drawn by clicking at the points in the drawing area. The draftsman may or may not draw the points before drawing the lines.

Example: Assume a surveyor has drawn four stations (A, B, C, and D) on a map, Figure 3-14b. Now, the stations are required to be connected by straight roads. The desired roads can be drawn as follows.

1. Activate the *Line* command.
2. Click at station A and then click at station B. A line segment is drawn from station A to station B, Figure 3-14b. Press the down arrow key of the keyboard to check the available options. Only the *Undo* option is available.

Figure 3-14b

3. Now, click at station C, a line segment is drawn from station B to station C, Figure 3-14c. Press the down arrow key from the keyboard to check the available options. Now, the *Close* option is available, too. The close option is available only after the user has clicked at least three points (that is, has drawn two line segments).
4. Repeat step (3) to draw a line from station C to station D.
5. Press the down arrow key from the keyboard and click on the *Close* option, Figure 3-14d. The selection of the *Close* option automatically draws a line from D to A and terminates the *Line* command.
6. To exit the command without creating a closed area, press the *Esc* or the *Enter* key.

Figure 3-14c

Figure 3-14d

3.7.2. Snap points

In snap point method, lines are drawn by counting and snapping at the grid points, Figure 3-15b.

Example: A travelling salesperson wants to travel 200 meters to the east from the station at (35, 55) meters; that is, the current station is located at x = 35 and y = 55 from the origin, Figure 3-15a. The salesperson's current location and destination can be drawn as follows.

1. Turn on the *Grid* (▦) and *Snap* (▦) options by clicking the respective buttons on the status bar. Now, the user is allowed to click only at the snap points.
2. Set the *Grid spacing* to be 10.0 and the *Snap spacing* to be 5.0.
3. The number of grid points can be accurately counted as:
    No. of grid points = Length of a line / Grid spacing

4. Calculate the coordinates of the current location and destination as follows:
    o   Current location of the salesperson is (35, 55); that is, 3.5 (35/10) grid points in the x-direction and 5.5 (55/10) grid points in the y-direction.

o Destination of the salesperson is at (200, 0) from the current location; that is, 200/10 grid points in x-direction. The value of the y-coordinate is not changed because the salesperson is travelling in the east direction.

5. Turn on the dynamic input option by clicking the dynamic input button ( ) on the status bar.

6. Activate the *Line* command.

7. For the current location of the salesperson (first point of the line), Figure 3-15a, click at (35, 55); that is, 3.5 and 5.5 grid points in the x- and y-direction, respectively.

8. For the salesperson's destination, click at (200, 0) from the current location; that is, 20 and 0 grid points in x- and y-direction, respectively, Figure 3-15b.

9. Press the *Enter* key to exit the command.

Figure 3-15a

Figure 3-15b

3.7.3. Cartesian coordinates

In Cartesian coordinate's method, lines are drawn by specifying the x-, y-, and z-coordinates of their end points.

Example: Draw a line from point P2 to point P3 using absolute and relative Cartesian coordinate.

1. Refer to Section 3.5.3.1 for the absolute Cartesian coordinates.
2. Refer to Section 3.5.3.2 for the relative Cartesian coordinates.

3.7.4. Polar coordinates

In polar coordinates method, a line is drawn by specifying its length and angle from a reference axis.

Example: Draw a line from point P2 to point P3 using absolute and relative polar coordinates.

1. Refer to Section 3.5.3.3 for the absolute polar coordinates.
2. Refer to Section 3.5.3.4 for the relative polar coordinates.

3.7.5.   Orthogonal command ⌐

The orthogonal lines mean that the lines are perpendicular, since the X- and Y-axes are at a right angle with respect to each other. Hence, lines parallel to the X- and Y-axes are perpendicular lines. In AutoCAD terminology, an orthogonal command means that the lines are parallel to the X- and Y-axis. By default, for the two-dimensional drawings, the X-axis is horizontal and the Y-axis is vertical. Figure 3-16a shows a pair of perpendicular or orthogonal lines. Figure 3-18b shows the angles between two orthogonal lines. The angle can be 0º, 90º, 180º, or 270º. In AutoCAD, by default the clockwise angles are negative, Figure 3-16b.

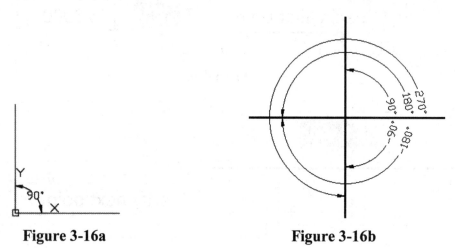

Figure 3-16a   **Figure 3-16b**

Example: Draw the object shown in Figure 3-17a using polar coordinates and orthogonal command. Recall that the polar coordinate needs length and angle. In the current example, there are 14 line segments. Hence, the user needs to specify 14 lengths and 14 angles. Since the lines are either horizontal or vertical, the AutoCAD user can increase productivity by using the *Ortho* command. This command allows the user to draw the orthogonal lines by specifying the lengths only, thus, saving 50% of the time required to draw the drawing!

Figure 3-17a

The user can draw the given shape using the following steps:

1. Turn *On* the dynamic input option by clicking the dynamic input button ( ) on the status bar.
2. Turn *On* the *Ortho* mode by clicking on the orthogonal mode button ( ) on the status bar.
3. Activate the *Line* command.
4. The drawing can be started at point A or B. However, in the current example, the drawing is started at point A.
5. To begin the drawing, click at a random point near the WCS.
6. Move the cursor in the direction of the line to be drawn, Figure 3-17b.

Figure 3-17b

7. Specify the length (300) and press the *Enter* key. **No need to specify the angle**. Now, move the cursor in the direction of the next line to be drawn, Figure 3-17c.

Figure 3-17c

8. Specify the length (100) and press the *Enter* key. No need to specify the angle. Now, move the cursor in the direction of the next line to be drawn, Figure 3-17d.
9. Repeat the above process and complete the drawing as shown in Figure 3-17a.

Figure 3-17d

3.8.   Circle

The user can draw a circle using six different methods (Figure 3-18a) using the *Circle* command. The circle command is used to draw a circle by specifying its center and the radius or diameter; a circle can also be drawn with two or three points on its circumference; and a circle of a known radius and tangent to two objects or a circle tangent to three objects can be drawn, too.

- The *Circle* command is activated using one of the following procedures.
  1. Panel method: From the *Home* tab and *Draw* panel, select the *Circle* tool, Figure 3-18a. Use the down arrow key from the keyboard to display the various options; select the desired option and the prompt for the selected option will open.
  2. Command line method: Type "circle", "Circle", or "CIRCLE" in the command line and press the *Enter* key.

Figure 3-18a

- The activation of the command results in the prompt shown in Figure 3-18b. Use the down arrow key from the keyboard to display the various options. However, if the user expands the *Circle*'s drop-down menu from the *Draw* panel, Figure 3-18a, then the user can select the desired option and the prompt is for the selected option. The user can use the left button of the mouse or dropdown arrow to select a particular option.

- The remainder of this section explains how to use Circle command to draw a circle.

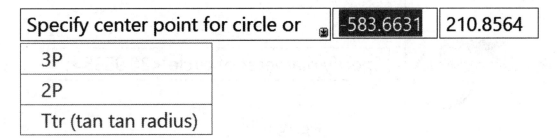

Figure 3-18b

- <u>Center point (default) option</u>: This option draws a circle based on the center point and the radius or the diameter of the circle.
    1. *Specify center point for circle or*: Either click at the desired location in the drawing area or specify the coordinates of the center of the circle and press the *Enter* key. The prompt to specify the radius appears on the screen, Figure 3-19a. Click the down arrow and check the available option. To draw the circle with

the radius option, perform step #2 and skip step #3; and for the diameter option skip step #2 and perform step #3.

Figure 3-19a

2. *Specify radius of circle or*: Press the up arrow to hide the options shown in Figure 3-19a. Type the radius (radius is the default option), Figure 3-19b. Press the *Enter* key or click with the right button of the mouse and select the *Enter* option from the menu. The circle of the specified radius appears on the screen.

Figure 3-19b

3. *Diameter option*: In Figure 3-19a, click the *Diameter* option. The prompt shown in Figure 3-19c appears. Type the diameter and press the *Enter* key. The circle of the specified diameter appears on the screen.

Figure 3-19c

• <u>Two points' option</u>: This option draws a circle based on the two endpoints of the diameter. The advantage of this command is that the user is not required to know the location of the center of the circle and its radius or diameter. This demonstration will use points *A* and *B* to draw the circle with *2P* option, Figure 3-20a.

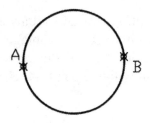

Figure 3-20a

1. Draw two points, *A* and *B*. Do not label them.
2. Activate the circle command. Either Press the down arrow and click on *2P* option, Figure 3-20b; or choose *2P* option from Figure 3-18a.

Figure 3-20b

3. *Specify the first end point of circle's diameter* (Figure 3-20c): Either type the comma separated coordinates of the first point or click at the desired location. For the current example, click at point *A*.

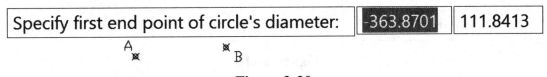

Figure 3-20c

4. *Specify the second end point of the circle's diameter* (Figure 3-20d): Either type the polar or Cartesian coordinates of the second point or click at the desired location. For the current example, click at *B*.
5. The resultant circle is shown in Figure 3-20a.

Figure 3-20d

- <u>Three points' option</u>: This option is used to draw a circle based on the three points on the circumference of the circle. The advantage of this command is that the user is not required to know the location of the center of the circle and its radius or diameter. This demonstration will use points *A*, *B*, and *C* to draw the circle with *3P* option, Figure 3-21a.

1. Draw three points, *A*, *B* and *C*. Do not label them.
2. Activate the circle command. Either Press the down arrow and click the *3P* option, Figure 3-21b; or choose the *3P* option from Figure 3-18a.

Figure 3-21a

Figure 3-21b

3. *Specify the first point on circle* (Figure 3-21c): Either type the comma separated coordinates of the first point or click at the desired location. In the current example, click at *A*.

Specify first point on circle:	-359.6948	34.2934

Figure 3-21c

4. *Specify the second point on circle* (Figure 3-21d): Either type the polar or Cartesian coordinates of the second point or click at the desired location. In the current example, click at *B*.

Figure 3-21d

5. *Specify third point on circle* (Figure 3-21e): Either type the polar or Cartesian coordinates of the third point or click at the desired location. In the current example, click at *C*.
6. The resultant circle is shown in Figure 3-21a.

Figure 3-21e

- <u>Tan, Tan, Radius (Ttr) option</u>: This option draws a circle of a specified radius that is tangent to two objects. This command can draw a circle tangent to two circles, two arcs, two lines, or combination of two objects. The current example draws a circle tangent to a circle and a line.

1. Open an "acad" file and draw a 15 inches long line. Choose any value for the angle. Now draw a circle of diameter 10 inches with its center at the lower end of the line, Figure 3-22a.

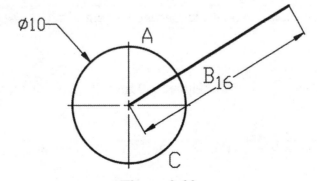

Figure 3-22a

2. Activate the circle command.
3. Press the down arrow and choose the "*Ttr*" option, Figure 3-22b. The prompt shown in Figure 3-24c appears on the screen.

Figure 3-22b

4. *Specify point on the object for first tangent of circle* (Figure 3-22c). Either enter the comma separated coordinates of the tangent on the first object, or click roughly in the vicinity of the tangent. In this example click near label *A* on the circle. Do not draw the labels *A* and *B*. These labels are used only for referencing.

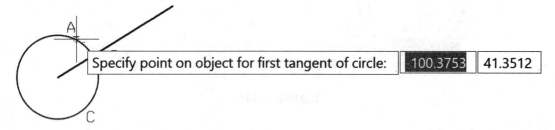

Figure 3-22c

5. *Specify point on object for second tangent of circle* (Figure 3-22d). Either enter the coordinates (Cartesian or polar) of the tangent on the second object, or click roughly in the vicinity of the tangent. In this example click near *B* on the line.

Figure 3-22d

6. *Specify radius of circle* (Figure 3-22e). Specify the radius to be 2.5 and press the *Enter* key.

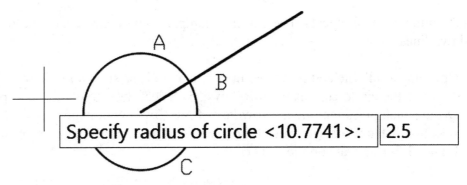

Figure 3-22e

7. This exits the command and draws the circle, Figure 3-22f.
8. If the specified radius is smaller than the smallest possible circle tangent to the selected objects, then the program does not draw a circle. In Figure 3-23b, a circle tangent to the smaller circles and of radius less than 3 inches cannot be drawn.
9. Repeat the process from step #2 - #6; click near point C in step #5. The resulting circle is shown in Figure 3-23a.

Figure 3-22f   **Figure 3-23a**

10. In Figure 3-23b and Figure 3-23c, a circle (shown as dashed line) is drawn tangent to two circles and tangent to two lines, respectively.

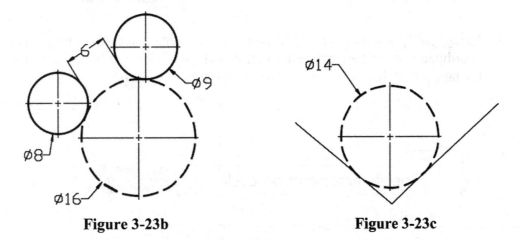

Figure 3-23b   **Figure 3-23c**

- <u>Tan, Tan, Tan option</u>: This option draws a circle that is tangent to three objects. This command can draw a circle tangent to three circles, three arcs, three lines, or combination of three objects. The current example draws a circle tangent to a circle and two lines.

1. Open an "acad" file and draw two lines and a circle as shown in Figure 3-24a.
2. Activate the circle command as follows: (i) Select the *Home* tab. (ii) From the *Draw* panel, press the down arrow key of the *Circle* command, Figure 3-24a; a selection list appears. (iii) Select the *Tan, Tan Tan* option. The prompt shown in Figure 3-24c appears on the screen.

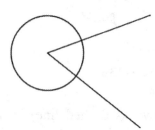

Figure 3-24a   **Figure 3-24b**

3. *Specify first point on circle: to* (Figure 3-24c). Either enter the comma separated coordinates of the tangent on the first object, or click roughly in the vicinity of the tangent. In this example click as shown in Figure 3-24c.

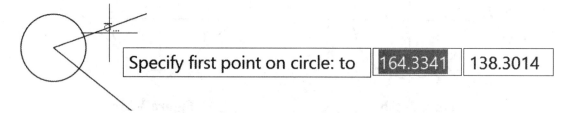

Figure 3-24c

4. *Specify second point on circle: to* (Figure 3-24d). Either enter the coordinates (Cartesian or polar) of the tangent on the second object, or click roughly in the vicinity of the tangent. In this example click as shown in Figure 3-24d.

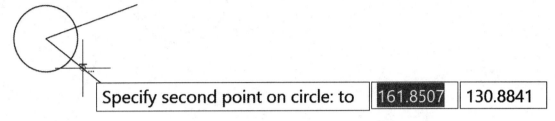

Figure 3-24d

5. *Specify third point on circle: to* (Figure 3-24e). Either enter the coordinates (Cartesian or polar) of the tangent on the second object, or click roughly in the vicinity of the tangent. In this example click as shown in Figure 3-24e.

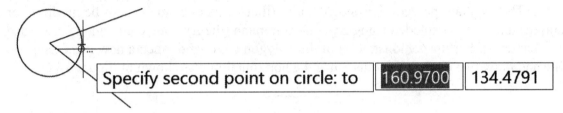

Figure 3-24e

6. This exits the command and draws the circle, Figure 3-24f.
7. Repeat the process from step #2 - #6; click near the end of the lines inside the circle in steps #3 - #4. The resulting circle is shown in Figure 3-24g.
8. If the circle cannot be drawn tangent to the three objects, then it is drawn tangent to one or two objects. Figure 3-25a shows three lines and the tangent points; and Figure 3-25b shows a circle which is tangent to two lines.

Figure 3-24f   **Figure 3-24g**

Figure 3-25a   **Figure 3-25b**

3.9.   Polygon

The *Polygon* command is used to draw a regular polygon, that is, a polygon with equal sides. The resultant polygon is a single entity (that is, its one side cannot be modified or erased) unless it is exploded using *Explode* command (the *Explode* command is discussed in Chapter 4). For the demonstration of the polygon command, open a new *acad* template file and draw two circles of radius 3in and a horizontal line as shown in Figure 3-26a.

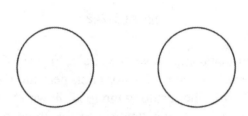

Figure 3-26a

- The *Polygon* command is activated using one of the following procedures.
  1. Panel method: From the *Home* tab and *Draw* panel, press the down arrow beside the rectangle and select the *Polygon* tool, Figure 3-26b.
  2. Command line method: Type "polygon", "Polygon", or "POLYGON" in the command line and press the *Enter* key.

Figure 3-26b

- The activation of the command will result in the prompt to enter the number of sides of the polygon, Figure 3-26c

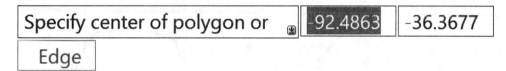

Figure 3-26c

- *Enter number of sides*: Specify a number between 3 and 1024 and press the *Enter* key. This example will create an octagon (8 sided polygon). Press the down arrow key from the keyboard to display the various options, Figure 3-26d.
- The user either specifies the center of the polygon or chooses the edge option.

Figure 3-26d

- <u>Center option</u>: This option creates a polygon by specifying its center (the user had already specified the number of edges), Figure 3-26c.
  1. *Specify center of polygon*: Either specify the coordinates of the center point and press the *Enter* key; or click in the drawing area at the desired location. For this example, click at the center point of one of the circles drawn earlier. The next prompt is shown in Figure 3-26e.
  2. *Enter an option [Inscribed in circle/Circumscribed about circle]* Figure 3-26e. Click on the *Inscribed in Circle* option. The prompt shown in Figure 3-26f appears on the screen.
  3. *Specify radius of circle*: Specify the radius (type 3 for the radius), Figure 3-26f, and press the *Enter* key.

Figure 3-26e

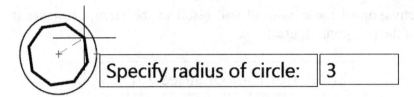

Figure 3-26f

4. The *Inscribed in Circle* option specifies the radius of a circle on which all the vertices of the polygon lie (that is, the polygon is drawn inside the circle), Figure 3-26g. *Circumscribed about Circle* option specifies the distance from the center of the polygon to the midpoints of the edges of the polygon (that is, the polygon is drawn outside the circle), Figure 3-26h.

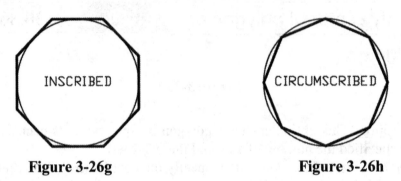

Figure 3-26g   **Figure 3-26h**

-   Edge option: This option creates a polygon by specifying the endpoints of one of the edges (the user had already specified the number of edges). This example also creates an 8 sided polygon.

    1. Click on the edge option as shown in Figure 3-27a. The prompt shown in Figure 3-27b appears.

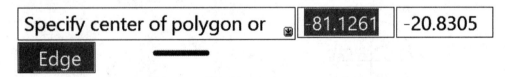

Figure 3-27a

    2. *Specify first endpoint of the edge*: Figure 3-27b, either specify the coordinates and press the *Enter* key; or click in the drawing area. Click on one of the two ends of the line drawn earlier in Figure 3-27a. The prompt shown in Figure 3-27c will appear.

Specify first endpoint of edge: -64.9218 -21.7617

Figure 3-27b

3. *Specify the second endpoint of the edge*: Figure 3-27c, either specify the coordinates and press the *Enter* key or click in the drawing area. The size of the polygon will change as the cursor is moved. Click on the other end of the line.

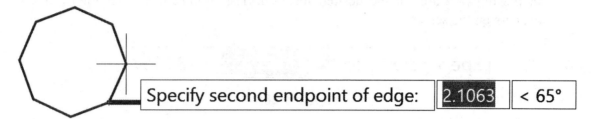

Figure 3-27c

4. The resultant polygon is shown in Figure 3-27d.

Figure 3-27d

3.10. Polyline

The *Polyline* command is used to draw an object composed of one or more connected line segments or circular arcs. The resultant polyline is a single entity; that is, one of its segments cannot be modified independently. A polyline can be converted to multiple entities using *Explode* command (the *Explode* command is discussed in Chapter 4).

- The *Polyline* command is activated using one of the following procedures.
  1. Panel method: From the *Home* tab and *Draw* panel, select the *Polyline* tool, Figure 3-28a.
  2. Command line method: Type "pline", "Pline", or "PLINE" in the command line and press the *Enter* key.

Figure 3-28a

- The activation of the command results in the prompt to specify the start point, Figure 3-28b.
- *Specify start point*: Either specify the coordinates and press the *Enter* key, or click in the drawing area at the desired location. The prompt shown in Figure 3-28c appears on the screen.

Specify start point:	308.9258	186.7970

Figure 3-28b

Figure 3-28c

- <u>Arc option</u>: The arc option creates arc segments in a polyline. Click on the *Arc* option in Figure 3-28c. The prompt shown in Figure 3-29 appears on the screen. Either specify the endpoint of the arc or press the down arrow key from the keyboard to display the options list, Figure 3-29.

Figure 3-29

1. <u>Angle</u>: The *Angle* option of Figure 3-29 allows for the specification of the included angle of an arc segment from the start point. A positive angle creates a counterclockwise arc segment and a negative angle creates a clockwise arc segment. (i) Activate the polyline command. (ii) Click at the Start point of Figure 3-30a. (iii) Press the down arrow on the keyboard and select the *Arc* option in Figure 3.28c. (iv) Press the down arrow on the keyboard and select the *Angle* option in Figure 3.29. The prompt shown in Figure 3-30b appears on the screen. (v) Specify the angle and press the *Enter* key, Figure 3-30c. (vi) For the *endpoint* option click at the End point of Figure 3-30a. For the *CEnter* option click at the CEnter of Figure 3-30a. For the *Radius* option specify its value. (vii) Press the *Enter* key. The resultant arc is shown in Figure 3-30a. The user is ready to draw the next command.

Figure 3-30a

Figure 3-30b

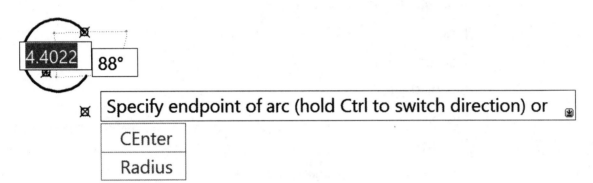

Figure 3-30c

2. <u>CEnter</u>: The *CEnter* option of Figure 3-29 allows for the specification of the center of the arc segment. (i) Activate the polyline command. (ii) Click at the start point of Figure 3-30a. (iii) Press the down arrow on the keyboard and select the *Arc* option in Figure 3.28c. (iv) Press the down arrow on the keyboard and select the *CEnter* option in Figure 3.29. (v) Specify the center of the arc segment, either through the coordinates or by clicking in the drawing area, Figure 3-31a. (vi) Choose endpoint, angle, or length option, specify the value, and press the *Enter* key, Figure 3-31b. For the current example, select the angle option, Figure 3-31c. (vii) Specify the included angle, Figure 3-31c. (viii) Press the *Enter* key. The resulting arc is shown in Figure 3-31d. Note that the positive angle resulted in a counterclockwise arc. The user is ready to draw the next command.

Figure 3-31a

Figure 3-31b

Figure 3-31c

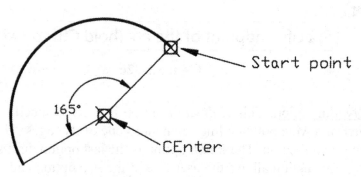

Figure 3-31d

3. <u>Direction</u>: The *Direction* option of Figure 3-29 allows for the specification of the direction of the arc segment. (i) Draw three points as shown in Figure 3-32a. Do NOT label the points. (ii) Activate the polyline command. (iii) Click at the point P1 for the start point. (iv) Press the down arrow on the keyboard and select the *Arc* option in Figure 3.28c. (v) Press the down arrow key on the keyboard and select the *Direction* option in Figure 3.29. (vi) Specify the starting direction for the arc segment. In order to draw an arc from point P1 to P3 as shown in Figure 3-32a, point P2 should be clicked for the tangent direction, Figure 3-32b. (vii) Finally, for the endpoint, click at P3, Figure 3-32c.

(viii) Press the *Enter* key. The resulting arc is shown in Figure 3-32a. The user is ready to draw the next command.

Figure 3-32a

Figure 3-32b

Figure 3-32c

4. Halfwidth option: This *Halfwidth* option is used to specify the width from the center of a wide polyline line segment to one of its edges. The process is similar to the *Width* option. The *Width* option is the last option discussed in this section.
5. Line: This option allows the user to exit the *Arc* option and returns to the initial polyline command prompts.
6. Radius option: The *radius* option requires the uset to specify the radius of the arc after the specification of its start point.
7. Second pt: Specifies the second point and endpoint of a three-point arc.
8. Undo option: The *Undo* option deletes the most recent line segment added to the polyline.
9. Width option: The *Width* option specifies the width of the next line segment of the polyline. (i) Activate the polyline command. (ii) Press the down arrow on the keyboard and select the *Arc* option in Figure 3.28c. (iii) Press the down arrow key from the keyboard and select the *Width* option in Figure 3.29. (iv) *Specify starting width*: Enter a value and press the *Enter* key, Figure 3-33a. (v) *Specify ending width*: Enter a value and press the *Enter* key, Figure 3-33b.

(vi) The ending width is the uniform width for all the subsequent segments until the width is changed again, Figure 3-33c.

Figure 3-33a

Figure 3-33b

Figure 3-33c

3.11.   Ellipse

The *Ellipse* command is used to draw elliptical shapes. An ellipse is determined by its two axes: the major (longer) and the minor (shorter) axis, Figure 3-34a.

- The *Ellipse* command is activated using one of the following procedures.
  1. Panel method: From the *Home* tab and *Draw* panel, select the desired *Ellipse* tool, Figure 3-34b.
  2. Command line method: Type "ellipse", "Ellipse", or "ELLIPSE" in the command line and press the *Enter* key.

Figure 3-34a   **Figure 3-34b**

- If the *Ellipse* command is activated from the command line, then the prompt shown in Figure 3-34c appears. Press the down arrow and select the desired option. However, if the user expands the *Ellipse*'s drop-down menu, Figure 3-34b, then the user can select the desired option and the prompt is for the selected option.

Figure 3-34c

- Center option: This option creates an ellipse by specifying its center.

  1. The user can draw the points as shown in Figure 3-35a before the activation of the *Ellipse* command. Do NOT label the points

Figure 3-35a

  2. Activate the *Ellipse* command and select the *Center* option, Figure 3-34b or Figure 3-34c. The resulting prompt is shown in Figure 3-35b.

Figure 3-35b

  3. Specify the center point. Either click at the desired location in the drawing area or specify the coordinates of the center of the ellipse and press the *Enter* key. The resulting prompt is shown in Figure 3-35c.
  4. Specify the endpoint of one of the two axes. Choose the end of the major or minor axis; that is, select point 1 or 2. This example clicks on point 2, Figure 3-35c. The resulting prompt is shown in Figure 3-35d.

Figure 3-35c

5. Specify the distance to the other axis. This example clicks on point 1, Figure 3-35d.
6. The resulting ellipse is shown in Figure 3-35e.

Figure 3-35d

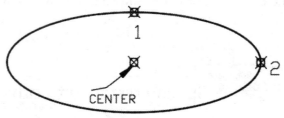

Figure 3-35e

- Axis endpoint option: This option draws an ellipse by specifying the end points of the two axes. **Note**: The order of the points' selection is important.

1. The user can draw the three end points as shown in Figure 3-36a or draw two perpendicular straight lines, representing the major and minor axes before the activation of the *Ellipse* command.

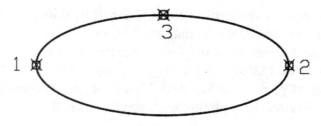

Figure 3-36a

2. Activate the *Ellipse* command and select the *Axis endpoint* option, Figure 3-35b or Figure 3-35c. The resulting prompt is shown in Figure 3-36b.

Figure 3-36b

3. Either click at points 1 of Figure 3-36a or specify its coordinates and press the *Enter* key. The prompt shown in Figure 3-36c appears.

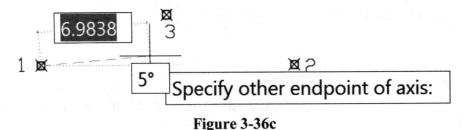

Figure 3-36c

4. Either click at points 2 of Figure 3-36a or specify its coordinates and press the *Enter* key. The prompt shown in Figure 3-36d appears.
5. Either click at points 3 of Figure 3-36a or specify its coordinates and press the *Enter* key. The ellipse is created as shown in Figure 3-36a.

Figure 3-36d

- <u>Arc option</u>: This option draws an elliptical arc. The order of the points' selection is important.

- <u>***Example:***</u> Draw an elliptical arc between points 6 and 7 of Figure 3-37a as follows.

1. The user can draw the points (do NOT label) as shown in Figure 3-37a before the activation of the *Ellipse* command.
2. Activate the *Ellipse* command and select the *Arc* option, 3-37b. The resulting prompt is shown in Figure 3-37c.
3. Either click at points 3 of Figure 3-37c or specify its coordinates and press the *Enter* key. The resulting prompt is shown in Figure 3-37d.

Figure 3-37a

Figure 3-37b

Figure 3-37c

4. Either click at points 4 of Figure 3-37d or specify its coordinates and press the *Enter* key. The resulting prompt is shown in Figure 3-37e.

Figure 3-37d

5. Specify the distance to the other axis by either clicking at points 5 of Figure 3-37e or specifying its coordinates and pressing the *Enter* key. The resulting prompt is shown in Figure 3-37f.

Figure 3-37e

6. Specify the start angle by clicking at point 6; either click on the point or specify the angle (52°), Figure 3-37f, and press the *Enter* key. The resulting prompt is shown in Figure 3-37g.

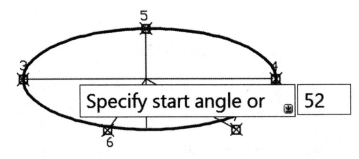

Figure 3-37f

7. Specify the end angle by clicking at point 7; either click on the point or specify the end angle (127°), Figure 3-37g, and press the *Enter* key. The resultant arc is shown in Figure 3-37h.

Figure 3-37g

Figure 3-37h

3.12. Elliptical Arc

To create an elliptical arc, follow the procedure of the *Arc option* explained in the Ellipse's section.

3.13. Circular Arc

To create a circular arc, follow the procedure of the *Arc option* explained in the Ellipse's section. However, the distance to point 5 should be equal to half of the distance between points 3 and 4.

3.14. Rectangle

The *Rectangle* command is used to draw a rectangular shape. Under this command a rectangle is created by specifying the distance between points diagonally apart. The resultant rectangle is a single entity; that is, one of its sides cannot be erased. A rectangle can be converted to multiple entities using the *Explode* command (the *Explode* command is discussed in Chapter 4).

- The *Rectangle* command is activated using one of the following procedures.
  1. Panel method: From the *Home* tab and *Draw* panel, select the *Rectangle* tool, Figure 3-38a.
  2. Command line method: Type "rectangle", "Rectangle", or "RECTANGLE" in the command line and press the *Enter* key.

Figure 3-38a

- The activation of the command results in the prompt shown in Figure 3-38b. Use the down arrow key to display the various options. The *Elevation* and *Thickness* options are useful for the 3D modeling. The *width* option specifies the width of the polyline used to draw a rectangle and is discussed in the polyline section. The *Chamfer* and *Fillet* options control the type of corners for the rectangle and are discussed in Chapter 4.

Figure 3-38b

- <u>Corner option</u>: This is the default option. This option creates a rectangle by specifying its diagonally opposite corners.

   1. Activate the *Rectangle* command; the resulting prompt is shown in Figure 3-38c.

Figure 3-38c

   2. *Specify the first corner point*: Either enter the coordinate's values and press the *Enter* key or click at the desired location. The next prompt is shown in Figure 3-38d. Press the down arrow key from the keyboard to check the option.

Figure 3-38d

3. *Specify the other corner point*: Press the up arrow on the keyboard to hide the option in Figure 3-38d. Either specify the coordinates of the diagonally opposite corner or click at the desired location. The resulting Rectangle is shown in Figure 3-38e.

Figure 3-38e

- Area option: This option creates a rectangle by specifying its area and either its length or width.

1. (i) Activate the *Rectangle* command; (ii) specify the first corner; and (iii) press the down arrow key on the keyboard and select the *Area* option, Figure 3-39a. The resulting command is shown in Figure 3-39b.

Figure 3-39a

2. *Enter area of a rectangle*: Specify area as a positive number (375 in this example) and press the *Enter* key. The resulting prompt is shown in Figure 3-39c.

Enter area of rectangle in current units <100.0000>: || 375

Figure 3-39b

3. *Calculate rectangle dimensions based on*: Press the down arrow key from the keyboard, Figure 3-39c. Select the *Length* or *Width* option. This example selects *Length* option. The resulting prompt is shown in Figure 3-39d.
4. *Enter rectangle length*: Specify length as a positive number and press the *Enter* key. This example chooses 25 units, Figure 3-39d.
5. The resultant rectangle of area 375 and length 25 is created, Figure 3-39e.

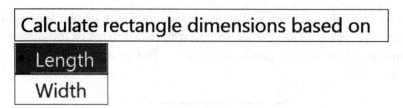

Figure 3-39c

Enter rectangle length <10.0000>:   25

Figure 3-39d

AREA = 375

25

Figure 3-39e

- <u>Dimensions option</u>: This option creates a rectangle by specifying its length and width.

    1. (i) Activate the *Rectangle* command; (ii) specify the first corner; and (iii) press the down arrow on the keyboard and select the *Dimensions* option, Figure 3-41a. The resulting prompt is shown in Figure 3-40b.
    2. *Specify length of the rectangle*: Specify length as a positive number (30 in this example) and press the *Enter* key, Figure 3-40b. The resulting prompt is shown in Figure 3-40c.

Figure 3-40a

Specify length for rectangles <25.0000>:   30

Figure 3-40b

3. *Specify width of the rectangle*: Specify width as a positive number (20 in this example) and press the *Enter* key, Figure 3-40c. The resulting prompt is shown in Figure 3-40d.

Specify width for rectangles <15.0000>: | 20

Figure 3-40c

4. A rectangle of specified dimensions is created and is pinned at the first corner point, point *C* in Figure 3-40e. As the cursor moves, the rectangle flips around the first corner point.

Specify other corner point or 2.4915 -6.1567

Figure 3-40d

5. Click in the desired direction. In this example, click on the diagonally opposite corner. The resulting rectangle of length 25 and width 20 is created and is shown in Figure 3-40e.

Figure 3-40e

- Rotation option: This option creates a rectangle at a specified rotation angle.

  1. (i) Activate the *Rectangle* command; (ii) specify the first corner; and (iii) press the down arrow on the keyboard and select the *Rotation* option, Figure 3-41a. The resulting prompt is shown in Figure 3-41b.
  2. *Specify rotation angle*: The default angle is 0°. Positive angles rotate the rectangle counterclockwise (Figure 3-41b) and negative angles rotate the rectangle clockwise (Figure 3-41c). Specify the rotation angle and press the *Enter* key. In this example, type 135, no need to type degree symbol.

Figure 3-41a

Figure 3-41b

Specify rotation angle or ⌄ -135

Figure 3-41c

3. Create the rectangle using *Area* or *Dimensions* options. Note that the positive angle creates the rectangle rotated counterclockwise, Figure 3-41d; and the negative angle creates the rectangle rotated clockwise, Figure 3-41e.

Figure 3-41d   **Figure 3-41e**

3.15.   Object Appearance

The usage of different line style and/or line thickness visually distinguishes objects from one another. Figure 3-42a and Figure 3-42b are two representations of the same drawing, a building, railway track, fences, and a gas line. In Figure 3-42a every object is drawn using same line style and thickness. However, the drawing shown in Figure 3-42b is easily readable because objects are drawn using different line style, color and thickness.

In AutoCAD terminology, the thickness of an object (line, circle, rectangle, etc.) is called its lineweight and the style (dotted, dashed, center, etc.) is called its linetype. The appearance of an object can be change by selecting appropriate property tools from the *Home* tab and *Properties* panel, Figure 3-42c.

Figure 3-42a   **Figure 3-42b**

Figure 3-42c

3.15.1. Color Control

The Figure 3-43a shows the available options under the *Color Control*. The figure shows only some of the colors available in AutoCAD. However, the user can select the colors not shown in the list, too. The color of most of the two-dimensional objects can be changed in two ways, (i) set the color before drawing the object or (ii) change the color after the object is drawn. This section uses a line to demonstrate the *Color Control*.

3.15.1.1. Set color of an object before it is drawn
The color of a line before it is drawn is changed as follows.

1. Under *Home* tab and in the *Properties* panel, click on the down arrow (⬛) of the *Color Control*. A dropdown list appears on the screen, Figure 3-43a.
2. Bring the cursor on the desired color and it is highlighted. In the example, *Green* color is selected.
3. Click on the highlighted color; this closes the list and the selected color appears in the *Color Control*, Figure 3-43b.
4. Now draw a line, the line is drawn with the selected color.
5. If the desired color is not listed in the color list, then click on *More Color* option of Figure 3-43a. The *Select Color* dialog box shown in Figure 3-43c appears on the screen. Click on the desired color and press the *OK* button and proceed with the drawing. In the example, color 10 is selected.

Figure 3-43a

Figure 3-43b

Figure 3-44c

3.15.1.2. Change color of an object after it is drawn
The user can change the color of the object after it is drawn as follows.

1. Draw a line, (the line labeled as *Before* in Figure 3-43d).
2. Select the line by clicking with the left button of the mouse, (the line with three square boxes in Figure 3-43e). The three blue squares are called grip points.
3. Click on the arrow (▾) of the *Color Control* dropdown list of the *Properties* panel; the color list appears on the screen, Figure 3-43a.
4. Bring the cursor on the desired color and it is highlighted.
5. Click on the highlighted color; this closes the list and the color of the selected object changes to the selected color, (the line labeled as *After* in Figure 3-43d).

Figure 3-43d

3.15.2. Lineweight Control
The Figure 3-45a shows the available options under the *Lineweight Control*. The figure shows all the possible lineweights available in AutoCAD. The lineweight (that is, line thickness) for most of the two-dimensional objects can be changed in two ways; (i) set the lineweight before drawing the object or (ii) change the lineweight after the object is drawn. This section uses a line to demonstrate the *Lineweight Control*.

In order to display thickness of an object in the drawing area, click the lineweight button (≡) on the status bar. The thickness of most of the two-dimensional objects can be changed in two ways.

3.15.2.1. Change thickness of a line before it is drawn
The thickness of a line before it is drawn is changed as follows.

1. In the *Properties* panel (under *Home* tab), click on the down arrow (▾) of the *Lineweight Control*. A dropdown list appears on the screen, Figure 3-44a.
2. Bring the cursor on the desired thickness and it is highlighted.
3. Click on the highlighted thickness; this closes the list and the selected thickness appears in the *Properties* toolbar, Figure 3-44b.
4. Now draw a line; the line is drawn with the selected thickness.
5. The user can set the lineweight properties using the *Lineweight Settings* dialog box, Figure 3-44c. This dialog box can be opened by clicking the *Lineweight Settings* option on Figure 3-44a. **Set the default line weight to *0.0*.**

Figure 3-44a

Figure 3-44b

Figure 3-44c

3.15.2.2. Change thickness of a line after it is drawn

The step-by-step process to change the thickness of a line after it is drawn is shown in Figure 3-45c.

1. Draw a line, (the line labeled as *Before* in Figure 3-44d).
2. Select the line by clicking with the left button of the mouse, (the line with three square boxes in Figure 3-44d). The three blue squares are called grip points.

3. Click on the arrow () of the *Lineweight Control* dropdown list in the *Properties* panel; the thickness list appears on the screen, Figure 3-44a.
4. Bring the cursor on the desired thickness and it is highlighted.
5. Click on the highlighted thickness; this closes the list and the lineweight of the selected object changes to the selected thickness of the selected object, (the line labeled as *After* in Figure 3-44d).

Figure 3-44d

3.15.3. Linetype Control

The Figure 3-45a shows the available options under the *Linetype Control*. The figure shows that only one linetype is available in AutoCAD. However, the user can select the linetypes not shown in the list, too. A line style (that is, linetype) for most of the two-dimensional objects can be changed in two ways; (i) set the linetype before drawing the object or (ii) change the linetype after the object is drawn. This section uses a line to demonstrate the *Linetype Control*. However, the user needs to load the desired line type before using it.

Figure 3-45a

3.15.3.1.   Load a linetype

- (i) Expand the *Linetype control*'s drop-down list, Figure 3-45a. (ii) Select the *Other* option; this opens a *Linetype Manager* (Figure 3-45b) dialog box.
- In the *Linetype Manager* dialog box, click the *Load* button; this open a *Load or Reload Linetypes* (Figure 3-45c) dialog box.

Figure 3-45b

- In the *Load or Reload Linetypes* dialog box, select a linetype and click the *OK* button. This closes the *Load or Reload Linetypes* dialog box and the selected line type appears in the *Linetype Manager* Dialog box, Figure 3-45d. This example selects the *TRACKS* pattern.

Figure 3-45c

- In the *Linetypes Manager* dialog box, click the *OK* button. This closes the dialog box and the *Zigzag* pattern appears in the linetype control, Figure 3-45e.

Figure 3-45d

3.15.3.2.   Change linetype before an object is drawn
The linetype of a line before it is drawn is changed as follows.

1. Click on the down arrow (▾) of the *Linetype Control* drop down list in the *Properties* panel; the linetype list will appear on the screen, Figure 3-45e.
2. Bring the cursor on the desired linetype and it is highlighted; *TRACKS* in the current example, Figure 3-45e.
3. Click on the highlighted linetype; this closes the list and the selected linetype appears in the *Properties* toolbar, Figure 3-46a.
4. Now draw a line, the line is drawn with the selected linetype.

Figure 3-45e

Figure 3-46a

3.15.3.3. Change linetype after an object is drawn

The step-by-step process to change the linetype of a line after it is drawn is shown in Figure 3-47c.

1. Draw a line, (the line labeled as *Before* in Figure 3-46b).
2. Select the line by clicking with the left button of the mouse, (the line with three square boxes in Figure 3-46b).
3. Click on the arrow (▼) of the linetype control dropdown list in the *Properties* toolbar; the linetype list appears on the screen, Figure 3-45e.
6. Bring the cursor on the desired linetype and it is highlighted.
4. Click on the highlighted linetype; this closes the list and the linetype of the selected line changes to the selected linetype; the line labeled as *After* in Figure 3-46b.
5. In Figure 3-46c every object is drawn using *Phantom* linetype; however, the pattern is not visible for some of the segment. A user can change the linetype scale to make the pattern visible.

Figure 3-46b

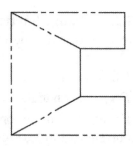

Figure 3-46c

3.15.3.4. Linetype scale

The *Linetype scale* capability is used to change the appearance of a pattern. In Figure 3-47d every object is drawn using *Phantom* linetype; however, the pattern is not visible for some of the segments. A user can change the linetype scale to make the pattern visible as follows:

- Select the lines, by clicking with the left button of the mouse, Figure 3-47a.
- Open the *Properties* palette (Figure 3-47b) using one of the techniques listed below.
  1. Panel method: Open the *Properties* palette using one of the two panel methods.
     a. From the *Home* tab and *Properties* panel, click on the dialog box launcher (a small arrow on the lower right corner of the panel), Figure 3-47c.
     b. From the *View* tab and *Palette* panel, click on *Properties* icon, Figure 3-47d.
  2. Object method: (i) Click on the object(s). (ii) Press the right button of the mouse and choose the *Properties* option, Figure 3-47e.
- Any of the above three methods opens the *Properties* palette of the selected object. On the upper left corner of the *Properties* palette, the type and number of the object (5 Lines in current example) is displayed. On the *Properties* palette, some of the properties are greyed indicating that those properties could not be changed. The properties palette is discussed in detail in Chapter 4.

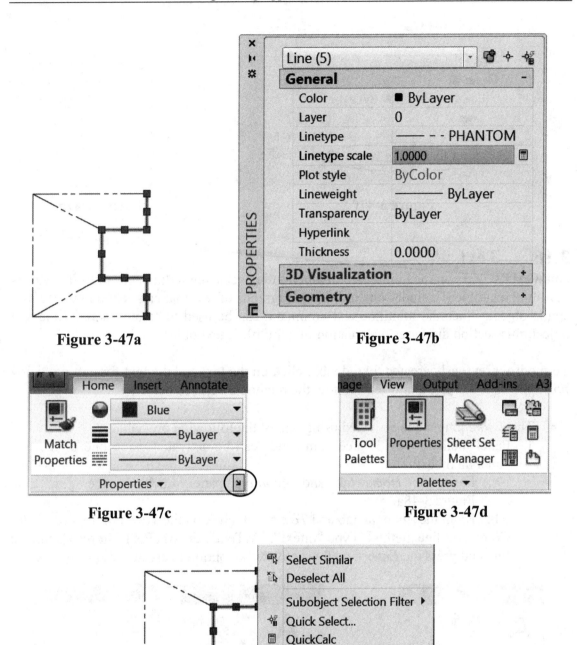

Figure 3-47a   Figure 3-47b

Figure 3-47c   Figure 3-47d

Figure 3-47e

- Select the *Linetype scale* (Figure 3-47f) and change the value to 0.6. If necessary, change the scale of other lines.
- The resultant drawing is shown in Figure 3-47g.
- **Important Note**: The user may need to reset the linetype scale in the layout.

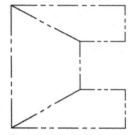

Figure 3-47f   **Figure 3-47g**

3.16. Text

AutoCAD's *Text* command makes a distinction between single line and multiline text. A multiline text object includes one or more paragraphs of text that can be manipulated as a single object. Since the multiline text command can be used to create a single line text object, this section discusses the creation of a multiline text object.

To modify previously created text, double click on the text and the text formatting dialog box appears. To create a new text, follow the method discussed below.

- The *Text* command is activated using one of the following procedures.
    1. Panel method: Text related commands can be activated using one of the two panel methods:
        a. From the *Home* tab and *Annotate* panel, click on the *Text* tool, Figure 3-48a.
        b. From the *Annotate* tab and *Text* panel, click on the *Text* tool, Figure 3-48b.
    2. Command line method: Type "mtext", "MText", or "MTEXT" in the command line and press the *Enter* key; this activates an option to create a multiline text.

Figure 3-48a   **Figure 3-48b**

3.16.1. Create multiline text

- Activate the multiline text command using one of the methods discussed above.
- The activation of the command leads to the specification of the diagonally opposite corner of the text bounding box, Figure 3-49a and Figure 3-49c. Note the appearance of *abc* at the cursor. The size of the *abc* depends on zoom factor. Try *Zoom in* and *Zoom out* commands and check the difference in *abc* size.

Figure 3-49a

- For the first corner, click at the desired location in the drawing area or specify the coordinate of the point and press the *Enter* key, Figure 3-49b.
- For the specification of the second point, click at a diagonally opposite corner. This will create a bounding box, Figure 3-49b, and open the text insertion box, Figure 3-49c. Also, the *Text Editor* tab becomes the current tab. The details of the *Text Editor* are discussed in next section.

Figure 3-49b

- Type in the text and click in the drawing area. The box will disappear and the text will appear in the drawing area.

Figure 3-49c

3.16.2. Text Editor

The *Text Editor* tab, Figure 3-50, provides the options to modify the style, format, paragraph properties, etc. of the selected multiline text object. These capabilities are available through the *Style, Formatting, Paragraph, Insert, Spell Check, Tools, Options,* and *Close* panels. The editor is available only if the text is open as shown in Figure 3-50 (double click on the text and the text editor opens). When the text editor is open, AutoCAD does not allow the user to access any other functionality. Exit the editor mode by clicking outside the text's bounding box or by pressing the *Esc* key from the keyboard.

The changes are in effect only for the selected text and the current text style is not changed. That is, the user must select the text to be changed and then select the facilities provided by the various panels. For example, in Figure 3-50 to make the word "AutoCAD" bold, the user should first select the text and then apply the bold option to the selected text. Most of the characteristics discussed in the remainder of this section, can be updated using the properties palette, too.

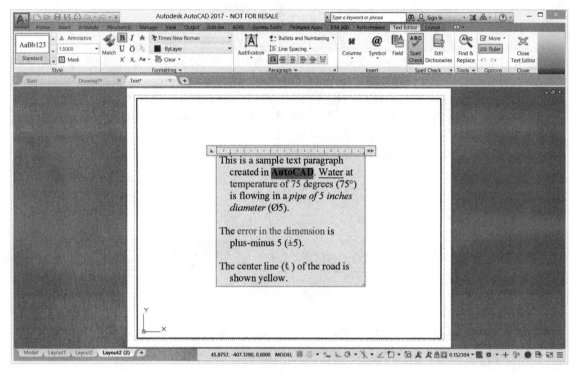

Figure 3-50

3.16.2.1. Style

The *Style* panel shown in Figure 3-51 provides the options to turns *on* or *off* the *Standard* and *Annotative* option, change font height, and background mask for the selected multiline text object.

Figure 3-51

3.16.2.1.1. Font height

The *Font height* option is used to change the text height. The font height setting specifies the height of the capitalized text.

3.16.2.1.2. Background mask

Notice the difference in Figure 3-52a and Figure 3-52b! A drafter can convert Figure 3-52a into Figure 3-52b by masking the background using the *Mask* command; this command hides the objects behind the text. A user can mask the background using one of the following two methods.

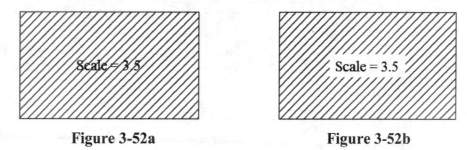

| Figure 3-52a | Figure 3-52b |

Dialog box method:

The background can be masked from the Background Mask dialog box as follows. (i) Double click the multiline text of Figure 3-52a and the *Text Editor* appears on the screen. (ii) From the *Style* panel, click the *Mask* option and the *Background Mask* dialog box appears on the screen, Figure 3-52c. (iii) Check both boxes on the *Background Mask* dialog box. (iv) Finally, click the *OK* button. The resultant masked text is shown in Figure 3-52b.

Figure 3-52c

Property palette method:

The background can be masked from the property palette as follows. (i) Select the multiline text. (ii) Press the right button. (iii) Choose the *Properties* option (the last option) to open the properties palette. (iv) From the *Text* panel of the property palette, select the *Background mask* option (Figure 3-52d) and ▣ appears in the left column. (v) Click on the ▣ button and the *Background Mask* dialog box appears on the screen, Figure 3-52c. (vi) Check both boxes on the *Background Mask* dialog box. (v) Finally, click the *OK* button. The resultant masked text is shown in Figure 3-52b.

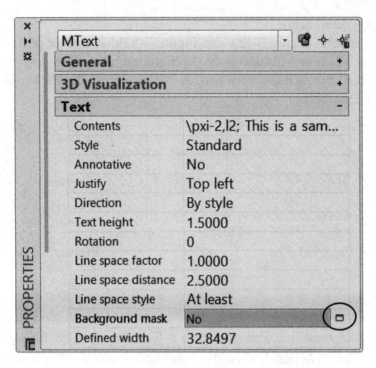

Figure 3-52d

3.16.2.2. Formatting

The expanded *Formatting* panel with the expanded *Clear* menu is shown in Figure 3-53. The user must select the text and then click on the desired command. This panel provides the options to change the font type and color of the selected text. The boldface and italics options are available for some of the fonts. The selected text can also be underlined, over lined, and/or strike through. The case change option allows the user to convert the lowercase to uppercase and vice versa by pressing the down arrow key from the keyboard and choosing the appropriate option. The *Clear* options removes the selected formatting. The remainder of this section discusses the stack capabilities.

Figure 3-53

3.16.2.2.1. Stacked characters

AutoCAD provides the capability to create stacked characters within multiline text. It uses special characters to indicate how the selected text can be stacked as shown in Figure 3-54a to Figure 3-54d.

- Slash symbol (/) stacks text vertically, separated by a horizontal line.
- Pound sign (#) stacks text diagonally, separated by a diagonal line.
- Carat sign (^) creates a tolerance stack, which is not separated by a line.

Text can be stacked as follows.
- Write 1/2, note that the stack option is inactive Figure 3-54a.
- Select 1/2, note that the stack option becomes active, Figure 3-54b.
- Click on the stack option.
- The desired effect is created, $\frac{1}{2}$, Figure 3-54c.
- Repeat the process with 1#2 and 1^2, Figure 3-54d.

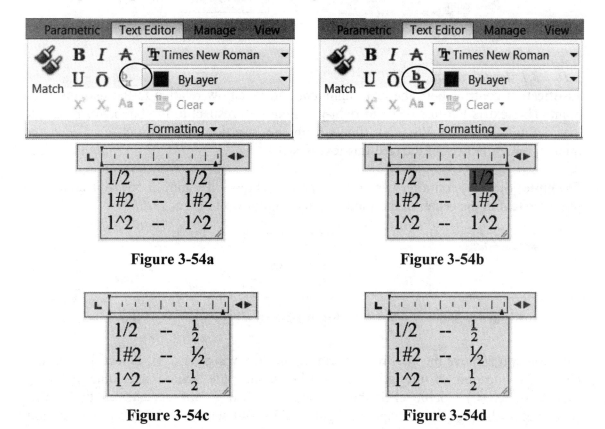

Figure 3-54a	Figure 3-54b

Figure 3-54c	Figure 3-54d

3.16.2.3. Paragraph

The *Paragraph* panel is shown in Figure 3-55a. This panel provides the options to change the paragraph properties of the selected text. Press the down arrow under the *Justification* on the *Paragraph* panel and check the various options, Figure 3-55b.

Figure 3-55a   **Figure 3-55b**

3.16.2.3.1. Justification

Justification controls both the text alignment and text flow relative to the text insertion point. The text is left-justified and right-justified with respect to the boundary rectangle that defines the text width. Text flows from the insertion point, which can be at the middle, top, or bottom of the resulting text object.

Example: Suppose a drafter has created the text shown in Figure 3-55c and desired to place the text in the center of the solid rectangle as shown in Figure 3-55d.

Figure 3-55c   **Figure 3-55d**   **Figure 3-55e**

The user can achieve the goal by performing the following steps. (i) Select the text and check the location of the grip points (the small blue square and blue triangle), Figure 3-55e. (ii) Double click the text and the *Text Editor* appears on the screen. (iii) Expand the *Justification* option, Figure 3-55b, and select the *Middle Center* option. (iv) Select the text and check the location of the grip points (the small blue square and blue triangle), Figure 3-55f. (v) Match the four arrows with the corresponding corner of the rectangle, Figure 3-55g. Click on one of the triangular grip point; keep pressing the left button; move the cursor to the nearest corner; repeat the process with the diagonally opposite grip pint. The resultant text is shown in Figure 3-55g. (vi) Click the *Esc* key from the keyboard to exit the command, Figure 3-55d.

Figure 3-55f   **Figure 3-55g**

3.16.2.3.2. List

The list can be created using bullets, uppercase or lowercase letters, or numbers. Press the down arrow under the *Bullets and Numbering* on the *Paragraph* panel and check the various options, Figure 3-56a.

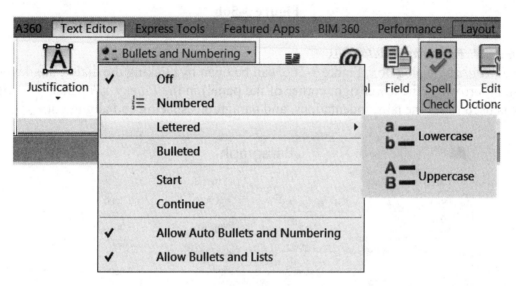

Figure 3-56a

3.16.2.3.3. Line spacing

The line spacing is the clear distance between the two consecutive lines in a multiple line paragraph. Press the down arrow under the *Line Spacing* on the *Paragraph* panel and check the various options, Figure 3-56b.

The line space factor applies to the entire multiline text object and not to the selected lines. Line spacing increment to a multiple of single line spacing and single line spacing is 1.66 times the height of the text characters.

To change the line spacing, (i) click on the drop-down arrow in line spacing option, Figure 3-56b, and (ii) select the *Line space factor*. The line spacing of the multiline text is updated.

The line spacing can also be changed as follows, (i) select the multiline text, (ii) press the right button, (iii) choose the *Properties* option to open the properties palette, (iv) set the *Line space factor* field (for the example, to 1.5), and (v) press the *Enter* key.

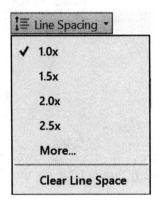

Figure 3-56b

3.16.2.3.4. Paragraph dialog box

The *Paragraph* dialog box, Figure 3-56c, can be open by clicking the dialog box launcher (a small arrow on the lower right corner of the panel) in the *Paragraph* panel. The dialog box is used to set the tabs, indentations, and paragraphs spacing and alignment.

Figure 3-56c

- Multiline text can be indented using tabs. The ruler in the in-place text editor shows the settings for the current paragraph, Figure 3-56d.
- Sliders on the ruler show indentation relative to the left side of the bounding box. The top slider indents the first line of the paragraph, and the bottom slider indents the other lines of the paragraph.

- Tabs and indents which are set before entering the text apply to the whole multiline text object. To apply different tabs and indents to individual paragraphs, click in a single paragraph or select multiple paragraphs and then change the settings.

Figure 3-56d

3.16.2.4.   Insert

The *Insert* panel is shown in Figure 3-57a. This panel provides the options to insert columns and symbols in the multiline text.

3.16.2.4.1. Column

The user can create and edit multiple columns. The various options are shown in the expanded *Columns* drop down menu, Figure 3-57b.

Figure 3-57a

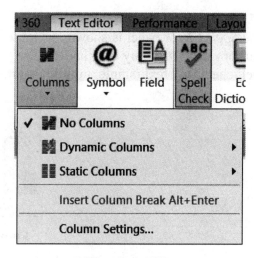

Figure 3-57b

3.16.2.4.2. Symbol

The user can create several symbols in the text. The various options are shown in the expanded *Symbol* drop down menu, Figure 3-57c. The most commonly used symbols are listed below and Figure 3-57d demonstrates their usage.

- Enter %%C in a text box to create ϕ (diameter symbol)
- Enter %%P in a text box to create $\pm$ (Plus Minus)
- Enter %%D in a text box to create $^\circ$ (symbol for degree)
- Set font to "gdt" and type q (symbol for the center line)
- To create the almost equal symbol, expand the *Symbol* drop down menu and select *Almost Equal \U+2248* option, Figure 3-57c.

Figure 3-57c   Figure 3-57d

3.16.2.5. Spell check

The *Spell Check* panel is shown in Figure 3-58a. By default, the spell check is *on*; a user can turn it *off* or *on* by clicking the *Spell Check* icon. This panel provides the options to spell check any text (single, multiline, dimension, qleader, etc.).

Figure 3-58a

- A user can open the *Dictionaries* dialog box, Figure 3-58b, by clicking *Edit Dictionaries* icon in the panel. A user can select a dictionary by pressing the down arrow in the *Main dictionary* group.
- A user can open the *Check Spelling Settings* dialog box, Figure 3-58c, by clicking the dialog box launcher (a small arrow on the lower right corner of the panel). This dialog box allows the user to set options for the spell checking.

Figure 3-58b

3.16.2.6. Tools

The expanded *Tool* panel is shown in Figure 3-59. This panel provides the options to find and replace a text, import text from other files, and type the uppercase text.

Figure 3-58c

Figure 3-59

3.16.2.7.   Options

The expanded *Options* panel is shown in Figure 3-60a. This panel provides the options to select a character set, display or hide the ruler on top of the text bounding box (Figure 3-57d), *Do*, and *Undo* buttons, click on the down arrow beside *More* (Figure 3-60b) and expand the *Character Set* to display the available character sets. In the current example, the *Western* character set is used.

3.16.2.8.   Close

The *Close* panel, Figure 3-61, is used to close the *Text Editor*. Click on the *Close Text Editor*, and the editor is closed. The user can also exit the editor mode by clicking outside the text's bounding box or by pressing the *Esc* key from the keyboard.

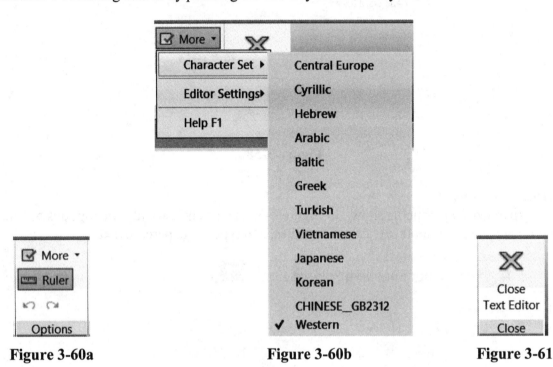

| **Figure 3-60a** | **Figure 3-60b** | **Figure 3-61** |

3.16.3.   Annotate tab and Text panel

The expanded *Text* panel from the *Annotate* tab is shown in Figure 3-61a. This panel provides the options to create a single and multiline text, spell checker, text alignment, justification, standard, text search, font height, and text scaling. The user can open *Text Style* dialog box from the dialog box launcher (small arrow in the lower right corner of the panel), Figure 3-61b.

Figure 3-61a

Figure 3-61b

3.16.4. Express Tools tab and Text panel

The expanded *Text* panel from the *Express Tools* tab is shown in Figure 3-62. This panel provides the options to mask and unmask, and modify (press the down arrow and check the options) the text. Some of these options were discussed earlier. This panel also provides the options to create text along an arc and to enclose a text object in a circle, rectangle, or slots. These two options are discussed here in detail.

Figure 3-62

3.16.4.1.1. Arc Aligned

As the name suggests, the *Arc Aligned* command allows creating text along a circular arc, Figure 3-63a and Figure 3-63b.

- **_Example:_** Create a text along a circular arc as shown in Figure 3-63b.
- Create a circular arc, Figure 3-63c.

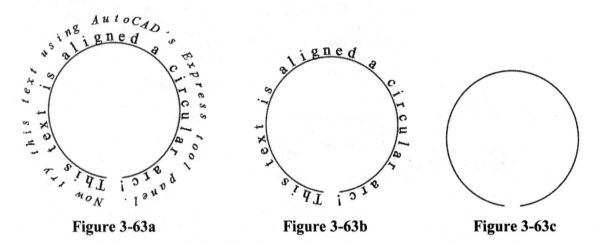

| Figure 3-63a | Figure 3-63b | Figure 3-63c |

- Activate the *Arc Aligned* command. The activation of the command results in the prompt shown in Figure 3-63d.

> ## Select an Arc or an ArcAlignedText:

Figure 3-63d

- Click at the arc; and *ArcAlignedText Workshop – Create* dialog box appears, Figure 3-63e.
- Type the desired text; and change the properties (if necessary).
- Click the *OK* button. This closes the dialog box and the text appears along the arc, Figure 3-63b.
- To edit the arc aligned text, double click at the text and the property palette appears on the screen, Figure 3-63f. Now the user can make the desired changes.
- The user should try to create the second text shown in Figure 3-63a. The *Offset from arc* distance should be the sum of *Text height* of the first row, *Offset from* arc for the first row, and space between the two rows.

Figure 3-63e

Figure 3-63f

3.16.4.1.2. Enclose in object

The *Enclose in Object* command can be used to enclose single or multiline text objects in a circle, rectangle, and a slot.

- ***Example:*** Enclose the text inside a slot (Figure 3-64a), circle (Figure 3-64b), and rectangle (Figure 3-64c).

Figure 3-64a   **Figure 3-64b**   **Figure 3-64c**

- Create the desired text.
- Activate the *Enclose in object* command. The activation of the command results in the prompt shown in Figure 3-64d.
- Click at the text and press the *Enter* key from the keyboard, Figure 3-64e.
- Specify the offset factor. It is the space between the text and outline of the enclosing object. Press the *Enter* key of the keyboard, Figure 3-64f.

Select objects:

Figure 3-64d

Enter distance offset factor <0.3500>: 0.3500

Figure 3-64e

- Select the type of the enclosing object. This example uses the *Rectangle* option. Click with the left button of the mouse, Figure 3-64f.

Figure 3-64f

- Select the *Constant* option for the size. Click with the left button of the mouse, Figure 3-64g.
- Select the *Both* option to maintain the object, Figure 3-64h. Press the *Enter* key of the keyboard.
- The text is enclosed in a rectangle, Figure 3-64a.
- Repeat the process for the slot (Figure 3-64a) and circle (Figure 3-64b).

Figure 3-64g

Figure 3-64h

3.17. Hatch

The *Hatch* command allows the user to create a hatch, that is, fill a space surrounded by closed boundary with a specified pattern, Figure 3-65a.

Figure 3-65a

- The *Hatch* command can be activated using one of the following procedures.
  1. Panel method: From the *Home* tab and *Draw* panel, select the *Hatch* tool, Figure 3-65b.
  2. Command line method: Type "hatch", "Hatch", or "HATCH" in the command line and press the *Enter* key.

Figure 3-65b

- The activation of the command will open hatch editor named as *Hatch Creation* tab, Figure 3-65c, with the *Boundaries, Pattern, Properties, Origin, Options*, and *Close* panels. Also, the *Hatch Creation* tab becomes the current tab.

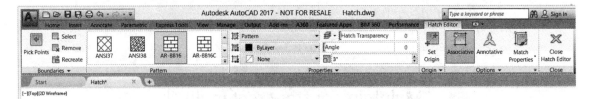

Figure 3-65c

3.17.1. Hatch creation tab

This section describes the basics of the hatch process by explaining most of the commands on the *Hatch creation* tab's panels.

3.17.1.1.1. Boundaries

The *Boundaries* panel is used to set the boundaries for creating a new hatch or modifying an existing hatch. When the *Hatch* command is activated from the *Draw* panel then the *Boundaries* panel appears as shown in Figure 3-66a. However, when the command is activated by clicking the existing hatch then the *Boundaries* panel appears as shown in Figure 3-66b. The difference is the availability of the *Remove* and *Recreate* tools (active in Figure 3-66b and inactive in Figure 3-66a). Hatch can be created using *Pick points* or *Select* commands as follows.

Figure 3-66a   **Figure 3-66b**

- **Pick Points:** The *Pick Points* option allows the user to select an area enclosed by one or more objects, Figure 3-66c. In the figure, the user has clicked inside the intersecting part of the circles. The area is hatched and the hatch boundary is highlighted.
- **Select:** The *Select* option allows the user to select a closed object. For example, a closed shape created using polyline, circle, polygon, etc., Figure 3-66d. In this figure, the user has clicked at the boundary of the circle on the right. Therefore, the part of the left circle inside the selected circle is hatched. The selected circle is hatched and the hatch boundary is highlighted.

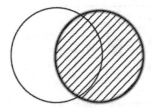

Figure 3-66c   **Figure 3-66d**

3.17.1.1.2. Pattern

The *Pattern* panel is used to set the hatch pattern, Figure 3-67a. The user can click up or down arrow to check the other patterns. The user can select a pattern before or after the hatch is created.

Figure 3-67a

- The user can change the pattern before the hatch command by clicking on the desired pattern.
- The user can change the pattern after the hatch command using the following steps: (i) Click on the hatch and a circular grip point appears, Figure 3-67b. (ii) Select the desired pattern. (iii) Press the *Esc* key from the keyboard. DO NOT PRESS THE *ENTER* KEY. The hatch appearance changes to the selected pattern, Figure 3-67c.

Figure 3-67b   **Figure 3-67c**

3.17.1.1.3. Properties

The *Properties* panel is used to set hatch color, background color, angle, and scale of the selected hatch, Figure 3-68.

- The user can change the pattern properties before the hatch command by selecting the desired properties.
- The user can also change the pattern properties after the hatch command using the following steps.

Hatch color

Background color

Hatch angle

Hatch scale

Figure 3-68

- ○ **Hatch color:** (i) Click on the hatch and a circular grip point appears, Figure 3-69b. (ii) Press the down arrow and select the desired color. (iii) Press the *Esc* key from the keyboard. DO NOT PRESS THE *ENTER* KEY. The hatch color changes to the selected color, Figure 3-69c. Similarly, change the background color, Figure 3-69d.

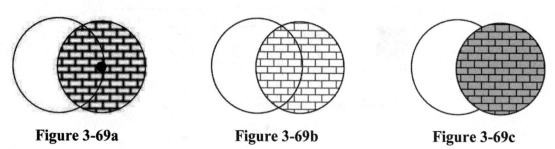

Figure 3-69a   **Figure 3-69b**   **Figure 3-69c**

- ○ **Hatch angle:** (i) Click on the hatch and a circular grip point appears, Figure 3-69a (angle = 0). (ii) Click at the *Angle* button and type the desired angle. (iii) Press the *Esc* key from the keyboard. DO NOT PRESS THE *ENTER* KEY. The hatch angle changes to the selected angle, Figure 3-69d (angle = 45°).
- ○ **Hatch scale:** (i) Click on the hatch and a circular grip point appears, Figure 3-69a (scale factor = 3.0). (ii) Press the down arrow and select the desired scale factor. (iii) Press the *Esc* key from the keyboard. DO NOT PRESS THE *ENTER* KEY. The hatch scale changes to the selected scale, Figure 3-69e (scale factor = 1.0). The scale factor should be selected such that the pattern is clearly visible.

Figure 3-69d   **Figure 3-69e**

3.17.1.1.4. Options
The *Options* panel, Figure 3-70a, is used to set various hatch properties.

- The user can open the *Hatch Editor* dialog box from the dialog box launcher (a small arrow on the lower right corner of the panel), Figure 3-70b. The sections in the dialog box are similar to the panels in the *Hatch Creation* tab or *Hatch Editor*.

Figure 3-70a

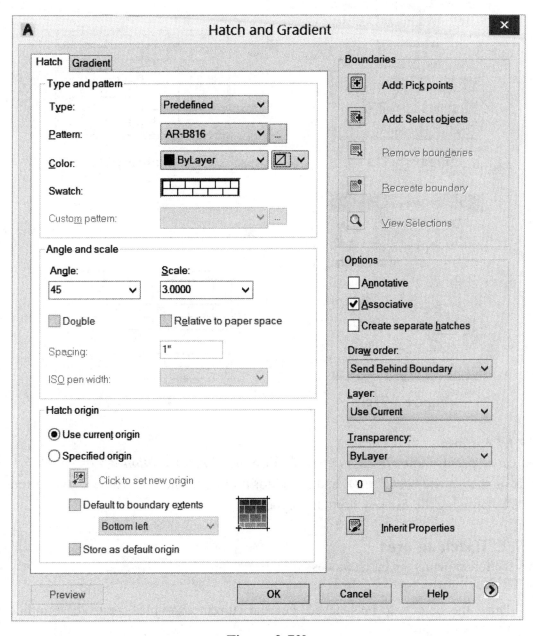

Figure 3-70b

3.17.1.1.5. origin

The expanded *Origin* panel is shown in Figure 3-71a. This panel is used to relocate the origin of the selected hatch. The default option is the Center, Figure 3-71a; in this case, the pattern begins in the center and the partial pattern is evenly distributed on all four edges, Figure 3-71b. Figure 3-71c shows the selection of the *Bottom Right* option; in this case, the pattern begins in the bottom right corner of the closed boundary and the partial pattern is distributed on the top and left edges.

Figure 3-71a

Figure 3-71b

Figure 3-71c

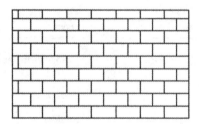

Figure 3-71d

3.17.1.1.6. Close

The *Close* panel, Figure 3-72, is used to close the *Hatch Creation* tab or *Hatch Editor*. Click on the *Close Hatch Editor*, and the editor is closed. The user can also exit the editor mode by pressing the *Esc* key from the keyboard.

3.17.2. Hatch an area

This section explains the hatch process.

- Draw the objects to be hatched. For the current example, create the building as shown in Figure 3-72a.

Figure 3-72

Figure 3-72a

- Activate the *Hatch* command.
- The activation of the command opens the *Hatch Editor* and the prompt shown in Figure 3-72b or Figure 3-72b appears on screen.
    o <u>Figure 3-72b:</u> Press the down arrow key from the keyboard and check the various options. This example uses the *pick internal point* option; press the up arrow and close the option list.
    o <u>Figure 3-72c:</u> Press the down arrow key from the keyboard and check the various options. This example uses the *pick internal point* option; click on the desired option. This closes the option list and the prompt shown in Figure 3-72d appears.

Figure 3-72b

Figure 3-72c

- Bring the cursor inside the large rectangle and the hatch pattern appears. However, if the hatch appears as shown in Figure 3-72d, then set the *Scale* factor in the *Properties* panel to a higher number. For the current example, the *Scale* is changed from 1 to 75.

- Now, bring the cursor inside the large rectangle and the hatch pattern appears as shown in Figure 3-72e. If necessary, change the scale factor, otherwise, press the *Enter* key and the hatch command is complete, Figure 3-72f.

Figure 3-72d

Figure 3-72e

Figure 3-72f

- Now, change the pattern and its scale. The pattern is changed to *AR-B816* (a brick pattern) and the scale to 2.0, Figure 3-72g; in this case the angle is set to 0.0°.
- Now, hatch the smaller triangle with *AR-B816* pattern, angle = 90°, and scale = 2.0, Figure 3-72g.
- Hatch the middle part using *AR-RSHKE* pattern, angle = 0.0°, and scale = 1.75, Figure 3-72g.

Figure 3-72g

3.18.   Table 🔳

A table is an object that is used to organize data in rows and columns as shown in Figure 3-73a. Commonly, tables (in drawings) are used for the dimensions of objects with multiple holes, to define coordinate data, to create part lists, and to create doors and windows schedules. In a table, every entry must be written with caps lock or upper case.

DIMENSION			
NAME	X-COORD	Y-COORD	Ø
A1	2.34	45.00	13.00
B1	-1.80	23.45	11.50
C1	4.98	35.12	9.00

Figure 3-73a

In AutoCAD, the *Table* command is used to create a table. Initially, the table is blank; however, it is populated as needed. If the height or width of a table is changed then the rows or columns change proportionally. If the width of a column is changed then the table widens or narrows to accommodate the change.

- *Example:* Create the table shown in Figure 3-73a.

- The *Table* command is activated using one of the following procedures.

    1. Panel method: The *Table* commands can be activated using one of the two panel methods:
        a. From the *Home* tab and *Annotation* panel, click on the *Table* tool, Figure 3-73b.
        b. From the *Annotate* tab and *Table* panel, click on the *Table* tool, Figure 3-73c.
    2. Command line method: Type "table", "Table", or "TABLE" in the command line and press the *Enter* key.

- The activation of the command opens the *Insert Table* dialog box, Figure 3-73d.

Figure 3-73b

Figure 3-73c

Figure 3-73d

3.18.1. Create a table

- A user can create a new table using *Insert Table* dialog box, Figure 3-73d, as follows.
    - From the *Table style* window, select a style from the list or click the button to create a new table style.
    - In the *Insert option* panel, select the *Start from empty table* option to create a table without any entries.
    - In the *Insertion behavior* panel, select the *Specify insertion point* option to insert the table in the drawing area.

o In the *Column & row settings* panel, set the number of columns and rows. For the current example, set the number of columns to 4 and number of data rows to 3. Assume the default values for the column width and row height.

o For the *Specify window* insertion method in the *Insertion behavior* panel, the user can enter only the number of columns and the rows height.

o Finally, click the *OK* button. This closes the dialog box and a prompt to specify the insertion point appears, Figure 3-73e.

• Specify the insertion point in the drawing area by clicking at the desired location. The resulting table is shown Figure 3-73f.

Figure 3-73e

Figure 3-73f

3.18.2. Table resize

This section uses grip points to resize the table. Grips are small, solid filled squares that are displayed at strategic points on the selected objects. Grips are discussed in detail in Chapter 4.

• Grip points can be used to reshape a table. To select a single cell, click inside the cell, Figure 3-74a. For multiple cells selection, use one of the following methods:

o Click inside a cell. Hold down the *Shift* key and click inside another cell to select those two cells and all the cells between them.

o Click inside the selected cell. Hold the left button of the mouse. Drag to the desired cell, Figure 3-74b, and release the button.

Figure 3-74a

Figure 3-74b

- <u>Change the row height</u>: To change the row height of the selected cell, drag the top or bottom grips point upward or downward, respectively. The resized table is shown in Figure 3-74c. If more than one cell is selected, then the row height changes equally for each row.
- <u>Change the column width</u>: To change the column width of the selected cell, drag the left or right grip point to the left or right, respectively. The resized table is shown in Figure 3-74c. If more than one cell is selected, then the column width changes equally for each column.

	A	B	C	D
1				
2				
3				
4				
5				

Figure 3-74c

- <u>Resize table</u>: Select the table. To stretch/shrink uniformly: use the grip point at the upper right corner to change the width, lower left corner to change the height, and lower right corner to change both the width and height of the table, Figure 3-74d. That is, all the rows and/or columns will be stretched by the same amount. Although Figure 3-74d shows multiple options selected, the software does not allow for multiple options selection simultaneously.
- Press the *Esc* key from the keyboard to remove the selection.

Figure 3-74d

- Move the table: Select the table; use the grip point at the upper left corner to move the table, Figure 3-74e.

- Break the table: Select the table; use the lower middle (light blue) grip point to break the table, Figure 3-74f. The user should avoid using this option.

Figure 3-74e

Figure 3-74f

3.18.3. Modify table's shape

Figure 3-75a shows the various options available to reshape the table. Bring the cursor on one of the cells and press the right button of the mouse and select the desired option. The figure shows the selection of multiple options simultaneously. However, the software does not allow for multiple options selection. These options are also available from the *Table Cell* tab shown in Figure 3-75b; this tab appears on the screen when a cell in a table is selected.

- Insert rows: To insert a row, select a cell as shown in Figure 3-75c and Figure 3-75d.
  - **Figure 3-75a method:** (i) press the right button of the mouse to open the options panel shown in Figure 3-75a. (ii) Click on the *Rows* option. (iii) Select the *Insert Above* or *Insert Below*. A row is added above or below the selected cell, respectively. In the current example, a row is added above the selected cell, Figure 3-75c. If '*n*' cells are selected than '*n*' rows are inserted, where n >1.

o **Figure 3-75b method:** Press the desired tool from the *Row* panel. In the current example, a row is added above the selected cell, Figure 3-75c. If '*n*' cells are selected than '*n*' rows will be inserted, where n >1.

- Insert Columns: The procedure to insert a column is similar to the row insertion process.

Figure 3-75a

Figure 3-75b

Figure 3-75c

Figure 3-75d

- Delete rows: To delete a row, select a cell in the row to be deleted.
  - **Figure 3-75a method:** (i) Press the right button of the mouse to open the options panel shown in Figure 3-75a. (ii) Click on the *Rows* option. (iv) Select the *Delete* option. A row will be deleted containing the selected cell. If '*n*' cells are selected than '*n*' rows will be deleted, where '*n*' >1.
  - **Figure 3-75b method:** Press the desired tool from the *Row* panel. A row will be deleted containing the selected cell. If '*n*' cells are selected than '*n*' rows will be deleted, where '*n*' >1.
- Delete columns: To delete a column, select a cell in the column to be deleted.
  - Same as deleting a row.
- Merge cells: To merge multiple cells, select the cells to be merged.
  - *By Row* merges the cells horizontally by removing the vertical gridlines and leaving the horizontal gridlines intact.
  - *By Column* merges the cells vertically by removing the horizontal gridlines and leaving the vertical gridlines intact, Figure 3-75d.
  - **Figure 3-75a method:** (i) Press the right button of the mouse to open the options panel shown in Figure 3-75a. (iii) Click on the *Merge* option and click on *By Row*. The selected cells will be merged into one cell. Similarly merge cells in a *Column*, or *All* (both directions, that is, row and column). Figure 3-75d shows the merge of cells using different options.
  - **Figure 3-75b method:** Press the desired tool from the *Merge* panel. The selected cells will be merged into one cell. Similarly merge cells in a *Column*, or *All* (both directions, that is, row and column). Figure 3-75e and Figure 3-75f shows a table and the merge of cells using different options.

Figure 3-75e

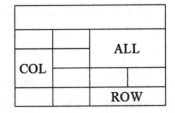

Figure 3-75f

- Split cells:
  - Cells cannot be split EXCEPT the cells that were merged previously.
- Press the *Esc* key on the keyboard to remove the selection.

3.18.4. The cursor movement

- Move the cursor to the next cell:
  - o If the cursor is inside a cell and the text is NOT selected then to move the cursor to the next cell press the *TAB* key; or use the arrow keys to navigate in all four directions (left, right, up, and down).

- Move the cursor in the same cell:
  - o *Left or right arrow keys:* If the cursor is inside a cell and the text is highlighted (that is, selected) then the left (or right) arrow key moves the cursor one character in the left (or right) direction. However, if the cursor is in the beginning (or end) of the text, then pressing the arrow key moves the cursor to the previous (or next) cell.
  - o *Up or down arrow keys* If the cursor is inside a cell and the text is highlighted (that is, selected) then the up (or down) arrow key moves the cursor to the beginning (or end) of the highlighted text.

3.18.5. Insert a multiline text in a cell

The row height of the selected cell increases to accommodate the number of lines of the text. If the length of the single line text is longer than the width of a cell, then the text wraps automatically to the next line. If the user presses the *Enter* key on the keyboard, the cursor moves to the next cell, Figure 3-76.

Figure 3-76

If a user desired to create a multiline line text object in a cell then hold the *Alt* key and press the *Enter* key to move the cursor to the next line. To format the text as shown in the right column of the table in Figure 3-76, the *Alt- Enter* keys are used twice to create a blank line between the two paragraphs.

3.18.6. The data type

The data in a table cell can be a text, a block, or a field. Select three cells of a column in the table and press the right button of the mouse, an options list appears on the screen, Figure 3-77a. Click on the *Data Format*, and the *Table Cell Format* dialog box appears on the screen, Figure 3-77b. In the current example, for the angle *Data type*, the Surveyor's units are used. The content of the *Preview* panel represents the selection of the *Data type*.

Figure 3-77a

Figure 3-77b

The Figure 3-77c shows the entries in the table are converted to Surveyor's units. Remember that the angles are measured counterclockwise from the east. To enter the data (i) type the data as decimal number, (ii) press the *Enter* key from the keyboard, and the data will appear selected data format (the Surveyor's units).

Figure 3-77c

3.18.7. Populate the table

When a new table is inserted, then its first cell is highlighted, the cursor is in the first cell, and the *Text Editor* tab becomes the current tab, Figure 3-78a. The table is ready to be populated (that is, to insert data).

- If necessary, set the data type for the cell.
- Populate the table using the cursor movement and multiline text entry discussed earlier, that is, insert the information shown in the table of Figure 3-78c.
- If necessary, click with the right button of the mouse and check the various options, Figure 3-78b.
- If necessary, resize the table. The table shown in Figure 3-78c is resized using table resizing techniques discussed earlier.

Figure 3-78a

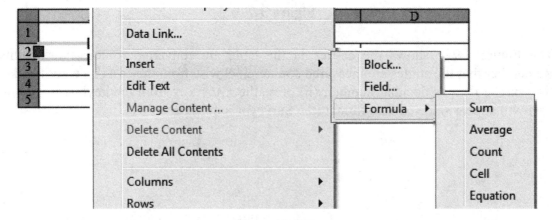

Figure 3-78b

DIMENSION			
NAME	X-COORD	Y-COORD	Ø
A1	2.34	45.00	13.00
B1	-1.80	23.45	11.50
C1	4.98	35.12	9.00

Figure 3-78c

3.18.8. Modify the contents of a table

Suppose a user has created the table shown in Figure 3-78c and wants to modify it to the format shown in Figure 3-79.

In the table of Figure 3-79, the *Title* cell is shaded blue, the *Header* cells are shaded orange, and the *Data* cells are shaded yellow. The line weight of the border is set to 0.5. The contents of the table are aligned in the middle center. The font is set to Times New Roman. The text height is 0.20 for the *Title* cell and 0.15 for the *Header* and the *Data* cells. The contents of the *Title* and the *Header* cells are set to *Bold* style whereas the contents of the *Data* cells are kept plain.

DIMENSION			
NAME	X-COORD	Y-COORD	Ø
A1	2.34	45.00	13.00
B1	-1.80	23.45	11.50
C1	4.98	35.12	9.00

Figure 3-79

There are multiple techniques to change the table format: (i) Use of the *Table Style* dialog box. This method changes the format of every table in the current drawing. (ii) Use of the property palette. This method only changes the format of the selected table. (iii) Update one cell at a time (long and exhaustive approach).

3.18.8.1. Table Style dialog box

This section uses the *Table Style* dialog box, Figure 3-80c, to change the table format. However, every table in the current drawing will be reformatted to the current style.

- Open the *Table Style* dialog box, using one of the following procedures.
  1. Panel method: (i) From the *Home* tab and expanded *Annotation* panel, select the *Table Style* tool, Figure 3-80a. (ii) From the *Annotate* tab and *Table* panel, click the dialog box launcher (a small arrow on the lower right corner of the panel).

2. Dialog box method: (i) From the *Home* tab and *Annotation* panel, select the *Table* tool. (ii) In the *Insert Table* dialog box Figure 3-80b, from the *Table style* panel click on the button to open the *Table Style* dialog box.

3. Command line method: Type "tablestyle", "Tablestyle", or "TABLESTYLE" in the command line and press the *Enter* key.

Figure 3-80a

Figure 3-80b

- Click on the *Modify* button of the *Table Style* dialog box to open the *Modify Table Style: Standard* dialog box, Figure 3-80d.

Figure 3-80c

Figure 3-80d

- On the *Modify Table Style: Standard* dialog box, perform the following actions.

    1. From the *Cell styles* panel (Figure 3-80d), click on the down arrow and select the *Data* option, Figure 3-81a.

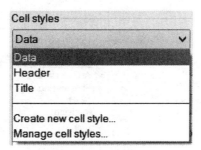

Figure 3-81a

    2. Select the *General* tab from the *Cell styles* panel and under the *Fill color* option, choose the desired color Figure 3-81b or click on the *Select Color* option to display more colors. In the current example, the yellow color is chosen.
    3. Select the *General* tab from the *Cell styles* panel and under the *Alignment* option, choose *Middle Center* option, Figure 3-81c.

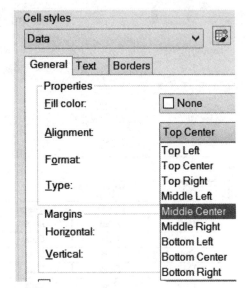

Figure 3-81b   **Figure 3-81c**

4. Select the *General* tab from the *Cell styles* panel, Figure 3-80d. (i) For the *Format* option, click on button (Figure 3-80d) to open the *Table Cell Format* dialog box shown in Figure 3-81d. (ii) Under the *Data Type* window choose *Decimal Number*. (iii) Under the *Format* window choose *Decimal*. (iv) Under the *Precision* window choose *0.00* (two decimal places). (v) Press the *OK* button to close this dialog box.

Figure 3-81d

5. Select the *General* tab from the *Cell styles* panel, Figure 3-80d. Under the *Type* option, choose *Data*, Figure 3-81e.

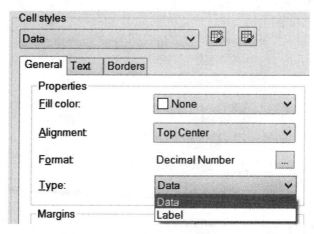

Figure 3-81e

6. Select the *Text* tab from the *Cell styles* panel, Figure 3-80d. Choose the options shown in Figure 3-82a. To set the font information, in Figure 3-80a, click on the ⬚ button to open the *Text Style* dialog box, Figure 3-82b.

Figure 3-82a

The *Text Style* dialog box shown in Figure 3-82b is used to set the properties of the text. (i) In the dialog box, choose the *Times New Roman* font under the *Font Name*. (ii) To create a new style click on the *New* button and this opens the *New Text Style* box, Figure 3-82c. (iii) Name the style with an easily recognizable name (*Data_Style* in the current example), save the style, and press the *OK* button. (iv) This closes the *New Text Style* box, activates the *Apply* button on the *Text Style* dialog box and converts the *Cancel* button to the *Close* button. (v) Press the *Apply* button followed by the *Close* button.

Figure 3-82b

Figure 3-82c

7. Select the *Border* tab from the *Cell styles* panel, Figure 3-80d. (i) Under the *Lineweight* option, choose the desired thickness (0.3mm in the example). (ii) Under the *Linetype* and *Color* options, select the *By Layer* option. The preview window on the lower left corner of the dialog box displays the changes.
8. Repeat steps #1 - #7 for the *Header* and *Title* cells.
9. The resultant table is shown in Figure 3-79. For the reader's convenience, the figure is shown again on the current page.

Figure 3-82d

DIMENSION			
NAME	X-COORD	Y-COORD	Ø
A1	2.34	45.00	13.00
B1	-1.80	23.45	11.50
C1	4.98	35.12	9.00

Figure 3-79

3.18.8.2.   Table update using the property palette

A table can also be updated using the *Properties* palette. The advantage of this technique is that only the selected table's format is changed. This section shows the process to modify the contents of the *Data cells*. The user can use the same process to modify the contents of the *Title cell* and the *Header cells*.

- To open the *Properties* palette, use one of the following methods.
  1. Select all the data cells, Figure 3-83a, press the right button of the mouse, and select the *Properties* option from the list of options.

  2. From the View tab and Palettes pane, select the *Properties* tool (▣). The *Properties* palette is shown in Figure 3-83b.

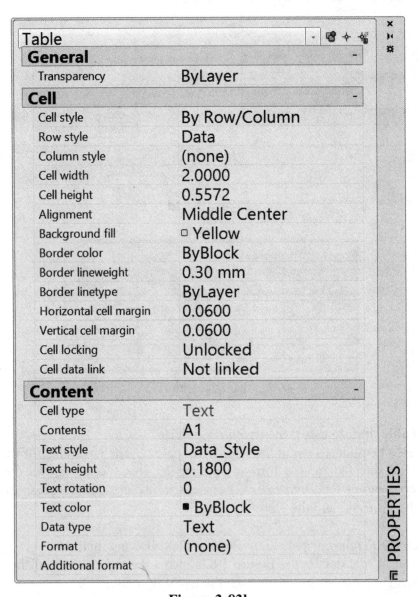

	A	B	C	D
1	DIMENSION			
2	NAME	X-COORD	Y-COORD	Ø
3	A1	2.3400	45.0000	
4	B1	-1.8000	23.4500	11.5
5	C1	4.9800	35.1200	

Delete All Contents
Columns ▶
Rows ▶
Merge ▶
Unmerge
Properties
Quick Properties

Figure 3-83a

Table

General −
Transparency   ByLayer

Cell −
Cell style   By Row/Column
Row style   Data
Column style   (none)
Cell width   2.0000
Cell height   0.5572
Alignment   Middle Center
Background fill   ☐ Yellow
Border color   ByBlock
Border lineweight   0.30 mm
Border linetype   ByLayer
Horizontal cell margin   0.0600
Vertical cell margin   0.0600
Cell locking   Unlocked
Cell data link   Not linked

Content −
Cell type   Text
Contents   A1
Text style   Data_Style
Text height   0.1800
Text rotation   0
Text color   ■ ByBlock
Data type   Text
Format   (none)
Additional format

PROPERTIES

Figure 3-83b

- The upper left corner of the *Properties* palette displays the name of the selected object.
- To expand the *General* panel (or contract the *Cell* panel) in Figure 3-83b, click the '+' or '-' sign in front of the panel name.
- A user cannot change the options shown in light gray background in the *Properties* palette. For example, the user cannot change the *Cell type* under the *Content* panel.

- To change the properties of the *Data cells*, perform the following actions in the *Properties* palette.
    1. In the *Cell* panel (i) click the *Alignment* option; a dropdown list arrow appears in the right column of the properties palette. (ii) Press the down arrow and click the desired alignments, Figure 3-83b. In the figure, the *Middle Center* option is selected. (iii) The drop-down list is closed and the contents of the data cell move in the middle center.
    2. In the *Cell* panel (i) select the *Background fill* option; a dropdown list arrow appears in the right column of the properties palette. (ii) Press the down arrow and click the desired color, Figure 3-83b. In the figure, the *Yellow* color is selected. (iii) The drop-down list is closed and the background color of the data cell is changed to the selected color.
    3. In the *Cell* panel (i) select the *Border Lineweight* option; the *Choose* button (▣) appears in the right column of the properties palette. (ii) Click the button and the *Cell Border Properties* dialog box appears, Figure 3-83c. (iii) For the border, select *All Border* option. (iv) Under the *Lineweight* option, choose the desired thickness (0.3mm in the example). (v) Under the *Linetype* and *Color* options, select the *By Layer* option. (vi) Click the OK button of the dialog box. This closes the dialog box; the *Choose* button disappears from the *Properties palette* and the border of the *Data cell* changes to the selected options.
    4. In the *Content* panel (i) select the *Text style* option; a dropdown list arrow appears in the right column of the properties palette. (ii) Press the down arrow and select the desired style. The *Data_Style* is a user defined style and the previous section describes the creation process. In this example, the *Data_Style* is selected. (iii) The drop-down list is closed and the background color of the data cell will change to the selected style.
    5. In the *Content* panel (i) select the *Text height* option, Figure 3-83b. (ii) Type the desired height in the right column. (iii) Press the *Enter* key on the keyboard. (iv) The selection is cleared and size of the content of the data cell will change to the selected height.
    6. Repeat steps #1 - #5 for the *Header* and *Title* cells.
    7. The resultant table is shown in Figure 3-79. For the reader's convenience, the figure is shown again on the current page.

Figure 3-83c

DIMENSION			
NAME	**X-COORD**	**Y-COORD**	**Ø**
A1	2.34	45.00	13.00
B1	-1.80	23.45	11.50
C1	4.98	35.12	9.00

Figure 3-79

4.   Basics of 2-Dimensional Editing

4.1.   Learning Objectives

After completing this chapter, you will demonstrate competency in the following areas:

- Grip points
- Object selection and de-selection
- Pan and Zoom capabilities
- Draw order (move object in front of or behind other objects)
- Object snap
- Editing commands (*Cancel*, *Erase*, *Undo*, *Redo*, *Oops*, *Copy*, *Array*, *Mirror*, *Offset*, *Move*, *Rotate*, *Scale*, *Stretch*, *Break*, *Explode*, *Join*, *Fillet*, *Chamfer*, *Trim*, *Extend*, and *Polyline Edit*)
- Properties Palette

4.2.   Introduction

A drafter can create unlimited design by creating new drawings and editing existing drawings. The focus of this chapter is the capability of AutoCAD to edit two-dimensional drawing objects. To achieve these capabilities, AutoCAD uses the *Modify* panel from the *Home* tab, Figure 4-1a, grip points, and the property palette. Figure 4-1a shows the expanded and pinned (check the pin at the lower left corner) panel.

Figure 4-1a

4.3.   Grips

Grips are small, solid-filled squares that are displayed at strategic points on the selected objects. By default, the *Grips* setting is *On* and the grip points are blue. In order to visualize the grip points, (i) press the *Esc* key to cancel any previously selected command, (ii) place the cursor on the desired object, and (iii) click with the left button of the mouse. The object is selected, that is, the blue boxes are shown at the ends and mid-point of a line (Figure 4-2a), four quadrants and the center of a circle (Figure 4-2b), and at the ends of the segments of a polyline (Figure 4-2c).

Figure 4-2a   **Figure 4-2b**   **Figure 4-2c**

4.3.1. Grips toggle

Grips can be turned *On* or *Off*. A user can toggle the grip capability as follows: (i) type "Grips" or "grips" or GRIPS" on the command line; (ii) press the *Enter* key; (iii) type "0" to turn *Off* ("1" or "2" to turn *On*); and (iv) press the *Enter* key, again.

4.3.2. Change the size and color of the grips

The size and color of the grip points can be changed from the *Options* dialog box as follows.

- Open the *Options* dialog box (Figure 4-3a) using one of the two methods
  1. Click with the right button in the *Drawing area* and select the *Options* option. The *Options* dialog box appears on the screen.
  2. Command line method: Type "options", "Options", or "OPTIONS" in the command line and press the *Enter* key.
- Click on the *Selection* tab of the *Options* dialog box.
- The slider in the *Grip size* panel, Figure 4-3a, is used to change the size of the grip points. Move the slider to the right (or left) to increase (or decrease) the size.
- Click on the *Grip Colors* button, Figure 4-3a, in the *Grip* panel to open the *Grip Colors* dialog box, Figure 4-3b. Make the desired changes and click *OK* button on both dialog boxes.

Figure 4-3a

Figure 4-3b

4.4.   Object Selection

The object selection is the prerequisite for the functionality of the editing commands. An object is defined as a graphical element for creation, manipulation, and modification. The graphical element can be a line, circle, polygon, text, dimension, polyline, etc. If one object needs to be modified, then the object selection process is very simple; click on the object and it is highlighted (its grip points appear). However, if a user needs to select multiple objects, then one of the following methods must be used.

4.4.1.   Method #1: Green Method

- Draw a circle, rectangle, polygon, and a line as shown in Figure 4-4a.
- Place the cursor below and to the right of the objects to be selected, Figure 4-4a; point labeled as 1 in the current example.
- Notice the change in the appearance of the cursor.
- The green color is the default color.

4.4.1.1.   Version #1

- (i) Click and press the left button of the mouse, (ii) keep pressing the left button and (iii) move the cursor to the left and upward (Figure 4-4a) such that all the objects to be selected are completely or partially in the green area.
- Release the left mouse button as shown in Figure 4-4a; the objects are highlighted (the grip points appeared), Figure 4-4b. In this method, the objects that are completely or partially inside the green area are selected.

Figure 4-4a

Figure 4-4b

4.4.1.2.   Version #2

- (i) Click the left button of the mouse and the prompt shown in Figure 4-4c appears (ii) move the cursor to the left and upward (Figure 4-4c) such that all the objects to be selected are completely or partially in the green rectangle.
- Click the left button again as shown in Figure 4-4c. In this method, the objects that are completely or partially inside the green rectangle are selected.

Figure 4-4c

4.4.2. Method #2: Blue Method
- Draw a circle, rectangle, polygon, and a line as shown in Figure 4-5a.
- Place the cursor above and to the left of the objects to be selected, Figure 4-5a; point labeled as 2 in the current example.
- Notice the change in the appearance of the cursor.
- The blue color is the default color.

4.4.2.1. Version #1
- (i) Press the left button of the mouse, (ii) keep pressing the left button and (iii) move the cursor to the right and downward towards point labelled as 1, such that all the objects to be selected are completely in the blue area.
- Release the left mouse button as shown in Figure 4-5a; the objects are highlighted (the grip points appeared), Figure 4-5b. In this method, the object that is completely inside the blue area is selected.

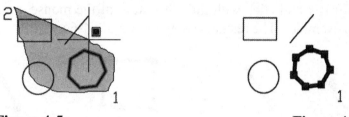

Figure 4-5a   **Figure 4-5b**

4.4.2.2. Version #2
- (i) Click the left button of the mouse and the prompt shown in Figure 4-5c appears, (iii) move the cursor to the right and downward (Figure 4-5c) such that all the objects to be selected are completely in the blue area.
- Click the left button again as shown in Figure 4-5c. In this method, the objects that are completely inside the blue area are selected, Figure 4-5d.

Figure 4-5c

4.4.3. Method #3
- If the objects to be selected cannot be enclosed in the green or the blue area because other objects may get selected, then select the objects individually by clicking them, Figure 4-5e.

Figure 4-5d   **Figure 4-5e**   **Figure 4-5f**

4.5.   Object De-selection

Although the object selection is the prerequisite for the functionality of the editing commands, the object de-selection is equally important. Figure 4-6a shows the selection of four objects. The user can de-select the entire selection by pressing the *Esc* key from the keyboard; Figure 4-6b shows the effect of pressing the *Esc* key. However, if the user wants to de-select a few objects from the set (for example wants to deselect the square), then hold the Shift key and click with the left button of the mouse on the desired object (the square in the example). The result is shown in Figure 4-6c.

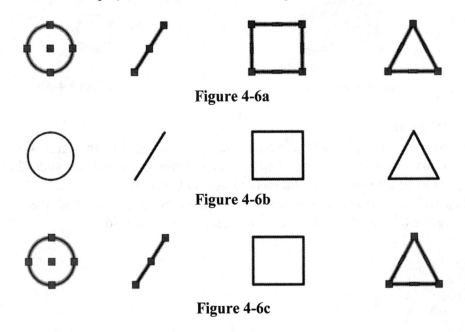

Figure 4-6a

Figure 4-6b

Figure 4-6c

4.6.   Zoom Capabilities

The zoom capabilities are used to change the magnification of the objects in the drawing area. The user accesses the zoom commands from the *View* tab and *Navigate* panel and clicking on the desired tool, Figure 4-7b. In the figure, the down arrow key is pressed to display the various options. Notice the change in the appearance of the cursor when zoom commands are activated.

By default, the *Navigate* panel is hidden. Therefore, the user must first display the navigate panel using the three step process listed here, Figure 4-7a. (i) Right click in the grey area after the last panel; (ii) click the *Show Panels* option; and (iii) click *Navigate*. Figure 4-7b shows the addition of the *Navigate* panel.

Figure 4-7a

Figure 4-7b

4.6.1. Zoom window

The *Zoom window* command is used to display the part of the drawing enclosed in a rectangular window. (i) Activate the *Zoom window* command by clicking the button, Figure 4-7b. The prompt shown in Figure 4-8a appears.

Figure 4-8a

(ii) Click below and to the right of the drawing as shown in Figure 4-8a. The prompt shown in Figure 4-8b appears. (iii) Click above and to the left of the drawing as shown in Figure 4-8b. This exits the command and the object is zoomed in. The first point can be any of the four corners of the rectangular window; however, the second point must be the diagonally opposite corner.

Figure 4-8b

4.6.2. Zoom scale

The *Zoom scale* command is used to zoom (in or out) using the scale factor. (i) Activate the *Zoom scale* command by clicking the button, Figure 4-7b. The prompt shown in Figure 4-9a appears. (ii) Specify the desired value. The value in Figure 4-9b (1.5x) makes every object in the drawing appear one and half times bigger than the original size. In Figure 4-9b the '*x*' implies that the scaling is relative to the current view. (iii) Figure 4-9c shows the original object whereas Figure 4-9d shows the scaled object.

Enter a scale factor (nX or nXP):   38.7399

Figure 4-9a

Enter a scale factor (nX or nXP):   1.5x

Figure 4-9b

Figure 4-9c   **Figure 4-9d**

4.6.3. Zoom center

The *Zoom center* command is used to zoom the center of the drawing using the scale factor. (i) Activate the *Zoom center* command by clicking the button, Figure 4-7b. The prompt shown in Figure 4-10a appears. (ii) Either specify the coordinated of the center of the desired object or click in the center. This example clicks at the center of the inner circle shown in Figure 4-10a. The prompt shown in Figure 4-10b appears. (iii) Specify the desired magnification value (this example uses 100) and press the *Enter* key. This zooms the object and exits the command. If necessary, this command also moves the object such that the center of the selected objects is at the center of the drawing area. In this command, zooming is inversely proportional to the magnification factor. For higher magnification numbers, the zooming is smaller.

Figure 4-10a

Figure 4-10b

4.6.4. Zoom object

The *Zoom object* command is used to zoom the selected object(s). (i) Activate the *Zoom object* command by clicking the button, Figure 4-7b. The prompt to select object appears. (ii) Click on the desired object and press the *Enter* key. This will zoom-in the object and exit the command. The center of the object is at the center of the drawing area and object appears as big as possible.

4.6.5. Zoom in

The *Zoom in* command is used to make the size of the drawing appear twice as big as the current size. (i) Activate the *Zoom in* command by clicking the button, Figure 4-7b. This zooms-in the drawing and exits the command. The center of the drawing stays in the center of drawing area.

4.6.6. Zoom out

The *Zoom out* command is used to make the size of the drawing appears half of the current size. (i) Activate the *Zoom out* command by clicking the button, Figure 4-7b.

This zooms-out the drawing and exits the command. The center of the drawing stays at the center of the drawing area.

4.6.7.   Zoom all

The *Zoom all* command is used to make every object in the drawing to appear in the viewing area of the drawing. (i) Activate the *Zoom all* command by clicking the button, Figure 4-7b. This makes every object in the drawing appear in the viewing area of the drawing and exits the command. The center of the drawing stays in the center of the drawing area.

4.6.8.   Zoom-wheel

The *Zoom wheel* command is NOT available through the *Navigate* panel. This command is ONLY available through the command line. The command is used to relate the magnification with the wheel of the mouse. (i) Type *Zoomwheel* on the command line and press the *Enter* key.

> *0:* Move wheel forward for zoom-in and backward for zoom-out.
> *1:* Move wheel backward for zoom-in and forward for zoom-out

4.7.   Pan

The pan capabilities are used to change the view without changing the viewing direction and /or magnification of the objects in the drawing. The user accesses the *Pan* command from the *View* tab and *Navigate* panel and clicking on the pan tool, Figure 4-11. Notice the change in the appearance of the cursor.

- The *Pan* command is activated as follows:
  1. Panel method: (i) From the *View* tab and *Navigate* panel, click on the pan tool.
  2. Command line method: Either type "pan", "Pan", or "PAN" and press the *Enter* key.

Figure 4-11

- The activation of the command changes the cross-hairs to the palm 👐 appearance.
- Click at a point and keep pressing the left button of the mouse; this changes the palm appearance to ✊.
- Click at a second point. Let d be the distance between the two clicks.

- Every object in the drawing is moved by distance d; in the direction from first point to the second point.
- Press *Esc* key on the keyboard to exit the command.

4.8.   Draw Order

The draw order capabilities are used to change the relative positions of overlapping objects. The user can access the commands through the *Draw Order* drop down menu (Figure 4-12a) or from a selection list as shown in, Figure 4-12b.

To understand the *Draw order* commands, draw two overlapping objects and change their color, Figure 4-12a. This example uses two overlapping objects a green line and red circle. The draw-order capabilities are discussed in the remainder of this section.

Figure 4-12a

4.8.1. Bring to front

The *Bring to Front* command is used to bring the selected object in front of every other object. The command can be activated using one of the following methods:

- The *Bring to Front* command is executed using one of the following procedures.
  1. Panel method: (i) From the *Home* tab and *Modify* panel, Figure 4-12a, expand the *Draw order* drop down menu, and select the *Bring to Front* tool. (ii) Click on the desired object, and circle in the current example. (iii) Press the *Enter* key. This closes the list and brings the selected object to the front.
  2. Selection list method: (i) Click on the desired object, a circle in the current example. (ii) Press the right button of the mouse. A selection list, Figure 4-12b, appears. (iii) Click on the desired option, *Bring to Front* in the current example. This closes the list and brings the selected object to the front.

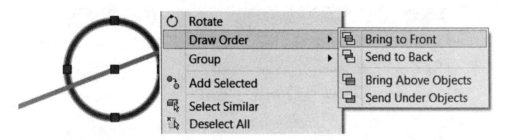

Figure 4-12b

4.8.2. Send to back

The *Send to Back* command is used to send the selected object back of every other object. The command can be activated using one of the following methods.

- The *Send to Back* command is executed using one of the following procedures.
  1. Panel method: (i) From the *Home* tab and *Modify* panel, expand the *Draw order* drop down menu, and select the *Send to Back* tool. (ii) Click on the desired object. (iii) Press the *Enter* key. This closes the list and sends the selected object to back.
  2. Selection list method: (i) Click on the desired object. (ii) Press the right button of the mouse. A selection list, Figure 4-12, appears. (iii) Click on the desired option. This closes the list and sends the selected object to back.

4.9. Object Snap

The *Object Snap* command allows snapping at strategic points on the selected objects in the drawing area, for example, end and mid points of a line, center and quadrant points of a circle, and point of intersection of two objects.

The *Drafting Setting* dialog box provides fourteen object snap modes; however, the user should select the modes related to the drawing objects in the current drawing. Turning *On* all the modes is NOT a good drawing practice.

4.9.1. Toggle object snap

Toggle the *Object snap* option using one of the following methods.

- Click the *Object Snap* button (□) on the status bar.
- Press the *F3* key on the keyboard.
- (i) Bring the cursor on the *Object Snap* button of the status bar. (ii) Click the down arrow key adjacent to the □. This opens a selection list. (iii) Click on the *Object Snap Settings* option, the *Drafting Settings* dialog box will open, Figure 4-13a (the *Object Snap* tab selected). (iv) Finally, check the *Object Snap On* box on the dialog box.
- Type "dsettings" or "osnap" on the command line and press the *Enter* key. This opens the *Drafting Setting* dialog box with the *Object Snap* tab selected. Finally, check the *Object Snap On* box, Figure 4-13a.

Figure 4-13a

The *Drafting Setting* dialog box provides fourteen object snap modes, Figure 4-13a. In order to distinguish various object snap points, AutoCAD provides different patterns for each mode. This dialog box can be opened during the execution of a command from the status bar, too; (i) bring the cursor on the *Object Snap* button of the status bar; (ii) click the down arrow key adjacent to the ⬜. This opens a selection list. (iii) Click on the *Object Snap Settings* option, the *Drafting Settings* dialog box with the *Object Snap* tab selected.

4.9.2.   Size and color of the object snap cursor

The user can change the size and color of the object snap cursor box. To change the size and color of the cursor box for the object snap, click on the *Options* (lower left corner) button in the *Drafting Setting* dialog box (Figure 4-13a) and the *Options* dialog box is opened. In the *Options* dialog box, select the *Drafting* tab, Figure 4-13b, and make the desired changes.

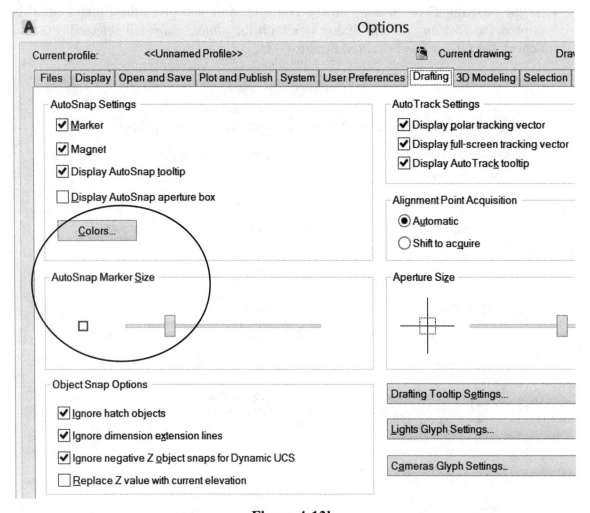

Figure 4-13b

4.9.3.   Object snap commands

Most of the *Object Snap* commands do not work independently but work in conjunction with other commands. For example, to draw a line starting at a quadrant point of a circle, use the following steps. (i) Activate the *Line* command. (ii) Activate the *object snap* command. (iii) Click on the quadrant tool in the *Drafting setting* dialog box (in the object snap tab). (iv) Bring the cursor on the circle and the nearest quadrant is highlighted.

(v) Now, proceed with the line construction process. **Important points**: It is good drawing practice to check two or three modes of *Object Snap* if those modes are used most of the time.

The *Object Snap* commands are activated by checking the corresponding box in the *Drafting setting* dialog box (first select *Object Snap* tab). *If the object snap command is activated by checking the box in the dialog box, then it is effective as long as the box is checked. **Therefore, for multiple uses, always activate the object snap commands from the dialog box.***

4.9.3.1.   Endpoint

The object snaps *Endpoint* mode snaps to the closet endpoint of an existing entity, for example, the ends of a line (Figure 4-14a), an arc (Figure 4-14b), and a polyline. The snap's point appears as a small square.

Example: Draw a circle with its center located at the end point of an existing line.
1. Draw a line.
2. Activate the *Circle* command.
3. Activate the object snap command and check the *Endpoint* box from the *Drafting setting* dialog box.
4. Bring the cursor near the end of the line, Figure 4-14a; the end of the line is automatically highlighted.
5. Click at the highlighted endpoint.
6. Continue with the *Circle* command.

| Figure 4-14a | Figure 4-14b |

4.9.3.2.   Midpoint

The object snap *Midpoint* mode snaps to the midpoint of an existing entity. For example, the midpoint of a line (Figure 4-14c), an arc (Figure 4-14d), and a polyline. The snap's point appears as a small triangle.

Example: Draw a circle with its center located at the midpoint of an existing line.
1. Draw a line.
2. Activate the *Circle* command.
3. Activate the object snap command and check the *Midpoint* box from the *Drafting setting* dialog box.
4. Bring the cursor near the mid of the line, Figure 4-14c; the midpoint of the line is automatically highlighted.
5. Click at the highlighted midpoint.
6. Continue with the *Circle* command.

Figure 4-14c   **Figure 4-14d**

4.9.3.3.   Node

The object snap *Node* mode snaps to a point Figure 4-15a. The figure shows three points. The snap's point appears as a small circle.

Example: Draw a circle with its center located at a given point.
1. Draw a point.
2. Activate the *Circle* command.
3. Activate the object snap command and check the *Node* box from the *Drafting setting* dialog box.
4. Bring the cursor near the point, Figure 4-15; the point is automatically highlighted.
5. Click at the highlighted point.
6. Continue with the *Circle* command.

Figure 4-15a

4.9.3.4.   Intersection

The object snap *Intersection* mode snaps to the intersection of two or more existing entities (arc, circle, line, polyline combination), Figure 4-15b. The figure shows the intersection of a circle and a line segment. The snap's point appears as a small x mark.

Example: Draw a circle with its center located at the intersection of a circle and a line.
1. Draw a circle and a line.
2. Activate the *Circle* command.
3. Activate the object snap command and check the *Intersection* box from the *Drafting setting* dialog box.
4. Bring the cursor near the intersection of the circle and the line, Figure 4-15b; the intersection point is automatically highlighted.
5. Click at the highlighted intersection.
6. Continue with the *Circle* command.

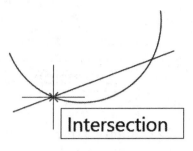

Figure 4-15b

4.9.3.5.   Extension

The object snap *Extension* mode creates a temporary extension of the object on its natural path. Figure 4-16a, Figure 4-16b, and Figure 4-16c show the extension of a circular arc, an elliptical arc, and a straight line, respectively. The snap's point appears as a small x mark.

Example: Draw a circle with its center located at the extension point of an object.
1. Draw the object (circular arc, elliptical arc, and a straight line).
2. Activate the *Circle* command.
3. Activate the object snap command and check the *Extension* box from the *Drafting setting* dialog box.
4. Bring the cursor near the end of the object and move the cursor on the natural path of the object, Figure 4-16a (circular arc), Figure 4-16b (parabolic arc), and Figure 4-16c (line).
5. The extension point is automatically highlighted.
6. Extend the object to the desired point.
7. Click at the extended point.
8. Continue with the *Circle* command.

Figure 4-16a

Figure 4-16b

Figure 4-16c

4.9.3.6.   Apparent intersection

The object snap *Apparent Intersection* mode snaps to the imaginary intersection of the two existing entities that would intersect if they were extended along their natural paths, Figure 4-17b. The snap's point appears as a small x mark.

Example: Draw a circle at the apparent intersection of a line and parabolic arc.
1. Draw a line and parabolic arc as shown in Figure 4-17a.
2. Activate the object snap command and check the *Apparent Intersection* and *Endpoint* commands box from the *Drafting setting* dialog box.
3. Activate the *Circle* command.
4. Bring the cursor on one of the lines and its endpoint appears, Figure 4-17a.
5. Bring the cursor on the arc and its endpoint appears, Figure 4-17b; also a small '+' mark appears at the selected end of the first line.
6. Move the cursor towards the apparent intersection of the two lines and a small 'x' mark appears at the apparent intersection, Figure 4-17c.
7. Click at the apparent intersection.
8. Continue with the *Circle* command.

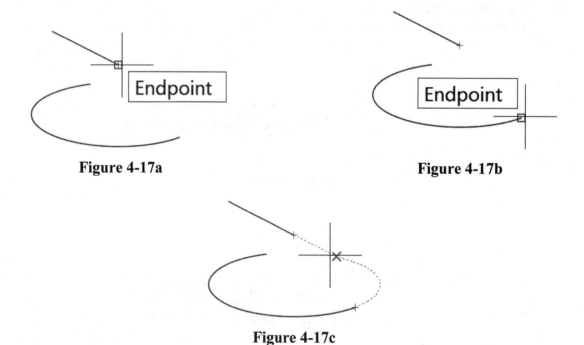

Figure 4-17a   **Figure 4-17b**

Figure 4-17c

4.9.3.7.   Center

The object snap's *Center* mode highlights the center of a circle to draw a line, arc, circle, and ellipse from or to the center of an arc/circle. The snap's point appears as a small plus sign.

Example: Draw a line through the center of an existing arc or a circle.
1. Draw an arc or a circle.
2. Activate the *Line* command.
3. Activate the object snap command and check the *Center* box from the *Drafting setting* dialog box.
4. Bring the cursor on the circumference of the circle, Figure 4-18a; the center of the circle is automatically selected.
5. Click at the highlighted center.
6. Continue with *Line* command.

4.9.3.8.   Quadrant

The object snap's *Quadrant* mode is used to snap directly to one of the quadrants of an existing arc or a circle. The snap's point appears as a small diamond mark.

Example: Draw a line between two quadrants of a circle as follows.
1. Draw a circle.
2. Activate the *Line* command.
3. Activate the object snap command and check the *Quadrant* box from the *Drafting setting* dialog box.
4. Bring the cursor on the circumference of the circle (Figure 4-18b), the closest quadrant is highlighted.
5. Click at the highlighted quadrant.
6. Continue with the *Line* command.
7. If in the *Drafting setting* dialog box both the *Center* and *Quadrant* boxes are checked, then the center and the closet quadrant are highlighted as the cursor is moved on the circumference, Figure 4-18c.

| Figure 4-18a | Figure 4-18b | Figure 4-18c |

4.9.3.9.   Geometric center

In AutoCAD terminology, the *Geometric Center* is the centroid or center of area of a closed polylines or polygons. The object snap *Geometric Center* mode highlights the geometric center of a closed polyline to draws a line, arc, circle, and ellipse from or to the center of the closed polyline. The snap's point appears as a small asterisk enclosed in a circle. Note: Geometric center command does not highlight the center of a circle.

Example: Draw a line through the center of an existing closed polylines or polygons.

1. Draw closed polylines and polygons as shown in Figure 4-18d, Figure 4-18e, and Figure 4-18f.
2. Activate the *Line* command.
3. Activate the object snap command and check the *Geometric Center* box from the *Drafting setting* dialog box.
4. Bring the cursor on the boundary of the closed polyline and the centroid of the selected object is automatically selected, Figure 4-18d, Figure 4-18e, and Figure 4-18f.
5. Click at the highlighted geometric center.
6. Continue with *Line* command.

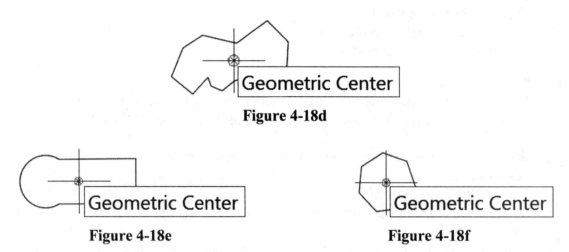

Figure 4-18d

Figure 4-18e   **Figure 4-18f**

4.9.3.10. Tangent

The object snap *Tangent* mode is used to draw an object tangent to an existing arc or a circle. The snap's point appears as a small circle with a horizontal line on top.

Example: Draw a line (the line's grip points are displayed in Figure 4-19a) with the starting point tangent to a circle and ending point is the intersection of two lines.

1. Draw two lines and a circle, Figure 4-19a.
2. Activate the *Line* command.
3. Activate the object snap command and check the *Tangent* box from the *Drafting setting* dialog box.
4. Bring the cursor on the circumference of the circle, Figure 4-19a. The point at the cursor location is highlighted.
5. Click for the start of the line.
6. The start point or tangent is called deferred, Figure 4-19a, because this is not the actual start of the line. If the cursor is moved around the circumference then the start point moves, too (Figure 4-19b).

Figure 4-19a

7. The location of the start point of the tangent is determined by the location of the end point.
8. Click at the intersection of the two lines for the end point of the line under construction. Notice how the start point has moved, Figure 4-19c.

Figure 4-19b

Figure 4-19c

4.9.3.11.   Perpendicular

The object snap's *Perpendicular* mode is used to draw a line perpendicular to an existing object. The snap's point appears as two small lines intersecting at 90° and parallel to the World coordinates system.

Example: Draw a line perpendicular to another line.
1. Draw a line.
2. Activate the *Line* command.
3. Activate the object snap command and check the *Perpendicular* box from the *Drafting setting* dialog box.
4. Bring the cursor on the line. The point at the cursor location is highlighted.
5. Click for the start of the line.
6. The start point is called deferred, Figure 4-20a, because this is not the actual start of the line. The location of the starting point of the perpendicular depends on the location of the ending point of the perpendicular. If the cursor is moved on the line then the start point also moves, Figure 4-20b.

Figure 4-20a   **Figure 4-20b**

4.10.   The Editing Commands

This section introduces the editing commands discussed in the remainder of this chapter. Based on the command functionality, Figure 4-21 shows the classification of the editing command.

- <u>Mistake correction</u>: Most of the commands are obvious from their names. The *Cancel* command is used to exit the currently active command and the *Erase* (⬛) command is used to erase the selected object(s). The *Oops* command is used to restore the object(s) deleted by the last erase command. The *Undo* (⬛) command is used to reverse the effect of one or more previous commands. The *Redo* (⬛) command is used to reverse the effect of one or more previous *Undo* commands.

- <u>Multiple occurrence</u>: The *Copy* (⬛) command is used to create copies at any location. The *Array* (⬛) command is used to create copies at specified location and in a specified pattern. The *Mirror* (⬛) command is used to create a copy that is a mirror image of the original object. The *Offset* (⬛) command is used to create a smaller or larger copy inside or outside the original object.

- <u>Relocate</u>: The *Move* (⬛) command is used to move the selected object to a new location. The *Rotate* (⬛) command is used to rotate the object; the entire object is rotated (relocated) except the point of rotation.

- <u>Resize</u>: The *Scale* (⬛) command is used to enlarge or shrink an object. The *Stretch* (⬛) command is used to stretch the selected part of the object.

- <u>Split</u>: The *Break* (⬛) command is used to break the selected object between two points. The *Break at a point* (⬛) command is used to break the selected object at a single point. The *Explode* (⬛) command is used to break the selected object into its basic components.

- <u>Object Connection</u>: The *Join* (⬛) command is used to connect multiple linear or curved objects to create a single object. The *Fillet* (⬛) command is used to connect two objects with an arc of the specified radius such that the arc is tangent to both the objects. The *Chamfer* (⬛) command is used to bevel the corners of objects or connect two non-parallel objects with a straight line.

- <u>Miscellaneous</u>: The *Delete duplicate objects* (⬛) command is used to retain one object if multiple and overlapping objects exist. The *Trim* (⬛) and the *Extend*

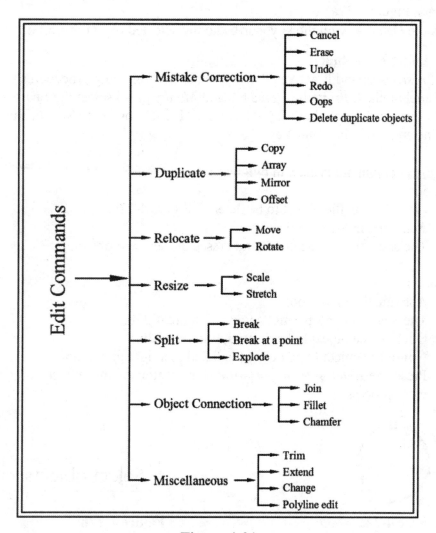 commands are used to trim and extend the edges of an object to meet the selected object, respectively. The *Polyline edit* (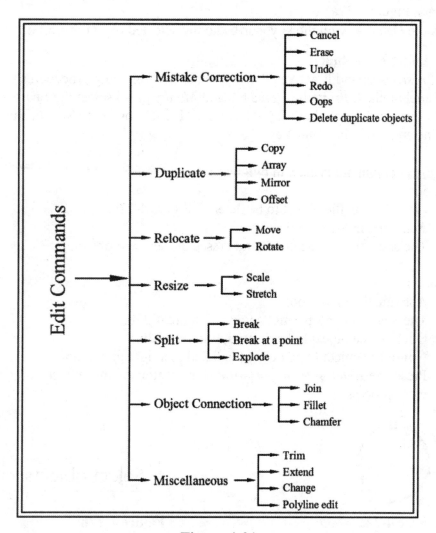) command is used to edit a polyline.

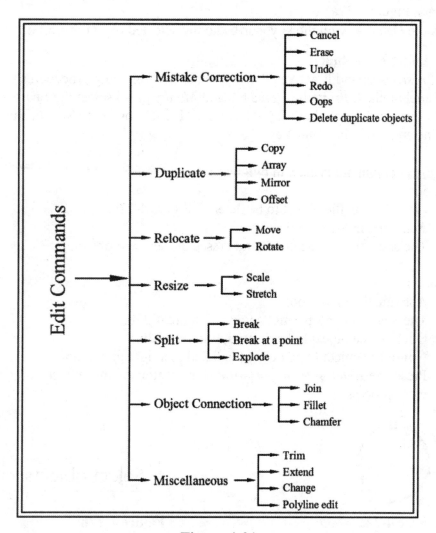

Figure 4-21

4.11. Cancel

A user of the AutoCAD can cancel any active command. If the user has activated a command intentionally or unintentionally; and needs to exit without completing it then simply press the *Esc* key on the keyboard and the command is canceled.

4.12. Erase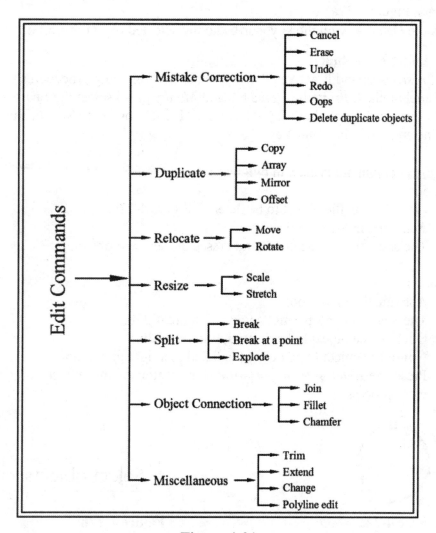

The *Erase* command is used to delete the selected objects from the drawing. A user can delete one or more objects using the methods discussed in this section.

4.12.1. Erase one object

4.12.1.1. Using delete key
- Click on the object to be deleted and the object is highlighted (that is, its grip points appear), Figure 4-22a.
- Press the *Delete* key on the keyboard, and the selected object is erased.

4.12.1.2. Using Erase tool
- The *Erase* command is activated using one of the following procedures.
  1. Panel method: From the *Home* tab and *Modify* panel select the *Erase* tool.
  2. Command line method: Type "erase", "Erase", or "ERASE" in the command line and press the *Enter* key.

- The *Erase* command is used in two ways.
  Method #1:
    o First click on the object to be deleted, Figure 4-22a.
    o Activate the *Erase* tool.
    o The activation of the command erases the selected object.

  Method #2:
    o Activate the *Erase* tool.
    o The *Select objects* prompt appears, Figure 4-22b.
    o Click on the object to be deleted, Figure 4-22b.
    o **Note:** The object to be deleted is faded to a light gray color.
    o Press the *Enter* key or press the right button of the mouse to complete the erase process.

Figure 4-22a   Figure 4-22b

4.12.2. Erase multiple object simultaneously
Multiple objects can be erased using the same procedure as used for erasing one object. The main difference is instead of selecting one object at a time, select multiple objects simultaneously using selection methods discussed earlier.

4.13. Undo ⟲
The *Undo* command is used to reverse the effect of one or more of the previous commands. However, the commands such as *Plot, Save, Open, Export* cannot be undone.

4.13.1. Undo one command

The following methods of undo are available during the activation of another command. For example, if a user is drawing a polyline, then the previous segment can be deleted using one of the two following methods.

- Hold the *Ctrl* key and press the '*z*' key on the keyboard. The most recent command is undone.
- Press the '*u*' or '*U*' key on the keyboard and press the *Enter* key. The most recent command is undone.

4.13.2. Undo several commands

The following methods of undo are available only if none of the other commands are active.

- Command line method: (i) Type "undo", "Undo", or "UNDO" in the command line and press the *Enter* key. The prompt shown in Figure 4-23a appears. (ii) Enter the number of commands to be undone. (iii) Press the *Enter* key.

> Enter the number of operations to undo or   ⟱ 3

Figure 4-23a

- Tool bar method: (i) Click the down arrow of the *Undo* tool (⟲) located on the upper left corner of the interface, Figure 4-23b. A drop-down list appears. (ii) Click the commands to be undone. The figure shows the selection of three commands.

Figure 4-23b

4.14.   Redo ⟳

The *Redo* command is used to reverse the effect of one or more previous *Undo* commands. However, the commands must be activated immediately after the *Undo* command, Figure 4-23c.

Figure 4-23c

4.14.1. Redo one command

Hold the *Ctrl* key and press the '*y*' key on the keyboard. The most recent *Undo* command is redone.

4.14.2. Redo several commands

This following method of redo is available only if none of the other commands are active.

- Command line method: Type "redo", "Redo", or "REDO" in the command line and press the *Enter* key.
- Tool bar method: (i) Click the down arrow of the *Undo* tool (⤵) located on the upper left corner of the interface. A drop-down list appears. (ii) Click the commands to be redone.

4.15.   Oops

The *Oops* command is used to restore only object(s) deleted from the last *Erase* command. The drawing of Figure 4-24a shows a bold triangle. The triangle is erased from the drawing of Figure 4-24b. In the drawing of Figure 4-24c, the user has added few more objects and realized that the bold triangle was deleted. The user wants to restore the triangle without deleting the newly created objects. The user can restore the recently deleted object using the *Oops* command.

- The *Oops* command can be activated only from the command line.
  1. Command line method: Type "oops", "Oops", or "OOPS" in the command line and press the *Enter* key.
- The object deleted in the previous *Erase* command appears on the screen. In the example, the triangle appears on the screen, Figure 4-24d.

Figure 4-24a   **Figure 4-24b**   **Figure 4-24c**   **Figure 4-24d**

4.16.   Delete Duplicate Objects

The *Delete Duplicate Objects* command is used for housekeeping. This command erases overlapping objects and combines small contiguous and collinear line, polyline, contiguous arcs with the same radius. In Figure 4-25a, AB and BC are contiguous (AB is touching BC at point B) and collinear (both lines are drawn at the same angle) lines. In Figure 4-25b, D and E are contiguous arcs with the same radius. Notice the difference in color, linetype, and lineweight of the objects.

Figure 4-25a   **Figure 4-25b**

- The *Delete Duplicate Objects* command can be activated using one of the following procedures.
    1. Panel method: From the *Home* tab and *Modify* panel select the *Delete Duplicate Objects* tool.
    2. Command line method: Type "overkill", "Overkill", or "OVERKILL" in the command line and press the *Enter* key.

- The activation of the command leads to the object selection prompt. Use one of the object selection methods discussed earlier, Figure 4-25c. Finally, press the *Enter* key to complete the object selection. This completes the object selection process and opens the *Delete Duplicate Objects* dialog box, Figure 4-25e.

Figure 4-25c

- *Delete Duplicate Objects* dialog box: The self-explanatory dialog box is shown in Figure 4-25e. The outcome of the command is shown in Figure 4-25d; notice, the color, linetype, and lineweight of the object. The resultant object adopts to the properties of the first component.

Figure 4-25d

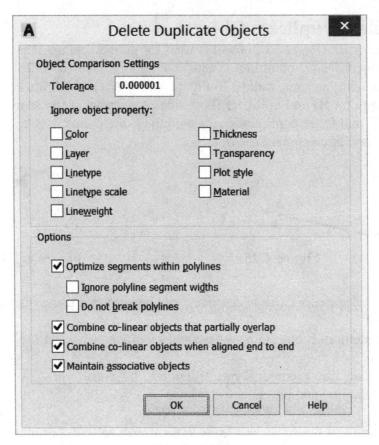

Figure 4-25e

4.17. Copy

The *Copy* command is used to create duplicates of drawing objects and place the duplicates at the specified location. This functionality is useful for creating multiple copies at a non-uniform spacing. Figure 4-26a shows five cars on two roads. The draftsman can create the car by drawing each car individually; a time consuming exhaustive process! The most efficient technique to complete the drawing is to use the *Copy* command. That is, create one car and use the copy command to create the other four buses.

Figure 4-26a

Example: Create four copies of the original car and place them at points B, C, D, and F.

- Draw the two roads, points A, B, C, D, and E, and the original car at point A as shown in Figure 4-26b using commands from the *Draw* and *Modify* Panel. The labels of the original car and the points can be ignored.

Figure 4-26b

- Activate the *Copy* command using one of the following procedures.
  1. Panel method: From the *Home* tab and *Modify* panel select the *Copy* tool.
  2. Command line method: Type "copy", "Copy", or "COPY" in the command line and press the *Enter* key.

- The most efficient technique to use the *Copy* command with the *Object snaps* mode *On* (copy-paste objects with precision).

- The activation of the command leads to the object selection prompt, Figure 4-26c. Select the original car using one of the object selection methods discussed earlier. Finally, press the *Enter* key to complete the object selection. **Notice the change in the appearance of the cursor.**

Figure 4-26c

- *Specify the base point*, Figure 4-26d: Either click on a point in the drawing or specify its coordinates (use the "," key to move from x's to y's input field) and press the *Enter* key. As a rule of thumb, the base point should be a point such that the copy can be pasted easily and precisely at its new location. In this example, the lower left corner of the side view mirror is selected as the base point, 4-26e.

Figure 4-26d

Figure 4-26e

- *Specify the second point*, Figure 4-26f: The second point is the location of the copy. Either click at the location of the copy or specify its coordinates (use the "," key to move from x's to y's input field) and press the *Enter* key. The coordinates of the second point are relative coordinates with respect to the base point. However, in the current example, click at point B of the top road, Figure 4-26g. This completes the process of creating the first copy. The prompt to create the second and subsequent copies is shown in Figure 4-26h.

Figure 4-26f

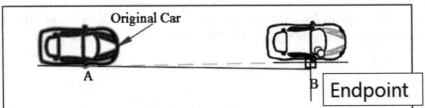

Figure 4-26g

- Make another copy: To create another copy, repeat the process of the specification of the second point. To exit the command, press the *Esc* or *Enter* key.
- The distance between the original to a copy location is determined by the distance and direction between the base and the second points.

Figure 4-26h

4.18.   Array

The *Array* command creates multiple copies of an object and arranges the copies in a specific pattern. The objects can be copied and arranged in a pattern using the *Copy*, *Rotate*, and *Move* commands, too. However, the drawing accuracy is increased and its creation duration is greatly reduced if the *Array* command is used to create the multiple copies in a pattern. AutoCAD allows users to create copies arranged in rectangular and circular patterns and along a specific path using *Rectangular*, *Polar*, and *Path* array commands, respectively.

The rectangular array command places copies in rows and columns, Figure 4-27a; the polar array command places the copies in a circular arrangement at a specific center, Figure 4-27b; and the path array command creates copies along a specified path, Figure 4-27c.

Figure 4-27a   **Figure 4-27b**

Figure 4-27c

4.18.1. Rectangular Array

The *Rectangular Array* command creates a rectangular array of the selected object. In a rectangular array, objects are arranged in rows and columns of an array. If an array contains one row then it must have more than one column and vice versa. By default, the maximum number of array elements generated in one command is 100000. The default number of elements in an array is 12 (3 rows and 4 columns).

- The ***ArrayRectangular*** command is activated using one of the following procedures.
    1. Panel method: From the *Home* tab and *Modify* panel, expand the *Array* drop down menu and select the *Rectangular Array* tool, Figure 4-28a.
    2. Command line method: Either type "array", "Array", or "ARRAY" and select the *ARRAYRECT* option; or type "arrayrect", "Arrayrect", or "ARRAYRECT" in the command line and press the *Enter* key.

Figure 4-28a   **Figure 4-28b**

Example: Create a three lane road with four cars in each lane; that is, create a drawing for a section of a road with four columns and three rows as shown in Figure 4-29a. The figure also shows the definition of the rows and column spacing.

Note: To practice the rectangular array command, a user can create a simple shape as shown in Figure 4-28b.

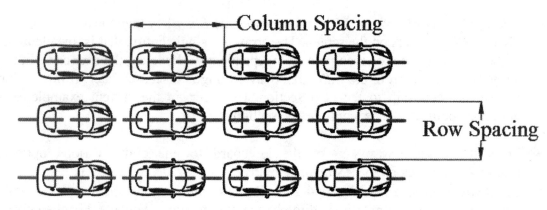

Figure 4-29a

- Create the basic element of the array, Figure 4-29b. Do not add dimensions.
- Activate the *Array Rectangular* command.
- The activation of the command displays the object selection prompt, Figure 4-29b.

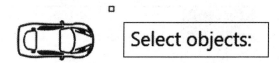

Figure 4-29b

- Select the desired objects and press the *Enter* key. The prompt shown in Figure 4-29c appears on the screen.

Figure 4-29c

- *Select grip to edit array or*: If the user presses the *Enter* key then the array shown in Figure 4-29c appears on the screen. The array is a single entity, that is, the elements of the array could not be manipulated independently. However, the user can edit the array using panels from the *Edit* tab. Array editing is discussed later. If this option is selected then skip to the next section. However, in the current example, this option is not used. Hence, continue the section.

- Press the down arrow key of the keyboard to check the various options, Figure 4-29c. Click on the *ASsociative* option.
- *Create associative array*, Figure 4-29d: The *Yes* option creates the array as a single entity and the user is not allowed to change one or more elements. For the current example, click on the *Yes* option.
- *Select grip to edit array or*, Figure 4-29e: Press the down arrow key of the keyboard and click on the *COUnt* option.

Figure 4-29d

Figure 4-29e

- *Enter the number of Columns*, Figure 4-29f: Specify the number of columns in the array (for the example array, type 4). Press the *Enter* key.

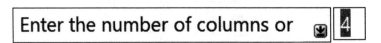

Figure 4-29f

- *Enter number of rows*, Figure 4-29f: Specify the number of rows in the array (for the example array, type 3). Press the *Enter* key.

Figure 4-29g

- *Select grip to edit array or*, Figure 4-29h: Press the down arrow key of the keyboard and click on the *Spacing* option.

Figure 4-29h

- *Specify the distance between columns or*, Figure 4-29i: Specify the spacing between the columns (for the example array, type 80). Press the *Enter* key. The column spacing is the summation of the width of a column and spacing between two consecutive columns, Figure 4-29a.

Figure 4-29i

- *Specify the distance between rows or*, Figure 4-29i: Specify the spacing between the rows (for the example array, type 70). Press the *Enter* key. The row spacing is the summation of the height of a row and spacing between two consecutive rows, Figure 4-29a.

Figure 4-29j

- *Select grip to edit array or*, Figure 4-29k: Press the *Enter* key to complete the array command. The resulting array is shown in Figure 4-29a.

Figure 4-29k

4.18.1.1. Rectangular array's grip points
This section explains the rectangular array's grip points.

- To use the options shown in Figure 4-30a and Figure 4-30b (i) bring the cursor on the desired grip point and it is highlighted (its color is changed) and its options appears; (ii) move the cursor to the desired option; (iii) finally, either press the *Enter* key or click with the left button of the mouse and follow the prompts.
  - The grip point at the lower right corner of the array can be used to change the number of columns, the column spacing, and the axis angle of the array, Figure 4-30a; the axis angle is shown in Figure 4-30e. The user can hold the Ctrl key and cycle through the available options.

Figure 4-30a

  - The grip point at the upper left corner of the array can be used to change the number of rows, the row spacing, and the axis angle of the array, Figure 4-30b.

Figure 4-30b

o The grip point at the upper right corner of the array can be used to change the number of rows and columns, and the row and column spacing of the array, Figure 4-30c.

Figure 4-30c

o The grip point at the lower left corner of the array can be used to move the array.

Figure 4-30d

Figure 4-30e

4.18.2. Polar array

The *Polar Array* command creates a circular array of the selected objects around a specified center point. Also, the objects are rotated to face the center point. This section explains the options available to create a polar array. The Figure 4-31a shows basic terminology of a polar array.

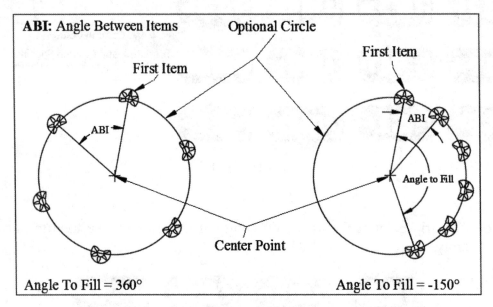

Figure 4-31a

- The ***ArrayPolar*** command is activated using one of the following procedures.
  1. Panel method: From the *Home* tab and *Modify* panel, expand the *Array* drop down menu and select the *Polar Array* tool, Figure 4-31b.
  2. Command line method: Either type "array", "Array", or "ARRAY" and select the *ARRAYPOLAR* option, Figure 4-31c; or type "arraypolar", "Arraypolar", or "ARRAYPOLAR" in the command line and press the *Enter* key.

Figure 4-31b

Example: Create a circular arrangement of seven chairs occupying three quarters of a circle and facing towards the center as shown in Figure 4-32a or Figure 4-32b. The two figures represent the same array. The Figure 4-32a is created using the fill angle of 270°; and the Figure 4-32b is created using the angle between items of 38.57°.

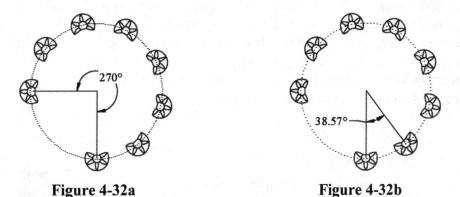

Figure 4-32a   **Figure 4-32b**

- Create the basic element of the array, Figure 4-32c and Figure 4-33a. In the current example, the circle of diameter 20 is drawn to show the arrangement of array elements.
- Activate the *Array Polar* command.
- The activation of the command opens the object selection prompt, Figure 4-33a.

Figure 4-32c   **Figure 4-33a**

- Select the desired objects and press the *Enter* key. The prompt shown in Figure 4-33b appears on the screen. Press the down arrow on the keyboard to display the various options.

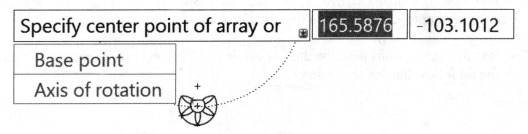

Figure 4-33b

- *Specify center point of array or*, Figure 4-33b: This example uses the *Center* option. (i) Press the up arrow of the keyboard to hide the option list. (ii) Turn *On* the *Center* option in the *Object snap*. (iii) Click on the center point of the circle. The prompt shown in Figure 4-33c appears on the screen.
- *Select grip to edit array or*, Figure 4-33c: If the user presses the *Enter* key then the array shown in Figure 4-33c appears on the screen; and the user should neglect the remaining bullets in this section. However, the user can edit the array using panels from the *Edit* tab. Array editing is discussed later. In the current example, press the down arrow key on the keyboard to check the various options.
- Select the *ASsociative* option, Figure 4-33d.

Figure 4-33c

- *Create associative array* Figure 4-33d: The *Yes* option creates the array as a single entity; that is, the elements of the array could not be manipulated independently. The user may need to change one or more elements. However, for the current example, click on the *Yes* option.

Figure 4-33d

- *Select grip to edit array or*, Figure 4-33e: Press the down arrow key of the keyboard and click on the *Items* option.
- *Enter number of items in array or*, Figure 4-33f: Specify the number of items (for the current example array, type 8). Press the *Enter* key.

The next two subsections describe the *Fill angle* and the *Angle between* options; and the user should follow the desired option.

Figure 4-33e

Enter number of items in array or ⊌ 8

Figure 4-33f

4.18.2.1.   Fill angle
- Continued from Section 4.16.2.
- *Select grip to edit array or*, Figure 4-34a: Press the down arrow key of the keyboard and click on the *Fill angle* option.

Figure 4-34a

- *Enter the angle to fill*, Figure 4-34b: Specify the fill angle (for the example array, type 270). Press the *Enter* key. Positive angles fill the circle counterclockwise.

Specify the angle to fill (+=ccw, -=cw) or ⊌ 270

Figure 4-34b

- *Select grip to edit array or*, Figure 4-34c: Press the *Enter* key to complete the array command. The resulting array is shown in Figure 4-32a.

Figure 4-34c

4.18.2.2.   Angle between

- Continued from Section 4.16.2.
- *Select grip to edit array or*: Press the down arrow key of the keyboard and click on the *Angle between* option, Figure 4-35a.

Figure 4-35a

- *Specify angle between items or*: Figure 4-35b, Specify the angle between two consecutive elements. For the example array, type 38.57. The positive angle creates a counterclockwise array. Press the *Enter* key.
- *Select grip to edit array or*, Figure 4-35c: Press the *Enter* key to complete the array command. The resulting array is shown in Figure 4-32b.

Figure 4-35b

Figure 4-35c

4.18.2.3.   Polar array and grip points

- Figure 4-36 shows the behavior of the grip point at the basic element of the array. These grip points can be used to change the number of items (*Item Count*) and the fill angle (*Fill Angle*) of the polar array. It is also used to change the radius (*Stretch Radius*) and the number of circles in the polar array using *Row Count* option.
- To use the options shown in Figure 4-36 (i) bring the cursor on the desired grip point and it is highlighted (its color changes) and its options appear; (ii) move the cursor to the desired option; (iii) finally, either press the *Enter* key or click with the left button of the mouse and follow the prompts.

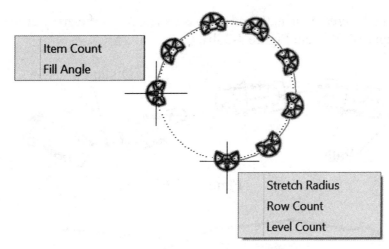

Figure 4-36

4.18.3. Path array

The *Array Path* command distributes the desired number of the object (to be arrayed) evenly on a path. The path can be a line, polyline, spline, helix, arc, circle, or ellipse. In the current example, the path is created using a polyline.

- The ***ArrayPath*** command is activated using one of the following procedures.
  1. Panel method: From the *Home* tab and *Modify* panel, expand the *Array* drop down menu and select the *Path Array* tool, Figure 4-37a.
  2. Command line method: Either type "array", "Array", or "ARRAY" and select the *ARRAYPATH* option; or type "arraypath", "Arraypath", or "ARRAYPATH" in the command line and press the *Enter* key.

Figure 4-37a   **Figure 4-37b**

Example: Show five cars on a road as shown in Figure 4-38a.

Note: To practice the path array command, a user can create a simple shape as shown in Figure 4-37b.

- For the example, create the path and the basic element of the array at the beginning of the path, Figure 4-38b and Figure 4-38b1.

Figure 4-38a

Figure 4-38b

Figure 4-38b1

- Activate the *Array Path* command.
- The activation of the command opens the object selection prompt, 4-38c.
- Select the desired objects and press the *Enter* key. The prompt shown in Figure 4-38d appears on the screen.

Figure 4-38c

- *Select path curve*, Figure 4-38d: Bring the cursor on the path and press the left button of the mouse. In the example, click the polyline labeled as Path.
- *Select grip to edit array or*, Figure 4-38e: If the user presses the *Enter* key then the array shown in Figure 4-38e appears on the screen; and the user should ignore the remaining steps in this section. The array is a single entity, that is, the elements of the

array could not be manipulated independently. However, the user can edit the array using panels from the *Edit* tab. Array editing is discussed later.

• In the current example, press the down arrow key of the keyboard to check the various options, Figure 4-38e. Click on the *ASsociative* option.

Figure 4-38d

Figure 4-38e

• *Create associative array*, Figure 4-39a: The *Yes* option creates the array as a single entity. The user may need to change one or more elements. However, for the current example, click on the *Yes* option.

Figure 4-39a

• *Select grip to edit array or*, Figure 4-39b: Press the down arrow key of the keyboard and click on the *Items* option.

Figure 4-39b

- *Specify the distance between items along path or*, Figure 4-39c: Press the down arrow key of the keyboard and check the various options. However, in this example specify the distance to be 95. Press the *Enter* key.

Figure 4-39c

- *Specify number of items or*, Figure 4-39d: The prompt displays the maximum number of items Figure 4-39d, calculated as the length of the path divided by distance between the two items. Press the down arrow key of the keyboard and check the various options. In the current example, select the *6* (number of items) option.

Figure 4-39d

- Press the *Enter* key again to complete the command. The resulting array is shown in Figure 4-38a.

Figure 4-39e

4.18.3.1.   Path array and grip points

- Figure 4-39f shows the behavior of the grip point at the basic element of the array. These grip points can be used to move the array to a different location (*Move*) and the number of paths in the path array using *Row Count* option.
- To use the options shown in Figure 4-39f (i) bring the cursor on the desired grip point and it is highlighted (its color changes) and its options appear; (ii) move the cursor to the desired option; (iii) finally, either press the *Enter* key or click with the left button of the mouse and follow the prompts.

Figure 4-39f

4.18.4. Edit array

The arrays can be edited using the grip points as discussed earlier. However, a user can also edit an array using the *Array* tab. Figure 4-40a shows the *Array* tab for the rectangular array; Figure 4-40b shows the *Array* tab for the polar array; and Figure 4-40c shows the *Array* tab for the path array created in Sections 4.18.1, 4.18.2, and 4.18.3, respectively.

A user can edit an array using the *Array* tab as follows: (i) Click the array that needs to be edited then the *Array* tab becomes the current tab. (ii) Now edit the array using the desired tool from the Array's panels and following the prompts.

Figure 4-40a

Figure 4-40b

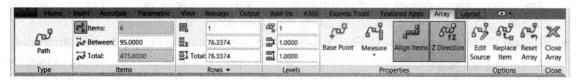

Figure 4-40c

4.19. Mirror

The *Mirror* command is used to flip an object about a specified axis (mirror line) to create a mirror image. This technique is useful for creating symmetrical models, Figure 4-41; the user is required to draw the repeating part of the model and then use the mirror command to complete the model.

Example: Create the window panel shown in Figure 4-41a. The figure also shows three lines of symmetry, A, B, and C. The window is created as follows.

Figure 4-41a   **Figure 4-41b**

- Draw the basic unit shown in Figure 4-41b. Do not add dimensions and the label *A*.
- Activate the *Mirror* command using one of the following procedures.
    1. Panel method: From the *Home* tab and *Modify* panel select the *Mirror* tool.
    2. Command line method: Type "mirror", "Mirror", or "MIRROR" in the command line and press the *Enter* key.

- The activation of the command leads to the object selection prompt, Figure 4-42a.
- *Select objects*: Select every object except the line labeled as mirror line using one of the selection methods discussed earlier in this chapter; press the *Enter* key to complete the object selection. The prompt shown in Figure 4-42b appears.

Figure 4-42a

- *Specify the first point of the mirror line*, Figure 4-42b: The user can select either of the two ends of the mirror line *A* as a first point. However, in the current example, the upper end is selected as the first point.
- Either click on upper end of the mirror line (follow the prompt) or specify its coordinates (use the "," key to move from x's to y's input field) and press the *Enter* key.

Figure 4-42b

- *Specify the second point of the mirror line*, Figure 4-42c: Either click on the lower end of the mirror line (follow the prompt) or specify the coordinates (use the "," key to move from x's to y's input field) and press the *Enter* key.

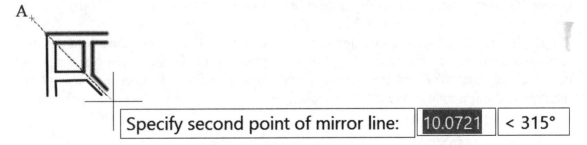

Figure 4-42c

- *Erase source objects? [Yes or No]*, Figure 4-42d: Click on *No*; the *No* option is used to flip the image by placing the mirrored image into the drawing and retaining the original objects. The *Yes* option is used to flip the image by placing the mirrored image into the drawing and erasing the original objects. Figure 4-42e shows the result of the mirror command.

Figure 4-42d

Figure 4-42e

- Draw the mirror line B and repeat the process. The resulting drawing is shown in Figure 4-43a. Repeat the mirror command using an imaginary vertical line used as a mirror line. The resulting object is shown in Figure 4-43b.
- Hatch the drawing to complete the drawing as shown in Figure 4-41a.

Figure 4-43a

Figure 4-43b

4.20.   Offset

The *Offset* command creates a new object whose shape is parallel to the shape of the selected object. A user can offset lines, arcs, circles, ellipses, polylines, construction lines, splines, and rays. Offsetting closed shapes and arcs creates smaller or larger shapes or arcs if offset is inside or outside, respectively (Figure 4-44a and Figure 4-44b).

2D polylines and splines are trimmed automatically when the offset shape is larger than can be accommodated inside the polyline or spline, Figure 4-44a. However, the offset object adopts the color and lineweight of the original object. If necessary, change the linetype and lineweight of the offset object.

Figure 4-44a

Figure 4-44b

An efficient and precise drawing technique is to offset objects (if possible) and then trim or extend their ends, Figure 4-44c.

Figure 4-44c

Example: Create the shape shown in Figure 4-45a, using the offset command.

Figure 4-45a

- Open a new "acad" file.
- Draw the basic shape using *Polyline* command as shown in Figure 4-45b. If necessary, use the *Join* command to connect the segments.

Figure 4-45b

- Activate the *Offset* command using one of the following procedures.
  1. Panel method: From the *Home* tab and *Modify* panel select the *Offset* tool.
  2. Command line method: Type "offset", "Offset", or "OFFSET" in the command line and press the *Enter* key.

- The activation of the command leads to the offset distance specification prompt, Figure 4-45c.

Figure 4-45c

- *Specify the offset distance or*, Figure 4-45c: Enter the offset distance and press the *Enter* key. In this example, the offset distance is 3.0. The prompt to select the object to offset (Figure 4-45d) appears.

Figure 4-45d

- *Select object to offset or*, Figure 4-45d: In order to select the object to offset, bring the cursor on the object and press the left button of the mouse, Figure 4-45e. The original object's color and appearance changes.

Figure 4-45e

- *Specify point on side to offset or*: In Figure 4-45e, the cursor is inside the selected object and the offset object's preview is displayed, too. For the current example, click inside the original object and a smaller object is created inside, and the prompt goes back to creating an offset, Figure 4-45f.
- Either click for another offset or exit the command by pressing the *Esc* key. However, in the current example, click on the offset object to create a new offset inside the previous offset, Figure 4-45g.

Figure 4-45f

- *Specify point on side to offset or*: Click on the offset object created in the previous step and click inside it, Figure 4-45f.

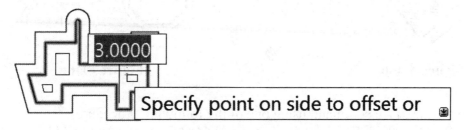

Figure 4-45g

- Exit the command by pressing the *Esc* key. The resultant objects are shown in Figure 4-45a. Notice, the shape of the innermost offset objects.

4.21.   Move

The *Move* command is used to relocate an object in a specified direction and at a specified distance from the original position. The user must activate the object snap command to move the objects with precision.

Figure 4-46a

Example: Move the screwdriver (Figure 4-46b) near the wrench (Figure 4-46c) as shown in Figure 4-46a using the *Move* command.

- Open a new "acad" file.

- Draw the screwdriver (Figure 4-46b) near the wrench (Figure 4-46c) using the basic drawing commands. The φ symbol represents the diameter. No need to add dimensions. The remainder of this section explains the move process.

Figure 4-46b   **Figure 4-46c**

- Activate the *Move* command using one of the following procedures.
    1. Panel method: From the *Home* tab and *Modify* panel select the *Move* tool.
    2. Command line method: Type "move", "Move", or "MOVE" in the command line and press the *Enter* key.

- The activation of the command leads to the object selection prompt, Figure 4-46d. Use one of the object selection methods discussed earlier. Finally, press the *Enter* key to complete the object selection. Notice the change in the appearance of the cursor. The prompt shown in Figure 4-46e appears.

Figure 4-46d

Figure 4-46e

4.21.1. Move in xy-plane

- *Specify the base point*, Figure 4-46e: As a rule of thumb, the base point should be a point such that the object can be relocated easily and precisely at its new location. Either click on a point in the object or specify the coordinates (use the "," key to move from x's to y's input field) and press the *Enter* key. In the current example, point A is selected as the base point.
- **Note:** As the cursor moves, the object at the original location is faded to light gray and the moving object maintains its color, Figure 4-47a.
- *Specify the second point*, Figure 4-47a: The second point is the new location of the object. Either click at the new location or specify its coordinates (use the "," key to move from x's to y's input field) and press the *Enter* key. The coordinates of the second point are relative coordinates with respect to the base point. This completes the process of moving the object from the original location to the new location and exits the command, too. For the current example, click at point B on the wrench. The resultant objects are shown in Figure 4-46a.
- The distance from the original to the new location is determined by the distance and direction between the base and second points.

Specify second point or <use first point as displacement>: 4.0811 < 312°

Figure 4-47a

4.21.2. Move in z-direction

The *Move* command can also be used to change the elevation of a drawing.

- Activate the *Move* command.
- Complete the object selection process and press the *Enter* key.
- *Specify the base point*, Figure 4-47b: Press the down arrow key on the keyboard. Select the *Displacement* option by clicking with the left button of the mouse.

Specify base point or -75.3342 -324.2460

• Displacement

Figure 4-47b

- *Specify displacement*, Figure 4-47c: Specify the coordinates, use the "," key to move from one input field to the next, and press the *Enter* key. In the example, for the vertical displacement x and y are set to "0" and 75 is entered for the z coordinate.

Specify displacement <0.0000, 0.0000, 0.0000>:   0 🔒 0 🔒 75

Figure 4-47c

- The base point's elevation (and every point's elevation) is incremented by 75. Initially, the elevation was zero. To check the elevation (or Z value) of the base point, (i) activate the *Line* command, (ii) bring the cursor on the base point, and (iii) check the coordinate in the lower left corner of the workspace.

4.22.   Rotate 🔄

The *Rotate* command is used to rotate objects in a drawing around a specified base point. The user must activate object snaps to rotate objects with precision.

Example: Rotate the screwdriver shown in Figure 4-48a at a counter-clockwise angle of 75°. Notice the change in the appearance of the cursor.

- Open a new "acad" file.
- Draw the screwdriver, also, draw the overlapping lines passing through the center of the screwdriver as shown in Figure 4-48a. For the dimensions of the screwdriver, refer to Figure 4-46b.

- Activate the *Rotate* command using one of the following procedures.
   1. Panel method: From the *Home* tab and *Modify* panel select the *Rotate* tool.
   2. Command line method: Type "rotate", "Rotate", or "ROTATE" in the command line and press the *Enter* key.

- The activation of the command leads to the object selection prompt, Figure 4-48a. Select the airplane and one of the horizontal lines, and then press the *Enter* key to complete the object selection.

Select objects:

Figure 4-48a

- *Specify the base point*, Figure 4-48b: In *Rotate* command, the base point is the pivot to rotate the object. Either click on a point in the object or specify the coordinates (use the "," key to move from x's to y's input field) and press the *Enter* key. In this example, click the nose of the airplane as a base point, Figure 4-48b.

Figure 4-48b

- **Note:** As the cursor moves, the object at the original position is faded to light gray and the rotated object maintains its color, Figure 4-48c.

Figure 4-48c

- *Specify rotation angle*, Figure 4-48c: Either click at the desired orientation or specify its value and press the *Enter* key. Positive angles rotate the object counterclockwise and negative angles rotate the object clockwise. In this example, the rotation angle is set to 20, Figure 4-48c.
- Figure 4.48d shows the rotated airplane.

Figure 4-48d

4.23.   Scale

The *Scale* command is used to enlarge or shrink the object in two-dimensions. Scaling is relative to the world coordinate system's origin; and the location of the drawing origin remains at the WCS origin

Example: Draw two cars as shown in Figure 4-49a. The second car size is 70% larger than the first car.

- Open a new "acad" file.
- Draw one of the cars as shown in Figure 4-49a. Use the copy command to create the second car. The car on the left will be used for the illustration of the *Scale* command.

Figure 4-49a

- Activate the *Scale* command using one of the following procedures.
    1. Panel method: From the *Home* tab and *Modify* panel select the *Scale* tool.
    2. Command line method: Type "scale", "Scale", or "SCALE" in the command line and press the *Enter* key.

- The activation of this command leads to the object selection prompt, Figure 4-49b.

Figure 4-49b

- Select the object (car on the right in the example) to scale and press the *Enter* key to complete the object selection, Figure 4-49c.
- *Specify the base point*, Figure 4-49c: When an object is scaled up or down; every point in the object moves from its current location except one point (the base point). For the *Scale* command, the base point is the point that stays at its current location. Either, click on a point in the object or specify its coordinates and press the *Enter* key. In this example, the lower left corner of the back of the car is chosen as the base point, therefore, just click on the lower left corner of the car. **Notice the change in the appearance of the cursor.**

Figure 4-49c

- *Specify scale factor*, Figure 4-49d: The car at the original scale is faded to light gray, and the scaled car maintains its color. Enter the desired value and press the *Enter* key. In this example, the goal is to enlarge the second car by 70%. Therefore, the scale factor of 1.7 is used.
- Every object in the second car is now 70% larger than the first car, Figure 4-49e.
- Repeat the above process; the goal is to reduce the second car by 20%. Hence, the scale factor is 0.8. The size of every object in the second car is decreased by 20%, Figure 4-49f.

Figure 4-49d

Figure 4-49e

Figure 4-49f

4.24.   Stretch

The *Stretch* command is used to lengthen or shorten an object (change in one-dimension).

Example: Stretch the model such that the right side is stretched from point A to point B, Figure 4-50a.

- Open a new "acad" file.
- Draw the objects shown in Figure 4-50a.
- Activate the *Stretch* command using one of the following procedures.
    1. Panel method: From the *Home* tab and *Modify* panel select the *Stretch* tool.
    2. Command line method: Type "stretch", "Stretch", or "STRETCH" in the command line and press the *Enter* key.

- The activation of this command leads to the object selection prompt, Figure 4-50a. The object selection in the *Stretch* command is slightly different then the object selection for the other command on the *Modify* panel.

Figure 4-50a

- *Select object*, Figure 4-50b: For the *Stretch* command, make the selection box starting below the lower right corner as shown in Figure 4-50b. Click below the lower left corner of the selection rectangle, keep pressing the left button of the mouse, and click at the diagonally opposite corner. The selected objects are shown in Figure 4-50b. Finally, press the *Enter* key.

Figure 4-50b

- *Specify the base point*, Figure 4-50c: For the *Stretch* command, the base point should be the point that needs to be stretched to the new location. Either click on the point or specify its coordinates and press the *Enter* key. In this example, click at point A.

Figure 4-50c

- *Specify second point*, Figure 4-50d: For the *Stretch* command, the second point is the new location of the base point. Either click on the point or specify its coordinates and press the *Enter* key. In this example, click at point B.
- **Note:** As the cursor moves, the original object is faded to light gray and the new object (that is, the stretched object) maintains its color, Figure 4-50d.
- The right side is stretched from point A to point B, Figure 4-50e.

Figure 4-50d

Figure 4-50e

- For the *Stretch* command, if the object is completely inside the selection rectangle, Figure 4-51a, then the object simply moves from the initial location A (clicked as base point) to the new location B (clicked as second point), Figure 4-51b.

Figure 4-51a

Figure 4-51b

4.25. Break

The *Break* command is used to create a gap or open space in the given object by specifying two points on the object.

Example: Consider a drafter drew the drawing shown in Figure 4-52a and now wants to create a gap between points A and B, Figure 4-52b. The drawing of Figure 4-52a can be modified to the drawing of Figure 4-52b using the *Break* command.

- Activate the *Break* command using one of the following procedures.
  1. Panel method: From the *Home* tab expand the *Modify* panel and select the *Break* tool.
  2. Command line method: Type "break", "Break", or "BREAK" in the command line and press the *Enter* key.

- The activation of the command displays the prompt to select the object, Figure 4-53a.

Figure 4-52a   **Figure 4-52b**   **Figure 4-53a**

- *Select object*, Figure 4-53a: Bring the cursor on the object and click with the left button of the mouse. The prompt shown in Figure 4-53b appears.
- *Specify second break point or*, Figure 4-53b: Press the down arrow key on the keyboard to display the available options. Select the First point option. The prompt shown in Figure 4-53c appears.

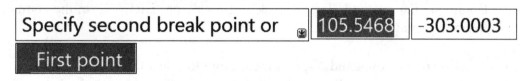

Figure 4-53b

- *Specify first break point or*, Figure 4-53c: Either click at the desired point or specify its coordinate and press the *Enter* key. In the current example, click at point A.

Figure 4-53c

- *Specify second break point or*, Figure 4-53d: Either click at the desired location or specify its coordinates and press the *Enter* key. In the current example, click at point B.
- The gap between point A and B is created as shown in Figure 4-52b.

Figure 4-53d

- The same effect can also be created by (i) drawing two temporary lines at points A and B, Figure 4-54a, (ii) using the *Trim* command to trim the objects between the two lines, Figure 4-54b, and (iii) deleting the lines using the *Erase* command, Figure 4-54c.

Figure 4-54a   **Figure 4-54b**   **Figure 4-54c**

4.26.   Break at a Point

The *Break at a point* command is used to break objects (line, polyline, and arcs) without creating a gap or open space in the object.

- Activate the *Break at a point* command using one of the following procedures.
    1. Panel method: From the *Home* tab expand the *Modify* panel and select the *Break at a point* tool.
    2. Command line method: Type "break", "Break", or "BREAK" in the command line and press the *Enter* key.

- The activation of the command displays the prompt to select the object.
- After the object selection, click at the desired point. The object is broken without creating a gap.
- *The same functionality can be achieved using the Break command. The user must click at the same point for both the first and second break points.*

4.27.   Explode

The *Explode* command is used to break a compound object into its basic component objects. The exploded objects cannot be joined to create the original object. To practice the command, create a rectangle, pentagon, circle, a closed polyline, and a dimension using the *Rectangle*, *Polygon*, *Circle*, *Polyline*, and *Dimension* commands, respectively, as shown in the left column of Table #1. Only one side of the rectangle is dimensioned.

- Activate the *Explode* command using one of the following procedures.
    1. Panel method: From the *Home* tab and *Modify* panel select the *Explode* tool.
    2. Command line method: Type "explode", "Explode", or "EXPLODE" in the command line and press the *Enter* key.

- The activation of the command leads to the object selection prompt. Select the object (bring the cursor on the rectangle) and press the *Enter* key. The object is broken into its basic component.
- The *Explode* command does not change the appearance of the object (left column of the Table #1). However, if the original and the exploded object are selected, then their grip points are different. The middle column of the Table #1 shows the original objects, whereas, the right column of the Table #1 shows the exploded objects.

- A circle cannot be exploded.
- The rectangle, pentagon, and the closed polyline are broken into line segments.
- The dimension is exploded into extension and dimension lines, the text, and the arrows.

Table #1: Explode command demonstration

Object	Original	Exploded
		 Circle cannot be exploded

4.28. Join

The *Join* command is used to connect multiple linear or curved objects to create a single object. The command can be used to connect lines, circular arcs, elliptical arcs, polylines, spline, and their combination. However, the command cannot be used to connect close objects. The order of the object selection effects the resultant object.

- Activate the *Join* command using one of the following procedures.
  1. Panel method: From the *Home* tab expand the *Modify* panel and select the *Join* tool.
  2. Command line method: Type "join", "Join", or "JOIN" in the command line and press the *Enter* key.

- The activation of the command leads to the source object selection prompt.
- *Select source object*, Figure 4-55a: Click the source object with the left button of the mouse. In this example, click on the line labeled as A.

Figure 4-55a

- *Select objects to join*, Figure 4-55b: Left click the object to be connected, Figure 4-55c. In this example, click on the line labeled as B.
- Press the *Enter* key. The joined object is shown in Figure 4-55d.

Figure 4-55b

Figure 4-55c

- In the *Join* command the order of the object selection effects the resultant object. In Figure 4-55d, the line labeled as A is selected as the source object. In Figure 4-55e, the line labeled as B is selected as the source object.

Figure 4-55d   **Figure 4-55e**

4.28.1.1. Lines

The *Join* command can connect non-intersecting collinear and coplanar lines with or without gaps. The collinear lines are in the same direction. The coplanar lines are in the same plane, that is, they have the same elevation. The resultant object is a single line.

Example: Connect A to B, C to D, and E to F.
- **A and B**: Two collinear and coplanar lines with a gap, Figure 4-56a. The lines A and B can be joined using the method discussed in section 4.28.
- **C and D**: Two collinear and coplanar lines without a gap, Figure 4-56b. The lines C and D can be joined using the method discussed in section 4.28.
- **E and F**: Two coplanar lines without a gap, Figure 4-56c. The lines E and F can be joined using the method discussed in section 4.28.

| Figure 4-56a | Figure 4-56b | Figure 4-56c |

4.28.1.2. Circular arc

The *Join* command can connect circular arcs with the same radius and same center point. The resultant object is an arc or a circle. The arcs are connected in counterclockwise direction starting from the source arc.

Example: Connect the arcs A to B and C to D, Figure 4-57a. The figure shows four arcs. Arcs labeled as A, B, and C have the same radius. Although the arc D has the same center its radius is different. Therefore, it cannot be joined to any arc of the figure.

Figure 4-57a

- **A and B**: Figure 4-57a, the arcs A and B can be joined using the method discussed in section 4.28. In this figure, A is the source arc. Arcs are connected in the counterclockwise direction starting from the source arc, Figure 4-57b.
- **B and A**: Figure 4-57a, the arcs B and A can be joined using the method discussed in section 4.28. In this figure, B is the source arc. Arcs are connected in the counterclockwise direction starting from the source arc, Figure 4-57c.

- **Note** the difference in the appearance and size of the resultant arcs of Figure 4-57b and Figure 4-57b.

Figure 4-57b   Figure 4-57c

- In Figure 4-57d, arcs A, B, and C have the same radius and same center. The three arcs can be connected as follows: (i) activate the *Join* command; (ii) click on A (source arc); (iii) click on B; (iv) click on C; and (v) finally, press the *Enter* key.

Figure 4-57d

- However, in Figure 4-57a, if the user desires to connect the arcs by setting C as the source arc, then after selecting C, A, and B and pressing the *Enter* key, the prompt shown in Figure 4-58a appears.
- Since there is no gap between B and C, if the user selects the *Yes* option (Figure 4-58a) then the circle shown in Figure 4-58b is created.
- However, if the user selects the *No* option then the arcs are not connected.

Figure 4-58a

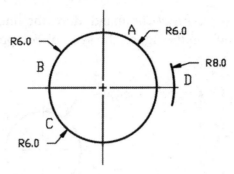

Figure 4-58b

4.28.1.3.   Polyline
The process to connect polylines is the same as for connecting the lines. The resultant object is a polyline.

4.28.1.4.   Spline
The process to connect splines is the same as for connecting the lines. The resultant object is a spline.

4.28.1.5.   Combination of objects
The *Join* command can be used to connect a combination of arcs, lines, polylines, and splines, too. However, the various objects should be contiguous, that is, one object ends at a point where the next object begins. Figure 4-59 shows a drawing composed of a combination of objects.

- Join line and arc: The resultant object is a polyline.
- Join polyline and arc: The resultant object is a polyline.
- Join line, polyline, and arc: Resultant object is a polyline.
- Join spline and arc: The resultant object is a spline.
- Join line, spline, and arc: The resultant object is a spline.
- Join line, polyline, spline, and arc: The resultant object is a spline.

Figure 4-59

4.29.   Fillet

The *Fillet* command is used to connect two objects with an arc of the specified radius such that the arc is tangent to both objects. The connecting objects can be arcs, circles, ellipses, elliptical arcs, lines, polylines, rays, splines, or the combination of any two.

Example: In order to follow the *Fillet* command, draw the lines and circles as shown in Figure 4-60a and Figure 4-60b. In the figure, the symbol ϕ represents the diameter.

Figure 4-60a   Figure 4-60b

- Activate the *Fillet* command using one of the following procedures.
  1. Panel method: From the *Home* tab and *Modify* panel expand the *Fillet* drop down menu and select the *Fillet* tool, Figure 4-61a.
  2. Command line method: Type "fillet", "Fillet", or "FILLET" in the command line and press the *Enter* key.

- The activation of the command leads to the first object selection prompt, Figure 4-61b. (i) Press the down arrow key, (ii) click on the Radius option with the left button of the mouse.
- *Specify fillet radius*: Specify the radius and press the *Enter* key, Figure 4-61c. In the current example, the radius is 2.

Figure 4-61a   Figure 4-61b

Specify fillet radius <25.0000>: 2

Figure 4-61c

- The remainder of this section describes how to fillet lines and circles.
- <u>Fillet lines</u>: The *Fillet* command draws the arc that meets the lines smoothly. If necessary, the command will also trim the corner, (fillet at corner D in Figure 4-62c and Figure 4-62d).
    1. Activate the *Fillet* command, if it is not active.
    2. Specify the radius (in this example, the radius is 2).
    3. For the first object, click in the vicinity of point A on line AD, Figure 4-62a.
    4. For the second object, click in the vicinity of point A on line AB, Figure 4-62b.

Figure 4-62a

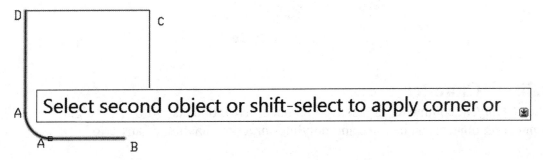

Figure 4-62b

5. An arc (of radius 2) is created from A to A which is tangent to lines AB and AD, Figure 4-62c.
6. Repeat the process from step #1 - #4 in the vicinity of points D. An arc (of radius 2) is created from D to D which is tangent to lines DA and DC. The corners of the lines are also trimmed, Figure 4-62d.

Figure 4-62c

Figure 4-62d

7. Repeat the process from step #1 - #4 in the vicinity of points B. At step #2, specify a radius of 0.0. An arc (of radius 0) is created from B to B tangent to lines BA and BC, Figure 4-62d. Notice the difference of an arc for *radius > 0* and *radius = 0*.

- Fillet Circles: The *Fillet* command does not trim the circles. However, the command draws an arc that meets the circles smoothly.

    1. Activate the *Fillet* command, if it is not active.
    2. Create a fillet with a specific radius (5 in the example) Figure 4-62e, by clicking in the vicinity of points labeled as A on both circles.
    3. Create a fillet with a specific radius (25 in the example) Figure 4-62e, by clicking in the vicinity of points labeled as B on both circles.

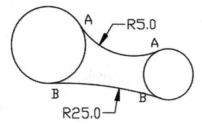

Figure 4-62e

4.30.   Chamfer

The *Chamfer* command is used to connect two objects with a straight line. The connecting objects can be lines and polylines or a combination of any two.

Example: In order to follow the *Chamfer* command, draw the lines and circles as shown in Figure 4-63a; the symbol ϕ represents the diameter. The figure also shows the angle and chamfer length for the corners A and B.

Figure 4-63a

Figure 4-63b

- Activate the *Chamfer* command using one of the following procedures.
  1. Panel method: From the *Home* tab and *Modify* panel expand the *Fillet* drop down menu and select the *Chamfer* tool, Figure 4-63b.
  2. Command line method: Type "chamfer", "Chamfer", or "CHAMFER" in the command line and press the *Enter* key.

- The activation of the command leads to the prompt shown in Figure 4-64a. Press the down arrow key to check the options list.
- *Select first line or*, Figure 4-64a: Select the *Angle* option, and press the *Enter* key.

Figure 4-64a

- *Specify chamfer length on the first line*, Figure 4-64b: Specify the length and press the *Enter* key. In the example, for corner A the length is 45.
- *Specify chamfer angle from the first line*, Figure 4-64c: Specify the angle and press the *Enter* key. In the example, for corner A the angle is 48.

| Specify chamfer length on the first line <23.0000>: | 45 |

Figure 4-64b

| Specify chamfer angle from the first line <57>: | 48 |

Figure 4-64c

- *Select the first line or*, Figure 4-64d: Click on the vertical line at corner A. The line changes its appearance, Figure 4-64e.

Figure 4-64d

Figure 4-64e

- *Select second line or shift-select to apply corner or*, Figure 4-64f: Bring the cursor on the horizontal line at corner A and the chamfer appears.
- *Select second line or shift-select to apply corner or*, Figure 4-64e: Click on the horizontal line at corner A. The chamfer line replaces the corner at A, Figure 4-64f.
- Repeat the chamfer process for corner B, Figure 4-64f.

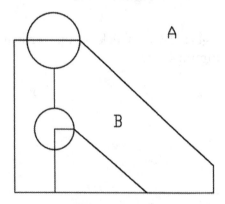

Figure 4-64f

- Repeat the chamfer process for corner A in Figure 4-63a as follows.
- Activate the *Chamfer* command.
- *Select first line or*, Figure 4-64a: Select the *Angle* option, and press the *Enter* key.
- *Specify chamfer length on the first line*, Figure 4-64b: Specify the length and press the *Enter* key. In the example, for corner A the length is 65.
- *Specify chamfer angle from the first line*, Figure 4-64c: Specify the angle and press the *Enter* key. In the example, for corner A the angle is 48.
- *Select the first line or*, Figure 4-64d: Click on the vertical line at corner A. The line changes its appearance, Figure 4-64e.
- *Select second line or shift-select to apply corner or*, Figure 4-64f: Bring the cursor on the vertical line at corner A, and the error message appears, Figure 4-65a.
- Click on the horizontal line at corner A. The error message shown in Figure 4-65b appears.
- Correct the error by specifying the correct length!

Figure 4-65a

Figure 4-65b

4.31. Trim

The *Trim* command is used to trim objects at a cutting edge. The cutting edge is defined by other objects. The concept of trim command can be better understood by comparing it to hair trimming at a barber shop. The barber holds the customer's hairs in their hands and then trims the hairs (above the fingers) with reference to their fingers. In this example, the barber's fingers are the cutting edge, and "above the fingers" is the desired side for trimming. The difference in the trim command and hair trimming is that the barber cuts hairs above their fingers. However, AutoCAD allows trimming on either side of the cutting edge.

__Example:__ Create the top of a patio umbrella (Figure 4-67a) using circle and trim commands.

- Draw the circles as shown in Figure 4-66b.
- Activate the *Trim* command using one of the following procedures.
    1. Panel method: From the *Home* tab and *Modify* panel expand the *Trim* drop down menu and select the *Trim* tool, Figure 4-66a.
    2. Command line method: Type "trim", "Trim", or "TRIM" in the command line and press the *Enter* key.

Figure 4-66a

- The activation of this command leads to the object selection prompt to choose which object serves as the cutting edge.
    1. *Select all the objects*, Figure 4-66b: To select all displayed objects as potential cutting edges, press the *Enter* key without selecting any of the objects.
    2. *Select one object*, Figure 4-66c: In the figure, circle #1 is selected as the cutting edge. (i) Bring the cursor on top of the circle and the circle is highlighted. (ii) Click the circle with the left button of the mouse. (iii) Press the *Enter* key, or the right button, to complete the object selection. The prompt shown in Figure 4-66d appears. If the *Enter* key or right button is pressed without pressing the left button of the mouse, then the selection process is complete but the object does not change its appearance.

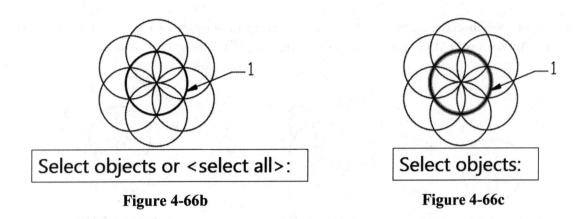

Figure 4-66b   **Figure 4-66c**

Figure 4-66d

- *Select the objects to trim*, Figure 4-66d: Bring the cursor on the top of the object to be trimmed. To create the object shown in Figure 4-67a, the parts of the circles outside circle #1 need to be removed. Therefore, bring the cursor on the outside part of circle #2, Figure 4-66e and Figure 4-66f.

Figure 4-66e

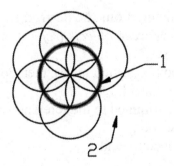

Figure 4-66f

- Repeat the previous step with the other circles to create the patio umbrella as shown in Figure 4-67a.
- Press the *Esc* or the *Enter* key to exit the command.

- Figure 4-67b and Figure 4-67c are created from the circles of Figure 4-66a. In these examples, every circle represents the cutting edge for one or more circles.

Figure 4-67a   **Figure 4-67b**   **Figure 4-67c**

4.31.1. Trim: FAQ

If the *Trim* command is not creating the desired effect, then do one or more of the following procedures.

1. **If the object exists after the *Trim* command is executed once then:**
   a. *Are there multiple objects lying on top of each other?*
   b. If the answer to the above question is **yes**, then delete the underlying objects until only the object to be trimmed is left using *Delete Duplicate Objects* command.

2. **The *Trim* command is executed but the desired result is not created then:**
   a. *Is the reference object and the object to be trimmed clicked in the correct order?*
   b. If the answer to the above question is **no**, then do the following steps:
   c. The object(s) clicked after the activation of the *Trim* command, are reference objects.
   d. Press the *Enter* key.
   e. The objects clicked after step d are the objects to be trimmed.

3. **The *Trim* command is executed but the desired result is not created then:**
   a. *Is there a clear space between objects (reference and to be trimmed) visible or invisible to the human eye?*
   b. If the answer to the above question is **yes**, then do the following steps:
   c. Activate the *Extend* command.
   d. Extend the object to be trimmed to the reference object. The *Extend* command is discussed in the next section.
   e. Now, perform the *Trim* command.

4. **The trim command cannot be continued:**
   a. *Is the layer containing the objects (reference and/or to be trimmed) locked?*
   b. If the answer to the above question is **yes**, then unlock the layers. Layers are discussed in the next chapter.

4.32.   Extend

The *Extend* command is used to extend an object to reach another object. The *Extend* command extends the object on its natural path. For example, a circular arc changes to a circle, an elliptical arc changes to an ellipse, a horizontal line stays horizontal, etc. The extend command is executed in a manner similar to the *Trim* command.

Example: In order to follow the extend capability; draw the lines (L1, l2, and L3), circular arcs (CA1 and CA2), elliptical arc (EA1), and a circle (C1) as shown in Figure 4-68. In the figure, the symbol ϕ represents the diameter.

Figure 4-68

- Activate the *Extend* command using one of the following procedures.
  1. Panel method: From the *Home* tab and *Modify* panel expand the *Trim* drop down menu and select the *Extend* tool, Figure 4-69.
  2. Command line method: Type "extend", "Extend", or "EXTEND" in the command line and press the *Enter* key.

Figure 4-69

- The activation of the command leads to choosing the object that serves as the bounding edge to which the other objects are extended, Figure 4-70a.

Select objects or <select all>:

Figure 4-70a

- *Select objects*, Figure 4-70b: In the figure, the circle C1 is selected as the bounding edge. In this example, every line and arc is extended to the circle. (i) Bring the cursor on top of the reference object (circle in the example) and it is highlighted. (ii) Click the circle with the left button of the mouse, and it changes its appearance (becomes a thick line). (iii) Press the *Enter* key or right button to complete the reference object selection. If the *Enter* key or right button is pressed without pressing the left button of the mouse, the selection process is complete but the object does not change its appearance.

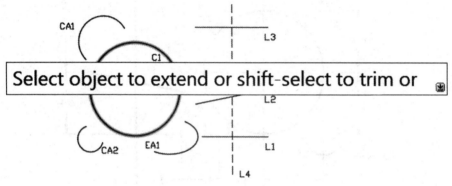

Figure 4-70b

- *Select the objects to extend*, Figure 4-70c: Bring the cursor on top of the object to be extended. For the arcs click near the ends of the arcs. In the example, the circular arc CA1 is selected. Bring the cursor near the end of the arc (Figure 4-70c) and press the left button of the mouse; the arc is extended to the circle, Figure 4-70d.

Figure 4-70c

Figure 4-70d

- *Select the objects to extend*: Repeat the process with the arc CA2, Figure 4-70e.
- *Select the objects to extend*: Now, extend the arc CA2 to the circle C1. Bring the cursor on the end of the arc and an error message (Figure 4-70e) appears; notice the appearance of the cursor. If CA2 is completed to be a circle it does not touch the circle C1. Hence, the *Extend* command does not extend CA2.

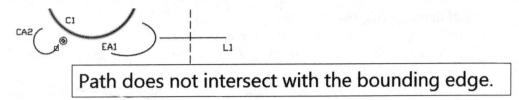

Figure 4-70e

- *Select the objects to extend*: Extend the other edge of CA1, and both edges of EA1, Figure 4-70f. Notice, changes in EA1, an elliptical arc.
- *Select the objects to extend*: Extend line L2. Bring the cursor on top of the *Select the objects to extend*: Now, extend the line L2. Bring the cursor on top of the line to be extended and it is highlighted. In the current example, click on the left of midpoint, (that is, to the left of L4) and L2 is extended to C1, Figure 4-70f. If the selection is made to the right of the midpoint (that is, to the right of L4), then L2 will not be extended.

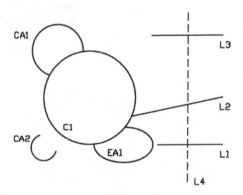

Figure 4-70f

- Repeat the process with the L1, L3.
  - o If L1 and L3 are extended on their natural paths, then these lines do not cross the circle C1. Hence, the *Extend* command does not extend L1 and L3.
- Press the *Esc* or the *Enter* key to exit the command.

4.33.   Polyline Edit

The polyline edit capabilities allow the drafter to modify the existing polylines.

- The *Edit Polyline* command is activated using one of the following procedures.

1. *Panel method:* From the *Home* tab expand the *Modify* panel and select the *Edit Polyline* tool. The activation of the command results in the polyline selection prompt, Figure 4-71a. Click on a polyline and an options list appears, Figure 4-72.
2. Command line method: (i) Type "pedit", "Pedit", or "PEDIT" in the command line and press the *Enter* key. The prompt shown in Figure 4-71b appears; follow one of the following two methods.
   - (i) Type *m* (to modify multiple polylines simultaneously), (ii) press the *Enter* key, (iii) click on multiple polylines, and (iv) press the *Enter* key. This opens the options list shown in the Figure 4-72.
   - (i) Press the *Enter* key, and (ii), select the polyline. This opens the options list shown in the Figure 4-72.

3. Polyline method: (i) Select a polyline, Figure 4-71c. (ii) Press the right button and select the *Polyline* option. (iii) Select the *Edit Polyline* option. (iv) This opens the options list shown in the Figure 4-72.

Figure 4-71a

Figure 4-71b

Figure 4-71c

Figure 4-72

- <u>Close</u>: The *Close* option is used to connect the starting point of a polyline with its ending point by drawing a straight segment between the two points. The selected polyline must contain at least two segments. Assume the drafter wants to close multiple segments polyline. (i) Draw two polylines as shown in Figure 4-73a. (ii) Activate the *PEdit* command. (ii) Choose the *Multiple* option. (iii) Select multiple polylines, Figure 4-73a. (iv) Press the *Enter* key. (v) Click on the *Close* option from the list of options, Figure 4-72. (vi) Press the *Enter* key. The closed polylines are shown in Figure 4-73b. To close a single polyline, activate the *PEdit* command and follow the above steps. Note, the closed polylines maintain their linetypes.

Figure 4-73a   **Figure 4-73b**

- Open: The *Open* option is used to remove the segment connecting the starting point of a polyline with its ending point. The selected polyline must be closed and contain at least three segments. Assume the drafter wants to open multiple polylines. (i) Draw two polylines as shown in Figure 4-74a. (ii) Activate the *PEdit* command. (ii) Choose the *Multiple* option. (iii) Select multiple polylines, Figure 4-74a. (iv) Press the *Enter* key. (v) Click on the *Open* option from the list of options. (vi) Press the *Enter* key, Figure 4-74b. To open a single polyline, activate the *PEdit* command and follow the above steps. Note, the open polylines maintain their linetypes.

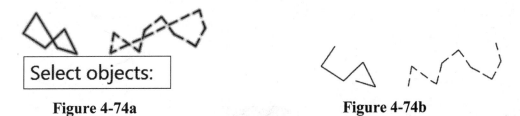

Figure 4-74a   **Figure 4-74b**

- Join: The *Join* option is used to connect multiple polylines, or a polyline with an arc and/or line segments. A drafter wants to join four polylines P1, P2, P3, and P4, Figure 4-75a. (i) Activate the *PEdit* command and select the single polyline option and select the polyline P1. (ii) Choose the *Join* option. (iii) Click on P2, P3, and P4. (iv) Press the *Enter* key twice.

Figure 4-75a   **Figure 4-75b**

- o *Important point to notice*: (i) Since the command was activated from P1, the new polyline follows the style of P1, Figure 4-57b. (ii) P4 is not joined to the other polylines because it did not share a vertex with the other polylines, Figure 4-75b.
- o *Join P4 with the other polylines*: (i) Activate the *PEdit* command. (ii) Choose the *Multiple* option. (iii) Click on both polylines. (iv) Press the *Enter* key. (v) Choose the *Join* option. (vi) The prompt shown in Figure 4-75c appears, press the down arrow to display the other options. (vii) Click on *Jointype*. (viii) Choose *Both* option from Figure 4-75d. (ix) The fuzz distance prompt appears, Figure 4-75e. (x) Specify a number (in the example 10 is used). (xi) Finally, press the *Enter* key, TWICE.

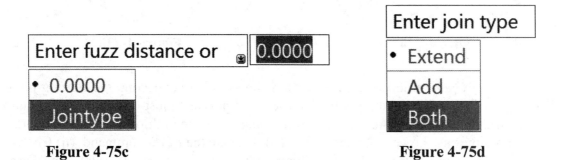

Figure 4-75c   Figure 4-75d

- o The new polyline is shown in Figure 4-75f. Since the polyline P1-P2-P3 was selected first in step (ii) above, the new polyline follows its style.

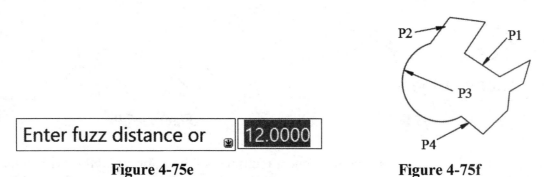

Figure 4-75e   Figure 4-75f

- • <u>Width</u>: The *Width* option is used to change the width of a polyline: (i) Activate the *PEdit* command. (ii) Click on a polyline. (iii) Choose the *Width* option. (iv) Specify the new width, Figure 4-76a. (iv) Press the *Enter* key, twice. The width of the polyline is changed. The width of the polyline shown in Figure 4-76a is increased to 2.2 and is shown in Figure 4-76b.

Figure 4-76a

Figure 4-76b

- Fit: The *Fit* option is used to replace a selected polyline with a smooth curve. The fitted curve passes through each vertex of the polyline. (i) Activate the *PEdit* command. (ii) Click on a polyline. (iii) Choose the *Fit* option. (iv) Press the *Enter* key. Figure 4-77a displays an original polyline and Figure 4-77b displays the polyline transformed into a fitted curve.

Figure 4-77a   **Figure 4-77b**

- Spline: The *Spline* option is used to replace the selected polyline with a quadratic spline curve. The curve passes through the starting and ending points of the polyline, other vertices may or may not be on the spline. (i) Activate the *PEdit* command. (ii) Click on a polyline. (iii) Choose the *Spline* option. (iv) Press the *Enter* key. Figure 4-78a and Figure 4-78b display a polyline and the corresponding splined curve, respectively.

Figure 4-78a   **Figure 4-78b**

- Decurve: The *Decurve* option is used to replace a curve fitted or splined polyline with a polyline of straight segments. (i) Activate the *PEdit* command. (ii) Click on a polyline. (iii) Choose the *Decurve* option. (iv) Press the *Enter* key. Figure 4-79a and Figure 4-79b display a curved and straight polyline, respectively.

Figure 4-79a   **Figure 4-79b**

- Edit vertex: The *Edit vertex* option is available only if the *Edit polyline* command is activated using a single polyline. This option is used to edit a selected vertex. (i) Select a polyline, Figure 4-80a. (ii) Press the right button and select the *Polyline* option. (iii) Select the *Edit Polyline* option. (iv) Select the *Edit vertex* command, Figure 4-80b. (v) The vertex editing option list appears and the first vertex is selected, Figure 4-80c. (iv) Choose the desired option and follow the prompt.

• <u>Undo</u>: As the name suggests, the *Undo* option cancels out the previous step.

Figure 4-80a   **Figure 4-80b**

Figure 4-80c

4.34.   Grips and Object Editing

The selection of an object results in the display of its grip points. These grip points can be used to edit the object using the pointing device instead of entering the respective commands. Some of the editing capabilities activated when grips are displayed on an object are: stretch, move, rotate, copy, erase, and scale.

4.34.1. Select a point

(i) Select an object. (ii) Place the cursor on any of the grip points and its color changes to RED, Figure 4-81a. (iii) Click with the right button of the mouse and a list of commands appears. The commands are object and grip point dependent. (iii) Click with the left button of the mouse on the desired command and follow the prompts.

Figure 4-81a

4.34.2. Stretch/shrink

Although, the *Stretch/shrink* command does not appear in the list of commands in Figure 4-81a, it is used to resize the object. (i) For a circle, select one of the quadrant points (for a line, select one of the endpoints). (ii) Move the cursor to the desired location, outward to stretch and inward to shrink, Figure 4-81b. (iii) Either click at the new location in the drawing area, or specify its coordinates (or distance) and press the *Enter* key.

Figure 4-81b

4.34.3. Erase

The *Erase* command is used to delete an object from the drawing. (i) Select a grip point. (ii) Click with the right button of the mouse and the option panel appears. (iii) Select the *Erase* option, Figure 4-81c. The object is deleted.

Figure 4-81c

4.34.4. Move

The *Move* command is used to relocate the object. (i) For a circle, select the center point (for a line, select the midpoint). (ii) Move the cursor to the desired location, Figure 4-81d. (iii) Either click at the new location in the drawing area; or specify its coordinates (or distance) and press the *Enter* key.

Figure 4-81d

4.34.5. Scale

The *Scale* command is used to resize an object. (i) Select a grip point. (ii) Click with the right button of the mouse and the option list appears. (iii) Select the *Scale* option, Figure 4-81e. (iv) The prompt to select the base point (the point that does not change its location) appears. (v) Click at the desired location. The command scales the selected object relative to the base point. (vi) The prompt to specify the scale factor appears. (vii) Increase the size of an object by dragging the cursor outward or decrease the size by dragging inward. Alternatively, specify the scale factor for the relative scaling (Figure 4-81f) and press the *Enter* key.

Figure 4-81e

Figure 4-81f

4.34.6. Rotate

As the name suggests, the *Rotate* command is used to rotate the object about a point. (i) Select a grip point. (ii) Click with the right button of the mouse and the options panel appears, Figure 4-81g. (iii) Select the *Rotate* option. (iv) The prompt to select the base point (point of rotation) appears. (v) Click at the desired location. (vi) The prompt to specify the angle of rotation appears, Figure 4-81h. (vii) Rotate the selected object around the base point by moving the cursor. Alternatively, specify the angle value (Figure 4-81h) and press the *Enter* key. This is an excellent method for rotating block references.

Figure 4-81g

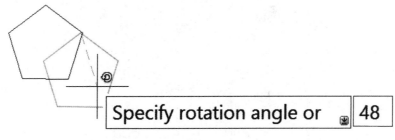

Figure 4-81h

4.35.   The Properties Palette and Object Editing

The *Properties* palette displays the properties of the selected object(s). The contents of the palette are object dependent. Figure 4-82a shows the properties for a table created in the previous chapter and Figure 4-82b shows the properties of a circle. The type of the object is displayed in the upper left corner of the property palette. The *Properties* palette not only displays the selected properties of the selected object, it allows the user to modify some of the properties of the selected object.

The prerequisite to open the properties palette is to first select the object (whose properties need to be checked or changed) and then use one of the following procedures to activate the *Properties* command.

1. *Panel method:* From the *View* tab and the *Palette* panel select the *Properties* tool.
2. Command line method: Type "properties", "Properties", or "PROPERTIES" in the command line and press the *Enter* key.
3. Hold the *Ctrl* key and press 1.
4. Press the right button of the mouse and choose the *Properties* option from the option panel.

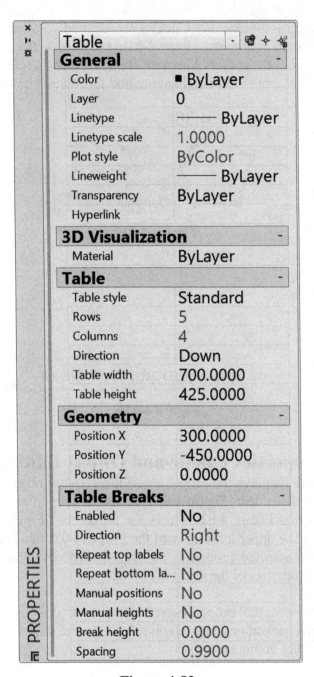

Figure 4-82a

Some of the characteristics of the *Properties* are listed here.

- The plus and minus buttons ([+] , [−]) are used to hide or display the option under a particular heading, Figure 4-82a.
- The content of the greyed fields cannot be altered. For example, in Figure 4-82a, under the *Table* heading, the number of rows and columns cannot be changed.

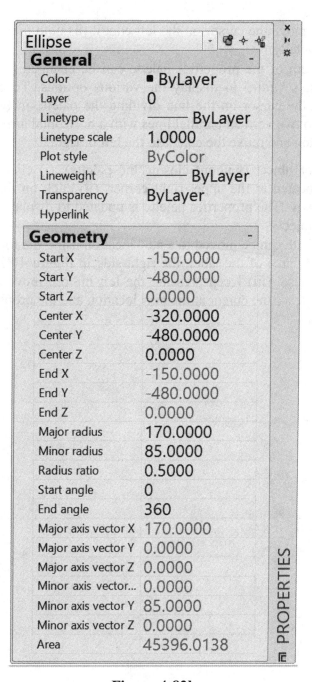

Figure 4-82b

- If desired, the content of the other fields can be altered. Type or choose the new value and press the *Enter* key. For example, in Figure 4-82b, under the *Geometry* heading, *Center X, Center Y*, etc. can be changed.
- The properties palette can be elongated or widened to see the various options. To elongate the palette, (i) move the cursor on the top or bottom edge (the cursor changes to a double headed arrow); (ii) hold the left button and move the cursor up or down. To widen the palette (i) move the cursor to the edge opposite to the palette heading

(in Figure 4-82a move the cursor on the left edge); (ii) hold the left button and move the cursor horizontally.

- The columns width of the properties palette can be changed (without changing the properties palette's width) to display the various options. To change the columns width, (i) move the cursor on the line dividing the palette in two columns and the cursor changes to two vertical parallel lines with a horizontal arrow on either side; (ii) hold the left button and move the cursor to the left or right.

- To select another object (without closing the palette), (i) click on the (*Select object*) button located in the upper right corner, (ii) click on the object(s), and (iii) press the *Enter* key. The properties palette is updated to display the properties of the newly selected object.

- The property palette can be moved to a new location using the following. (i) Place the cursor in the grey area of the label, the right side in Figure 4-82b. (ii) Press the left button of the mouse. (iii) Keep pressing the left button; move the cursor to a new location. (iv) Release the cursor at the new location and the property palette moves to the new location.

Notes:

5. Layers

5.1. Learning Objectives

After completing this chapter, you will demonstrate competency in the following areas:

- Drawings with multiple layers
- Objects' appearance and layers
- Objects' movement from one layer to the other
- Objects' visibility and layers

5.2.   Introduction

Prior to the computer use in drafting, architects drew different parts of the drawing on transparent overlays. The base drawing and the overlays maintained matching points for the alignment. Figure 5-1a demonstrates the base drawing (floor plan) and the roof overlay, and both the base drawing and the roof overlay have four matching points (A, B, C, and D). Figure 5-1b shows the roof overlay placed on the base drawing by aligning the matching points.

Figure 5-1a

Figure 5-1b

The use of overlays provided a technique of managing, organizing, and controlling the visual layout of a drawing. In order to see the drawing more clearly, the drafter may want to remove all the text and dimensions from the drawing. **The drafter wants to keep the information, but just wants to hide it from the view**. Deleting the information would not be appropriate as the drafter would lose all the work. Hence, just hiding the selected overlays would solve the problem.

In AutoCAD, an overlay is replaced by a layer. A layer can be thought of as a large piece of clear plastic of the size of the drawing area. In other words, the layer is invisible and the objects drawn on the layer are visible. An entire drawing (or part of a drawing) can be made visible or hidden. Figure 5-1c shows a drawing with three layers, the floor plan, roof plan (shown as dashed lines), and the dimensions.

Figure 5-1c

5.3.   Layers in AutoCAD

Layers are controlled by the *Home* tab and the *Layers* panel, Figure 5-2a and the layer properties manager button (labeled as *Layer Properties*) which is located on the *Layers* panel, Figure 5-2a. The tools on the toolbar are not the command tool, but the indicator of the status. For example, the light bulb shows that the selected layer is *On* (visible) or *Off* (hidden). The yellow and grey colors of the bulb represent that the layer is *On* or *Off*, respectively.

In AutoCAD, by default, everything is drawn on the default layer which is set as the current layer. When a new file is created, *Layer 0* is the current layer; the user can create a new layer. Normally, it is recommended to create a different layer for different parts of a drawing. Each layer should be assigned its own color, linetype, and line thickness so that every object drawn on that layer appears in the same color, linetype, and line thickness. Figure 5-2b shows the layers created for the drawing shown in Figure 5-1a. Figure 5-2c shows the basic characteristic of a layer.

Figure 5-2a

Figure 5-2b

Figure 5-2c

5.4.   Layer Command

The *Layer* command is used to create new layers and modify the existing layers.

- The *Layer* command is activated using one of the following procedures.
    1. Panel method: From the *Home* tab and the *Layers* panel click on the *Layer Properties* tool (⬛).
    2. Command line method: Type "layer," "Layer," or "LAYER" on the command line and press the *Enter* key.

- The activation of the command opens the *Layer Properties Manager* palette as shown in Figure 5-3.

5.5.   Layer Properties Manager

The *Layer Properties Manager* palette, for the drawing shown in Figure 5-1c, is shown in Figure 5-3. This palette is used to create a new layer, delete an empty layer, and change the characteristics of new and existing layers.

Figure 5-3

5.5.1.   Characteristics of a layer

The *Layer Properties Manager* palette, shown in Figure 5-3, is used to change the characteristics of the layers. Each layer has the following characteristics.

1. *Status*: The *Status* field shows if a layer is the current layer. In Figure 5-3, the current layer has a green check mark (✔), and the other layers have small parallelograms (▱) in this field. In Figures 5-2a, 5-2b, and 5-2c, the current layer's name is displayed on the top.

2. *Name*: The *Name* field displays the layer's name. The Layer *0* cannot be renamed; however, the user created layers can be renamed. The layers' names should be based on their functionality (this helps if there are several layers), Figure 5-2b and Figure 5-3. For example, a layer for the doors is named *Door*. To rename a layer, (i) press the *F2* key or click inside the name field, (ii) type the new name, and (iii) press the *Enter* key.

3. *On*: The *On* option controls the visibility of a layer. Select the light bulb (💡) to turn the layer *Off* on the drawing. The drawing of an *On* layer is visible and available for plotting. The drawing of an *Off* layer is invisible and is unavailable for drawing and plotting. The visibility can be switched by using one of the following two methods.
   a. Click the bulb button in the *Layer Properties Manager* palette, Figure 5-3.
   b. Press the down arrow of the *Layer* toolbar and click the bulb icon of the desired layer, Figure 5-2b and Figure 5-2c.

4. *Freeze*: This option is available for layouts. The layouts are discussed in Chapter 7. The *Freeze or thaw in current view port* option (⧉) is used to hide a layer for a longer period of time. If a layer is turned *Off* in the *Model* space then it disappears from the *Model* space and from all the viewports, too. However, freezing a layer in a particular viewport will only hide the contents of the layer in question in

the selected viewport. Freezing of layers improves the performance and reduces the object regeneration time. The freeze option should be used only for those layers that need to be invisible for long periods. Otherwise, the *On/Off* option should be used. **Before freezing the layer, the viewport must be selected. The viewport is selected by double clicking inside the viewport. For the selected viewport, its boundary's line thickens and the coordinate system appears in the viewport.** The freeze option can be set by using one of the following two methods.

   a.   Click the *Freeze* button in *Layer Properties Manager* palette.
   b.   Press the down arrow of the *Layer* toolbar and click the *Freeze* icon of the desired layer.

5. *Lock*: The *Lock* option (🔓) is used to lock a layer. The contents of a lock layer cannot be modified. The lock option can be set by using one of the following two methods.

   a.   Clicking the lock button in *Layer Properties Manager* palette.
   b.   Press the down arrow of the *Layer* toolbar and click the lock icon of the desired layer.

6. *Color*: The *Color* option is used to set the color of the objects drawn on the layer. To change the color (i) open the *Layer Properties Manager* palette, Figure 5-3, (ii) click on the small colored box (■) under the *Color* column to open the *Select Color* dialog box, Figure 5-4a, (iii) select the desired color from the *Select Color* dialog box, and (iv) press the *OK* button of the *Select Color* dialog box. This closes the *Select Color* dialog box and change the color of the small box to the selected color. All the objects drawn on the layer are displayed in the chosen color, provided that the *Color Control*'s setting in the *Properties* panel of *Home* tab is set to *By Layer*, Figure 5-4b.

Figure 5-4a

Figure 5-4b

7. <u>Linetype</u>: The *Linetype* option sets the default linetype for all the objects drawn on the layer. All objects drawn on the layer are displayed in the chosen linetype style, provided that the *Line Type Control*'s setting in the *Properties* panel of *Home* tab is set to *By Layer*, Figure 5-5a. Linetype is discussed in detail in Chapter 3. The linetype of a layer can be changed as follows. (i) Open the *Layer Properties Manager* palette, Figure 5-3, and (ii) Click on *Continuous* under the *Linetype* column to open the *Select Linetype* dialog box, Figure 5-5b. (iii) Click on the *Load* button to open the *Load or Reload Linetype* dialog box, Figure 5-5c. (iv) Select the desired linetype (Figure 5-5b shows the selection of *Phantom*) and press the *OK* button. The *Phantom* linetype appears in the *Select Linetype* dialog box, Figure 5-5d. (v) Select the *Phantom* linetype and press the *OK* button. This closes the *Load or Reload Linetype* dialog box and changes the linetype to the selected style.

Figure 5-5a

Figure 5-5b

Figure 5-5c

Figure 5-5d

8. <u>Lineweight</u>: The *Lineweight* option sets the thickness of the lines drawn on the layer. All objects drawn on the layer are displayed in the chosen lineweight, provided that the *Line Weight Control*'s setting in the *Properties* panel of the *Home* tab is set to *By Layer*, Figure 5-6a. Lineweight is discussed in detail in Chapter 3. The lineweight of a layer can be changed as follows. (i) Open the *Layer Properties Manager* palette, Figure 5-3. (ii) Click on the *Default* under the *Lineweight* column to open the *Lineweight* dialog box, Figure 5-6b, (iii) select the desired lineweight (Figure 5-6 shows the selection of *0.60mm*) and press the *OK* button. This closes the *Lineweight* dialog box and change the lineweight to the selected lineweight.

To display the lineweight of the drawing, toggle (*On /Off*) the LWT option by pressing the ▤ button in the status bar.

Figure 5-6a

Figure 5-6b

9. <u>Plot</u>: The *Plot* option (🖨) is used to allow the objects on the layer to be printed if the drawing is plotted (printed). If the content of a particular layer need not to be printed, then turn *Off* the plot option by clicking on the printer icon (a no entry sign appears on the printer, and its appearance changes to 🖨).

5.5.2. Create a new layer 🎨

To create a new layer, click on the *New Layer* button (🎨) in the *Layer Properties Manager* palette shown in Figure 5-3. The new layer inherits the properties of the current layer, Figure 5-7. If necessary, change the properties of the new layer. By default, the new layers are named as *Layer1*, *Layer2*, etc. To rename a layer, (i) press the *F2* key or click inside the name field, (ii) type the new name, and (iii) press the *Enter* key,

Figure 5-7. To make the change permanent, close the *Layer Properties Manager* palette by clicking the cross on the upper left corner of the toolbar.

Figure 5-7

5.5.3. Delete an existing layer

To delete a layer, in the *Layer Properties Manager* palette shown in Figure 5-3, (i) select the layer by clicking on it; (ii) click on the *Delete Layer* button ( ) in the *Layer Properties Manager* palette, Figure 5-8a. The selected layer is deleted only if it is not one of the layers shown in Figure 5-8b. Close the *Layer Properties Manager* palette to make the change permanent.

Figure 5-8a

Figure 5-8b

5.5.4. Make a layer a current layer

AutoCAD provides three ways to make a layer the current layer.

1. Use the down arrow in *Layer* toolbar (*Home* tab and *Layer* panel) to display the layers in the drawing, and choose the desired layer, Figure 5-9a.

2. Click on the *Make Current* tool () in the *Layer* panel from *Home* tab, Figure 5-9b, and follow the prompts.

3. In the *Layer Properties Manager* palette, click on a layer, and click on the *Set Current* (⬚) button, Figure 5-9c; a check mark (✓) appears under the *Status* column. Close the *Layer Properties Manager* palette to make the change permanent.

Figure 5-9a

Figure 5-9b

Figure 5-9c

5.6. Drawing and Layers

In order to draw on a specific layer, the drafter must make the desired layer a current layer and then draw on it. Also, **remember** to turn *On* and *thaw* (not freeze) the current layer before drawing any object.

5.7. The *Defpoints* Layer

Both the Figure 5-10a and Figure 5-10e shows a layer named as "*Defpoint.*" The *Defpoint* layer is created by the system during the dimensioning process. The user has no control over this layer. That is, the layer cannot be renamed or deleted and its contents cannot be printed. Therefore, the user should turn *Off* this layer.

5.8. Move Objects Between Layers

The drafter desired to place the dimensions on the dimension layer. The *DIM* layer was created and its properties are shown in Figure 5-10a.

After drawing the objects and adding the dimension, Figure 5-10b, the drafter realized that the dimensions are not on the DIM layer. The drafter can correct the mistake by moving the dimensions to the DIM layer, Figure 5-10c.

Status	Name	⌃ On	Freeze	Lock	Color	Linetype	Lineweight
✔	0	♀	☼	🔓	■ white	Continuous	—— Default
▱	Defpoints	♀	☼	🔓	■ white	Continuous	—— Default
▱	Dim	♀	☀	🔓	▢ magenta	Continuous	—— Default
▱	Door	♀	☼	🔓	■ white	Continuous	▬▬ 0.70...

Figure 5-10a

If objects are created on one layer, and later it is necessary to move them to another layer, then use the following steps to move the objects.

1. Select the objects to be moved, Figure 5-10d, dimensions in the example.
2. Select the layer as shown in Figure 5-10e, that is, press the down arrow in the *Layers* toolbar and click on the desired layer.
3. The selected objects (dimensions in the example) move to the selected layer (DIM layer in the example). The dimensions were created on *Layer 0* but are now moved to the *DIM* layer.
4. The objects (dimensions) are moved to the desired layer (DIM), Figure 5-10e; however, the current layer is still the *Layer 0*.
5. **_Check_**: To make sure that the objects have moved to the selected layer, turn *Off* the selected layer and if the objects disappear then it means that the objects have moved. If the objects do no disappear then repeat steps #1 - #3.

Figure 5-10b   **Figure 5-10c**

Figure 5-10d   **Figure 5-10e**

5.9.   Update Layer Properties

In order to draw on specific layers with the layer properties, it is important that on the *Properties* panel, the color, linetype, and lineweight are set to *By Layer*, Figure 5-11 (shown below). Any update for these properties using *Layer Properties Manager* palette is reflected in the drawing.

1. <u>Color</u>: All objects drawn on the layer are displayed in the chosen color provided that the objects' color setting in the *Properties* toolbar is set to *By Layer*, Figure 5-11. The color is discussed in detail in Chapter 3.

2. <u>Lineweight</u>: All objects drawn on the layer are displayed in the chosen lineweight, provided that the objects' lineweight setting in the *Properties* toolbar is set to *By Layer*, Figure 5-11. The lineweight is discussed in detail in Chapter 3.

3. <u>Linetype</u>: All objects drawn on the layer are displayed in the chosen linetype, provided that the objects' linetype setting in the *Properties* toolbar is set to *By Layer*, Figure 5-11. The linetype is discussed in detail in Chapter 3.

If the properties of the object drawn are not set *By Layer*, then any change in the layer properties will **NOT** reflect on the drawing.

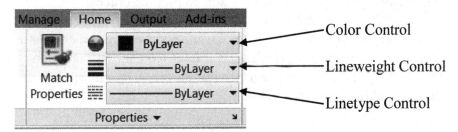

Figure 5-11

5.10.   Layers: FAQ

The user may come across one or more problems during a drawing creation, modification, and plotting using layers. This section describes some of the problems and their solution. **Remember** that the drafter can DRAW ONLY on the CURRENT layer and objects appear based on the options selected in the controls of the *Properties* toolbar.

1. **Problem:** *The drafter is creating an object but it is not appearing on the screen in the drawing area.*
   Reason: This problem occurs if the current layer is either *Off* or frozen.
   Solution: This problem can be solved by turning *On* the current layer (if it is *Off*) or thawing the current layer (if it is frozen).

2. **Problem:** *The drafter has created an object but its color/lineweight/linetype is different for the object's layer color/lineweight/linetype.*
   Reason: This problem occurs if the current layer is not the object's layer or the layer toolbar is not set correctly.
   Solution: This problem can be solved as follows.
   1. If the object is not drawn on the correct layer then move the object to its layer.
   2. If the properties toolbar is not set correctly then select the object and set the *color/lineweight/linetype* controls to *By Layer*. Also, make sure that the three controls are set to *By Layer* before drawing the objects.

3. **Problem:** *The drafter is changing the layers color/lineweight/linetype in the Layer Properties Manager* palette *but the objects are not changing their color/lineweight/linetype in the drawing area.*
   Reason: This problem occurs if the *color/lineweight/linetype* of the *Properties* toolbar is not set to the *By Layer* option.

Solution: This problem can be solved as follows: (i) Select the objects; (ii) press the down arrow of the *color/lineweight/linetype Control* in the *Properties* toolbar; and (iii) select the *By Layer* option.

4. **Problem:** *The drafter can see the objects but cannot plot them.*
   Reason: This problem occurs if the objects in question are drawn in the *defpoints* layer or the layer's plot option is *off* ([icon]).
   Solution: This problem can be solved as follows.
   1. If the objects are drawn on the *defpoints* layer, then move them to their respective layers and the drafter is able to plot the objects.
   2. If the objects are drawn on their respective layer then open the *Layer Properties Manager* palette. If the layer's (containing the objects in question) plot option is *off*, that is, the layer's printer icon shows the no entry sign ([icon]) then just click on the printer icon. The no entry sign disappears ([icon]) and the drafter is able to plot the drawing.

5.11.   Illustrative Example

Example: Draw the objects shown in Figure 5-12a using layers. The drafter can use the following commands to create the drawing.

- Open a new acad template file.
- Create three layers and name them as *Circle*, *Rectangle*, and DIM. Set the properties (color, linetype, and lineweight) of the layers as shown in Figure 5-12b.
- In order to draw on different layers with the layer properties, it is important that on the *Properties* toolbar, the *Color*, *Linetype*, and *Lineweight* controls must be set to *By Layer*, Figure 5-11.

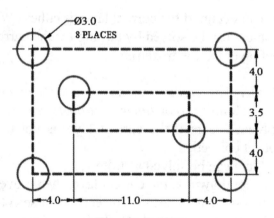

Figure 5-12a

Status	Name	▲	On	Freeze	Lock	Color	Linetype	Lineweight
✔	0		♀	☼	🔓	■ white	Continuous	—— Default
▱	Circle		♀	☼	🔓	■ red	Continuous	▬▬ 0.70 mm
▱	Defpoints		♀	☼	🔓	■ white	Continuous	—— Default
▱	Dim		♀	☼	🔓	■ white	Continuous	—— Default
▱	Rectangle		♀	☼	🔓	■ blue	HIDDEN	▬▬ 0.70 mm
▱	Triangle		♀	☼	🔓	■ magenta	ZIGZAG	▬▬ 0.70 mm

Figure 5-12b

- Make the *Rectangle* layer the current layer and draw the rectangles.
- Make the *Circle* layer the current layer and draw the circles.
- The resulting drawing is shown in Figure 5-13a.

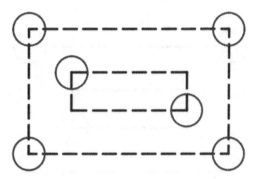

Figure 5-13a

- Make the *Dim* layer the current layer and add the dimensions. If the user has not learnt the dimensioning techniques, then skip this step.
- Although the linetype of the rectangles shown in Figure 5-13a and Figure 5-13d is the same, the line appearance is different because the linetype scale is different.
- To change the linetype scale, select the rectangles, Figure 5-13b.

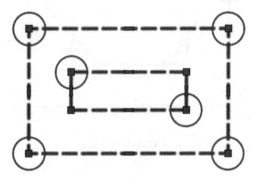

Figure 5-13b

- Press the right button of the mouse and choose the *Properties* option.
- This opens the *Properties* palette, Figure 5-13c.
- Select the *Linetype scale* and type 0.5 in the corresponding right column.

- Press the *Enter* key on the keyboard.
- The resulting drawing is shown in Figure 5-13d.

Figure 5-13c

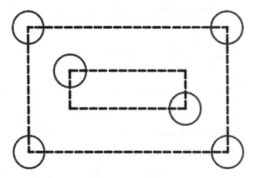

Figure 5-13d

Now, make the *Triangle* layer to be the current layer and draw the triangles as shown in Figure 5-14. If necessary, set the linetype scale.

Figure 5-14

Notes:

6.   Blocks

6.1.   Learning Objectives

After completing this chapter, you will demonstrate competency in the following areas:

- Different types of blocks
- Create and insert blocks
- Combine blocks
- The *Design Center*

6.2.   Introduction

In AutoCAD, block is a general term for one or more objects that are combined to create a single entity. That is, a block is a group of entities saved as a single unit. If an object (or group of objects) is used frequently, then time can be saved if the object is created once and used as many times as needed in the same or a different drawing.

A Block can be classified, Figure 6-1, based on its availability or its contents.

- **Availability:** A basic block is available for insertion only in the native file (that is, in the file in which it is created), the Wblocks (also known as write blocks) can be inserted in any AutoCAD's ".dwg" file, and the dynamic blocks can be updated in real time.

- **Contents:** A drawing block contains only the drawing objects (circle, line, polyline, etc.). A text block is composed of text objects. An attributes block is created using attributes, (attributes are the sections of text added to a block that prompts the user to add information to the drawing). A miscellaneous block can contain any combination of drawing objects, texts, and attributes.

A drawing, text, attributes, or combination block can be saved as a basic or Wblocks. This chapter discusses in detail the creation of basic and Wblock using drawing, text, and attributes and their insertion in native or other files.

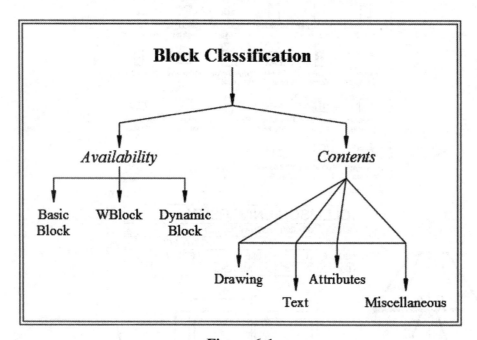

Figure 6-1

6.3.   Basic Block

A basic block is a block that can be inserted only in the native drawing file. That is, it can be inserted only in the drawing file in which it was created. In order to follow a block creation process, draw the lamp stand shown in Figure 6-2a (the drawing units are in inches). The dimensions, point, and label *A* are added for illustration and are not necessary for the block creation process.

Figure 6-2a

6.3.1.   Create a basic block

- The *Make Block* command is activated using one of the following procedures.
  1. Panel method: Either from the *Home* tab and *Block* panel select the *Create Block* ( ) tool, or from the *Insert* tab and *Block Definition* panel select the *Create Block* tool.
  2. Command line method: Type "block," "Block," or "BLOCK" on the command line and press the *Enter* key.

- The activation of the command opens the *Block Definition* dialog box as shown in Figure 6-2b.

6.3.2.   Block definition dialog box
The main features of the *Block Definition* dialog box (Figure 6-2b) are briefly discussed here.

- *Name*: The *Name* field is used to name the block. The name can be 255 characters long and can include letters, numbers, and blank spaces. However, blocks should be given meaningful names. In the current example, the block is named *Stand*.
- *Base point*: The *Base point* information group is used to choose an insertion base point (or a reference point) for the block. The selection of a proper base point is an important factor in the block creation process because it will help during the insertion process. Its default value is (0,0,0). However, to make the insertion process efficient, select the base point on the object itself. In the current example, point 'A' is selected to be the base point. The base point is selected using one of the following techniques.
  - ***Specify On-screen***: The selection of this box makes the other two options inactive. The prompts to specify the base point appear when the *Block Definition* dialog box is closed. In the current example, check this box.

- o **Pick point**: In order to choose the base point using the pointing device: (i) click on the pointing device button (⧉), this temporarily closes the dialog box and allows the user to select a point; (ii) turn on the *object snap* option and click on the desired point. This reopens the dialog box. In the current example, point '*A*' is selected as the base point using the pointing device.
- o **X, Y, Z**: Specify the coordinates of the base point.

Figure 6-2b

- • *Object*: The *Object* panel is used to select the objects to be included in the block.
  - o **Specify On-screen**: The selection of this box makes the other two options inactive. The prompts to select the object appears when the *Block Definition* dialog box is closed.
  - o **Select objects**: In the current example, this option is used. (i) Click on the object selection pointing device button (⊕). This temporarily closes the dialog box and allows the user to select the objects. (ii) Select the objects using one of the object selection methods; this reopens the dialog box. In this example, the dimensions are excluded from the block.
  - o **Retain**: This option retains the selected objects as distinct objects in the drawing after the block is created.
  - o **Convert to block**: This option converts the selected objects to a block in the drawing after the block is created. In the current example, this option is used.
  - o **Delete**: This option deletes the selected objects from the drawing after the block is created.

- *Behavior*: The behavior panel is used to specify the behavior for a block.
  - o **Scale uniformly**: During the insertion process the user may want to (i) scale the object uniformly (same scale factors in *X*, *Y*, and *Z* direction) or (ii) use different scale factors in *X*, *Y*, and *Z* direction. Since a block can only be scaled uniformly from the second option, do not check this box. In the current example, this box is not checked.
  - o **Allow exploding**: This box specifies whether or not a block can be decomposed to the basic object (exploded). Checking of this box allows the user to modify the block. In the current example, check this box.
- *Setting*: The setting panel is used to specify the settings for a block.
  - o **Block units**: This option specifies the insertion units for the block reference.
- *Open in block editor*: This option inserts the block in the block editing mode. In the current example, this box is not checked.
- *Description*: In this box, the user can add a description of the block.
- *OK*: Click the *OK* button to save the changes and to close the dialog box.

- When the user clicks the *OK* button, the prompt shown in Figure 6-2c appears.

Specify insertion base point: 36.1519 3.7041

Figure 6-2c

- Turn on the object snap and click at point *A*.
- The object selection prompt appears, Figure 6-2d.
- In this example, the dimensions and the label *A* are excluded from the block. Therefore, the dimension layer is turned off. Select the objects as shown in Figure 6-2d.
- Either press the right button of the mouse or press the *Enter* key.
- This completes the basic block creation process.
- Click on the block; the block only has one grip point. The base point is the only grip point, Figure 6-2e.

Figure 6-2d

Figure 6-2e

6.4.   Wblock

Wblocks (write blocks) are the blocks that can be inserted into any drawing. These blocks are saved as independent drawing files.

6.4.1.   Create a Wblock

Create a basic block. This example uses the *Stand* block created in the basic block section.

- The *Wblock* command is activated using one of the following procedures.
  1. Panel method: From the *Insert* tab and *Block Definition* panel select the *Write Block* ( ), Figure 6-3a.
  2. Command line method: Type "wblock," "WBlock," or "WBLOCK" on the command line and press the *Enter* key.

- The activation of the command opens the *Write Block* dialog box as shown in Figure 6-3b.

Figure 6-3a

6.4.2.   Write block dialog box

In the *Write Block* dialog box, perform the following actions.

- *Source*: Select the *Block* option. The list of blocks (basic or Wblock) in the current file is available. Press the down arrow to choose the block. Select the *Stand* block created in the basic block section.
- *Base point*: This option is deactivated if the *Block* option is selected in the *Source* panel.
- *Object*: This option is deactivated if the *Block* option is selected in the *Source* panel.
- *Destination*: Select the location to store the Wblock file by clicking the ( ) destination button. This opens the *Browse for Drawing File* dialog box, Figure 6-3c. Specify the location and click the *Save* button.
- *OK*: Now, click the *OK* button in the *Write Block* dialog box to save the changes.

- This will close the *Write Block* dialog box, and the *Wblock Preview* window shown in Figure 6-3d pops up for a very short time. This is the indication that the *Wblock* is created properly.

Figure 6-3b

Figure 6-3c

Figure 6-3d

6.5.   Block With Attributes

Attributes are the sections of text added to a block that prompt the user to add information to the drawing. This section will create a title block with attributes shown in Figure 6-4. The title block includes the information to uniquely identify the drawing. The title block is generally located on the lower right corner of a drawing. A title block's entries depend on a company. The block created in this section is typically used in academic institutions.

CLEMSON UNIVERSITY		
ENGR 2100 - 000	NIGHAT YASMIN	
EX A5-1	A5	SHT 1 OF 2
SCALE: 1:1	TABLE 0	LETTER
05/05/2017	MILLIMETERS	

Figure 6-4

6.5.1.   The initial setup

Before creating the attributes, create the initial setup for the title block.

- Open a new acadiso file.
- Create a layer and rename it to be *Title Block*; set the linetype to *Continuous* and lineweight to be *0.0mm*.
- Make the *Title Block* layer the current layer.
- Do not add the dimensions.
- Use the *Line* command to draw the lines shown in Figure 6-5a.
- Use the *Offset* command with the offset distance of 3 to create the thin lines (above or to the right of the existing lines) as shown in Figure 6-5b. The thin lines are created to locate the attributes.
- The start point of an attribute is the intersection of the thin lines. The thin lines are deleted after adding the attributes, that is, before creating the block.

Figure 6-5a

Figure 6-5b

An attribute is defined through the *Attribute Definition* dialog box, Figure 6-5c, and the dialog box is opened using one of the following procedures.

1. Panel method: Either from the *Home* tab and expanded *Block* panel select the *Define Attributes* (⬚) tool, or from the *Insert* tab and *Block Definition* panel select the *Define Attributes* tool.
2. Command line method: Type "attdef," "Attdef," or "ATTDEF" on the command line and press the *Enter* key.

6.5.2. Attribute definition dialog box
The main features of the *Attribute Definition* dialog box (Figure 6-5c) are briefly discussed here.

- *Mode*: The *Mode* panel is used to set the options of attribute for inserting the attributes in the drawing.
  - *Lock position*: This option allows for locking the position of the attribute within the block reference. In the current example, this box is checked.
- *Insertion Point*: The *Insertion Point* panel is used to set the location of an attribute in the drawing. The user can specify either the coordinates or pick the location in the drawing area. In the current example, the *Specify on-screen* box is checked because the drafter has defined the location of the attributes, the intersection of the thin lines.
- *Align below previous attribute definition*: If this box is checked then the second and subsequent attribute tags are placed directly below the previously defined attribute. This option is not available for the first attribute. In the current example, this option

is not checked because the drafter has defined the location of the attributes, the intersection of the thin lines.

- *Attribute*: The *Attribute* panel is used to set attribute data. An attribute has three components.
    - o *Tag*: Tag is the name (one word with no space) of the attribute that identifies an attribute for the filing and referencing purpose. The *Tag* field is used to enter the attribute's name using any combination of characters except spaces. Lowercase letters are changed to uppercase letters. If the tag field is left blank and the *OK* button is pressed then the software displays an error message.
    - o *Prompt*: The prompt is the message that is displayed when the block is inserted. The *Prompt* field is used to specify the prompt that is displayed when a block containing attribute is inserted. If the prompt field is left blank then the tag is used as a prompt.
    - o *Value*: The value is the information that is stored in an attribute. The *Value* field is used to specify the default attribute value. Although, this field could be left blank, it is good drawing practice to specify a reasonable default value.
- *Text Settings*: The *Text* panel is used to set the justification, style, height, and rotation of the attribute's text.

Figure 6-5c

6.5.3. Create attributes

The tag, prompt, and values of the attributes used in the title block are shown in Table #1. The first entry in each cell is the tag, the second entry is the prompt, and the third entry is the default value of the attribute.

Table #1: Tag, prompt, and default values for attributes

COMPANY-NAME Enter the company's name: CLEMSON UNIVERSITY		
SECTION_NO Enter section #: ENGR 2100 - 000	NAME Enter your name: NIGHAT YASMIN	
EX-NO Enter the exercise #: EX A5-1	ASSIGNMENT Enter Assignment no.: A5	SHEET-NO Enter sheet #: SHT 1 OF 2
SCALE Scale of the drawing: SCALE: 1:1	TABLE-NO. Your table #: TABLE 0	PAPER Enter the paper type: LETTER
DATE Enter today's date: 05/05/2017	UNITS Enter the units of the drawing: MILLIMETERS	

1. Open the *Attribute Definition* dialog box.
2. Create the company's name attribute as shown in Figure 6-5c. The text style and height is standard and 10, respectively.
3. Press the *Enter* key. This closes the *Define Attributes* dialog box.
4. The prompt to specify the start point of the attribute appears, Figure 6-6a.

Figure 6-6a

5. Click at the lower left corner of the thin lines intersection in the topmost cell, Figure 6-6b.

Figure 6-6b

6. Repeat steps #2 to #5 to create the remaining attributes. Set the text height to 6, Figure 6-6c.
7. The resulting title block is shown in Figure 6-6c.
8. Delete the thin lines, and the final version of the title block is shown in Figure 6-6d.

COMPANY-NAME		
SECTION_NO	NAME	
EX-NO	ASSIGNMENT	SHEET-NO
SCALE	TABLE-NO.	PAPER
DATE	UNITS	

Figure 6-6c

COMPANY-NAME		
SECTION_NO	NAME	
EX-NO	ASSIGNMENT	SHEET-NO
SCALE	TABLE-NO.	PAPER
DATE	UNITS	

Figure 6-6d

6.5.4. Create block with attributes

1. Activate the *Make Block* command to open the *Block Definition* dialog box.
2. Set the *Name* of the block to be the Title Block; choose the lower right corner of the block as the base point. Press the *OK* button.
3. This closes the *Block Definition* dialog box and opens the *Edit Attributes* dialog box, Figure 6-7b. This box can display at most eight attributes; therefore, use the *Next* button to see the remaining attributes.
4. Make any changes (if necessary) and press the *OK* button.
5. This closes the *Edit Attributes* dialog box. The block displays the default values of the various attributes, Figure 6-7a.

CLEMSON UNIVERSITY		
ENGR 2100 - 000	NIGHAT YASMIN	
EX A5-1	A5	SHT 1 OF 2
SCALE: 1:1	TABLE 0	LETTER
05/05/2017	MILLIMETERS	

Figure 6-7a

Figure 6-7b

6.5.5. Convert to Wblock

The process to convert a block with attributes into a Wblock is identical to converting a basic block into a Wblock.

6.6.   Block with Text Boxes

This section will create a block that contains several text boxes. This example will create a release block. A release block contains a list of approval signatures or initials required before the drawing is released for production. Create a release block as follows.

- Open a new acadiso file.
- Create a layer and rename it to be a *Release Block*; set the linetype to *Continuous* and lineweight to be *0.0mm*.
- Make the *Release Block* layer the current layer.
- Do not add the dimensions.
- Use the *Line* command to draw the lines shown in Figure 6-8a.

- Use the *Offset* command with the offset distance of 3 to create the thin lines (above or to the right of the existing lines) as shown in Figure 6-8a. The thin lines are created to place the text.
- Use the *Text* command to create the text shown in Figure 6-8b. Select the font type as Arial and the text height as 10 for the team manager and 6 for the others.
- Remove the thin lines, Figure 6-8c.
- Create a basic block, set the *Name* of the block to be the Release Block, and choose the lower right corner of the block as the base point.
- Convert it to a Wblock.

Figure 6-8a

TEAM MANAGER		
DRAWN BY		
DESIGNED BY		
CHECKED BY		
CLIENT		

Figure 6-8b

TEAM MANAGER		
DRAWN BY		
DESIGNED BY		
CHECKED BY		
CLIENT		

Figure 6-8c

6.7.   Basic Block Insertion

The basic block, *Stand*, created earlier is used to demonstrate the block insertion process. The blocks are inserted using the *Insert Block* command.

- The *Insert Block* command is activated using one of the following procedures.
  1. Panel method: Either from the *Home* tab and *Block* panel, select the *Insert Block* tool; or from the *Insert* tab and *Block* panel, select the *Insert Block* tool. If one or more blocks are available to insert in the current file, then the activation of the command expands the dropdown menu as shown in Figure 6-9a. The expanded menu shows the blocks in the current file and *More Options* option. Click on the *More Options* to open the *Insert* dialog box, Figure 6-9b.
  2. Command line method: Type "insert," "Insert," or "INSERT" on the command line and press the *Enter* key.

Figure 6-9a

6.7.1. Insert dialog box

The activation of the *Insert Block* command opens the *Insert* dialog box shown in Figure 6-9b. The main features of the *Insert* dialog box are briefly discussed here.

- *Name*: The *Name* field is used to choose a named block. By default, it displays the block just created. The down arrow or *Browse* button can be used to choose any other block.
- *Path*: The *Path* option displays the location of the block. If the selected block is a basic block then *Path* is empty and the block is shown in the preview area in the upper right corner of the *Insert* dialog box. However, if the block is saved as a wblock then the *Path* displays the location of the selected block and the preview area is blank, Figure 6-9b.

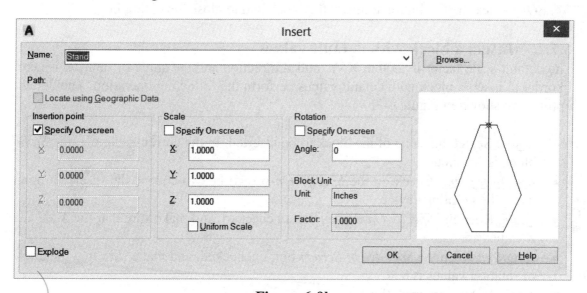

Figure 6-9b

- *Insertion point*: This panel is used to specify the insertion point in the drawing for the block.
  - *Specify On-screen*: Check this box to choose the insertion point using the pointing device.
  - *X, Y, Z*: These boxes are used to set the coordinate values. If the *Specify On-screen* option is selected, then these boxes are not available.
- *Scale*: This panel is used to specify the scale for the inserted block. The negative value for the X, Y, and Z scale factors inserts a mirror image of the block.
  - *Specify On-screen*: Check this box to specify scale factors during the insertion process using the pointing device.
  - *X, Y, Z*: These boxes are used to set the scale factors in the respective directions. If the *Specify On-screen* option is selected then these boxes are not available.
  - *Uniform Scale*: This box is checked to specify a single scale value for the *X, Y,* and *Z* coordinates. In this case, the *Y* and *Z* fields are deactivated by the software and the value specified for X is displayed in the *Y* and *Z* fields, too.
- *Rotation*: This panel is used to specify the rotation angle for the inserted block.
  - *Specify On-screen*: Check this box to specify the angle during the insertion process using the pointing device.
  - *Angle*: Specify the value of the rotation in the dialog box.
- *Block Unit*: This panel is used to display the information regarding the inserted block. The user cannot control the content of this panel.
  - *Unit*: Displays the unit's value for the inserted block.
  - *Factors*: Displays the unit scale factor, which is calculated based on the units used in the block creation and the drawing units.
- *Explode*: If this box is checked, then the block is exploded and its parts are inserted as the individual objects. Generally, this box is not checked.
- *OK*: Click the *OK* button to insert the block and to close the dialog box.

6.7.2. Insert a block with default values

The default scale factor is 1.00 in X, Y, and Z direction and the angle of rotation is zero. In order to insert a block with default values perform the following operation. The default options are shown in Figure 6-9b.

- *Name*: Select the name of the block to be inserted. In the current example, the *Stand* block is selected.
- *Insertion point*: Check on the *Specify On-screen* box to choose the insertion point using the pointing device.
- *Scale*: Keep the *Specify On-Screen* box unchecked, and make sure that the *X, Y,* and *Z* values are 1.
- *Rotation*: Keep the *Specify On-Screen* box unchecked, and make sure that the angle of rotation values is 0.
- *Explode*: Do not check this box.
- *OK*: Click the *OK* button to insert the block. The dialog box is closed and the block insertion process starts.

- o The prompt shown in Figure 6-10a appears on the screen. The block appears on the screen with its insertion (base point in the block creation process) point aligned with the cursor. The block moves with the cursor.
- o Specify the insertion point using one of the two methods. (i) Either move the cursor to the desired location and press the left button of the mouse. Or (ii) type the values of the x and y coordinates of the insertion point and press the *Enter* key.
- o The block shown in Figure 6-10b appears on the screen. Recall that the dimensions are not selected as a part of the block.

Figure 6-10a

Figure 6-10b

6.7.3. Change the scale of the block at the insertion

Figure 6-11c shows the effect of changes in the scale factors. Activate the *Insert Block* command.

- • <u>Name</u>: Select the name of the block to be inserted. In the current example, the *Stand* block is selected.
- • <u>Insertion point</u>: Check the *Specify On-screen* box to choose the insertion point using the pointing device.
- • <u>Scale</u>: Check the *Specify On-Screen* box.
- • <u>Rotation</u>: Keep the *Specify On-Screen* box unchecked, and make sure that the angle of rotation values is 0.
- • <u>Explode</u>: Do not check this box.
- • <u>OK</u>: Click the *OK* button to insert the block. The dialog box will be closed and the block insertion process will start.

- o The prompt to specify the insertion point appears on the screen.
- o Specify the insertion point.
- o The prompt to specify the scale factor appears on the screen, Figure 6-11a. Specify the *X* scale factor and press the *Enter* key. In the current example, the scale factor is 2.
- o The prompt to specify the *Y* scale factor appears on the screen, Figure 6-11b. Specify the Y scale factor and press the *Enter* key. In the current example, the scale factor is 0.5.
- o The block is inserted at the specified insertion point and at the specified scale factor, Figure 6-11c.

Figure 6-11a

Figure 6-11b

Figure 6-11c

- Repeat the process with the following changes: (i) in the *Scale* panel, do not check the *Specify On-Screen* box; (ii) type the values (1,0, 1.0,1.0) for the (x, y, z) fields. The representations are shown in Figure 6-11d.
- Repeat the process with the following changes: (i) in the *Scale* panel, do not check the *Specify On-Screen* box (ii) type the values (0.5, 2.0,1.0) for the (x, y, z) fields. The representations are shown in Figure 6-11e.

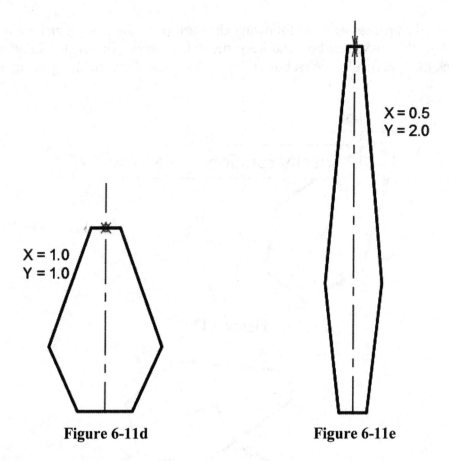

Figure 6-11d   **Figure 6-11e**

6.7.4. Rotate the block at the insertion

Figure 6-12a shows the effect of changes in the rotation angle. Activate the *Insert Block* command.

- *Name*: Select the name of the block to be inserted. In the current example, the *Stand* block is selected.
- *Insertion point*: Check the *Specify On-screen* box to choose the insertion point using the pointing device.
- *Scale*: Keep the *Specify On-Screen* box unchecked, and make sure that the scale factors value is 1.
- *Rotation*: Check the *Specify On-Screen* box.
- *Explode*: Do not check this box.
- *OK*: Click the *OK* button to insert the block. The dialog box will be closed and the block insertion process will start.

  - The prompt to specify the insertion point will appear on the screen; specify the insertion point.
  - The prompt to specify the rotation angle will appear on the screen; specify the angle and press the *Enter* key Figure 6-12a. In the example, the angle is 75.
  - The block will be inserted at the specified insertion point and rotated at the specified angle, Figure 6-12b.

- Repeat the process with the following changes: (i) in the *Scale* panel, do not check the *Specify On-Screen* box and keep the default scale; (ii) in the *Rotation* panel, check the *Specify On-Screen* box and type -75 in the *Angle* field; figure not shown.

Figure 6-12a

Figure 6-12b

6.7.5.   Insert a Wblock

The insertion process of a Wblock is similar to the insertion process of a basic block. In the *Name* field of the *Insert* dialog box, use the browse button to load the Wblock created and saved earlier. Furthermore, the Wblocks can be combined or exploded in a manner similar to a basic block.

6.7.6.   Insert a block with attributes

1. Activate the *Insert Block* command to open the *Insert* dialog box.
2. Choose the *Title Block*, set the various options as discussed earlier. Press the *OK* button.
3. Specify the insertion point.
4. The *Edit Attributes* dialog box appears on the screen, Figure 6-13.
5. If necessary, change the value of the data field. This box can display at most fifteen attributes; therefore, use the *Next* button to see the remaining attributes.
6. Press the *OK* button to close the box. The *Title Block* appears with the specified value.

Figure 6-13

6.7.7.   Insert a block with text boxes
The insertion process of a block with the text boxes is similar to the insertion process of a basic block. In the *Name* field of the *Insert* dialog box, use the browse button to load the respective block created and saved earlier. Furthermore, a block with the text boxes can be combined or exploded in a manner similar to a basic block.

6.8.   Combine Blocks
Complicated shape objects can be created by inserting different blocks at the desired locations. Figure 6-14c shows a lamp created by combining a *Stand* and a *Shade* block.

Blocks can be combined as follows.
- Create the *Stand* block with point *A* selected as the base point, Figure 6-14a.
- Create the *Shade* block with point *B* selected as the base point, Figure 6-14b.
- Insert the *Stand* block with desired scale factors.

- Insert the *Shade* block on top of the *Stand* block with the desired scale factors, Figure 6-14c. Points A and B should overlap.

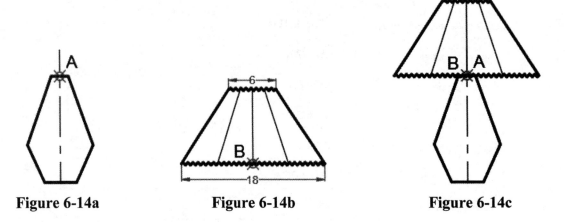

| Figure 6-14a | Figure 6-14b | Figure 6-14c |

6.9.　　Modify Block

In some situations, a user of the block is required to modify the block. Figure 6-15 shows the modification of *Shade* block's top and bottom rims (remove the zig-zag linetype). The process is given as:

- Create the lamp (Figure 6-14c) and it becomes part of the current drawing.
- From the Home tab and *Modify* toolbar, use the *Explode* command to explode the block.
- Edit the block as desired; that is, change the linetype of the top and bottom rims.
- If the new shape is used frequently then save it as *Lamp* block (a new block).

Figure 6-15

6.10.　　Design Center

AutoCAD provides a *Design Center* (Figure 6-16a), a blocks and symbols library. The *Design Center* is the collection of blocks and symbols that can be inserted in both ANSI and ISO file. The *Design Center* can be opened using one of the following procedures.

1. Panel method: Either from the *Insert* tab and *Content* panel select the *Design Center* tool, Figure 6-16b, or from the *View* tab and *Palettes* panel select the *Design Center* tool, Figure 6-16c.
2. Command line method: Type "adCenter," "Adcenter," or "ADCENTER" on the command line and press the *Enter* key.
3. Hold the *Ctrl* key and press the '*2*' key.
4. Open the *Design Center* option by expanding *Program File* → *Autodesk* → *AutoCAD 2018* → *Sample* → *en-us* → *Design Center*, Figure 6-16a. The path is also shown on the lower edge of the dialog box.

Figure 6-16a

Figure 6-16b

Figure 6-16c

- The remainder of this section explains how to insert a block from the *Kitchens.dwg* of the *Design Center*.

- Expand the *Design Center* and select the *Kitchens.dwg*, Figure 6-17a.
- Either click on the *Blocks* in the left column or double click on the *Blocks* in the preview window; the content of the drawing appears in the preview window, Figure 6-17b. The figure displays the available blocks under the *Kitchen.dwg* file.

Figure 6-17a

Figure 6-17b

6.10.1. Insert a block (known dimension)

This section explains how to insert a block from the *Design Center* whose dimensions are known by explaining the insertion process of the *"Wall Cabinet 18 X 36 in front"* block.

Example: The drafter wants to draw a cabinet in the elevation (front view). The size of the desired cabinet is shown in Figure 6-18a. The dimensions of the cabinet are in inches.

- The size of the cabinet block in the design center is shown in Figure 6-18b.

Figure 6-18a

Figure 6-18b

- Insert the cabinet as follows (Figure 6-18c). (i) Click with the left button of the mouse on the cabinet; this highlights the cabinet icon and displays it in the preview window. (ii) Press the right button of the mouse. (iii) Click on the *Insert Block* option. The Insert block dialog box appears on the screen. (iv) Follow the procedure to insert a block.
- In this example, the desired size is different than the actual size. Hence, the cabinet must be scaled before the insertion. The scale factor is calculated as:

  Scale factor = (Desired size) / (Actual size in the *Design Center*)
  Therefore,

  X-Scale factor = 45 / 36
  Y-Scale factor = 32 / 18   and
  Z-Scale factor = 1

Figure 6-18c

6.10.2. Insert a block (unknown dimension)

This section explains how to insert a block from the *Design Center* whose dimensions are unknown by explaining the insertion process of the "*Microwave*" block.

Example: The drafter wants to draw a microwave in the elevation (front view). The size of the desired microwave is shown in Figure 6-19a. The dimensions of the microwave are in inches.

Figure 6-19a   **Figure 6-19b**

- The microwave's block in the Design Center does not contain any dimension. Therefore, the first step is to find out the block dimension.
- To find the dimension of a block, (i) insert the block in question at the scale factor of 1.0 in X, Y, and Z-direction and Angle = 0. (ii) Add the dimensions to the block. Figure 6-19b shows the trial block.
- Now insert the microwave block at the desired location and the desired scale factor.

    Scale factor = (Desired size) / (Actual size in the *Design Center*)
    Therefore,

    X-Scale factor = 30 / 24
    Y-Scale factor = 27 / 18   and
    Z-Scale factor = 1

- Finally, delete the trial block and its dimensions.

Notes:

7.   Layouts and Template Files

7.1.   Learning Objectives

After completing this chapter, you will demonstrate competency in the following areas:

- Layout manipulate (add, delete, rename, move)
- Layers in layouts
- Scale list
- Template file
- Plot from a layout

7.2.   Introduction

In AutoCAD, a layout is a drawing environment mainly used for printing or plotting the drawing. New layouts can be created and existing layouts can be modified. This chapter explains the usage and advantages of layouts. Furthermore, this chapter creates template files using layouts and title and release blocks created in the previous chapter.

7.3.   Layout

Generally, layouts are used for printing or plotting the drawing. By default, AutoCAD creates two layouts. The user can switch to a layout by selecting the *Layout1* or *Layout2* tab, respectively, from the lower left corner of the AutoCAD's interface, Figure 7-1a.

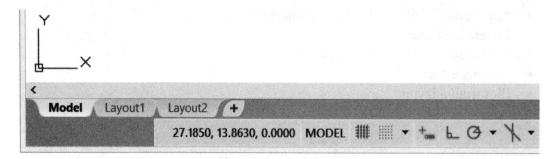

Figure 7-1a

When a user clicks on a layout tab, the drawing area appears as shown in Figure 7-1b. The dashed rectangle is the limits of the printing area. The solid rectangle is the boundary of the viewport. A viewport is a bounded area that displays a portion of the model space of a drawing in a layout. The user can change the size and location of the viewport.

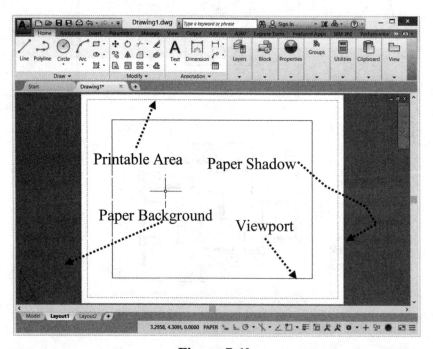

Figure 7-1b

7.3.1. Paper background and shadow

The paper background and shadow does not affect the quality or efficiency of a drawing. However, it is good drawing practice to keep the two options *On*. The user can hide or display the paper background and/or shadow of the layouts as follows. (i) Type the *Options* in the command line. This opens the *Options* dialog box. (ii) Select the *Display* tab, Figure 7-2. The lower left corner contains the layout controls, Figure 7-2. (iii) Clear or check the appropriate boxes. (iv) Finally, click the *OK* button to make the changes effective and close the dialog box. The changes are applied to each layout in the current drawing file.

Figure 7-2

7.3.2. Printable area

The printable area does not affect the quality of a drawing. However, it may affect the productivity of the draftsmen. If the printable area limits are not displayed, then the draftsmen may draw outside the printable area, and will be required to adjust the drawing before printing. Hence, it is good drawing practice to display the printable area in layouts.

The user can hide or display the printable area of the layouts as follows. (i) Type the *Options* in the command line. This will open the *Options* dialog box. (ii) Select the *Display* tab, Figure 7-2. The lower left corner contains the layout controls, Figure 7-2. (iii) Clear or check the *Display printable area* box. (iv) Finally, click the *OK* button to make the changes effective and close the dialog box. The changes will be applied to each layout in the drawing file.

The user can adjust the printable area of the layouts as follows.

- (i) Click the *Layout1* tab. (ii) Bring the cursor on the *Layout1* tab. (iii) Press the right button of the mouse and the option selection panel, Figure 7-3a, appears. (iv) Move the cursor to the *Page Setup Manager* option and press the left button of the mouse. This opens the *Page Setup Manager* dialog box, Figure 7-3b.

- Click the *Modify* button of the *Page Setup Manager* dialog box. This opens the *Page Setup – Layout1* dialog box, Figure 7-3c.

Figure 7-3a

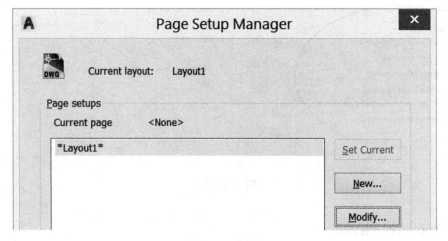

Figure 7-3b

- Select the printer from the *Page Setup – Layout1* dialog box in the *Printer/plotter* panel and click the *Properties* button. This opens the *Plotter Configuration Editor* dialog box, Figure 7-3d.

Figure 7-3c

- Select the *Modify Standard Paper Sizes (Printable Area)* from the *Plotter Configuration Editor* dialog box, Figure 7-3d, and click the *Modify* button. This opens the *Custom Paper Sizes - Printable Area* dialog box, Figure 7-3e.

Figure 7-3d

- In the *Custom Paper Sizes - Printable Area* dialog box, Figure 7-3e, set the value for the *Top*, *Bottom*, *Left*, and *Right* limits and click the *Next* button. This opens the *Custom Paper Sizes – File name* dialog box, Figure 7-3f.

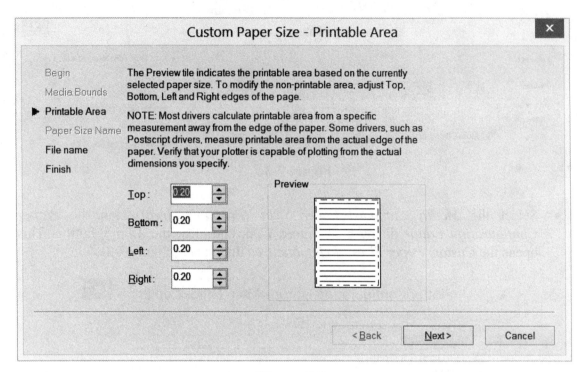

Figure 7-3e

- In the *Custom Paper Sizes – File name* dialog box, Figure 7-3f, specify the file name and click the *Next* button. This opens the *Custom Paper Sizes - Finish* dialog box, Figure 7-3g.

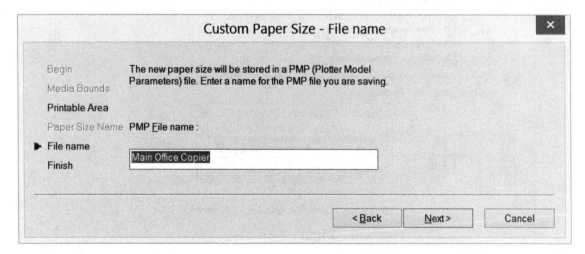

Figure 7-3f

- In the *Custom Paper Sizes - Finish* dialog box, Figure 7-3g, click the *Finish* button. This closes the *Custom Paper Sizes – Finish* and *Custom Paper Sizes – File name* dialog boxes.

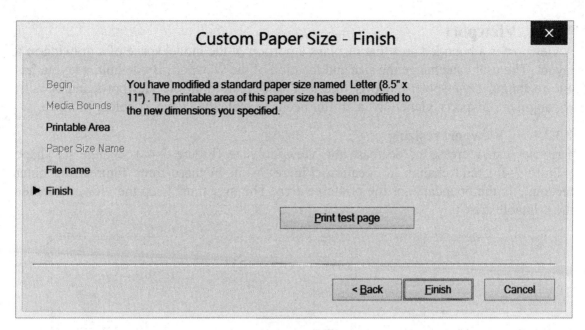

Figure 7-3g

- Click the *OK* button of the *Plotter Configuration Editor* dialog box.
- Click the *OK* button of the *Page Setup – Layout1* dialog box.
- Click the *Close* button of the *Page Setup Manager* dialog box.
- The new printable area is shown in Figure 7-3h.

Figure 7-3h

7.3.3. Viewport

A viewport is a bounded area that displays a portion of the model space of a drawing in a layout. The user can change the size and location of the viewport. By default, a layout has one rectangular viewport; however, the user can create multiple viewports and/or non-rectangular viewports. Generally, a drafter needs to scale the viewport before plotting.

7.3.3.1. Viewport resizing

The user can increase or decrease the viewport size (Figure 7-4a), change its shape (Figure 7-4b), and change its location (Figure 7-4c). In these three figures, the outer rectangle is the boundary for the printable area. The user must keep the viewport inside the printable area.

Figure 7-4a   **Figure 7-4b**   **Figure 7-4c**

A viewport can be relocated or resized as follows.

- Select the viewport, Figure 7-4d. The corner grip point appears.
- Use the *Move* command to relocate inside the printable area.
- Use the *Grips and Object editing* technique to resize the viewport. That is, click on a grip point and stretch it outward or inward as needed, Figure 7-4e.
- For further details, use the *Grips and Object editing* technique (discussed in Chapter 4) to resize the viewport.

Figure 7-4d   **Figure 7-4e**

7.3.3.2. Multiple viewports

By default, a layout has one rectangular viewport; however, the user can create multiple viewports, Figure 7-5f. A user can create multiple viewports as follows.

- Select the current viewport, Figure 7-4d. The corner grip point appears.
- Delete the current viewport.
- Activate the *MVIEW* command. (i) Type "mview," "Mview," or "MVIEW" on the command line and press the *Enter* key. The prompt shown in Figure 7-5a appears.
- *Specify corner of viewport or*, Figure 7-5a: Press the down arrow of the prompt and an option list appears. Click on *4*; the prompt shown in Figure 7-5b appears.
- *Specify first corner or*, Figure 7-5b: Click near the upper left corner of the layout. The prompt shown in Figure 7-5c appears.
- *Specify opposite corner*, Figure 7-5c: Click at a diagonally opposite corner as shown in Figure 7-5c.
- The resulting viewports are shown in Figure 7-5d.

Figure 7-5a

Figure 7-5b

Figure 7-5c

Figure 7-5d

- Activate the *MVIEW* command, again. (i) Type "mview," "Mview," or "MVIEW" on the command line and press the *Enter* key. The prompt shown in Figure 7-5a appears.
- *Specify corner of viewport or*, Figure 7-5a: Press the down arrow of the prompt and an option list appears. Click on *3*. The prompt shown in Figure 7-5e appears.
- *Enter viewport arrangement*, Figure 7-5e: Click on the *Below* option. This option creates a horizontal viewport below the two vertical viewports.
- Follow the prompts.
- The resulting viewports are shown in Figure 7-5f.

Figure 7-5e

Figure 7-5f

7.3.3.3.   Non-rectangular viewports

By default, a layout has one rectangular viewport; however, the user can create non-rectangular viewports, too.

- Select the current viewport, Figure 7-4d. The corner grip point appears.
- Delete the current viewport.
- Draw a circle, a polygon, and a closed polyline, Figure 7-6a.

- (i) Activate the *MVIEW* command: Type "mview," "Mview," or "MVIEW" on the command line and press the *Enter* key. The prompt shown in Figure 7-6b appears. (ii) Press the down arrow of the prompt, and an option list appears. (iii) Click on the *Object* option. (iv) The prompt shown in Figure 7-6c appears. (v) Click on the closed shape created using polyline. The closed polyline is converted into a viewport. Double click inside the viewport to check the creation of the viewport, Figure 7-6d.
- Repeat the above process with the polygon and the circle.
- The resulting viewports are shown in Figure 7-5d.

Figure 7-6a   Figure 7-6b

Figure 7-6c

Figure 7-6d

7.3.3.4.   Viewport scaling

Consider the floor plan of a three bedroom house shown in Figure 7-7a. The architect wants to show the client the entire floor plan and the details of the kitchen as shown in Figure 7-5a and Figure 7-7b, respectively. The architect can achieve the desired goal by creating two layouts at two different scale factors. In the figures, the floor plan is at the scale of 1:132 and the kitchen plan is at the scale of 1:30.

Figure 7-7a

Figure 7-7b

7.3.3.5.   Rescale a viewport

A viewport can be rescaled using one of the following two methods.

Method #1: The Properties Palette
- Select the viewport, Figure 7-4d. The corner grip point appears.
- Press the right button of the mouse and select the *Properties* from the options list.
- The above selection opens the *Properties* palette, Figure 7-7c.
- From the *Misc* panel, click the down arrow in front of the *Standard scale*.
- Click on the desired scale. This action closes the list and the viewport (that is, its content) sets itself to the selected scale.

Method #2a: The Status bar
- Select the viewport, Figure 7-4d. The corner grips point appears.
- Either click on the down arrow beside the scale factor (right oval on Figure 7-7d), or click on the scale button (⊡) on the status bar (middle oval on Figure 7-7d).
- The scale selection appears.
- Click on the desired scale. This action closes the list and the viewport (that is, its content) sets itself to the selected scale.

Method #2b: The viewport method
- Double click inside the viewport, Figure 7-7e; the viewport boundary becomes bold and the coordinates system appears.
- Either click on the down arrow beside the scale factor (right oval on Figure 7-7d), or click on the scale button (⊡) on the status bar (middle oval on Figure 7-7d).
- The scale selection appears.
- Click on the desired scale. This action closes the list and the viewport (that is, its content) sets itself to the selected scale.

Figure 7-7c

Figure 7-7d

Figure 7-7e

7.3.3.6. Lock the scale of a viewport

The draftsman should lock the viewport scale to avoid rescaling of the viewport accidentally using zoom/unzoom commands. By locking the viewport scale, the user can zoom into the viewport (or zoom out) at different levels of detail without altering the viewport (or drawing) scale. A viewport can be locked using one of the following two methods.

Method #1: *The Properties Palette*
- Select the viewport, the corner grips point appears, Figure 7-4d.
- Press the right button of the mouse and select the *Properties* from the options list.
- The above selection opens the *Properties* palette, Figure 7-8a.
- From the *Misc* panel, click in the cell on the right side of the *Display locked*, Figure 7-8b.
- A down arrow appears in the cell labeled as *No*.
- Press the down arrow and select the *Yes* option, Figure 7-8c. Notice, that the scale is greyed; that is, the user cannot change it.

Figure 7-8a

Figure 7-8b

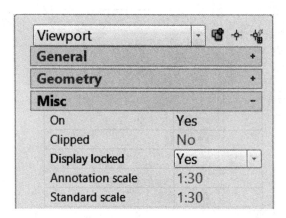

Figure 7-8c

Method #2a: *The Status bar*
- Select the viewport, Figure 7-4d. The corner grips point appears.
- Click on the lock button (🔒) on the status bar (left oval on Figure 7-7d).

Method #2b: *The viewport method*
- Double click inside the viewport, Figure 7-4e; the viewport boundary becomes bold and the coordinates system appears.
- Click on the lock button (🔒) on the status bar (left oval on Figure 7-7d).

7.4.   Add an Entry in The Scale List

A situation may arise when the user needs to use a scale factor not available in the default scale list of AutoCAD.

__Example:__ Add *1:120* entry in the scale list. The user can add a new scale factor in the edit scale list as follows.

- From the *Annotate* tab and *Annotation Scaling* panel, select the *Scale List*, Figure 7-9a. This opens the *Edit Drawing Scales* dialog box, Figure 7-9b.
- On the dialog box, select the entry labeled as 1:100. This helps in the addition of the new entry at its correct location. (1:120 should be after 1:100).
- Click the *Add* button of the *Default Scale List* dialog box. This opens the *Add Scale* dialog box, Figure 7-9c.

Figure 7-9a   **Figure 7-9b**

Figure 7-9c

- Enter the desired values, Figure 7-9c. Press the *OK* button on the *Add Scale* dialog box. This action will accept the new scale factor and close the dialog box.
- The new scale will appear in the *Edit Scale List* dialog box, Figure 7-9d.
- If the new scale is not created at its correct location, then use the *Move Up* or *Move Down* button to move the newly created scale to the appropriate location.
- Click the *OK* button to close the *Edit Drawing Scale* dialog box.

Figure 7-9d

7.5.　　Layout Manipulation

By default, AutoCAD creates two layouts: *Layout1* and *Layout2*, Figure 7-10a. However, a user can delete, move, copy, or rename existing layouts and insert more layouts. The Figure 7-10b shows the layouts created for the floor plan drawing shown in Figure 7-7a and renamed based on their functionality.

If the labels of the layouts cannot fit on the lower left side of the interface, then the labels are collapsed in a list. The user can visualize the list by pressing the ⩔ button on the right side of the layouts labels, Figure 7-10b.

Figure 7-10a

Figure 7-10b

7.5.1. Delete a layout
This section describes the process of deleting layouts.

__Example:__ Delete the layout labeled *WWDim* in Figure 7-10b.
(i) Bring the cursor on the *WWDim* tab. (ii) Click the *WWDim (2)* tab. (iii) Press the right button of the mouse and the option selection panel shown in Figure 7-11a appears. (iv) Move the cursor to the *Delete* option and press the left button of the mouse. (v) The AutoCAD warning shown in Figure 7-11b appears. (vi) Finally, click the *OK* button to complete the deletion process. Figure 7-11c shows that the *WWDim* layout is deleted.

Figure 7-11a   **Figure 7-11b**

Figure 7-11c

7.5.2. Move a layout

This section describes the process of moving a layout.

Example: In Figure 7-10b, move the *RmSize* layout in front of *BPorch* layout.

Method #1:

(i) Bring the cursor on the *RmSize* tab. (ii) Click the *RmSize* tab. (iii) Press the left button of the mouse and keep pressing it. (iv) Move the cursor to the desired location, Figure 7-12a. A small triangle appears at the cursor's location. (v) Release the left button. The moved layout is shown in Figure 7-12b.

Figure 7-12a

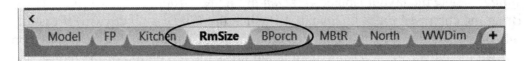

Figure 7-12b

Method #2:

(i) Bring the cursor on the *RmSize* tab. (ii) Click the *RmSize* tab. (iii) Press the right button of the mouse and the option selection panel shown in Figure 7-12d appears. (iv) Move the cursor to the *Move or Copy* option (Figure 7-12c), and press the left button of the mouse. This opens the *Move or Copy* dialog box, Figure 7-12d. (v) Select the new location. Since, the *RmSize* is required to move in front of *BPorch*, *BPorch* is selected. (vi) Click the *OK* button to complete the move command. The moved layout is shown in Figure 7-12b.

Figure 7-12c

Figure 7-12d

7.5.3. Copy a layout
This section describes the process of copying a layout.

Example: Make a copy of the *North* layout and place the copy before the *Kitchen* layout.

(i) Bring the cursor on the *North* tab, Figure 7-13a. (ii) Click the *North* tab. (iii) Press the right button of the mouse and the option selection panel shown in Figure 7-12c appear. (iv) Move the cursor to the *Move or Copy* option (Figure 7-12c), and press the left button of the mouse. This opens the *Move or Copy* dialog box, Figure 7-13b. (v) Check the *Create a copy* box. (vi) Select the location of the copy. Since the *copy* is required to be on the layout before the *Kitchen, Kitchen* is selected. (vii) Click the *OK* button to complete the copy command. The copied layout, *North (2)*, is shown in Figure 7-13c.

Figure 7-13a

Figure 7-13b

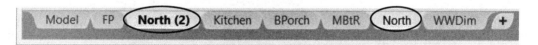

Figure 7-13c

7.5.4. Rename a layout
This section describes the process of renaming a layout.

Example: Rename the layout labeled as *North (2)* in Figure 7-13c.

Method #1:
Double click on the name of the layout *North (2)* and its name is highlighted, Figure 7-14. Type the new name and press the *Enter* key.

Figure 7-14

Method #2:
(i) Bring the cursor on the *North (2)* tab. (ii) Click the *North (2)* tab. (iii) Press the right button of the mouse and the option selection panel shown in Figure 7-11a appears. (iv) Move the cursor to the *Rename* option. The selected layout is highlighted, Figure 7-14. Type the new name and press the *Enter* key.

7.5.5. Insert a layout
AutoCAD allows its user to insert two types of layouts: a default layout or a layout from a specific template file. Template files are discussed in the later sections of this chapter.

7.5.5.1. Default layout
Example: Insert a default layout.
The user can insert a default layout as follows: (i) Bring the cursor on any of the layout tabs. (ii) Press the right button of the mouse and the option panel appears, Figure 7-15. (iii) Move the cursor to the *New layout* option. (iv) Finally, press the left or right button of the mouse. (v) The option panel is closed and a new layout is added to the drawing.

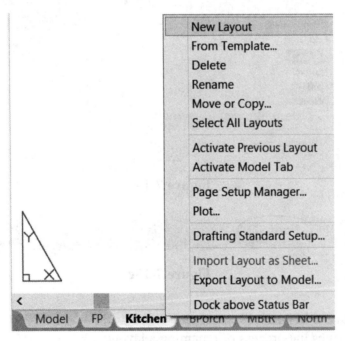

Figure 7-15

7.5.5.2. Layout from template
Example: Insert a "My_acad_Landscape" from "My_Template."
The user can insert a layout from a template as follows: (i) Bring the cursor on any of the layout tabs. (ii) Press the right button of the mouse and the option panel appears, Figure 7-15. (iii) Move the cursor to the *From Template...* option. (iv) This opens the

Select Template From File dialog box, Figure 7-16a. (v) Choose the appropriate template and press the *Open* button. (iv) This opens the *Insert Layout(s)* dialog box, Figure 7-16b. (v) Select the desired layout, My_acad_Landscape in the example. (vi) Press the *OK* button in the *Insert Layout(s)* dialog box. (vi) Press the *Open* button in the *Select Template From File* dialog box to complete the layout insertion process.

Figure 7-16a

Figure 7-16b

7.5.6. Grid and Snap commands
The *Grid* command is used to display the visible grid (similar to graph or engineering paper) background on the drawing screen. The *Snap* command is used to set an invisible grid background on the drawing screen and to limit the movement of the cursor to the snap grid's points only. The snap grid is completely independent of the visible grid. The process of grid and snap manipulation in the layout is the same as in the model space and is discussed in detail in Chapter 2.

7.6. Layers freezing and layouts
A draftsman needs to create a drawing of the model shown in Figure 7-17a. However, the draftsman needs to display different parts of the drawing to different clients. The drafter

has two choices: (i) create multiple drawings specific to each client (wastage of resources and time) or (ii) create one drawing with multiple layers and multiple layouts and display the desired views to the clients. The drafter has decided to follow the second choice. This section explains the process of freezing layers to create the desired views.

Figure 7-17a

- File: Open a new acadiso file.
- Layouts: Create the layouts and label them as shown in Figure 7-17b.
- Layers: Create the layers and label them as shown in Figure 7-17c.

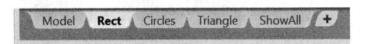

Figure 7-17b

Filters	«	Status	Name	On	Freeze	Lock	Color	Linetype	Lineweight
□ All		✓	0	♀	☼	🔓	■ white	Continuous	—— 0.00 mm
└ All Used		⊘	Circles	♀	☼	🔓	■ 160	ZIGZAG	■■ 0.50 mm
		⊘	Defpoints	♀	☼	🔓	■ white	Continuous	—— 0.00 mm
		⊘	Rectangles	♀	☼	🔓	■ 92	TRACKS	■■ 0.50 mm
		⊘	Triangles	♀	☼	🔓	■ 210	HIDDEN	■■ 0.50 mm

Current layer: 0   Search for layer

Figure 7-17c

- Important point: The names of the layers and layouts should be small and descriptive. The naming of a layer and layouts are independent processes. The names can be the same or different; note the names of the layouts in Figure 7-17b and the layers in Figure 7-17c. In the example, only two layers and two layouts have the same name.

- Create the drawing: Figure 7-18a, (i) Make the *Rectangles* layer the current layer and draw the rectangles. (ii) Make the *Circles* layer the current layer and draw the circles. (iii) Make the *Triangles* layer the current layer and draw the triangles. However, the user can skip the dimensioning step.

Figure 7-18a

- Create the views: (i) Select the layout tab labeled as *ShowAll*. (ii) Either double click inside the viewport or click on `PAPER` button on the status bar (lower right corner of the interface). The layout appears as shown in Figure 7-18a. **Note that, the viewport boundary is bold and the coordinate and the viewcube appear inside the viewport**. (iii) Press the down arrow on the layer toolbar and freeze the '*0*' and *Defpoints* layers by clicking its *Freeze or thaw in current viewport* button as shown in Figure 7-18b. (iv) The resulting layout is shown Figure 7-18c.

Figure 7-18b

Figure 7-18c

- Repeat the process: Repeat the above process with each layout. The layouts and corresponding layers manipulation are shown in Table #1.
- Important point: Freezing a layer is an independent process from the current layer. In the layers of Table #1, *Circle* is the current layer in all four cases; it is frozen in the *Rectangles* and *Triangles* layouts.

Table #1: Layouts and layers

Layouts	Layers

Cirles

Rectangles

Triangles

ShowAll

7.7.   Object Appearance and Layouts

Figure 7-19a shows the objects (created in the previous section) in the model space and Figure 7-19b shows the same objects in the layout. The two figures have the same lineweight and linetype (Figure 7-17c), and the same linetype scale; the linetype scale (not shown in Figure 7-17c) is changed from the *Properties* palette. Every property is the same, yet the object appearance is different in the two drawing environments.

The user must decide about the drawing environment for the demonstration of the drawing and activation of the plotting command before setting the lineweight and the linetype scale. **If the user is planning to plot or demonstrate the drawing from the layout, then set the lineweight and the linetype scale for the layout and ignore the appearance in the model space and vice versa.** Generally, the lineweight is a higher number in the layout; however, the linetype scale is a pattern and the lineweight a dependent number. Lineweight can be changed for a layer from the layer manager. On the other hand, the linetype scale is changed from the *Properties* palette.

Figure 7-19a   **Figure 7-19b**

A property of an object can be changed using the *Properties* palette as follows.

- Select the object and its grip points appear. In the current example, select all three circles.
- Press the right button of the mouse and select the *Properties* option from the list of options.
- On the *Properties* palette, under the *General* panel, change the *Linetype scale* to 0.25, Figure 7-19c.

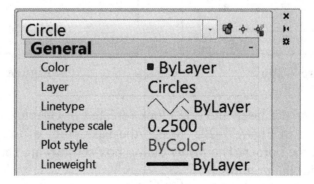

Figure 7-19c

7.8.   Template File

A template file is a mold or a pattern file that gives consistency to every drawing file in the company. AutoCAD provides a few template files for its users. However, this section creates a typical template file used in academia.

This section creates template files for ISO (millimeters) and ANSI (inch) units. The title and release blocks created in the previous chapters are inserted in a layout and then the file is saved as a template file.

7.8.1. Landscape template for ISO units

A landscape template for ISO units is created using the following steps. The template file is shown in Figure 7-22c.

1. Open a new acadiso.dwt file.
2. Create a layer *TemplateFile*; set its color to be *White*, linetype to be *Continuous*, and lineweight to be *0.0*.
3. Make the *TemplateFile* layer to be the current layer.
4. Select the *Layout1*; double click inside the viewport and turn *off* the grid.
5. Click on the *Layout1* tab and rename it to My_acadiso_Landscape. Figure 7-20a shows the viewport and the printable area of the layout.
6. *Add the border*: Every drawing requires a border and the viewport's boundaries are not printed; therefore, the draftsman must draw the border. The border of a drawing is 1/2 inches from the edge of the plotting paper. However, in this section the border is created with respect to the printable area. Hence, draw a rectangle slightly smaller than the printable area, Figure 7-20b.

Figure 7-20a

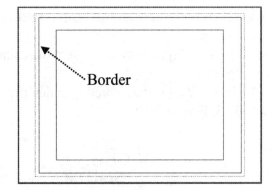

Figure 7-20b

7. *Insert the title block*: Insert the title block (created in Chapter 6) in the lower right corner as shown in Figure 7-20c. Match the base point of the block to the lower right corner of the border. The *Insert* dialog box settings are shown in 7-20d. Press the *Enter* key for the prompts.
8. *Scale down the title block*: If the title block is overpowering the drawing, then scale it down; if it is too small then scale it up. As a rule of thumb, the height of the title block should be about 1/6 of the height of the printable area. If necessary, scale the block as follows: (i) Activate the *Scale* command. (ii) In response to the prompt *Select objects*, click on the title block and press the *Enter* key. (iii) In response to the prompt *Specify the base point*, click on the lower right corner of the title block and press the *Enter* key. (iv) In response to the prompt *Specify scale factor*, type 0.5 and press the *Enter* key. (v) The title block is reduced by 50%, Figure 7-20e.

Figure 7-20c

Figure 7-20d

9. *Insert the release block*: Insert the release block in the lower left corner of the title block, Figure 7-20f. The *Insert* block dialog box shows the entries for the release block insertion. Notice that the release block is scaled down during the block insertion process, Figure 7-20g.

Figure 7-20e

Figure 7-20f

Figure 7-20g

10. *Adjust the viewport*: (i) Select the upper left grip point of the viewport and move it to the upper left corner of the border rectangle, Figure 7-21a. (ii) Select the lower right grip point of the viewport and move it to the upper right corner of the title block, Figure 7-21b.

Figure 7-21a

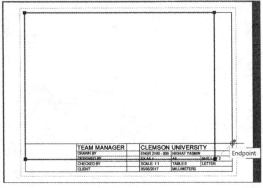

Figure 7-21b

11. *Delete layout 2.*

12. *Save the template file*: (i) From the *Quick Access* toolbar, click the *Save As* (⊟) icon and this opens the *Save Drawing As* dialog box. (ii) In the dialog box, for the *Files of type* field press the down arrow to display the option list, Figure 7-22a. (iii) Click with the left mouse button on *dwt* type, Figure 7-22a, and this opens the template folder. (iii) Specify the template file name, for the example, My_acadiso_Landscape. (v) Press the *Save* button and this opens the *Template Options* dialog box, Figure 7-22b. (vi) Press the *OK* button to complete the template creation process.

13. By default, the template file is saved in *Template* folder. However, if the software is reloaded frequently then save the template file in a different folder (for example, in the user folder).

14. The template file is shown in Figure 7-22c.

15. User created template files can also be saved as *dwg* files in a manner similar to the way software created files are saved as *dwg* files.

Figure 7-22a

Figure 7-22b

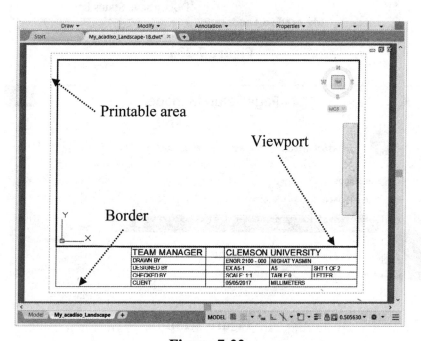

Figure 7-22c

7.8.2. Portrait template for ISO units

A portrait template for ISO units is created using the following steps. The template file is shown in Figure 7-23e.

1. Open a new acadiso.dwt file.
2. Create a layer *TemplateFile*; set its color to be *White*, linetype to be *Continuous*, and lineweight to be *0.0*.
3. Make *TemplateFile* layer to be the current layer.
4. Select the *Layout1*; double click inside the viewport and turn *off* the grid.
5. Click on the *Layout1* tab and rename it to My_acadiso_Portrait.
6. Click on the My_acadiso_Portrait layout and press the right button of the mouse. The options panel appears, Figure 7-23a.
7. Move the cursor to the *Page Setup Manager* option and press the left button of the mouse. The *Page Setup Manager* dialog box shown in Figure 7-23b appears.
8. Bring the cursor on the My_acadiso_Portrait tab, if necessary.
9. On the *Page Setup Manager* dialog box, Figure 7-23b, click on the *Modify* button. The *Page Setup – My_acadiso_Portrait* dialog box shown in Figure 7-23c appears.
10. Select the *Portrait* for the *Drawing orientation* option (on the lower right corner of the dialog box), select the *Letter* for the *Paper size* option (on the upper left corner of the dialog box), and press the *OK* button.

Figure 7-23a

Figure 7-23b

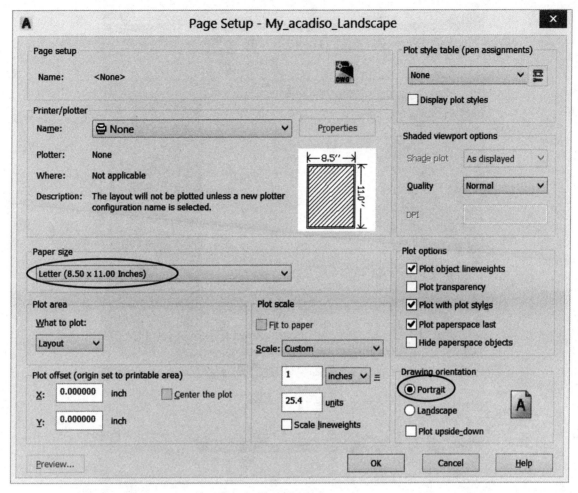

Figure 7-23c

11. Press the *Close* button on the *Page Setup Manager* dialog box.
12. The layout format changes to the portrait style as shown in Figure 7-23d; and the viewport is outside the layout. This is corrected in the template creation process.
13. Now, follow step #6 to step #13 from the procedure used for the landscape template file and save the portrait template file.
14. Save the template file as My_acadiso_Portrait.
15. The Figure 7-23e shows the portrait template file.

7.8.3. Template for ANSI units
Open a new acad.dwt file and repeat the process of creating acadiso templates (landscape and portrait) to create the ANSI template files.

Figure 7-23d

Figure 7-20e

7.9.   Modify Attribute of a Block in a Template File

1. Open a new *My_acadiso_Portrait* file.
2. This example changes the *Scale* field in the title block.
   a. Bring the cursor on top of the *Scale* field in the title block (Figure 7-24a) and double click with the left button of the mouse; this opens the *Enhanced Attribute Editor* dialog box, Figure 7-24b.
   b. Select the *Attribute* tab.
   c. If necessary, click the desired attribute and change its value in the *Value* field. This activates the *Apply* button.
   d. If necessary, change the value of the other attributes, too.
   e. Press the *Apply* or the *OK* button. The *Apply* button makes the changes permanent and does not close the dialog box. However, the *OK* button makes the changes permanent and closes the dialog box, too.

Figure 7-24a

Figure 7-24b

Notes:

8.   Dimensioning Techniques

8.1.   Learning Objectives

After completing this chapter, you will demonstrate competency in the following areas:

- Art of creating and reading a dimensional drawing
- Basics of dimensioning techniques
- Characteristics of the dimension and extension lines, spacing of the dimensions, arrowheads, etc.
- Different type of dimensions
- Standard practice to dimension circles, arcs, and inclined surfaces
- Basics of smart dimensioning
- Basics of quick dimensioning

8.2.   Introduction

A dimension describes the size and location of the feature of a model. Irrespective of the type of the drawing and units used in the drawing, a dimension is given in the form of a distance, an angle, and/or a note. In AutoCAD, a draftsman can add dimensions to a drawing, from the *Home* tab using the *Annotation* panel (Figure 8-1a) and from the *Annotate* tab using the *Dimension* panel (Figure 8-1b). This chapter explains the concepts and techniques used to add dimensions to a drawing.

Figure 8-1a   Figure 8-1b

8.3.   Dimensioning in General

In addition to visually representing the shapes of objects, an engineering drawing must also show the sizes of the objects so that the workers can build the structure or fabricate the parts that fit together. This is accomplished by placing the required values (measurements) along the dimension lines and by giving additional information in the form of notes which are referenced to the parts in question by angled lines called leaders.

A dimensioned drawing should provide all the information necessary for a finished product or part to be manufactured. Dimensions are always drawn using continuous thin lines. Two projection lines indicate where the dimension starts and ends. The projection lines do not touch the object and are drawn perpendicular to the element being dimensioned. In general, units can be omitted from the dimensions if a statement of the units is included on the drawing. All notes and dimensions should be clear and easy to read. In general, all notes should be written in capital letters to aid legibility and all lettering should be of the same size.

8.4.   Terminology

For the following terms, refer to Figure 8-2a and Figure 8-2b.

- *Dimension*: A dimension is the numerical value that defines the size, shape, location, or geometrical characteristics of a feature. Normally, dimension text is 3mm (or 0.125") high and the space between lines of text is 1.5mm (or 0.0625").
- *Dimension lines*: A dimension line is a thin continuous line that shows the extent and direction of the dimension; usually located outside the outlines of the object.
- *Extension lines*: An extension line is a thin, continuous line positioned perpendicular to the dimension line that extends from the object. It allows the dimension to be located off the object.
- *Leader lines*: A leader line is a thin, continuous line used to indicate the feature with which a dimension, note, or symbol is attached. Leader lines begin with an arrowhead or dot.
  - *For the best appearance make leader lines*
    - near each other and parallel, and
    - across as few lines as possible.
  - *Do not make leader lines*
    - parallel to the nearby line,
    - through the corner of the view,
    - longer than needed, and
    - horizontal or vertical.
- *Center lines*: A center line is a thin line with alternate long and short dashes.
- *Linear dimensions*: A linear dimension is a straight line distance between two points; it can only be horizontal and/or vertical.
- *Align dimensions*: An align dimension is a straight line distance between two points and can be horizontal, vertical, or inclined (that is, it is always parallel to the feature).
- *Angular dimensions*: An angular dimension is a dimension that defines the angular value, measured in degrees, between two straight lines.
- *Diameter symbol*: The diameter symbol is ϕ, which precedes a numerical value, to indicate that the dimension shows the diameter of a circle or a circular arc. (The symbol can be created by typing %%c in the text object). The circles and circular arcs equal or greater than $180°$ are dimensioned using the diameter symbol.
- *Radius symbol*: The radius symbol is R, which precedes a numerical value, to indicate that the dimension shows the radius of a circular arc. The circular arcs less than $180°$ are dimensioned using the radius symbol.
- *Architectural drawing*: In an architectural drawing:
  - The dimension lines end with tick marks, and the dimension value is located above the dimension line, Figure 8-2a.
  - The leader lines can end with a dot or an arrow.

Figure 8-2a

Figure 8-2b

8.5.   Important Points to Remember

Figure 8-2a, Figure 8-2b, and Figure 8-3 shows rules for placing dimensions. If possible, turn on the *Grid* so dimension placement becomes faster.

- <u>Space between dimension lines</u>: Dimension lines should be uniformly spaced.
- <u>Alignment of the dimensions</u>: Align and group dimensions for neatness and easy understanding.
- <u>Center line used as an extension line</u>: For the circled and circular arcs, use the end of the centerline as the beginning of the extension lines.

- Dimension placement:
  - o Place dimensions near the features they are dimensioning.
  - o Do not place dimensions on the surface of the object.
  - o Avoid crossing extension lines.
  - o Place smaller dimensions closer to the object than the larger ones.
  - o Always place overall dimensions the farthest away from the object.
- Gap between the object and the extension line: There should be a noticeable gap between the object and the extension line to create a visual break. The visual effects can also be enhanced by using different colors for the dimensions.
- Line of symmetry: If a drawing is symmetrical at a certain axis (two sides are mirror images) then show the line of symmetry. It is enough to show the dimension for one side.

Figure 8-3

8.6. Dimension Styles

The appearance of dimensions can be controlled by changing various settings using the *Dimension Style Manager* dialog box or the *Properties* palette.

- The *Dimension Style Manager* dialog box can be launched using one of the following procedures.
  1. Panel method: (i) From the *Annotate* tab and the *Dimension* panel, click on the dialog box launcher (the small arrow on the lower right corner of the panel). (ii) From the *Home* tab, expand the *Annotation* panel, and select the *Dimension Style* tool.
  2. Command line method: Type "dimstyle," "Dimstyle," or "DIMSTYLE" on the command line and press the *Enter* key.

- The activation of the command opens the *Dimension Style Manager* dialog box, Figure 8-4. The dialog box provides the capability to create new styles, sets the current style, modifies existing styles, overrides the current style, and compares styles. This chapter discusses the capabilities to modify the current dimension style.

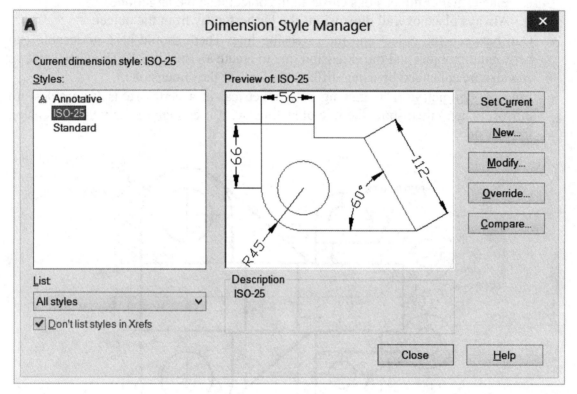

Figure 8-4

- Click on the *Modify* button (Figure 8-4) to modify an existing style. This opens the *Modify Dimension Style Manager* dialog box, Figure 8-5a. The *: Standard* means that the standard style is modified. Also, the *New Dimension Style* and *Override Current Style* dialog boxes provide these capabilities.

8.7.   Modify Dimension Style Dialog Box

The *Modify Dimension Style* dialog box allows for changes in lines (dimension and extension), symbol and arrows (arrowheads, center mark, jog dimension etc.), text (appearance, placement, and alignment), fit (placement of the dimension text and arrowheads), primary units (linear and angular, measurement, and zero suppression), and tolerance (format, alignment, and zero suppression).

8.7.1. Lines

The *Lines* tab (Figure 8-5a) sets the format and properties for the dimension and extension lines. The most commonly used features are shown in Figure 8-2a, Figure 8-2b, and Figure 8-5a. The effect of some of the commonly used features are shown in Figure 8-5b.

Figure 8-5a

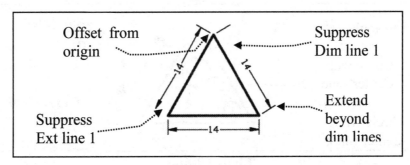

Figure 8-5b

8.7.2. Symbols and arrows

The *Symbols and Arrows* tab, Figure 8-6a, sets the format and size of the arrowhead, center marks, dimension break, arc length symbol, radius jog dimension, and linear jog dimension. The effect of some of the commonly used features are shown in Figure 8-6b.

Figure 8-6a

Figure 8-6b

8.7.3. Text

The selection of the *Text* tab (Figure 8-7a) sets the format, placement, alignment, and size of the dimension text. The effect of some of the commonly used features are shown in Figure 8-7b.

Figure 8-7a

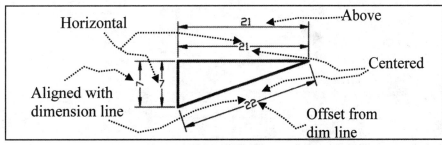

Figure 8-7b

8.7.4. Fit

The *Fit* tab controls the placement of the dimension text and arrowheads based on the space available between the extension lines, leader lines, and dimension lines.

8.7.5. Primary units

The *Primary Units* tab, Figure 8-8, sets the format and precision of the primary dimension units for both the linear and angular dimensions. Most of the fields are self-explanatory, except for the scale factor, which needs some explanation. The *Scale factor* is used to set a scale factor for the linear dimension measurements. It is recommended that the value of the *Scale factor* should not be changed from the default value of 1.00. If the *Scale factor* is changed from 1 to some number n, then every dimension is multiplied by n except the angular dimensions, rounding values, and the plus/minus tolerance values. For example, if the original dimension is 15 and the *Scale factor* is 2 then the dimension appears as 30.

Figure 8-8

8.7.6. Alternate units

The selection of the *Alternate Units* tab specifies the display of alternate units in dimension measurements and sets their format and precision.

8.7.7. Tolerance

The selection of the *Tolerances* tab controls the display and format of dimension text tolerances. Although, theoretically possible, it is economically unfeasible to manufacture products to the exact dimensions displayed on an engineering drawing. The cost of a part rapidly increases as an absolute correct size is approached. Hence, accuracy depends largely on the manufacturing process used and the care taken to manufacture a product. Since different companies make different parts of a system, it is very important that these parts should be interchangeable. A tolerance value shows the manufacturing department the maximum permissible variation from the basic dimension. Tolerance is discussed in detail in Chapter 9.

8.8.   Modify Dimension Style

A user can modify the dimension style using the dialog box or the properties palette.

8.8.1. Modify dimension style using the dialog box

If the user desired to change the settings for all the dimensions in the drawing then open the *Modify Dimension Style* dialog box. Using the functionality of the dialog box, change the dimension setting. For example, if *Suppress Dim line 1* option under the *Lines* tab is selected, then the first dimension line is suppressed from every dimension (both linear and angular dimensions).

8.8.2. Modify dimension style using the properties palette

If the user desired to change the settings for one (or more but not all) dimension then use the *Properties* palette, Figure 8-9; and perform the following steps.

- Select the desired dimension(s) by clicking with the left mouse button.
- Open the option panel by pressing the right button of the mouse.
- Click on the last option; this opens the *Properties* palette, Figure 8-9.
- The *Properties* palette has a panel for every tab in the *Modify Dimension Style* dialog box.
- On the *Properties* palette, select the desired panel.
- In Figure 8-9a under the *Primary Units* panel and *Dim units* command, the current option is *Decimal*. The user is changing it to the *Architectural* type unit. Modifying the desired option will only affect the selected dimension(s).
- In Figure 8-9b under the *Lines & Arrow* panel and *Dim line 1*, the current option is *on*. The user is changing it to the *off*. Modifying the desired option will only affect the selected dimension(s).
- In Figure 8-9c under the *Text* panel and *Text view direction*, the current option is *Left-to-Right*. The user can change it to the *Right-to-Left*. Modifying the desired option will only affect the selected dimension(s).

Figure 8-9a

Figure 8-9b

Figure 8-9c

8.9.   Dimensioning Techniques

This section describes basic technics of dimensioning. For example, how to dimension a horizontal or vertical line, sloping lines, angles, circles, etc.

8.9.1.   Linear dimensions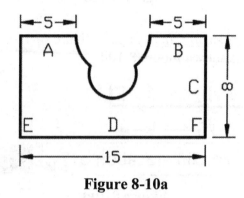

The *Linear* dimension command is used to create only horizontal and vertical dimensions. In Figure 8-10a, the dimension for the sides labeled as A, B, C, and D are the linear dimensions.

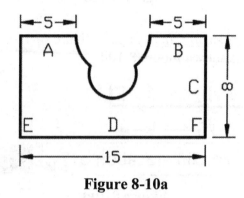

Figure 8-10a

Example: Add the linear dimension for the side A, B, C, and D, Figure 8-10a. The linear dimensions can be added using the following procedure.

- The *Linear* dimension is activated using one of the following methods.
  1. Panel method: The *Linear* dimension command can be activated from two panels. (i) From the *Home* tab, expand the *Annotation* panel, expand the *Linear* dropdown menu and click the *Linear* tool. (ii) From the *Annotate* tab and the *Dimension* panel, expand the *Dimension* dropdown menu and click the *Linear* tool.
  2. Command line method: Type "dimlinear," "Dimlinear," or "DIMLINEAR" on the command line and press the *Enter* key.

- The remainder of this section discusses the addition of linear dimension, text justification, text rotation, and space adjustment between multiple linear dimensions.

8.9.1.1.   Extension lines
- Linear dimensions can be added using extension lines as follows:

  o *Activate the command*: The activation of the command leads to the extension line specification prompt, Figure 8-10b.

Specify first extension line origin or <select object>:   164.0760   -112.7220

Figure 8-10b

o *Specify first extension line origin*, Figure 8-10a: Turn on the object snap with *Endpoints* option. Click on point *F* and a rubber band appears originating from point *F* and terminating at the cursor, Figure 8-10c.

Figure 8-10c

o *Specify second extension line origin* Figure 8-10c: Click on point *E*, the resulting prompt is shown Figure 8-10d.

Figure 8-10d

o *Specify the dimension line location*, Figure 8-10d: Locate the dimension line by moving the crosshairs, following the dimension placement rules. Press the left mouse button at the desired location, Figure 8-10e.
o Figure 8-10a: Similarly, add dimensions to sides A, B, and C.

Figure 8-10e

8.9.1.2.   Object selection

- Linear dimensions can be added by selecting the object to be dimensioned as follows:

  o *Activate the command*: The activation of the command leads to the extension line specification prompt, Figure 8-10b.
  o Press the *Enter* key, Figure 8-10f.
  o *Select object to dimension*, Figure 8-10f: Bring the cursor on the side D and press the left mouse button, Figure 8-10d

    ○ *Specify dimension line location*, Figure 8-10d: Locate the dimension line by moving the crosshairs, following the dimension placement rules. Press the left mouse button at the desired location.

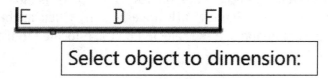

Figure 8-10f

8.9.1.3. Text relocation

Figure 8-11a shows a part of a drawing with several linear dimensions. The user can increase the readability by relocating the dimension's text as shown in Figure 8-11b.

Figure 8-11a

Figure 8-11b

- Justification commands are used as follows:
- The text can be relocated using three different methods as follows:
  1. Panel method: (i) Activate the justification command from the *Annotate* tab, and expanded *Dimension* panel, Figure 8-11c. (ii) Click on ⊢⊣, ⊢⊣, or ⊢⊣ tools for the left, center, or right justification commands, respectively. The figure shows the activation of the left justification. The activation of the command leads to the *Select dimension* prompt, Figure 8-11d. (iii) Click on the desired text. In the current example, click on 150. This exits the command and the selected text is relocated to the new location, Figure 8-11b.

Figure 8-11c

Figure 8-11d

2. Command line method: (i) Type "dimtedit," "Dimtedit," or "DIMTEDIT" on the command line and press the *Enter* key. (ii) The activation of the command leads to the *Select dimension* prompt, Figure 8-11d. (ii) Click on the desired text. In the current example, click on 150. The cursor is attached to the text and the prompt shown in Figure 8-11b appears. (iii) Click at the desired location. This exits the command and the selected text is relocated to the new location.

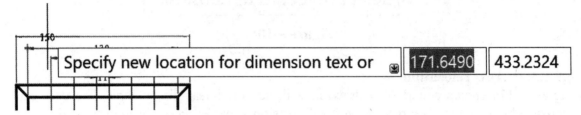

Figure 8-11e

3. Grip point method: (i) Click the desired dimension, 150 in the current example, and its grip points appear, Figure 8-11f. (ii) Click on the grip point on the text. The grip point's color is changed and the prompt shown in Figure 8-11f appears. (iii) Click at the desired location. This exits the command and the selected text is relocated to the new location.

Figure 8-11f

8.9.1.4. Space adjustment

Figure 8-12a shows a part of a drawing with unevenly spaced horizontal dimensions and the scattered vertical dimensions. The same drawing is shown in Figure 8-12b with evenly spaced horizontal dimensions and properly aligned vertical dimensions.

-   The user can convert Figure 8-12a into Figure 8-12b using the *Adjust Space* command as follows:
    1. Panel method: (i) Activate the *Adjust Space* command from the *Annotate* tab, and *Dimension* panel and click on the *Adjust Space* tool. The activation of the command leads to the prompt shown in Figure 8-12c.
    2. Command line method: (i) Type "dimspace," "Dimspace," or "DIMSPACE" on the command line and press the *Enter* key. The activation of the command leads to the prompt shown in Figure 8-12c.
    3. Grip point method: Exhaustive approach! Match the grip points manually, one dimension at a time.

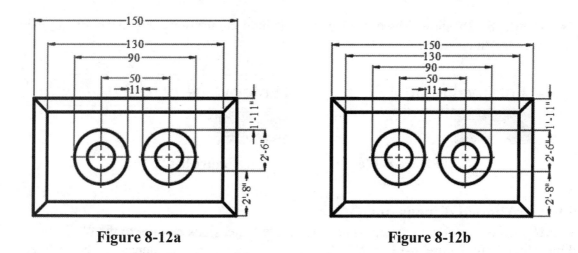

Figure 8-12a   **Figure 8-12b**

- *Select base dimension*: Click on the dimension 11, Figure 8-12c; and the prompt shown in Figure 8-12d appears.

Figure 8-12c

- *Select dimension to space*: Select the remaining horizontal dimensions as shown in Figure 8-12d. Press the *Enter* key and the prompt shown in Figure 8-12e appears.

Figure 8-12d

- *Enter value or*: Click on the *Auto* option. This exits the command and evenly spaces the horizontal dimensions. For the *Auto* option, the software automatically calculates the spacing and the spacing is equal to twice the text height. If desired, the user can specify the spacing.
- Repeat the above process for the vertical dimensions as follow. (i) Select 1'-11" dimension as the base dimension. (ii) In response to *Enter value or* prompt, type 0 as shown in Figure 8-12f.

- Figure 8-12b shows evenly spaced horizontal dimensions and properly aligned vertical dimensions.

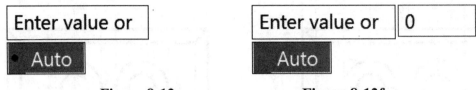

Figure 8-12e   **Figure 8-12f**

8.9.2. Aligned dimensions

The *Aligned* dimension command is used to create dimensions parallel to the object being dimensioned. In Figure 8-13, every dimension is an aligned dimension. Every linear dimension (dimensions 5, 10, and 23) is an aligned dimension. However, every aligned dimension (dimensions for the side dimensions for the sides AB, BC, and CD) is NOT a linear dimension.

Example: Add the dimension for the sides AB, BC, and CD, Figure 8-10g.

- The process of creating aligned dimensions is the same as the linear dimensions.
- The *Aligned* command is activated using one of the following procedures.
  1. Panel method: The *Aligned* dimension command can be activated from two panels. (i) From the *Annotate* tab and the *Dimension* panel, expand the *Dimension* dropdown menu and click the *Aligned* tool. (ii) From the *Home* tab, expand the *Annotation* panel, expand the *Linear* dropdown menu and click the *Aligned* tool.
  2. Command line method: Type "dimaligned," "Dimaligned" or "DIMALIGNED" on the command line and press the *Enter* key.

Figure 8-13

8.9.3. Angular dimensions

The *Angular* dimension command is used to create angular dimensions. The Figure 8-14 shows two angular dimensions for the path labeled as ABC; one of the angles is less than 180° and the other is greater than 180°. This section explains how to add the two angles.

- The *Angular* command is activated using one of the following procedures.

  1. Panel method: The *Angular* dimension command can be activated from two panels. (i) From the *Home* tab, expand the *Annotation* panel, expand the *Linear* dropdown menu and click the *Angular* tool. (ii) From the *Annotate* tab and the *Dimension* panel, expand the *Dimension* dropdown menu and click the *Angular* tool.
  2. Command line method: Type "dimangular," "Dimangular" or "DIMANGULAR" on the command line and press the *Enter* key.

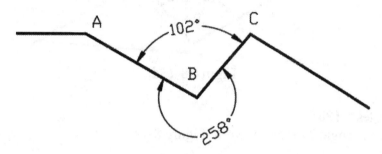

Figure 8-14

8.9.3.1.   Angles < 180°
Example: Add the angle 87° as shown in Figure 8-14.

- Activate the *Angular* command. The activation of the command leads to the line selection prompt, Figure 8-15a.

Select arc, circle, line, or <specify vertex>:

Figure 8-15a

- *Select arc, circle, line*: Click on the line AB, Figure 8-15b.

Figure 8-15b

- *Select second line*: Click on the line BC, Figure 8-15c.
- *Specify dimension line location*: Locate the dimension line by moving the crosshairs, following the dimension placement rules. Press the left mouse button at the desired location, Figure 8-15d.
- Figure 8-15d shows the angled dimensions added to the drawing.

Figure 8-15c

Figure 8-15d

8.9.3.2.   Angles > 180º

Example: Add the angle 273º as shown in Figure 8-14.

- Activate the *Angular* command. The activation of the command leads to the line selection prompt, Figure 8-16a.

- *Select arc, circle, line or <specify vertex>*: Press the *Enter* key and the prompt shown in Figure 8-1a appears. This option allows the specification of three points for an angular dimension.

Figure 8-16a

- Turn on the object snap with *Endpoint* option. Click at point B (the intersection of the AB and BC) and the prompt shown in Figure 8-16c appears.

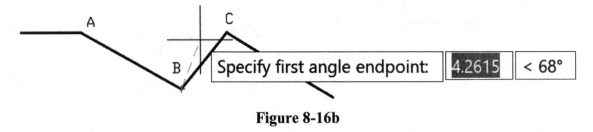

Figure 8-16b

- Click at point C (the endpoint of line BC) and the prompt shown in Figure 8-16c appears.
- Click at point A (the endpoint of line BA) and the prompt shown in Figure 8-16d appears.

Figure 8-16c

Figure 8-16d

- Finally click a point on the side that the angle is desired as shown in Figure 8-16e.

Figure 8-16e

8.9.4. Dimensioning radii

The *Radius* dimension command is used to create radius dimensions. Circular arcs less than 180° are dimensioned using the radius. Figure 4-17a shows four circular arcs less than 180° (notice the grip points). Figure 4-17b shows the arcs dimensions; all radial dimensions are preceded by the uppercase *R*. Notice, in the figure, the arc labelled as C extends itself to show the radial dimensions.

Figure 8-17a   **Figure 8-17b**

Example: Add the dimension for the arc A, B, C, and D as shown in Figure 8-17a.

- The *Radius* command is activated using one of the following procedures.
  1. Panel method: The *Radius* dimension command can be activated from two panels. (i) From the *Home* tab, expand the *Annotation* panel, expand the *Linear* dropdown menu and click the *Radius* tool. (ii) From the *Annotate* tab and the *Dimension* panel, expand the *Dimension* dropdown menu and click the *Radius* tool.
  2. Command line method: Type "dimradius," "Dimradius" or "DIMRADIUS" on the command line and press the *Enter* key.

- The activation of the command leads to the arc/circle selection prompt, Figure 8-17c.

Select arc or circle:

Figure 8-17c

- *Select arc or circle*: Click on the arc A.
- *Specify dimension line location*, Figure 8-17d: Locate the dimension line by moving the crosshairs, following the dimension placement rules. Press the left mouse button at the desired location.
- Position the radius dimension so that the leader line is neither horizontal nor vertical, Figure 8-17b.
- The radius tool automatically includes the center mark or centerline based on the option selected in the *Dimension Style* dialog box → *Modify Dimension Style* dialog box → *Arrow and Symbol* tab.

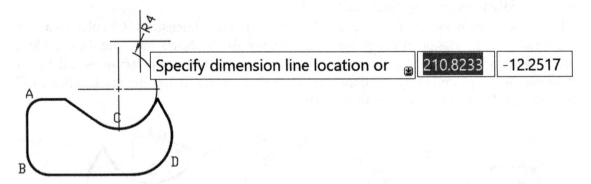

Figure 8-17d

8.9.5. Dimensioning circles

The *Diameter* dimension command is used to create diameter dimensions. The circles, semicircles, or arcs greater than 180 degrees are dimensioned using the diameter, Figure 8-18b. All the diameter dimensions are preceded by the symbol ϕ. The symbol ϕ can be created by typing %%c in a text box.

Example: Draw a circle and circular arcs, Figure 8-18a; and add the dimension, Figure 8-18b. In the figures, the arc A is greater than 180°, and B is a semicircle (notice the grip points).

Figure 8-18a

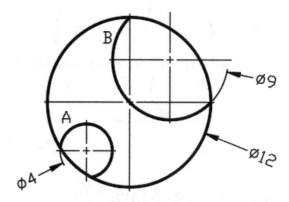

Figure 8-18b

- The *Diameter* command is activated using one of the following procedures.
  1. Panel method: The *Linear* dimension command can be activated from two panels. (i) From the *Home* tab, expand the *Annotation* panel, expand the *Linear* dropdown menu and click the *Diameter* tool. (ii) From the *Annotate* tab and the *Dimension* panel, expand the *Dimension* dropdown menu and click the *Diameter* tool.
  2. Command line method: Type "dimdiameter," "Dimdiameter" or "DIMMETER" on the command line and press the *Enter* key.

- The activation of the command leads to the arc/circle selection prompt, Figure 8-18b.

Select arc or circle:

Figure 8-18c

- *Select arc or circle*: Click on arc B, Figure 8-18d.
- *Specify dimension line location*: Locate the dimension line by moving the crosshairs, following the dimension placement rules. Press the left mouse button at the desired location, Figure 8-18b.
- Position the diameter dimension so that the leader line is neither horizontal nor vertical.
- Similarly add dimensions to the arc A and the circle, Figure 8-18b.
- The diameter tool automatically includes the center mark. However, the user can replace the center mark with the centerline based on the option selected in the *Dimension Style* dialog box → *Modify Dimension Style* dialog box → *Arrow and Symbol* tab.

Figure 8-18d

8.10. Center Mark

The *Center mark* command is used to draw a center mark (Figure 8-19a) or center line (Figure 8-19b) at the center of a circle or circular arc. The *Center Mark* command is activated either by the command line method or the panel method.

Figure 8-19a   **Figure 8-19b**

8.10.1. Command line method

The advantages of the command line method are that (i) it allows the user to create both the center mark and center line and (ii) the user can change the diameter of the circle or circular arc after adding the centerlines (in Figure 8-19c, the diameter of the circle labeled as A is reduced). However, the drawback of this method is that the user is required to activate the command for each circle or circular arc in the drawing. For example, for Figure 8-19c, the user is required to activate the command five times.

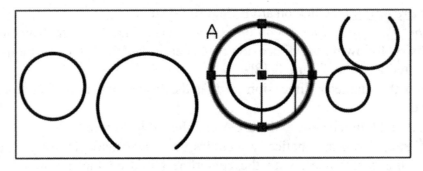

Figure 8-19c

In the command line method, the *Center Mark* command is activated by typing "dimcenter," "Dimcenter" or "DIMCENTER" on the command line and pressing the *Enter* key.

- The activation of the command leads to the prompt for the arc or circle selection, Figure 8-19d.

Select arc or circle:

Figure 8-19d

- Click at the circumference of the circle and the center mark is drawn at the center of the circle, Figure 8-19a.
- However, if the user wants to display the center line, Figure 8-19b, then perform the following steps. (i) Delete the center mark from the circle. (ii) Open the *Dimension Style Manager* dialog box (Section 8.6). (iii) Click on the *Modify* button to open *Modify Dimension Style* dialog box (Section 8.7.2), Figure 8-19e. (iv) Click on the *Symbols and Arrow* tab. (v) Under the *Center marks* panel, select the *Line* option; press the *OK* button. (vi) Activate the *Center marks* command and click at the circumference of the circle. The center line is drawn at the center of the circle, Figure 8-19b. (vii) If the center line does not appear as shown in Figure 8-19b, then increase/decrease the number field in the *Center marks* window.

Figure 8-19e

8.10.2. Panel method

The advantage of the panel method is that the user can add centerlines to multiple circles or circular arcs in a single activation of the command. For example, for Figure 8-19c the user is required to activate the command only once. However, the drawbacks of this method are that (i) it allows the user to create only the center line and (ii) the user cannot change the diameter of the circle or circular arc after adding the centerlines.

In the panel method, the *Center Mark* command is activated as follow: from the *Annotate* tab and the *Centerlines* panel click the *Center Mark* tool, Figure 8-20a.

- The activation of the command leads to the prompt for the arc or circle selection, Figure 8-20b.

Figure 8-20a

Select circle or arc to add centermark:

Figure 8-20b

- Click at the boundary of the desired circle or circular arc.
- To exit the command, press either the *Esc* key or the *Enter* key on the keyboard.

8.11. Leader Lines

The *Leader* command is used to create a line that connects an annotation to a feature. A leader line has three parts: (i) an arrowhead at the starting end of the line, (ii) a line, and (iii) a multiline text near the other end of the line, Figure 8-21a.

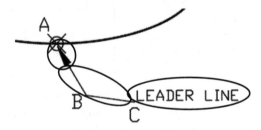

Figure 8-21a

The *Leader* command is activated using one of the following procedures. However, the prompts by the two methods are slightly different.
1. Panel method: From the *Home* tab and *Annotation* panel click the *Leader* tool.
2. Command line method: Type "qleader," "Qleader" or "QLEADER" on the command line and press the *Enter* key.

- The activation of the command by the command line method leads to the prompt shown in Figure 8-21b.
- *Specify first leader point, or*, Figure 8-21b: Click on the desired location. The arrowhead is created at the first point. This example creates a leader to point *A*, therefore, click at point *A*.

Figure 8-21b

- *Specify next point*, Figure 8-21c: This point represents the first limb of the arrow in the current example, line AB. Click in the vicinity of point B, Figure 8-21c. The prompt shown in Figure 8-21d appears.

Figure 8-21c

- *Specify next point*, Figure 8-21d: This point represents the second limb of the arrow in the current example, line BC. Click in the vicinity of point C, Figure 8-21d. The prompt shown in Figure 8-21e appears.

Figure 8-21d

- *Specify text width*, Figure 8-21e: Specify the width. In the current example, use the default value and press the *Enter* Key. The prompt shown in Figure 8-21f appears.
- *Enter first line of annotation text*, Figure 8-21f: Type the multiline text and press the *Enter* key twice. The text can be edited just like multiline text. The leader is shown in Figure 8-21g.
- Figure 8-21g also shows the grip point. Click at a grip point, keep pressing the left button, and move the cursor. Note the behavior of the various grip points.

Figure 8-21e

Figure 8-21f

Figure 8-21g

8.11.1. Arrow

The user can draw an arrow (without the text) using the *Leader* command as follows.

- Activate the *Leader* command.
- *Specify first leader point*, Figure 8-21b: The arrowhead is created at the first point. Click on the desired location. This example creates a leader to point *A*, therefore, click at point *A*.
- *Specify next point*, Figure 8-21c: This point represents the first limb of the arrow in the current example, line AB. Click in the vicinity of point B, Figure 8-21c. The prompt shown in Figure 8-21d appears.
- **Press the *Esc* key on the keyboard to exit the *Leader* command without writing the text.**

8.11.2. Arrowhead size

The arrowhead size depends on the length of the segment AB and the lineweight of the arrow. This section explains the process to adjust the head size if it is too big/small or not visible.

Head size too big/small, Figure 8-22a:
- Click on the arrow and its grip points appear.
- Right click and select the *Properties* option from the option list to open the *Properties* palette.
- From the *Lines & Arrows* tab, click on the *Arrow size* and decrease/increase the number such that the arrowhead appears to be 3mm on the drawing.

Figure 8-22a

Arrow without head:
- Zoom in at the starting end of the qleader.
- Click on the arrow and its grip points appear.
- Right click and select the *Properties* option from the option list to open the *Properties* palette.
- From the *Lines & Arrows* tab, click on the *Arrow size*.
- If the arrowhead is not displayed, then change the *Arrow size* using one of the following criteria such that the arrowhead appears to be 3mm on the drawing.
  - If the *Arrow size* is a **large** number then **decrease** the number, Figure 8-22b.
  - If the *Arrow size* is a **small** number then **increase** the number, Figure 8-22c.

                    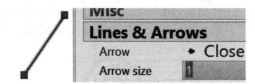

      Figure 8-22b   **Figure 8-22c**

8.12.   Smart Dimensions

Consider a simple object shown in Figure 8-23a. In order to dimension the object, the user needs to activate **eight** dimension commands (2*Angular* + 2*Aligned* + 2*Circle* + *Linear* + *Radius*). The user productivity can be greatly enhanced by using the smart dimensioning technique. In this technique, the user is required to activate only **ONE** command to add the above mentioned dimensions as follow: (i) hover over the object; (ii) the software recognizes the geometry and displays the appropriate dimension. The remainder of this section describes the smart dimensioning technique.

- The smart dimensions command is activated using one of the following procedures.
  1. Panel method: From the *Annotate* tab and the *Dimension* panel, click the *Dimension* tool.
  2. Command line method: Type "dim," "Dim" or "DIM" on the command line and press the *Enter* key.

Figure 8-23a

- The user must turn off the ORTHO option by clicking ⬛ button on the status bar.
- Activate the *Dimension* command; the resulting prompt is shown in Figure 8-23b.

Select objects or specify first extension line origin or ⬇ 68.8548 -26.8252

Figure 8-23b

- Bring the cursor on top of the object to be dimensioned and the software displays the appropriate dimensions as shown in Figure 8-23c (align), Figure 8-23d (linear), Figure 8-23e (circular), and Figure 8-23f (radial) dimensions. Click at the desired location to place the dimension; and the prompt is changed to the prompt shown in Figure 8-23b. Continue the dimensioning process.

Figure 8-23c

Select line to specify extension lines origin:

Figure 8-23d

Figure 8-23e

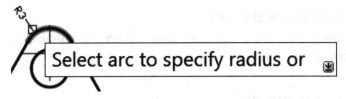

Figure 8-23f

- The angular dimension can be added as follow. (i) Bring the cursor on one of the lines of the angle to be dimensioned, Figure 8-24a. (ii) Click on the line, Figure 8-24b. (iii) Bring the cursor on the second line of the angle to be dimensioned, Figure 8-24c; angles are displayed. (iv) Click on the line, Figure 8-24d. (v) Click at the desired location to place the angle, and the prompt is changed to the prompt shown in Figure 8-23b. Continue the dimensioning process.

Figure 8-24a

Figure 8-24b

Figure 8-24c

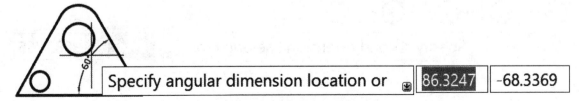

Figure 8-24d

8.13.   Types of Dimensions

This section describes different types of dimensions (continues, baseline, ordinate, tabular, and combine dimensions) used in a drawing.

8.13.1. Continue dimension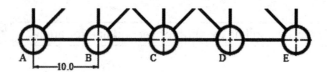

The *Continue* dimension is a type of linear dimension that uses the second extension line's origin (of a selected dimension) as the first extension line's origin for the next dimension, Figure 8-25c. This type of dimensioning is also known as the *Chains of dimension*. This technique breaks one long dimension into shorter segments that add up to the total measurement. However, the continue dimension should only be used if the functionality of the object is not affected by the accumulation of the error.

- The *Continue* dimensions command is activated using one of the following procedures.
    1. Panel method: From the *Annotate* tab and the *Dimension* panel, expand the *Continue* dropdown menu and click the *Continue* tool.
    2. Command line method: Type "dimcontinue," "Dimcontinue" or "DIMCONTINUE" on the command line and press the *Enter* key.

- In Figure 8-25c, the object is dimensioned using the continue dimensioning technique. The *Continue* dimensions can be added as follows.
    1. Create a linear dimension for the first feature. In Figure 8-25a, the dimension between the circles labeled as A and B is a linear dimension.

Figure 8-25a

2. Activate the *Continue* command; the resulting prompt is shown in Figure 8-25b. Bring the cursor on the second extension line of the linear dimension and it is highlighted.
3. Now click on the second extension line for the origin of the second dimension, Figure 8-25b. That is, for the second extension line, click at the center of the circle C.

Figure 8-25b

4. Since circles D and E can be dimensioned with respect to the dimension of circles A and B, repeat step #3 for the circles D and E, Figure 8-25c.
5. Press the *Esc* key to exit the command.
6. The location of the text and arrowheads can be changed using the *Fit* tab of the *Modify Dimension Style* dialog box.
7. The current example is based on the linear dimension. However, the continue dimensions option can be used with the aligned and angular (Figure 8-25d) dimensions, too.

Figure 8-25c

Figure 8-25d

8.13.2. Baseline dimensions

The *Baseline* dimension is a dimensioning technique in which multiple dimensions are measured from the same baseline or datum; that is, several dimensions originate from one extension line as shown in Figure 8-26b and Figure 8-26c. This dimensioning technique is also called *parallel dimensions* and *datum dimensions*. The baseline dimensions are useful because they help eliminate error build up associated with each dimension. However, it requires a large area on the drawing.

- The *Baseline* dimensions command is activated using one of the following procedures.
  1. Panel method: From the *Annotate* tab and the *Dimension* panel, expand the *Continue* dropdown menu and click the *Baseline* tool.
  2. Command line method: Type "dimbaseline," "Dimbaseline" or "DIMBASELINE" on the command line and press the *Enter* key.

- In Figure 8-26b and Figure 8-26c, the object is dimensioned using the baseline dimensioning technique. The *Baseline* dimensions can be added as follows.

    1. Create a linear dimension for the first feature. In Figure 8-26a, the dimension between the circles labeled as A and B is a linear dimension.
    2. Activate the *Baseline* command; the resulting prompt is shown in Figure 8-19a.

Figure 8-26a

    3. Now click at the center of circle C; this causes the dimension from the datum line to be created.
    4. Repeat step #3 for circles D and E, Figure 8-26b.
    5. Press the *Esc* key to exit the command.

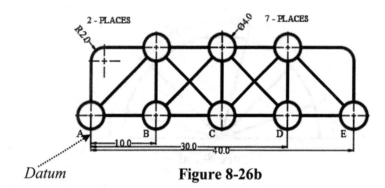

Figure 8-26b

- The appearance of the baseline dimension can be enhanced using one of the following two methods.
- Figure 8-26b, perform the following procedure:
- To enhance the appearance of Figure 8-26b, perform the following procedure:
    1. Use the *Adjust space* command.
    2. Dialog box method.
        a. Open the *Dimension Style Manager* and *Modify Dimension Style* dialog boxes.
        b. Select the *Text* tab under the *Text Alignment* panel and choose the *Aligned with dimension line* option.
        c. Select the *Lines* tab under the *Dimension lines* panel and increase the *Baselines spacing*.
        d. Click the *OK* and *Close* buttons to close the two dialog boxes, respectively.
        e. This changes the alignment of every dimension in the drawing. However, it does not update the baseline spacing.
        f. To reflect the change in the baseline spacing, delete the baseline dimensions and re-dimension the object.

- Figure 8-26c shows the updated version.
- Also, the vertical baseline dimensions are added, Figure 8-26c

Figure 8-26c

- The current example is based on linear dimension. However, the baseline dimensions can be used with the aligned and angular (Figure 8-26d) dimensions, too.

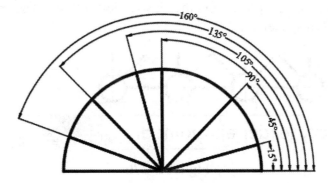

Figure 8-26d

8.13.3. Ordinate dimensions

The *Ordinate* dimensions are based on the X, Y coordinates; and the ordinates are calculated from the user defined origin. The technique is useful when dimensioning an object with many holes. Instead of using extension and dimension lines and arrowheads, the ordinate dimensioning includes horizontal and vertical leader lines originating directly from the features of the object.

Since the ordinates are based on the origin, it is important that the origin of the coordinate system is located on the object, as shown in Figure 8-27c. This can be achieved in two ways: (i) either start the drawing from the origin (the center of the lower left circle at the origin of WCS) or (ii) move the drawing to origin (the center of the lower left circle at the origin).

- The *Ordinate* dimensions command is activated using one of the following procedures.
  1. Panel method: (ii) From the *Home* tab, expand the *Annotation* panel and click the *Ordinate* tool.
  2. Command line method: Type "dimordinate," "Dimordinate" or "DIMORDINATE" on the command line and press the *Enter* key.

- In Figure 8-27c, the object is dimensioned using the ordinate dimensioning technique. The *Ordinate* dimensions can be added as follows.
  1. Relocate the origin (if necessary).
  2. Turn the ORTHO command *On* by clicking the ⬚ button on the status bar.
  3. Activate the *Ordinate* command. The prompt is shown in Figure 8-27a.

Figure 8-27a

4. Select the center point for the lower left circle. The prompt shown in Figure 8-27b appears.

Figure 8-27b

5. Specify the endpoint for the leader line by moving parallel to the y- or x-axis for the x- or y-ordinate, respectively.
6. Repeat steps #4 - #6 for every hole in the drawing and any other feature in the drawing.
7. The dimensioned drawing is shown in Figure 8-27c.

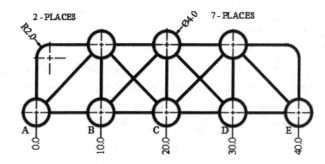

Figure 8-27c

8.13.4. Tabular dimensions

The tabular dimension stores the *coordinate* dimensions in a table. The tabular or *coordinate* dimensions are useful when dimensioning an object that has many holes. The coordinate dimension uses a chart (or a table), Figure 8-28a and Figure 8-28b. Holes are labeled by letters and numbers; holes of the same diameter are labeled with the same letters.

The coordinate dimension can be added as follows:

- Define X and Y-axis as baselines.
- Label the circles (or holes).
- Create a table, Figure 8-28b.
- Populate the table using the coordinates for the centerlines of the circles.
- The diameter symbol is created by typing %%c in the text box.

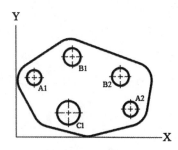

COORDINATE TABLE FOR HOLES			
HOLE	X-COORD	Y-COORD	Ø
A1	3.2100	10.2100	2
A2	21.1200	4.8000	2
B1	9.9400	13.7600	3
B2	18.5300	10.3700	3
C1	9.2800	4.1400	4

Figure 8-28a   **Figure 8-28b**

8.13.5. Combined dimensions

A combined dimension uses the combination of the dimensioning techniques discussed in the previous sections.

8.14.   Quick Dimensions ⊞

The *Quick* dimension command is useful to create series of dimensions in single step.

- The *Quick* dimensions command is activated using one of the following procedures.
    1. Panel method: (ii) From the *Home* tab, expand the *Annotation* panel and click the *Quick* tool.
    2. Command line method: Type "qdim," "Qdim" or "QDIM" on the command line and press the *Enter* key.

- Activation of the *Quick* dimensions command leads to the prompt shown in Figure 8-29a.

> Select geometry to dimension:

Figure 8-29a

- *Select geometry to dimension,* Figure 8-29a: Select the objects to be dimensioned. In the current example, select the circles and press the *Enter* Key. The prompt shown in Figure 8-29b appears.
- *Specify dimension line position, or,* Figure 8-29b: Press the down arrow and display the available options. The default option is the baseline dimensions. Select the desired option. This closes the option list and the prompt does not change.
- *Specify dimension line position, or,* Figure 8-29b: Click for the dimension location. This exits the command and the selected type dimensions appear.
- If necessary, adjust the dimension spacing and text and arrow size.

Figure 8-29b

8.15.   Dimensioning Fillets and Rounds

Fillets and rounds may be dimensioned individually or by a note. Figure 8-30 shows different methods of dimensioning fillets and rounds.

Figure 8-30a   **Figure 8-30b**   **Figure 8-30c**

Figure 8-30d

Figure 8-30e

8.16. Centerline

The centerlines are used to indicate the center of an individual component or the entire object. A centerline has two parts: the line and its label, Figures 8-31. A centerline can be drawn as follows.

- _For the centerline_: (i) Load linetype _Center_, (ii) either select linetype _Center_ and then draw a line in the center or draw a line and then change its type to _Center_. The user may need to change the linetype scale (from the _Properties_ palette).
- _For the centerline symbol_: (i) Activate the _Text_ command, (ii) select the font "gdt", and (iii) type lower case q. The center line symbol (℄) is created.

Figure 8-31

8.17. Line of Symmetry

The line of symmetry indicates that the object is a mirror image on either side of the line of symmetry. The advantage of the line of symmetry is that it reduces the time to draw the object; only draw the repeating part of the object and then use the mirror command to complete the object, Figure 8-32a, Figure 8-32b, Figure 8-32c, and Figure 8-32d.

Figure 8-32a

Figure 8-32b

Figure 8-32c   **Figure 8-32d**

The line of symmetry can be shown in two ways.

- <u>Method #1</u>: Draw two parallel lines perpendicular to the line passing through the axis of symmetry, Figures 8-33a.
- <u>*Method #2*</u>: Write a note OBJECT IS SYMMETRICAL ABOUT THIS AXIS pointing to the line passing through the axis of symmetry, Figures 8-33b.

Figure 8-33a   **Figure 8-33b**

<u>**Notes:**</u>

9.   Tolerance

9.1.   Learning Objectives

After completing this chapter, you will demonstrate competency in the following areas:

- Basics of tolerance
- Placement of the tolerance text
- Different types of tolerance's format
- Selection of a tolerance
- Art of creating and reading dimensions appended with tolerances

9.2.   Introduction

A dimension describes the size and location of features of an object; therefore, dimensions are given in the form of distance, angle, and/or notes irrespective of the units used in the drawing. Although theoretically possible, it is economically unfeasible to manufacture products to the exact numbers displayed on an engineering drawing. The cost of a part rapidly increases as an absolute correct size is approached. Hence, accuracy depends largely on the manufacturing process used and the care taken to manufacture a product. Since different companies make different parts of a model, it is very important that these parts should be interchangeable. A tolerance value shows the manufacturing department the maximum permissible variation from the basic dimension. The size and location of a tolerance depends on the design objective of the model, how it is manufactured, how it is inspected, and how it is used.

In AutoCAD, a draftsman can add tolerance to a dimension using the *Tolerance* tab from the *Modify Dimension Style* dialog box, Figure 9-1.

Figure 9-1

9.3.   Terminology

Use Figure 9-2 with the following definitions.

- *Basic dimension*: The basic dimension is the theoretical dimension of an object.
- *Actual dimension*: The actual dimension is the measured size of the finished product.
- *Allowance*: The allowance is the minimum clearance or maximum interference between parts.
- *Tolerance*: The tolerance is the total amount by which a given dimension may vary, known as plus-minus or limits (the difference between the maximum and minimum acceptable sizes).
- *Tolerance range*: The tolerance range is the difference between the maximum and minimum allowable sizes of the feature, and is given as

  Tolerance range = maximum allowable size - minimum allowable size

Figure 9-2

9.4.   Tolerance Methods

There are two methods to include tolerance as a part of the dimension: plus-minus, and limits tolerance.

9.4.1. Plus-minus method

The plus-minus tolerance defines the range for manufacturing and is shown in Figure 9-3a. In the plus-minus tolerance representation, the plus tolerance is always on the top. If the dimensions of the finished product are within the specified tolerance range then it is correct (ok); otherwise, it is either discarded or fixed. The plus-minus tolerance is further subdivided as unilateral and bilateral.

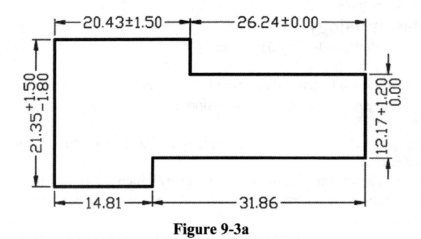

Figure 9-3a

9.4.1.1. Unilateral

When the dimension can vary only in one direction from the basic dimension, either larger or smaller, then the tolerance is known as a unilateral (known as *Deviation* in AutoCAD, Figure 9-1). That is, the tolerance is either plus (Figure 9-3b) or minus (Figure 9-3c) but not both.

Figure 9-3b   **Figure 9-3c**

9.4.1.2. Bilateral

When the dimension can vary in both directions from the basic dimension (larger and smaller), then the tolerance is known as a bilateral. The tolerance in both directions can have the same value (known as *Symmetrical* in AutoCAD, Figure 9-1 and Figure 9-3d) or different (known as *Deviation* in AutoCAD, Figure 9-1 and Figure 9-3e).

9.4.1.3. Tolerance expression

The dimension and tolerance values are written differently for inch and millimeter dimension values Figure 9-4.

9.4.1.4. Unilateral values

- *Millimeter values*: Specify zero limit with one zero only.
- *Inch values*: The zero limits must include the same number of decimal places as given for the dimension.
- *Angular values*: A single "0" can be used for zero limits.

9.4.1.5. Bilateral values

- *Millimeter values*: The dimension values and tolerance values may have different precisions.
- *Inch values*: The dimension values and tolerance values must have the same precisions.
- *Angular values*: The dimension values and tolerance values must have the same precisions.

Figure 9-3d

Figure 9-3e

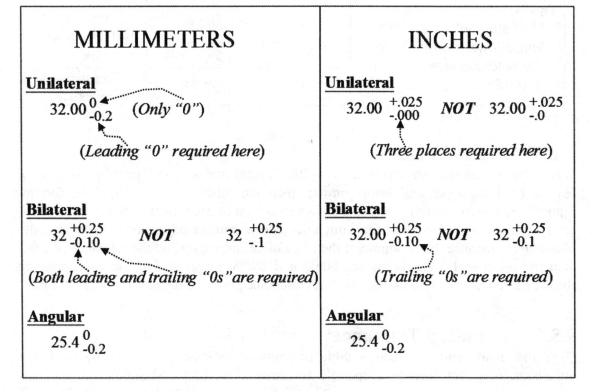

Figure 9-4

9.4.1.6.   Usage of Plus-minus tolerance

In Table #1 the dimension is in millimeters. Consider a basic dimension (Bd) of 60 with the tolerance values of *+0.25* and *-0.12*. The maximum and minimum allowable sizes and the tolerance range can be calculated as follows:

Maximum allowable size (Mx): 60 + 0.25 = 60.25
Minimum allowable size (Mn): 60 – 0.12 = 59.88
Tolerance range (Tr):
    60.25 – 59.88 = 0.37 OR 0.25 - (-0.12) = 0.25 + 0.12 = 0.37

After the object is manufactured and inspected, if *Mn <= Bd <= Mx* then the object is *OK* (that is, it is accepted), otherwise it is rejected, Table #1. Objects larger than the *Mx* can be reworked to fit the acceptable size; and the objects smaller than the *Mn* are rejected.

Table #1

Given (mm)
+0.25
60
-0.12
 	
That is:
  Max. allowable size = 60.25
  Min. allowable size = 59.88
  Tolerance range =
    (60.25 – 59.88) = 0.37
	Object	Measured Size (mm)	Acceptable

	1	60.160	OK
	2	60.020	OK
	3	60.253	Too long (can be fixed)
	4	59.920	OK
	5	59.79	Too short (Rejected)

9.4.2.   Limits tolerance

When the dimensions are represented by the largest and smallest possible sizes of a feature (that is, upper and lower limits), then the tolerance is in the *limit* format, Figure 9-5. The two limiting values are stacked on top of each other with the larger limit always on the top. Generally, the limit tolerance is considered easier to read than the plus-minus tolerance. For example, if the basic dimension is 60 and the tolerance is ± 0.2 then the upper and lower limits are 60.02 and 59.98, respectively. The final distance should lie between the two limits. The limit tolerance gives the range for manufacturing.

9.5.   Standard Tolerance

Generally, manufacturers create a table of standard tolerances that can be used if a dimension does not include a specific tolerance. Figure 9-6 shows some standard tolerances. If the dimension is given as *60.000*, then the implied tolerance is *0.005* and if the dimension is given as *60.0*, then the implied tolerance is *0.1*.

Figure 9-5

x ± 1

.x ± .1

.xx ± .01

.xxx ± .005

x° ± 1°

.x ° ± .1°

Figure 9-6

9.6.   Double Dimensioning

If the dimension of a feature is given twice than it is called a double dimensioning. In Figure 9-7a, the lower edge is dimensioned twice. (i) The overall length is given as 34. (ii) The overall length can also be calculated from the dimensions on the top (5 + 5 + 12 + 12 = 34).

Figure 9-7a

9.6.1.   Double dimensioning: an error

In technical drawings, a double dimension is an error. Mathematically the two dimensions (34 and 5 + 5 + 12 + 12) are equal, Figure 9-7a. On the other hand, in technical drawings these dimensions are not equal when tolerance is applied. Assume the tolerance is "1" then

Sum of top dimensions = (5+1) + (5+1) + (12+1) + (12+1) = 38
Bottom dimension = (34+1) = 35

9.6.2. Solution #1

One possible solution to the double dimensioning problem is to make one of the top dimensions a floating dimension; that is, do not provide its dimension, Figure 9-7b. Instead of providing "12" for one side, called A in the figure, allow that side to have floating dimension; it absorbs the cumulated tolerance. In this case, A is equal to $(34 + 1)$ $- (5 + 1) - (5 + 1) - (12 + 1) = 10$ (the assumption is that every side has the maximum error).

9.6.3. Solution #2

A different possible solution is to use a reference dimension, Figure 9-7c. Keep the dimension "12" and change the overall dimension to a reference dimension by enclosing it in parentheses, Figure 9-7c. In this case, the top three dimensions are used for manufacturing and inspecting the object. The reference dimension is used only for the mathematical convenience.

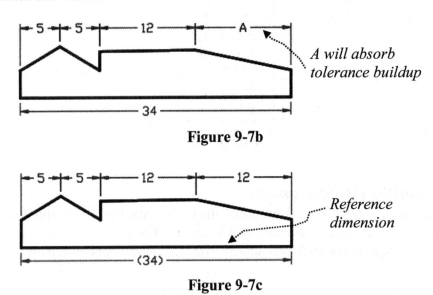

Figure 9-7b

Figure 9-7c

9.7. Chain and Baseline Dimension

The chain dimension relates the dimension of one feature to the next feature and the baseline dimension relates all features to a single baseline or datum.

- The drawback of the chain dimension is that it accumulates tolerance. The tolerance buildup can be eliminated by using floating dimension (Figure 9-7b), reference dimension (Figure 9-7c) or baseline dimension (Figure 9-7d).
- If the distance between individual features is more important, then use the chain dimension because the error between the two consecutive features is the least. If the distance of a feature from the baseline is more important, then use baseline dimension.

Figure 9-7d

9.8. Tolerance Study

The tolerance study is the process of analyzing the effects of tolerances of different features on each other and on the object. In Figure 9-8 the incline distance AB is not dimensioned. Its length depends on the tolerances of horizontal distances AE and CD and the vertical distance BC and DE. Let AB_x and AB_y equal the horizontal and vertical components of AB, respectively. The maximum and minimum length of AB_x and AB_y can be calculated as shown in Table #2.

Table #2

Object	Maximum value	Minimum Value
AB_x	= Max AE – Min CD = (34+1.50) – (8-1.31) = 28.81	= Min AE – Max CD = (34-1.10) – (8+0.85) = 24.05
AB_y	= Max BC + Max DE = (8.95) + (10+1.50) = 20.45	= Min BC + Min DE = (6.50) + (10-1.5) = 15

Figure 9-8

9.9.   Tolerance in AutoCAD

The appearance of tolerance can be controlled by changing the settings in *Dimension Style Manager* and *Modify Dimension Style* dialog boxes or the *Properties* palette.

- The *Dimension Style Manager* dialog box can be launched using one of the following procedures.

  1. Panel method: (ii) From the *Home* tab, expand the *Annotation* panel, and select the *Dimension Style* tool. (ii) From the *Annotate* tab and the *Dimension* panel, click on the dialog box launcher (the small arrow on the lower right corner of the panel).
  2. Command line method: Type "dimstyle," "Dimstyle" or "DIMSTYLE" on the command line and press the *Enter* key.

- The activation of the command opens the *Dimension Style Manager* dialog box, Figure 9-9a. The dialog box provides the capability to create new styles, sets the current style, modifies existing styles, overrides the current style, and compares styles. This chapter discusses the capabilities to modify the current dimension style.
- Click on the *Modify* button to modify an existing style. This opens the *Modify Dimension Style Manager* dialog box, Figure 9-9b. The *: Standard* means that the standard style will be modified. Also, the *New Dimension Style* and *Override Current Style* dialog boxes provide these capabilities.

Figure 9-9a

Figure 9-9b

9.9.1. Tolerance tab

This section explains the AutoCAD capabilities to add or modify the tolerance of a dimension using the *Tolerance* tab of the *Dimension Style Manager* dialog box, Figure 9-9b.

9.9.1.1. Tolerance format

The *Tolerance format* panel sets the format of the tolerance and its members are discussed below.

- *Upper value*: The *Upper value* option sets the maximum or upper bound to the tolerance value, Figure 9-9b.
- *Lower value*: The *Lower value* option sets the minimum or lower bound to the tolerance value, Figure 9-9b.
- *Method*: Press the down arrow and expand the *Method* list, Figure 9-9b. The *Method* list allows the selection of the method to calculate and represent the tolerance. AutoCAD provides five different options, Figure 9-10a.

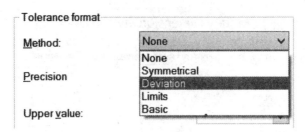

Figure 9-10a

1. *None*: The *None* option indicates that the tolerance is not added to the dimension, Figure 9-10a and Figure 9-10b.
2. *Symmetrical*: The *Symmetrical* option adds a bilateral (symmetrical) tolerance to the dimension measurement, Figure 9-10a and Figure 9-10b. A plus-minus sign appears automatically. For this option, specify the tolerance value in the *Upper value* box: either type the number and press the *Enter* key or use up/down arrow to increase/decrease the value; the *Lower value* box is deactivated.
3. *Deviation*: The *Deviation* option adds a bilateral (asymmetrical) and unilateral tolerances to the dimension measurement, Figure 9-10a and Figure 9-10b. For this option, specify the tolerance value in the *Upper* and *Lower value* boxes: either type the numbers and press the *Enter* key or use the up/down arrow to increase/decrease the values. Do not type the plus-minus signs in the *Upper* and *Lower value* boxes, the software adds these signs automatically. **Note**: To create unilateral tolerances type *0* in the *Upper* or *Lower value* box.
4. *Limits*: The *Limits* option creates a limit dimension and displays a maximum and a minimum value, Figure 9-10a and Figure 9-10b; the maximum value is on top of the lower value. The maximum value is the dimension value plus the value entered in the *Upper value* box, and the minimum value is the dimension value minus the value entered in *Lower value* box.
5. *Basic*: The *Basic* option creates a basic dimension, which displays a box around the dimension, Figure 9-10a and Figure 9-10b.

Figure 9-10b

- *Precision*: This option sets the number of decimal places in the tolerance value.
- *Vertical position*: The *Vertical position*'s list allows the selection of the text justification for symmetrical and deviation tolerances. AutoCAD provides three different options, Figure 9-10c.

Figure 9-10c

1. *Top*: The *Top* option aligns the tolerance text with the top of the main dimension text, Figure 9-10d.
2. *Middle*: The *Middle* option aligns the tolerance text with the middle of the main dimension text, Figure 9-10d.
3. *Bottom*: The *Bottom* option aligns the tolerance text with the bottom of the main dimension text, Figure 9-10d.

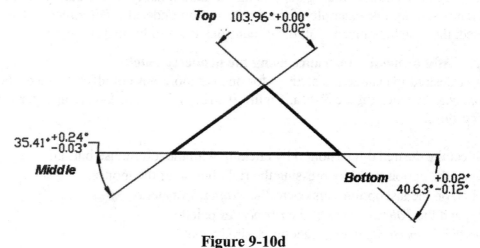

Figure 9-10d

9.9.1.2.   Tolerance Alignment

The *Tolerance Alignment* panel sets the alignments of upper and lower values, Figure 9-9b. This option is available for the *Deviation* and *Limits* methods.

- *Align decimal separator*: The upper and lower values are stacked by aligning the decimal, Figure 9-10e.
- *Align operational symbols*: The upper and lower values are stacked by aligning the operational symbols (+ and -), Figure 9-10e.

9.9.1.3.   Zero Suppression

The *Zero suppression* panel is used to suppress the *Leading and Trailing* zeroes (independently) by checking the corresponding box, Figure 9-9b.

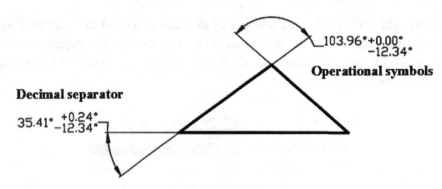

Figure 9-10e

9.9.2. Add or modify tolerance
A user can add or modify the tolerance value and style using the dialog box or the property palette.

9.9.2.1. Add or modify tolerance using the dialog box
If the user desired to change the settings for the tolerance of all the dimensions then open the *Modify Dimension Style* dialog box; using the functionality of the dialog box, change the tolerance setting. For example, if the *Limits* option under the *Tolerance format* panel is selected, then the tolerance for all the dimensions is set to limits format.

9.9.2.2. Add or modify tolerance using the property palette
If the user desired to change the settings for one (or more but not all) tolerances then use the *Properties* palette, Figure 9-11a, Figure 9-11b, and Figure 9-11c, and perform the following steps.

- Select the desired dimension(s) by clicking with the left mouse button.
- Open the option panel by pressing the right button of the mouse.
- Click on the last option; this opens the *Properties* palette.
- Expand the *Tolerance* tab of the *Properties* palette.
- On the *Properties* palette select the desired panel.
- In Figure 9-11a, the *Tolerance alignment* panel is expanded and the *Operational symbols* option is selected.
- In Figure 9-11b, the *Tolerance display* panel is expanded and the *Limits* option is selected.
- In Figure 9-11c, the *Tolerance position vertical* panel is expanded and the *Middle* option is selected.

Figure 9-11a

Figure 9-11b

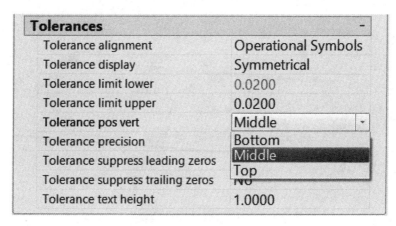

Figure 9-11c

Notes:

10. Land Survey

10.1. Learning Objectives

After completing this chapter, you will demonstrate competency in the following areas:

- Different types of survey systems
- Draw survey data using AutoCAD
- Deed and parcel of land
- Find/calculate area of a parcel

10.2.   Introduction

According to Webster New Collegiate Dictionary, survey is defined as "To determine and delineate the form, extent, position, of (as a tract of land) by taking linear and angular measurements and by applying the principles of geometry and trigonometry." Thus, surveying is an art of measuring (angles, distances, etc.), calculating quantities (area, volume, etc.), and plotting of the measurements (profile, contour maps, etc.). Generally, in surveying the point of measurement is known as a station and stations are identified using their position and direction with respect to a reference location.

10.3.   Location

The position of a station on the surface of the earth can be specified by its longitude and latitude.

10.3.1. Longitudes

The longitudes, or meridians, are imaginary lines connecting the North Pole to the South Pole. The longitudes are an angular distance measured in degrees towards east or west. The 0° longitude is known as the prime meridian, Figure 10-1a. The angles going east are measured as positive and angles going west are measured as negative. For example, station A is at -40° longitude whereas station B is at 60° longitude, Figure 10-1a.

10.3.2. Latitudes

Latitude represents the position of a station measured north or south of the equator, Figure 10-1b. The equator is zero-degrees latitude. The north and south poles are 90° north and south latitude, respectively. The angles toward the north are measured as positive, and angles toward the south are measured as negative. However, the latitudes are generally written with N or S. For example, the latitude of station A is 40° N whereas the latitude of station B is 60° S, Figure 10-1b.

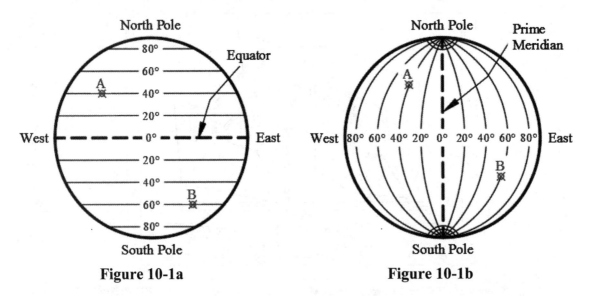

Figure 10-1a   **Figure 10-1b**

10.3.3. Location on a map

The latitudes and longitudes can be used as a coordinate system to find the location of a station on a map. Figure 10-1c shows a map with two longitudes (85° and 75°), two latitudes (27° and 23°), and four stations (*R, H, T,* and *C*). For example, C is located east of 85° longitude and to the south of 27° latitude. Also, latitudes and longitudes can be used to find the location of places with respect to each other. For example, Figure 10-1c shows that *R* is to the north of every other station and *C* is to the east of every other station (on the map). It is clear from Figure 10-1c, that both *H* and *T* are to the north of 23° latitude and south of 27° latitude; on the other hand *H* is to the west of *T*.

Figure 10-1c

10.4.   Angular Measurement

In land survey, the direction of a line represents the angular relationship between the given line and a reference (or datum) line. Generally, either the North-South or the East-West line is used as the reference line. In Figure 10-2a, α is the angle of line *L1* with respect to the East-West line, and β is the angle of the same line with respect to the North-South line.

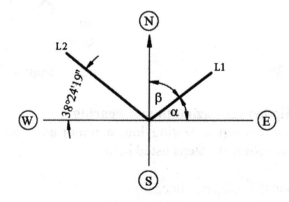

Figure 10-2a

10.4.1. Units of measurement

The angles are measured in degrees or radians. The degrees are denoted by the symbol '°'. Each degree is divided into 60 minutes (denoted by the symbol ') and each minute is subdivided into 60 seconds (denoted by the symbol "). In Figure 10-2a, the angle of the line *L2* with respect to the East-West datum line is 38 degrees, 24 minutes, and 19 seconds (or 38° 24' 19").

10.4.2. Direction

The angular measurement is represented either as an azimuth or a bearing.

10.4.2.1.   Azimuth

The azimuth of a line is the horizontal angle between the given line and the datum line. Generally, the datum is the north-south line. An azimuth is measured clockwise from the north with its value ranges from 0° to 360°. In Figure 10-2b, the azimuth of L1 is 53° and of L2 is 308°.

10.4.2.2.   Bearing

The bearing of a line is the angle between the line and a datum line. Generally, the datum can be either the north or south meridian. Hence, the angle can be measured clockwise or counter-clockwise ranging from 0° to 90°. To measure the bearing of a line, the angle of a circle (360°) is divided into four quadrants: NE, SE, SW, and NW, Figure 10-2c. Therefore, the value of the bearing angle is preceded by *N* or *S* and followed by *E* or *W*. For example, the bearing of the line L1 in Figure 10-2c is N39°E and of *L2* is S71°E.

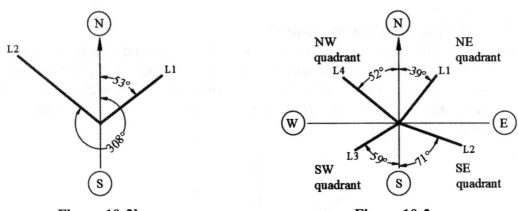

Figure 10-2b   **Figure 10-2c**

10.4.2.3.   Relationship between azimuth and bearing

If necessary, a user can convert a bearing into azimuth and vice versa. To convert a bearing into an azimuth, follow the steps listed below.

- Sketch the line and the reference line.
- Table #1 shows the process for converting bearings into the corresponding azimuths. In the figures of the Table #1, the angles with the dimension lines ending with dots are the azimuths and the angles with the dimension lines ending with arrowheads are the corresponding bearings.

Table #1: Conversion of bearing to azimuth

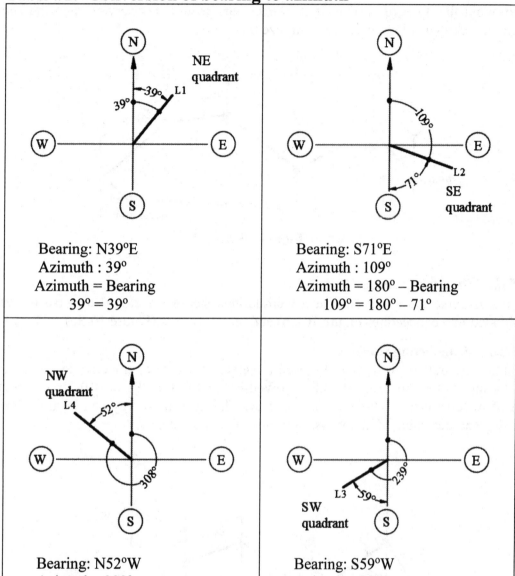

Bearing: N39°E Azimuth : 39° Azimuth = Bearing 39° = 39°	Bearing: S71°E Azimuth : 109° Azimuth = 180° – Bearing 109° = 180° – 71°
Bearing: N52°W Azimuth : 308° Azimuth = 360° – Bearing 308° = 360° – 52°	Bearing: S59°W Azimuth : 239° Azimuth = 180° + Bearing 239° = 180° + 59°

10.5.   Traverse

Traverse is a series of interconnected lines between a series of points. The connecting lines are called courses, and the points are called traverse stations. The main purpose of a traverse survey is to find out the distance between the traverse stations and angle of the courses. A traverse can be classified as an open or a closed traverse.

10.5.1. Open traverse

This type of survey is commonly used for exploratory purposes. As the name suggests, the open traverse neither create a loop nor does it end at a point of known position,

Figure 10-3a. This type of traverse cannot be checked for accuracy. Therefore, if possible try to avoid this type of survey. If it is necessary to use this survey, then the survey should be repeated at least twice to minimize the errors.

Figure 10-3a

10.5.2. Closed traverse

A close traverse starts and ends at a well-defined station. A closed traverse is further subdivided into connecting (Figure 10-3b) and loop traverses (Figure 10-3c).

10.5.2.1. Connecting traverse

A connecting traverse is a type of closed traverse. This type of traverse does not end at the starting station; however, it ends at a well-defined station, Figure 10-3b. Hence, this type of traverse can be checked for accuracy. This type of survey can be used for the planning and designing of highways, railroads, pipelines, etc.

Figure 10-3b

10.5.2.2. Loop traverse

A loop traverse is a type of a closed traverse that starts and ends at the same station, thus creating a closed path, Figure 10-3c. This type of traverse can be checked for its accuracy. This type of survey is used for the boundary line of a piece of land.

Figure 10-3c

10.6. Drawing a Traverse Using AutoCAD

This section explains how to draw traverses using azimuth and bearings. Although the examples create loop traverses, the process is similar for any other traverse.

10.6.1. Traverse for the given azimuths

In the current section, a closed traverse is drawn using the length of the courses and their azimuth, Figure 10-4e. The drawing units are Engineering (Feet-Inches), and the angles are the azimuths from the North (that is, the angles are measured in the clockwise direction from North).

- Create the drawing as follows.

1. Open a new landscape template file for ANSI units created in Chapter 7.
2. Type *Units* in the command line and press the *Enter* key. This opens the *Drawing Units* dialog box, Figure 10-4a.
3. In the *length*'s panel, choose the *Engineering* option, Figure 10-4a. Now the user can specify the information in engineering units (feet and inches). The length 5'-6" is entered as follows: (i) activate the *Line* or *Polyline* commands. (ii) Type 5. (iii) Type the apostrophe (') key. (iv) Type 6. (v) Press the *Enter* key. (vi) DO NOT TYPE hyphen (-) to separate feet from inches and double apostrophe to represent inches.
4. Click on the *Direction* button and the *Direction Control* dialog box opens, Figure 10-4b. Choose the *North* option for the *Base Angle*; and press the *OK* buttons on both dialog boxes.
5. Start the *Line* command and click at point *A* (a random point in the drawing area) to start the traverse.
6. First, draw the 114' long line with the azimuth of 137° from North.
7. The clockwise angles are specified with negative signs because positive angles are measured in the counterclockwise direction.

8. (i) Press the @ key to specify the relative coordinates; the prompt is shown in Figure 10-4c. (ii) Specify the length (114'), (iii) press the *Tab* key, (iv) specify the angle (-137), and (iv) press the *Enter* key. The first line segment is drawn.
9. Similarly, draw the line of length 119' at 211° azimuth.
10. Repeat the process with the remaining traverse.
11. The resulting traverse is shown in Figure 10-4e.
12. Find the length and azimuth for the last course, *BA*.

Figure 10-4a

Figure 10-4b

Figure 10-4c

Figure 10-4d

10.6.2. Traverse for the given bearings

In the current section, a closed traverse shown in Figure 10-5 is drawn. The drawing units are Engineering (Feet-Inches), and the angles are the bearing from the North or South (that is, the angles are measured in the clockwise or counterclockwise direction). Create the drawing as follows.

1. Open a new landscape template file for ANSI units created in Chapter 7.
2. Type *Units* in the command line and press the *Enter* key. This opens the *Drawing Units* dialog box, Figure 10-4a.
3. Click on the *Direction* button and the *Direction Control* dialog box opens, Figure 10-4b. Choose the *North* option for the *Base Angle*, and press the *OK* buttons on both dialog boxes.
4. The clockwise angles are specified with negative signs because the positive angles are measured counterclockwise.

Figure 10-4e

Figure 10-5

5. The *Direction* control box can be activated even if the line command is active. (i) Type *Units* in the command line and press the *Enter* key. This opens the *Drawing Units* dialog box. (ii) Click on the *Direction* button and the *Direction Control* dialog box opens. (iii) Choose the *South* option for the *Base Angle*. (iv) Press the *OK* button on both of the dialog boxes.

6. Start the *Line* command and click at point *A* (a random point in the drawing area) to start the traverse.

7. First draw the 114' long line with the bearing of S43°E. (i) Press the @ key to specify the relative coordinates; the prompt is shown in Figure 10-4c. (ii) Specify the length (114'), (iii) press the *Tab* key, (iv) specify the angle (-43), and (iv) press the *Enter* key.

8. Similarly draw lines of lengths and angles (119', S31°W).

9. Repeat the process with the remaining courses. Change the base angle as needed.

10. The resulting traverse is shown in Figure 10-5.

11. Find the length and bearing for the last course, *BA*.

10.7. Add Dimensions to a Traverse

Every course needs both the linear and angular dimensions. The linear dimension is the length of the course and the angular dimension is its azimuth or bearing.

10.7.1. Length

Add the length to a course as follows.

1. (i) Create a layer for the linear dimension and name it as Length. (ii) Make the Length layer to be the current layer.

2. Display the *Linear* or *Aligned* dimensions as necessary, Figure 10-6a.

3. Figure 10-6b displays only two courses, however, the user must select every linear or align dimension in the traverse.

4. Click with the left button of the mouse on the length dimensions, and the grip points appear, Figure 10-6b.

5. Press the right button of the mouse, and options list appears.

6. Select the *Properties* option with the left button of the mouse.

7. In the *Properties* palette, under the *Lines & Arrows* panel, turn *Off* the *Dim line 1*, *Dim line 2*, *Ext line 1*, and *Ext line 2*; press the down arrow in the right column and then choose the *Off* option, Figure 10-7.

8. The resultant dimensions are shown in Figure 10-6c.

Figure 10-6a   **Figure 10-6b**   **Figure 10-6c**

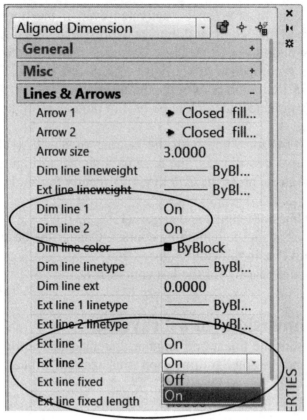

Figure 10-7

10.7.2. Add reference line to a traverse

To make the dimensioning process faster and accurate draw an arrow, north label, and the reference line at every traverse station using the following steps. The reference line is necessary because the leader (arrow) cannot be used for angular dimensions.

1. Create a layer for NS reference lines and name it as *NS_Reference*; set the linetype to be *Continuous* and lineweight to be *0.0*.
2. Make the *NS_Reference* layer to be the current layer.
3. The North direction is created by drawing a leader. (i) Turn on the ORTHO option by clicking the ▣ icon on the status bar. (ii) Activate the *QLEADER* command, and draw a vertical arrow with the arrowhead pointing upward. (iii) Press the *Esc* key from the keyboard to exit the *QLEADER* command without completing it, Figure 10-8a.
4. Activate the *Line* command and draw a line on top of the arrow. The user must draw a straight line on top of the arrow because the angular dimension does not recognize an arrow created using *QLEADER* command.
5. Write N using a text command, Figure 10-8a.
6. Enclose N in a circle using *Express Tool* tab → *Text* panel → *Enclose in Object* command; use circle option, Figure 10-8a.
7. Activate the *Copy* command and paste the north at each station, Figure 10-8b.

Figure 10-8a **Figure 10-8b**

10.7.3. Azimuth angle

As explained earlier, the azimuths are measured with respect to North in the clockwise direction, and the angle's value can range from 0° to 360°.

1. Create a layer for the azimuth dimension and name it *Azimuth*; set its linetype to be *Continuous* and lineweight to be *0.0*.
2. Make the *Azimuth* layer the current layer.
3. Display the *Angular* dimension (Angle > 180° technique) between a course and NS reference, as shown in Figure 10-4d.

10.7.4. Bearing angle

As explained earlier, the bearings are measured either with respect to North or South and towards East or West; and the angle's value can vary from 0° to 90°.

1. Create a layer for the bearing dimension and name it *Bearing*; set its linetype to be *Continuous* and lineweight to be *0.0*.
2. Make the *Bearing* layer the current layer.
3. Display the *Angular* dimension (Angle < 180° technique) between a course and NS_reference, as shown in Figure 10-5.

10.7.5. Save the file

Save the traverse file named as *Traverse.dwg*.

10.8. Parcel

In real estate terminology, a parcel is defined as a contiguous area of land, with or without buildings, owned by one or multiple owners and described by a single deed. For example, a residential area plot owned by a single owner and a form land owned by multiple owners (may be one family) is a parcel. In Figure 10-9, person X is the owner of lot #3 and person Y is the owner of lot #4, whereas lot #1 and #2 are owned by multiple (A, B, and C) owners.

10.9. Deed

A deed is a legal document (written certificate) indicating ownership of a land. In terms of real estate, a deed shows the ownership of a parcel of land. It is also used to convey an ownership from the previous owner to the current owner. A deed must show the limits and the detailed description of the boundary of the property. A deed uses specific phrases such as *"Commencing at," "Point-of-Beginning," "thence," ";", "in a _____ly direction"* (for example, northerly, northeasterly, easterly, etc.), *"–most," "along," "a distance of," "to," "to a point,"* etc. Due to the importance of a deed, the landowner keeps the original deed and the local courthouse keeps its copy.

Figure 10-9

10.10. Land Survey

The basic purpose of the land survey is to measure existing boundaries and lay out new boundaries. Based on the size of the area to be surveyed, the survey is carried out by government agencies or private surveyors. In the United States, a parcel of land is usually described using the *rectangular* system, *metes and bound*, and *lots and blocks* methods.

10.11. Rectangular System

The rectangular system is used by the Public Land Survey System (PLSS) of the United States. The system was created by the *Land Ordinance of 1785*. It has been expanded and slightly modified but is still in use in the states of Alabama, Alaska, Arizona, Arkansas, California, Colorado, Florida, Idaho, Illinois, Indiana, Iowa, Kansas, Louisiana, Michigan, Minnesota, Mississippi, Missouri, Montana, Nebraska, Nevada, New Mexico, North Dakota, Ohio, Oklahoma, Oregon, South Dakota, Utah, Washington, Wisconsin, and Wyoming. In the rectangular system, the basic units of the land are the township and range. The townships and ranges are formed by the intersection of the reference lines (baseline and meridians).

10.11.1. Reference lines

In a rectangular system, the baseline and meridians are the two commonly used reference lines. The baseline (or latitude) runs east-west, and the principle meridian (or longitude) runs north-south. Lines parallel to the principle meridian and the baseline with six mile intervals are created, Figure 10-10a and Figure 10-10b. The intersection of these lines forms a grid of 6 miles by 6 miles which is used as the base for the rectangular survey, Figure 10-10c.

The initial point of the PLSS survey is the intersection of the meridian and baselines or lines running parallel to the baseline and meridian. The parallel lines to the principle meridian are named. The first surveys in the rectangular system were carried out in eastern Ohio; hence, its west boundary is the first principal meridian. The first six principal meridians are labeled as first, second, third, fourth, fifth, and sixth principal meridians. The rest of the meridians are named using local names. For example, in Louisiana the PLSS uses *Louisiana meridian*.

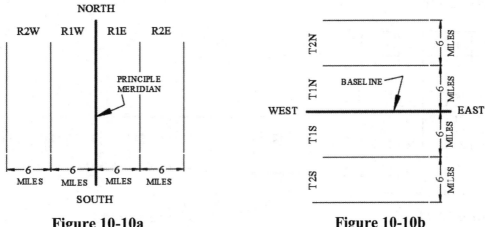

| Figure 10-10a | Figure 10-10b |

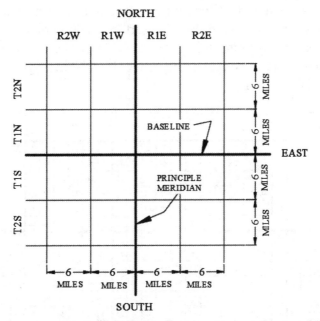

Figure 10-10c

10.11.2.   Township and range

The columns of the grid shown in Figure 10-10c are called range, and the rows are called township. Each cell of the grid is called a township. Each township is further subdivided into 36 sections of one square mile (area equal to 640 acres), Figure 10-11a. The numbering of the sections (of a township) starts from the upper right corner and follows the zigzag pattern as shown in Figure 10-11a. Each section can be further subdivided into two half-sections of 0.5 square mile (320 acres) each. Each section can also be further subdivided into four quarter-sections of 0.25 square mile (160 acres) each. The federal government typically surveys only to the quarter-section level. If necessary, smaller parcels are usually surveyed later by private surveyors. In governmental surveys, the township corner is established every six miles and followed by the marking of the section, half-section and the quarter- section corners, denoted as $\top$, S, $\frac{1}{2}$, and $\left|\frac{1}{4}\right.$ as shown in Figure 10-11b.   .

6	5	4	3	2	1
7	8	9	10	11	12
18	17	16	15	14	13
19	20	21	22	23	24
30	29	28	27	26	25
31	32	33	34	35	36

←———— 6 MILES ————→

Figure 10-11a

Figure 10-11b

This technique allows for the identification of any parcel of land by specifying section, township, and range numbers. This format is used in deeds to delineate the property. For example, a parcel located in range R1E, township T4S, and in section 15 is shown in Figure 10-11c, and the deed contains the entry 15-4S-1E. Figure 10-11d shows the further subdivisions of 15- 4S-1E.

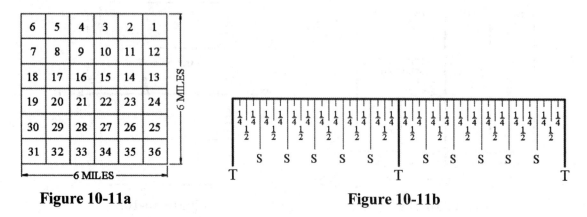

Figure 10-11c

The area of the subdivisions shown in Figure 10-11d can be obtained by multiplying "the product of the factors" with "640 ACRES." The area calculations for four of the subsections shown in Figure 10-11d are shown in Table #2.

Table #2: Area calculation

Subdivision	Product of Factor	Area (Acres)
SW1/4 NE1/4 SE1/4	1/4 * 1/4 * 1/4 = 1/64	1/64 * 640 = 10
S1/2 SE1/4 SE1/4	1/2 * 1/4 * 1/4 = 1/32	1/32 * 640 = 20
N1/2 NE1/4	1/2 * 1/4 = 1/8	1/8 * 640 = 80
NW1/4	1/4	1/4 * 640 = 160

Figure 10-11d

10.12. Metes and Bounds

The term *metes* refers to a boundary defined by the measurement of each straight run. A run is specified by a distance between the terminal points and an orientation (or direction). A direction may be a simple compass bearing or a precise orientation determined by accurate survey methods. The term *bounds* refers to a more general boundary description, such as along a certain watercourse, a stone wall, an adjoining public road way, or an existing building.

The metes and bounds system is often used to define larger pieces of property (e.g. farms), and political subdivisions (e.g. town boundaries) where a precise definition is not required or would be far too expensive, or previously designated boundaries can be incorporated into the description.

Typically the system uses physical features of the local geography, directions, and distances, to define and describe the boundaries of a parcel of land. The boundaries are described in a running style (from a point of beginning) working around the parcel of the land in sequence (returning back to the same point). It may include references to other adjoining parcels of land (and their owners), and it in turn could also be referred to in later surveys. At the time the description was compiled, it may have been marked on the ground with permanent monuments placed where there were no suitable natural monuments.

In many deeds, the angle is described not by a degree measure out of 360 degrees, but instead by indicating a direction north or south (N or S) followed by a degree measure out of 90 degrees and another direction west or east (W or E). For example, such a bearing might be listed as *N 42°35' W*, which means that the bearing is 42°35' counterclockwise (to the west) from north. This has the advantage of providing the same degree measure regardless of which direction a particular boundary is being followed; the boundary can be traversed in the opposite direction simply by exchanging N for S and E for W. In other words, *N 42°35' W* describes the same boundary as *S 42°35' E*, but is traversed in the opposite direction.

Once such a survey takes place, traditionally long use establishes the boundaries. The description might refer to *landmarks* such as the *large oak tree* which could die, rot, and disappear. Streams might dry up or change course. Man-made features such as roads, walls, markers, or stakes also have been used to determine the real boundaries. But these features move, change, and disappear over time. When it comes time to re-establish these boundaries (for sale, subdivision, or building construction) it can become difficult, even impossible, to determine the original location of the boundary. Court cases are sometimes required to settle the matter.

10.12.1. Land description using metes and bounds

A typical description for a small parcel of land using metes and bounds is illustrated below, and the corresponding parcel of land is shown in Figure 10-12a. In the description below, POB is the abbreviation for the Point Of Beginning.

Beginning at a point 212' 7.1" south of the NW corner NW/4 NE/4 of section13-T8N-R1E,

Thence S0° 15' 0" E a distance of 74' 6.7", Thence S89° 55' 0" W a distance of 151' 2.4",

Thence N0° 15' 0" W a distance of 74' 6.7", Thence N89° 55' 0" E a distance of 151' 2.4" to POB.

Figure 10-12a

10.12.2.   AutoCAD and Metes and Bounds

If the surveyor's angles are used when specifying the polar coordinates, then clearly indicate whether the surveyor's angles are in the north or south direction and towards east or west direction.

Example: Draw the boundary of the parcel described using metes and bounds as follows.

1. Open a new file landscape template file for ANSI units created in Chapter 7.
2. Type *Units* in the command line and press the *Enter* key. This opens the *Drawing Units* dialog box, Figure 10-12b.
3. In the *length*'s panel, choose the *Engineering*'s option, Figure 10-12b.
4. Now the user can specify the information in engineering units (feet and inches). The length 5'-6" is entered as follows: (i) activate the *Line* or *Polyline* commands. (ii) Type 5. (iii) Type the apostrophe (') key. (iv) Type 6. (v) Press the *Enter* key. (vi) DO NOT TYPE hyphen (-) to separate feet from inches and double apostrophe to represent inches.
5. In the *Angle*'s panel, choose the *Surveyor's Units* option, Figure 10-12b. Using image editing techniques, this figure shows multiple selections; however, AutoCAD allows for only one selection at a time.

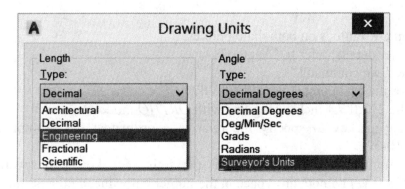

Figure 10-12b

6. Click on the *Direction* button, Figure 10-12b, and the *Direction Control* dialog box opens, choose the *North* option for the *Base Angle*, and press the *OK* buttons on both dialog boxes.

7. Open the *Drafting Settings* dialog box and select *Dynamic Input* tab, Figure 10-12c.

8. Click on the *Settings* option under the *Pointer Input* panel. This opens the *Pointer Input Settings* dialog box, Figure 10-12d.

9. In the *Pointer Input Settings* dialog box, under the Format panel, select the Polar format option, Figure 10-12d.

Figure 10-12c

Figure 10-12d

10. Click on *OK* buttons on both dialog boxes.

11. For further details, refer to Chapter 3.

12. Start the *Line* command.

13. Click for the first point at the *NW* of *NW/4 NE/4* corner.

14. Draw the 212 ft 7.1 inches long line with *ORTHO* mode *On*.

15. Press the @ key to specify the relative coordinates; the prompt is shown in Figure 10-12e.

16. (i) Specify the length (151'2.4), (ii) press the *Tab* key, (iii) specify the angle (N 89d55'0 W) without any space in the numerical value, and press the *Enter* key.

17. Repeat the process to complete the course.

| Specify next point or ⊡ | @ | 503'-3.3" | < S 24d8'54" E |

Figure 10-12e

10.13. Lots and Blocks

10.13.1.   Terminology
- Suburb: A suburb is defined as a residential area on the outskirts of a city or a large town adjacent to the main employment centers. Most of the time it has a lower population density than the inner-city neighborhoods.
- Exurb: An exurb, also known as a bedroom community or dormitory town, is defined as a residential area where residents sleep, but mostly work elsewhere because there are very few local businesses.
- Subdivision: Subdivision is the act of dividing land into pieces that are easier to sell or otherwise develop. If it is used for housing it is typically known as a housing subdivision or housing development, although some developers tend to call these areas communities.

10.13.2.   Lots and Blocks
The *Lot and Block* Survey System is used in the United States and Canada to locate and identify land, particularly for lots in densely populated metropolitan areas, suburban areas, and exurbs. It is sometimes referred to as the Recorded Plat Survey System or the Recorded Map Survey System.

This system is the most recent and may be the simplest of the three main survey systems. In this system, a large parcel is defined by metes and bounds or the PLSS. The owners of the parcel would divide the land into smaller parcels known as blocks. Blocks are further subdivided into even smaller parcels known as lots. Blocks and lots can be of any size. However, usually the municipality restricts their sizes. Each block and lot is given identification (a number or a letter). In some cases, blocks may be part of a subdivision. All surveys and identification are recorded with an official government record keeper. The officially recorded map then became the legal description of all of the lots in the subdivision.

A legal description of a lot in a Lot and Block system must identify the following:
  i.   an individual lot number,
  ii.   the block in which the lot is located, if applicable,
  iii.   a reference to a platted subdivision or a phase thereof,
  iv.   a reference to find the cited plat map (i.e., a page and/or volume number), and
  v.   a description of the map's place of official recording (e.g., recorded in the files of the County Engineer).

The legal description of a 0.3542 acre property under the *Lot and Block* system may be something like (i) Lot 11 of (ii) Block 8 of the (iii) White Oak Subdivision (iv) as recorded in Map Book 35, Page 64 (v) at the Recorder of Deeds office, Figure 10-13. Some simple maps may only contain a lot and map number, such as Lot C of the Riverside Subdivision map as recorded in Map Book 12, Page 8 in the office of the City Engineer. The more technical details of the legal description are contained in the recorded plat map and there is no need to reiterate them in a deed or other legal description.

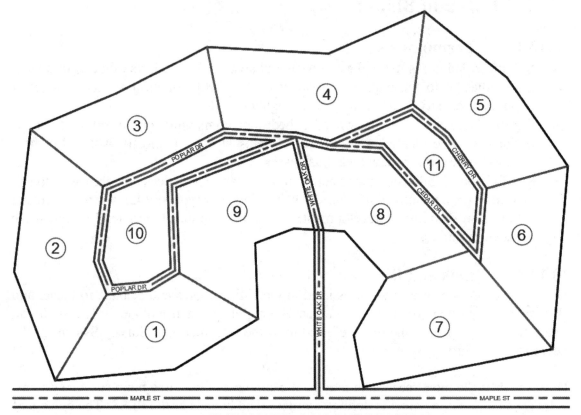

THE WHITE OAK SUBDIVISION

Figure 10-13

10.13.3.   AutoCAD and Lot and Block
In AutoCAD, a lot and block system can be created by following the step-by-step directions given below.

1. Launch AutoCAD 2018.
2. Units: Engineering (i.e. ANSI).
3. Open file
   • Open the Traverse.dwg file created in Section 10.6 and saved in Section 10.7.
4. Units format
   • Change units to *Engineering* units as follows: (i) Type *Units* on the command line to open the *Drawing Units* dialog box; (ii) expand the *Length* panel; and (iii) select the *Engineering* option, Figure 10.14a.
   • Now the user can specify the information in architectural units (feet and inches). The length 5'-6" is entered as follows: (i) activate the *Line* or *Polyline* commands. (ii) Type 5. (iii) Type the apostrophe (') key. (iv) Type 6. (v) Press

the *Enter* key. (vi) DO NOT TYPE hyphen (-) to separate feet from inches and double apostrophe to represent inches.

Figure 10-14a

5. Layers
   - Create the layers as shown in Figure 10.14b

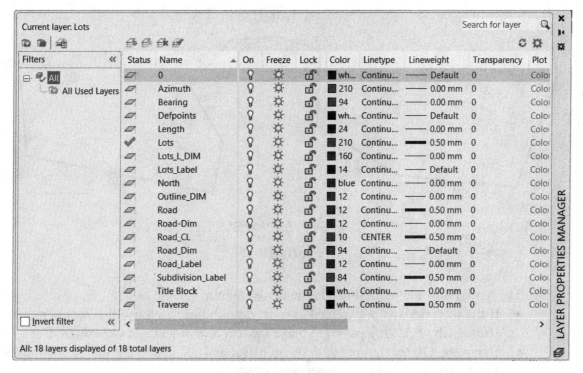

Figure 10-14b

6. Outline: Draw the outline of the subdivision.
   - The closes traverse will be used as the outline for the Lots and Block drawing file.
   - Freeze the layers displaying the angle and north direction.
   - The complete outline is shown in Figure 10-15.

7. <u>Outline Dimension:</u> Add the dimensions to the outline of the subdivision.
   - The linear dimensions in the outline of the traverse were added in the Traverse.dwg, Figure 10-15.

8. <u>Save the subdivision:</u> Save the subdivision.
   - Save the subdivision as *LotsBlocks.dwg*.

THE WHITE OAK SUBDIVISION

Figure 10-15

9. <u>The road:</u> Draw the roads and add the roads' labels.
   - If the traverse was not created as a single polyline, then use the *Join* command (*Home* tab → *Modify* panel) to make the traverse as a single closed polyline.
   - Using the Offset command, draw an offset at 160' inside the outline boundary, Figure 10-16a. This is the inner edge of the road.
   - Using the Offset command, draw an offset at 16' outside the offset drawn in the previous step, Figure 10-16b. This is the inner edge of the road.
   - Move these offsets to the *Road* layer.
   - Using the Offset command, draw an offset at 8' in the middle of the two offsets drawn earlier and move this offset to the *Road-CL* layer, Figure 10-16c. If necessary, set the linetype scale. In the current example, set the linetype scale (from the *Property* palette) to 0.25.

Figure 10-16a

Figure 10-16b

Figure 10-16c

- Draw the remaining roads of the subdivision, Figure 10-16d.
- Create the offset, Figure 10-16e.
- Clean the roads using the *Trim* command, Figure 10-17.
- Make the *Road_DIM* the current layer and add the dimensions of the roads.

Figure 10-16d

Figure 10-16e

10. <u>The road label:</u> Add the roads labels.
   - Make the *Road_Label* the current layer and add the labels to the roads, Figure 10-17. The roads names are: *Maple Street*, *White Oak Dr.*, *Cedar Dr.*, *Cherry Dr.*, *Poplar Dr.*, and *Palm Dr.*

Figure 10-17

11. <u>The subdivision label:</u> Add the dimensions to the outline of the subdivision.
   - Make the *Subdivision_Label* the current layer. Add the label to the subdivision of the subdivision using the *Text* command (text height 20'), Figure 10-18.

THE WHITE OAK SUBDIVISION

Figure 10-18

12. <u>The lots:</u> Draw the lots of the subdivision.
   - Make the *Lots* to be the current layer and connect the corners as shown in Figure 10-19a and Figure 10-19b.
   - Make the *Lots_DIM* the current layer and add the dimensions to the lots.

Figure 10-19a

- Make the *Lots_Label* the current layer and add the labels, Figure 10-17b. (i) Create a label using the *Text* command, text size 20'. (ii) Encircle the text from *Express tools* tab → Text panel → *Enclose in Object* command with the *Circle* option. (iii) Using the *Mirror* and *Copy* and *Geometric center* option in object snap, create a label for every lot.

Figure 10-19b

13. Finally, display the drawing in a layout and update the Title block, Figure 10-20.
   a. Set the scale of the drawing's viewport to be 1:1800, Figure 10-20.
   b. Lock the viewport.
   c. Update the Title block.
   d. The resultant drawing in the layout is shown in Figure 10-20.

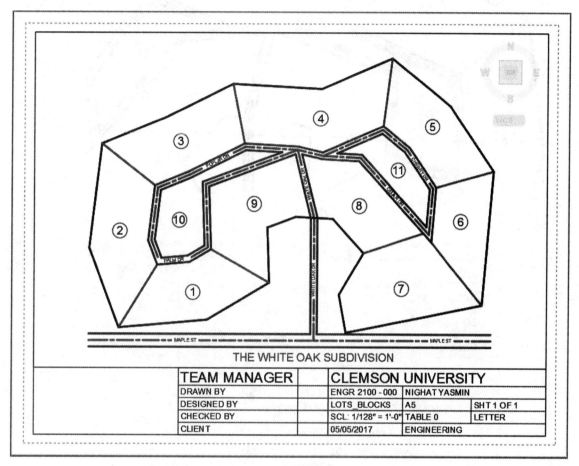

Figure 10-20

10.13.4.   Area of a lot
In the Lot and Block system shown in Figure 10-20, the area of a lot can be determined using the closed boundary, hatch or *Area* command method.

10.13.4.1. Closed boundary method
Area of a lot can be determined using the closed boundary as follow.
- Using a *Polyline* command, create a closed boundary of the lot in question, Figure 10-21a. In the current example, a closed boundary of lot 10 is created.
- Select the boundary and its grip points will appear.
- Open the *Property* palette and the area of the lot can be found under the *Geometry* panel, Figure 10-21b.

(handwritten annotations)

0.9121 acre

1. 5721266 sq in. (39731 sq ft)

4. 8108669 sq in (56310)

8. 5421288 (37648)

5. 8093522 (42316)

9a. 6447778 sq in. (44755 sq ft) 1.0280

10. 4019292 (27912)

6. 4790354 (33266)

2. 6872525 sq in. (44755 sq ft)

11. 2553535 (17733)

7. 7640598 (53099)

3. 6288943 sq in. (43632 sq ft)

Figure 10-21a

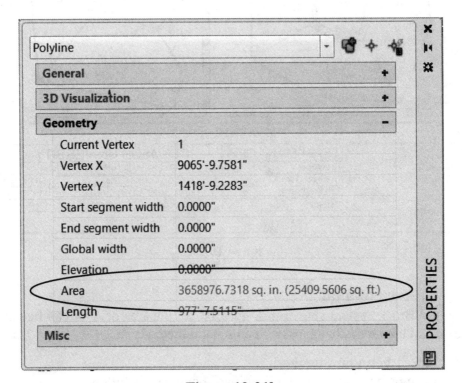

Figure 10-21b

10.13.4.2. Hatch method
Area of a lot can be found using the hatch as follows.

- Make *Lots_A-DIM* the current layer.
- Add independent hatch to each lot in question, Figure 10-22a. That is, activate the hatch command and add the hatch to Lot 1; activate the hatch command again and

add hatch to Lot 2; repeat the process for every lot in question. In the current example, hatch is added to only Lot 10.

- Select the hatch of one of the lots. In the current example, select Lot 10.
- Open the *Property* palette and the area of the hatch can be found under the *Geometry* panel, Figure 10-22b.

Figure 10-22a

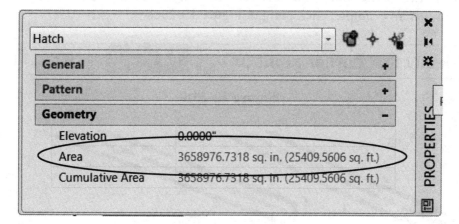

Figure 10-22b

10.13.4.3. Area command method

The *Area* command uses the points on the boundary. All the points must lie in a plane parallel to the XY plane of the UCS.

- The *Area* command is activated using one of the following procedures.
  1. Panel method: from the *Home* tab and the *Utilities* panel, expand the *Measure* dropdown menu and click the *Area* option, Figure 10-23a.
  2. Command line method: Type "area," "Area" or "AREA" in the command line and press the *Enter* key.

Figure 10-23a

- The activation of the command results in the prompt shown in Figure 10-23b.
- This example measures the area of Lot 10 shown in Figure 10-20.
- Turn on the object snap.
- For the first corner point, the user can click any point on the boundary of the area. In the current example, click point *a*, Figure 10-23c.

Specify first corner point or   8445'-9.4"   -82'-11.0"

Figure 10-23b

Specify next point or   71'-3.9060"   < 278°

Figure 10-23c

- For the second point, the user can click on the two adjacent points (*b* or *i*). In the current example, click point *b*, Figure 10-23d.

Figure 10-23d

- For the third and subsequent points, the user can click only on the next adjacent point. Click at point *c*, followed by *d*, Figure 10-23e.
- Press the *Enter* key. The area and perimeter information are shown in Figure 10-23e.
- Either choose the *eXit* option in Figure 10-20e or press the *Esc* key to exit the command.
- The area and perimeter are also available on the command line.
- If the green area is not closed then the area is calculated as if a straight line is drawn from the last point to the first. For the perimeter calculation, the length of that line is added to the existing lines.
- Convert the area into acres using the relationship: 1 acre = 43560 sq. ft.
- Save the drawing!

Figure 10-23e

Notes:

11. Contours

11.1. Learning Objectives

After completing this chapter, you will demonstrate competency in the following areas:

- Identify different types of contour lines
- Identify streams, ridges, peaks, depressions, and saddles on a contour map
- Identify steep and mild slopes on a contour map
- Create a contour map
- Mark and label the index contours

11.2.   Introduction

Consider a cup of coffee and assume that the coffee has evaporated. Figure 11-1a shows the coffee marks as circular rings in the top view and straight lines in the front view. In the coffee marks plotting, the parameter is the time when the coffee was evaporated. Similarly, isobars and isotherms are wavy or closed looped lines representing constant pressure and constant temperature, respectively. These wavy or looped lines, representing a constant value of a parameter, are called contour. In a land survey, a contour line is an imaginary horizontal line passing through the points of the same elevation drawn on a topographic map, Figure 11-1b. Shorelines are a good example of contour lines, since the water receding marks create non-intersecting loops, Figure 11-1c.

Figure 11-1a   **Figure 11-1b**

Figure 11-1c

11.3.   Characteristics Of A Contour Line

A contour line is an imaginary line representing a constant value of a parameter. Some of the characteristics of contour lines are listed here.

- A contour line represents a constant parameter. For example, Figure 11-1b represents elevation contours. The elevation is 10 units for every point on the loop labeled as 10 in the figure.
- If a large enough area is available, then the contour lines loop around and join themselves.
- Contour lines never end.
- Contour lines neither join with other contour lines nor bifurcate.
- Contour lines never cross each other.

11.4.   Terminology

- *Bench Mark*: A bench mark is a point of reference for the measurement. In a land survey, a bench mark is the point of known elevation.
- *Mean sea level*: The average elevation between the low and high tide of a sea is called the mean sea level.
- *Elevation*: The elevation of a point is the vertical distance from a bench mark, a datum line, or a reference plane. In the Figure 11-2a, the vertical distance of point A is 5ft from the datum line aa. Generally, the elevation of a geographic location is its height above (or depth below) the mean sea level. The mean sea level is the datum line. Figure 11-2b shows the elevation of one of the trees on the shore with respect to the mean sea level (datum).

Figure 11-2a   **Figure 11-2b**

- *Contour interval*: The contour interval of a map is the vertical distance between two consecutive contour lines. The contour intervals are closely related to the terrain, purpose of the map, and scale of the drawing. On a given map, the contour interval should be constant. Assuming the unit of measurement is feet, the contour interval is 2ft in Figure 11-1b.

- *Types of contour lines*: Contour lines can be classified into three groups.
  - o *Index contour*: To make the reading of contour maps easy, every fifth contour is labeled. The labeled contour lines are called index contour, Figure 11-3. The index contour line is broken at certain places and text labels are added. The labels represent the elevations with respect to the mean sea level. Usually, the index contours are drawn thicker than the other contour lines. The index contours can be marked as follows: (i) Identify the elevation of the first index contour (FIC). (ii) Specify the contour interval (CI). (iii) If the elevation is increasing, then the elevation of the second index contour (SIC) is calculated as *Elevation of SIC = FIC + 5*CI*. If the elevation is decreasing, then the second index contour (SIC) is calculated as *Elevation of SIC = FIC - 5*CI*. In Figure 11-3, the contour interval is 10 feet.
  - o *Intermediate contour*: The unlabeled contour lines between any two index contours are called intermediate contours. Conventionally, these contours are not labeled but can be labeled in special cases. Usually, the intermediate contours are drawn lighter than the index contours, Figure 11-3.
  - o *Supplementary contour*: The supplementary contours are the special type of contour lines and are drawn only when the contour interval is large and a user wishes to display the features between two consecutive contour lines. As a rule of thumb, the elevation of the supplementary contour is the average of the two contours on its either side, Figure 11-3.

Figure 11-3

- *Peak*: The peak of a hill or mountain is shown by the closed looped contour lines of decreasing diameters and increasing elevation. Figure 11-4a shows the contour map of a peak and Figure 11-4b shows the corresponding peak in a 3D contour map.

Figure 11-4a

Figure 11-4b

- _Depression_: A depression (hole or excavation pit without any drainage outlets) is shown by the closed looped contour lines of decreasing diameters and decreasing elevation. Figure 11-5a shows the contour map of a depression and Figure 11-5b shows the corresponding depression in a 3D contour map. The innermost circle is marked with small lines on the inside, Figure 11-5a. These small lines are called hachures.

Figure 11-5a

Figure 11-5b

- _Saddle_: Two peaks side by side form a saddle. Figure 11-6a shows the contour map of a saddle and Figure 11-6b shows the corresponding peaks in a 3D contour map. In Figure 11-6a, the arrow shows the downward slope.

Figure 11-6a

Figure 11-6b

- _Streams_: Contour lines are roughly parallel to stream. The contour lines cross the streambed upstream by creating V's with the closed end of the V's pointing upstream and the open end of the V's pointing downstream. Figure 11-7a shows a contour map of a stream, and Figure 11-7b shows the corresponding stream in a 3D contour map.

Figure 11-7a   **Figure 11-7b**

- *Ridge or hill or mountain*: Contour lines are roughly parallel to a ridge, and the contour lines cross the ridge downstream by creating V's or U's. The closed end of the V's or U's points downstream and the open end of the V's or U's points upstream. Figure 11-8a shows a contour map of a stream and ridge line and Figure 11-8b shows the corresponding stream and ridge in a 3D contour map.

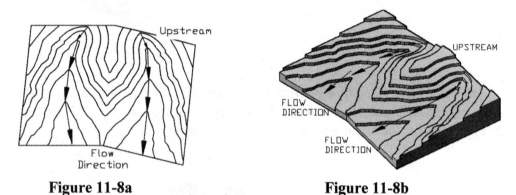

Figure 11-8a   **Figure 11-8b**

- *Slope verses space*: The closely spaced contour lines represent steep slope and widely spaced contour lines represent mild slope. The top portion of Figure 11-9a shows a contour map and the lower parts show the profile indicating. On the left side of the top part, the contour lines are closely spaced and its lower parts show the profile indicating the steep slope. Similarly, on the right side of the top part, the contour lines are widely spaced and its lower parts show the profile indicating the mild slope. Figure 11-9b shows the corresponding 3D contour map.

Figure 11-9a   **Figure 11-9b**

- _Topographic map_: A topographic (contour) map is a two dimensional representation of the three dimensional earth. The three dimensions are the longitude, latitude, and the elevation. A topographic map is used to represent the shape of the earth using contour lines. On these maps, the contour interval depends upon the gradient of the land, and it is represented on the map. A typical map is shown in Figure 11-10. In these maps the contour lines are shown in brown color, water bodies (lakes, rivers, streams, etc.) in blue color, man-made structures (buildings, roads, etc.) in black color, and woodlands in the green color.

Figure 11-10

11.5.   AutoCAD And Contour Map

In AutoCAD contour maps can be created by drawing polylines through the elevation data. This section assumes that the user has interpolated the field data and has created a script file. To draw a contour map, the color of the point is not important. However, for better understanding, every elevation is assigned its distinct color. The remainder of this section provides step-by-step instructions to create a contour map.

11.5.1. Create Script file

- Create a script file or download the script files. The script file is saved with ".*scr*" extension and can be created in *Notepad*. The Figure 11-11a shows part of a script (Script.scr) file and Figure 11-11b explains the contents of the script file.

color 20 *point* *13.20,8.80,00.00* *text* *13.20,8.80* *0.20 0 930* *point* *12.00,9.67,00.00* *text* *12.00,9.67* *0.20 0 930*	• **"color 20" assigns color to a point** • **"point" activates the *Point* command** • **"13.20,8.80,00.00" (no spaces) are the coordinates of the point** • **"text" activates the *Text* command** • **"13.20,8.80" is the coordinate of the first corner of the text box** • **"0.20" is the text height** • **"0" is the rotation of the text** • **"930" is the text that appears in the text box.** • **......**

Figure 11-11a   **Figure 11-11b**

11.5.2. Create layers

- Launch AutoCAD 2018.
- Open a new portrait file (your template file for the ANSI units).
- (i) Create a *Data* layer for the elevation data pint. (ii) Create a *Contour* layer for the contour lines. (iii) Create a *Label* layer for the contours' labels.

11.5.3. Change point style

- From the *Home* tab and the expanded *Utilities* panel click at *Point Style...* tool. This opens the *Point Style* dialog box.
- Change point style to circle (second style in the second row), Figure 11-12.
- Change the point size to 0.5 *Units*.
- Select the *Set Size in Absolute Units* option.
- Press the *OK* button.

11.5.4. Read the script files

- Make the *Data* layer to be the current layer.
- Read the script file by activating the script command.
  - Command line method: Type "script," "Script" or "SCRIPT" on the command line and press the *Enter* key.
- Figure 11-13a shows the close-up of the selected elevation data points.
- The complete elevation data is shown in Figure 11-13b.

Figure 11-12

Figure 11-13a

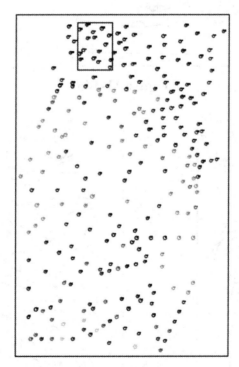

Figure 11-13b

11.5.5. Create the contour map

- Select the 'Contour' layer.
- Activate the *Polyline* command and draw a polyline through the points of the same elevation without intersecting any contour line. Figure 11-14a shows the contour line for the points shown in 11-13a.
- Repeat the process with the remaining data points, Figure 11-14b.
- Fit a curve through each polyline, Figure 11-14c. Curve fitting is discussed in the next section.
- If polylines are created in the multiple activations of the command, then first join the line and then perform the curve fitting operation. The *Join* operation is described in detail in Chapter 4.

Figure 11-14a

Figure 11-14b

Figure 11-14c

11.5.6. Curve fitting

Curve fitting is optional; however, this section explains the curve fitting technique.

- Select a polyline for the elevation 930 (the grip points appear), Figure 11-15a.
- Press the right button of the mouse, and the options list appears.
- Choose the *Polyline* from the list, Figure 11-15a.
- Another list of options appears; choose the *Curve Fit* option, Figure 11-15a.
- The *Curve Fit* option passes the curve through the data points. A smooth curve is drawn through the points, Figure 11-15b.
- Repeat the process with the other contour lines, Figure 11-14c.

Figure 11-15a

Figure 11-15b

11.5.7. Add the labels to the index contours

- If polylines are created in the multiple activations of the commands, then first join the line, and then perform the labeling and masking operation. The *Join* operation is discussed in detail in Chapter 4.
- Mark the index contours (that is, increase the lineweight for the index contours).
- Use the *Text* command from the *Home* tab and *Annotate* panel to create the text of the label. The text should be parallel to the polyline. If necessary, use the *Rotate* command from the *Home* tab and *Modify* panel to rotate the text.
- The Figure 11-16 shows a contour map with only two labeled index contours.
- Similarly add labels to the other contours.
- Hide the contour line behind the label using the *Background mask* option from the *Properties* palette. The *Background mask* command is discussed in Chapter 3.
- Finally, add the *North* direction block from the *Design Center* → *Landscaping.dwg* → *North Arrow*; scale the north block appropriately, Figure 11-16.

Figure 11-16

Notes:

12. Drainage Basin

12.1.   Learning Objectives

After completing this chapter, you will demonstrate competency in the following areas:

- Basics of a water cycle
- Fundamentals of a drainage basin
- Delineate a drainage basin of a channel using AutoCAD

12.2.   Introduction

Hydrology is a Greek word, and it means the study of water. In the engineering community, hydrology is the scientific study of the movement, distribution, and quality of water throughout the earth. Hydrology addresses both the hydrologic cycle and water resources.

12.3.   Hydrologic cycle

The hydrologic cycle, also known as the water cycle, is the continuous movement of the water above, on, and below the surface of the earth. Hence, there is no beginning or ending of this cycle. In the various stages of this cycle, water is available in one of the three different possible states: gas (water vapor), liquid, and solid (snow, ice). The most simplified representation of the hydrologic cycle (Figure 12-1) is as follows. *The major driving force of the hydrologic cycle is the sun. It heats the water in the oceans, lakes, rivers, streams, etc. and causes some of it to evaporate. The vapors rise into the air where cooler temperatures cause vapors to condense into clouds. These clouds drift over the land and the vapors fall as precipitation (rain, hail, snow, fog, etc.). The rainwater flows into lakes, rivers, or aquifers. The water in lakes, rivers, and aquifers then either evaporates back to the atmosphere or eventually flows back to the ocean, completing the cycle.*

The hydrological cycle can be affected by environmental effects and by humans. The following list shows some of the human factors affecting the water cycle.

- Agriculture
- Alteration of the chemical composition of the atmosphere
- Construction of dams
- Deforestation and afforestation
- Removal of groundwater from wells
- Water abstraction from rivers
- Urbanization

12.4.   Terminology

Refer to the Figure 12-1 for the terms discussed in this section.

- Condensation: Condensation is the transformation of water vapor to liquid water, for example, the droplets in the air that produce clouds and fog.
- Precipitation: Precipitation is the process of condensed water vapor falling to the earth's surface. Generally, precipitation occurs as rain. It also occurs as snow, sleet, hail, and fog drip.
- Interception: Interception is the precipitation that is intercepted by buildings, plant foliage, etc. Part of the intercepted precipitation reaches the ground surface and the remaining part evaporates back to the atmosphere.
- Snowmelt: Snowmelt is the runoff produced by the melting snow.
- Groundwater: Groundwater is the water found below the ground surface. It may be available as soil moisture, in liquid form, or frozen form.

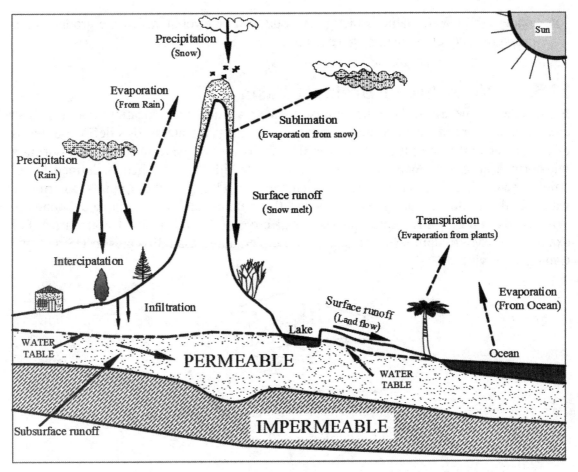

Figure 12-1

- <u>Runoff</u>: Runoff is the method by which water moves across the land. This includes both surface runoff and channel runoff. As water flows, it may infiltrate into the ground, evaporate into the air, become stored in lakes or reservoirs, or be extracted for agricultural or other human uses.
- <u>Infiltration</u>: Infiltration is the percolation of the water from the ground surface into the ground. Once infiltrated, the water becomes soil moisture or groundwater.
- <u>Subsurface flow</u>: Subsurface flow is the underground flow of water. It may return to the surface as a spring or by extraction using pumps.
- <u>Advection</u>: Advection is the movement of water (in solid, liquid, or vapor states) through the atmosphere. Without advection, water that evaporated over the oceans could not precipitate over the land.
- <u>Evaporation</u>: Evaporation is the transformation of water from a liquid to a gaseous state.
- <u>Sublimation</u>: Sublimation is the transformation of water from a solid (ice) to gaseous (vapor) state.
- <u>Transpiration</u>: Transpiration is the evaporation of water from vegetation.
- <u>Evapotranspiration</u>: Evaporation and transpiration are collectively known as evapotranspiration.

- <u>Water table</u>: Water table is the underground water level at which the ground water pressure is equal to the atmospheric pressure.

12.5.   Watershed or Drainage basin

A watershed is the area of land that drains into a stream at a given location; that is, it is an area of land bounded by a hydrologic system. Generally, a watershed is defined in terms of a point or outlet and all the land area that sheds (pours) water to the outlet during a rainstorm. Using the concept that "water runs downhill," a watershed is defined by all points enclosed within an area from which the rain falling at these points contributes water to the outlet. Figure 12-2 represents the delineation of a watershed boundary. Watersheds come in all shapes and sizes and cross state and national boundaries. For example, the Mississippi river drainage basin covers more than 30 states in US and two Canadian provinces.

Outlet

Figure 12-2

A drainage basin is a region of land where the precipitation's water flows downhill into a river, lake, dam, or ocean. The drainage basin includes both the channels and the land from which water drains into those channels. Each drainage basin is separated topographically from adjacent basins by a ridge, hill, or mountain, which is known as a water divide. In Figure 12-2, the dashed line is the main water divide of the hydrographic basin. In North America, watershed refers to the drainage basin itself. The terms catchments, catchment area, catchment basin, drainage area, river basin, and water basin are also used to represent the same concept.

The majority of water that discharges from the basin outlet originated as the precipitation falling on the basin. In hydrology, the drainage basin is a logical unit of focus for studying the movement of water within the hydrological cycle. A portion of the water that enters the groundwater system beneath the drainage basin may flow towards the outlet of another drainage basin because groundwater flow directions do not always match those of their overlying drainage network. The measurement of the discharge of water from a basin may be made by a stream gauge located at the basin's outlet.

12.6. Watershed characteristics

12.6.1. Drainage area
The drainage area (A) is probably the single most important watershed characteristic for a hydrologic design. It reflects the volume of water that can be generated from rainfall. The drainage area is used to indicate the potential for rainfall to provide a volume of water. It is common in hydrologic design to assume a constant depth of rainfall occurring over the watershed. Under this assumption, the volume of the water available for the runoff would be the product of rainfall depth and the drainage area. Thus the drainage area is required as input to models ranging from simple linear prediction equations to complex computer models.

12.6.2. Watershed length
The length (L) of a watershed is the second greatest characteristic of interest. While the length increases as the drainage increases, the length of a watershed is important in hydrologic computations. The watershed length is usually defined as the distance measured along the main channel from the watershed outlet to the basin divide. Since the channel does not extend to the basin divide, it is necessary to extend a line from the end of the channel to the basin divide following a path where the greatest volume of water would travel. The straight-line distance from the outlet point on the watershed divide is not usually used to compute L because the travel distance of floodwaters is conceptually the length of interest. Thus, the length is measured along the principal flow path. Since it is used for hydrologic calculations, this length is more appropriately labeled the hydrologic length. The length is usually used in computing as a time parameter, which is a measure of the travel time of water through the watershed.

12.6.3. Watershed slope
The flood magnitudes reflect the momentum of the runoff. The slope is an important factor in the momentum. Both watershed and channel slope may be of interest. The watershed slope reflects the rate of change of elevation with respect to distance along the principal flow path. Typically, the principal flow path is delineated, and the watershed slope (S) is computed as the difference in elevation (ΔE) between the end points of the principal flow path divided by the hydrologic length of the flow path (L).

The elevation difference, ΔE, may not necessarily be the maximum elevation difference within the watershed since the point of highest elevation may occur along a side boundary of the watershed rather than at the end of the principal flow path.

12.6.4. Miscellaneous
Some of the other important watershed factors are listed here.
- Land cover and use
- Surface roughness
- Hydrologic soil groups
- Soil characteristics such as texture, structure, and moisture contents

12.7.   Major steps in a watershed delineation

The major steps in the watershed delineation process are listed below.

Step 1: Create a contour map of the area.
Step 2: Mark the centerline of the channel by joining the V's. For a channel, the tip of the V is upstream.
Step 3: Show the direction of flow. A channel flows from a higher elevation (upstream) to the lower elevation (downstream).
Step 4: Delineate the watershed boundary by connecting the ridge lines in the elevation contour lines map. For a ridge, the tip of the V or U is downstream.
Step 5: Choose and label the point of the watershed outlet. The outlet is usually a monitoring location or hydraulic structure.
Step 6: Find the length of the channel and the area of the watershed.

12.8.   Watershed delineation using AutoCAD

In AutoCAD the watershed delineation can be performed using the following steps.

1. Launch AutoCAD 2018.
2. Contour map
   - Open the contour map previously created or a downloaded map.
   - Create the layers as shown in Figure 12-3.
   - Change the color, linetype, and lineweight of the layers.

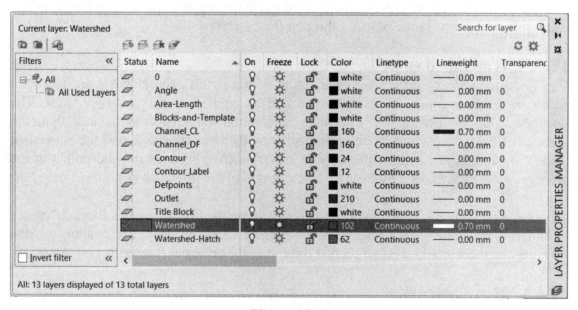

Figure 12-3

3. Contour labels, Figure 12-4
   - Make the *Contour_Labels* layer to be the current layer.
   - Label the index contour using the *Text*, *Background Mask*, and the *Rotate* commands. The text height is 12 feet in the sample watershed.

Figure 12-4

4. Center line, Figure 12-5
    - Make *Channel_CL* to be the current layer.
    - A channel flows from the higher elevation to the lower elevation. As mentioned earlier, the contour lines cross the streambed upstream by creating V's with the bottom of the V's pointing upstream.
    - Draw the centerlines for the channel.
      - o Activate the *Polyline* command.
      - o Draw a polyline through the bottom of the V's as shown in Figure 12-5.

Figure 12-5

5. Direction of the flow, Figure 12-6
   - Make *Channel_DF* to be the current layer.
   - Show the direction of the flow for the channels using the leader line. Use the first part of the *qleader* command to draw arrows; arrowhead size is 25ft – 40ft.
   - The direction of flow label's text height is 13'.

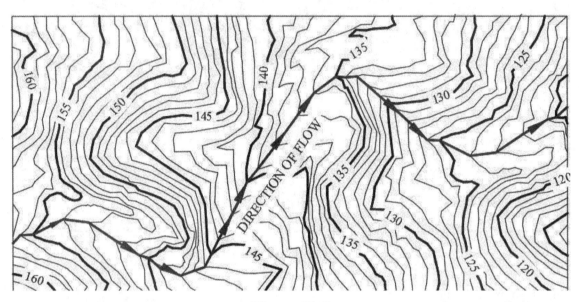

Figure 12-6

6. Outlet point
   - Make the *Outlet* layer to be the current layer.
   - In Figure 12-7, the intersection of the channel and the edge of the contour map is selected as the outlet point for the watershed.
   - Draw a point at the outlet and label it.
   - The outlet label's text height is 13'.

Figure 12-7

7. Delineate the watershed, Figure 12-8
    - Make the *Watershed_Boundary* layer to be the current layer.
    - The contour lines cross the ridge downstream by creating V's or U's pointing downstream.
    - Draw the boundary lines for the channel.
        o Activate the *Polyline* command.
        o Draw a polyline through the bottom of *U's* as shown in Figure 12-8.

Figure 12-8

8. Hatch the watershed, Figure 12-9a
    - Make the *Watershed_Hatch* layer to be the current layer.
        o Turn off all the layers except the *Watershed_Boundary* and *Watershed_Hatch* layers.

Figure 12-9a

- o Draw polylines to close the open ends of the watershed boundary.
- o Join the polylines (using the polyline edit command) to form a single closed polyline.
- o Activate the *Hatch* command.
- o Hatch the watershed, using the *GRASS* pattern and the scale of 60, Figure 12-9b and Figure 12-9c.

Figure 12-9b

Figure 12-9c

9. <u>Channel length</u>
   - Make the *Area-Length* the current layer.
   - Set the drawing units to engineering as follows. (i) Type *Units* on the command line and press the *Enter* key. This opens *Drawing Units* dialog box. (ii) In the *Drawing Units* dialog box, under the *Length* panel, select the *Engineering* units, Figure 12-10a.

Figure 12-10a

   - Find the length of the channel in feet (length of the channel's center line). The length of the channel in feet can be obtained using one of two techniques.

   (a) Using the *Property* palette
      o The easiest and the fastest method is the property palette.
      o Select the centerline of the channel and open its property palette, Figure 12-10b
      o The last entry in the *Geometry* panel is the length of the channel.

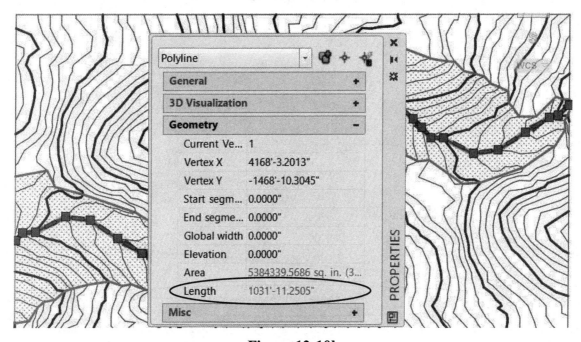

Figure 12-10b

(b) Using the *Distance* command
   o Lengthy method!
   o From the *Home* tab and *Utilities* panel, expand the *Measure* drop down

   menu and select the *Distance* ( ) tool.
   o Follow the prompts.

10. Watershed area
   - Make the *Area-Length* to be the current layer.
   - Find the area of the watershed in acres. The area of the watershed can be obtained using one of two techniques.
   (a) Using the *Property* palette
      o Select the boundary of the watershed, and connect and close the polyline, Figure 12-11a.
      o Open its property palette, Figure 12-11b.
      o The second to last entry in the *Geometry* panel is the area of the watershed.
      o The area is in square feet.

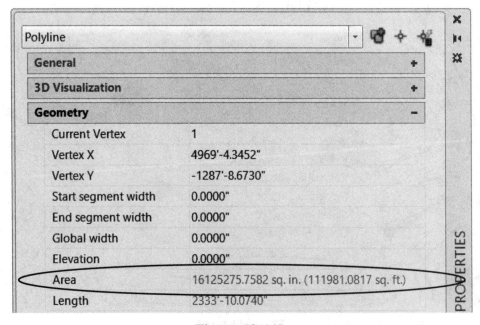

Figure 12-11a

Figure 12-11b

(c) Using the *Distance* command
  o From the *Home* tab and *Utilities* panel, expand the *Measure* drop down
    menu and select the *Area* () tool.
  o The prompt shown in Figure 12-11c appears.
  o Use the down arrow and choose the *Object* option.

Specify first corner point or ⊡ 4138'-0.4996" -1068'-4.6702"

| Object |
| Add area |
| Subtract area |
| eXit |

Figure 12-11c

  o Click on the watershed boundary (make sure the boundary is represented
    by a single closed polyline, Figure 12-11a.
  o The area information appears on the screen, Figure 12-11d.
  o Press the *Esc* key to exit the command.

Area = 16125275.7582 square in. (111981.081654 square ft.), Perimeter = 2333'-10.0740"
Enter an option

| Distance |
| Radius |
| Angle |
| • ARea |
| Volume |
| eXit |

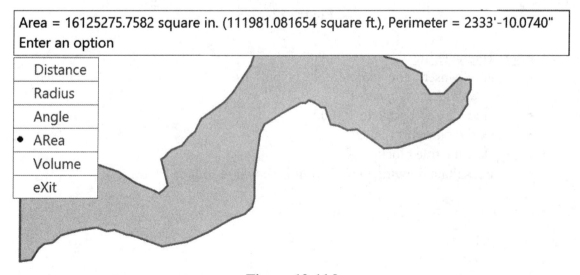

Figure 12-11d

- Convert   the   area   into   acres   using   the   conversion   factor   of
  1 Acres = 43560 sq. ft.

11. Display the length and area on the drawing
   • Create two texts boxes (or two tables) to show the length in feet and the area in acres on the drawing, Figure 12-12.

| HYDROLOGIC LENGTH: 1032 FT | WATERSHED AREA: 2.5707 ACRES |

Figure 12-12

12. Insert Template file
   • Finally, insert the *Landscape* layout from the template file labeled as "*My_acad Landscape.dwt.*"
   • Set the viewport scale to 1:1000.
   • Lock the viewport scale.
   • Update the title block.
   • The resultant drawing in the layout is shown in Figure 12-13.

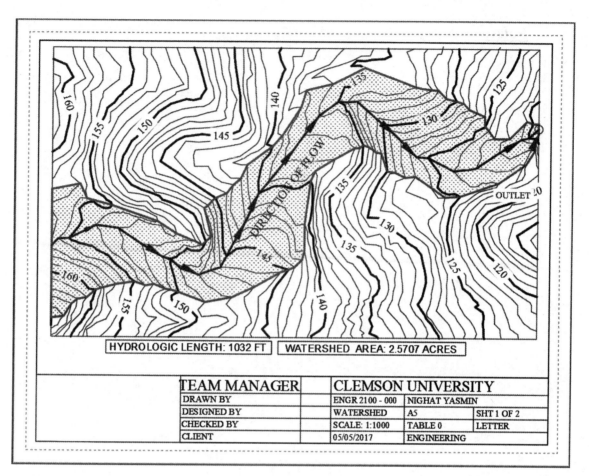

Figure 12-13

Notes:

13. Floodplains

13.1. Learning Objectives

After completing this chapter, you will demonstrate competency in the following areas:

- Basics of floodplains
- Basics of hydrographs
- Delineate floodplains of a channel using AutoCAD

13.2.   Introduction

Generally, a floodplain is the dry and flat (or mild sloped) land area adjacent to a river, stream, creek, or lake which is subject to inundation by floodwaters from the source. In order to save life and property on the floodplain, it is important to estimate their extent and geometry. The area of the floodplain can be determined by delineating the boundaries of the floodplain. The focus of this chapter is floodplain delineation.

13.3.   Terminology

- Open channel flow: An open channel flow is a surface water flow with a free surface, e.g., flow in rivers, streams, or partially filled pipes.
- Flooding/flood: A flood, also known as flooding, is the phenomenon by which water level exceeds the capacity of a stream, river, or a drainage channel. Flooding occurs due to excessive rainfall, snowmelt, or a dam break upstream.
- Main channel: The main channel is referred to as the normal capacity of a channel, Figure 13-1a and Figure 13-1b.
- Bankfull: The bankfull capacity of a channel is referred to as the maximum capacity of a channel without overflowing, Figure 13-1a and Figure 13-1c.
- Floodplain: A floodplain is defined as the dry and flat (or mild slope) land area adjoining a river, stream, creek, or lake which is subject to inundation by floodwaters from the source, Figure 13-1a and Figure 13-1d.

Figure 13-1a

Figure 13-1b

Figure 13-1c

Figure 13-1d

- Encroachment: An encroachment is defined as any construction or modification of the topography in the floodplain that reduces the area available to convey the floodwater. In Figure 13-2, the construction of the building on the left bank reduces the area for the flood wave. This encroachment leads to higher flood elevation on the right bank and a larger area is inundated by the flood.

Figure 13-2

- <u>100 year flood</u>: A 100 year flood is defined as the flood water level expected to occur at least once in a 100-year period. More precisely the 100 year flood is known as a 1% flood because this is the probability of occurrence of the flood. Although, very unlikely, depending on rainfall or snowmelt in an area it is possible that two 100 year floods occur in the same year.

- <u>Floodplain study</u>: Due to the continuous change in the floodplain, these areas need to be examined in order to find out how they might affect or be affected by the development. The purpose of a floodplain study is to delineate the 100-year floodplain limits within or near a development. The study helps to preserve the natural resources within the 100-year floodplain, to protect property and persons, and to apply a unified, comprehensive approach to floodplain management.

- <u>Hydrograph</u>: Hydrograph is the flow data represented as a graph (Figure 13-3a) or in a tabular format (Figure 13-3b). Hydrographs are classified as discharge, stage, and station-stage hydrographs.

- <u>Discharge hydrograph</u>: A discharge hydrograph, at a gauging station, represents the rate of flow with respect to time usually as cubic feet per second or cfs. Figure 13-3a shows a discharge hydrograph in a graphical representation and its equivalent tabular form is shown in Figure 13-3b.

- <u>Stage hydrograph</u>: A stage (or elevation) hydrograph represents water surface elevation of flow at a gauging station with respect to time, Figure 13-3c.

- <u>Station-Stage hydrograph</u>: A station-stage hydrograph represents water surface elevation of flow at a given time for several gauging stations, Figure 13-3d.

Figure 13-3a

13.4.   Major Steps In A Floodplain Delineation

The major steps in watershed delineation process are listed below.

Step 1: Create a contour map of the area.
Step 2: Mark the centerline of the channel by joining the V's. For a channel, the tip of the V is upstream.
Step 3: Show the direction of flow. A channel flows from a higher elevation (upstream) to the lower elevation (downstream).
Step 4: Draw the main channel.
Step 5: Draw the bankfull discharge.

Step 6: Draw the floodplain's boundary.
Step 7: Find the length of the channel and the area of the floodplains.

Discharge Hydrograph	
Time (Hour)	**Discharge (cfs)**
0	2
2	6
4	5
6	3
8	6
10	9
12	3
14	6
16	8
18	5
20	6
22	1
24	4

Figure 13-3b

Stage Hydrograph	
Time (Hour)	**Stage (Feet)**
0	1
2	2
4	3
6	4
8	5
10	6
12	7
14	6
16	5
18	4
20	3
22	2
24	1

Figure 13-3c

13.5.   Floodplain Delineation Using AutoCAD

The term delineate is defined as outlining the boundary. The floodplain delineation is the technique to mark the floodplain for the given stage. This section provides step-by-step instruction to delineate a floodplain. The station-stage hydrograph for a 100-year flood shown in Figure 13-3d is used to delineate the floodplain.

Station-Stage Hydrograph May 17, 2017			
Station	*Stage (Feet)*	*Station*	*Stage (Feet)*
P1	156	P11	138
P2	155	P12	137
P3	154	P13	136
P4	153	P14	134
P5	151	P15	132
P6	148	P16	128
P7	146	P17	127
P8	143	P18	124
P9	141	P19	123
P10	140	P20	122

Figure 13-3d

1. Launch AutoCAD 2018.
2. <u>Contour map</u>
   - Open the previously created contour map or a downloaded map.
   - Create the layers as shown in Figure 13-4.
   - Change the color, linetype, and lineweight of the layers.

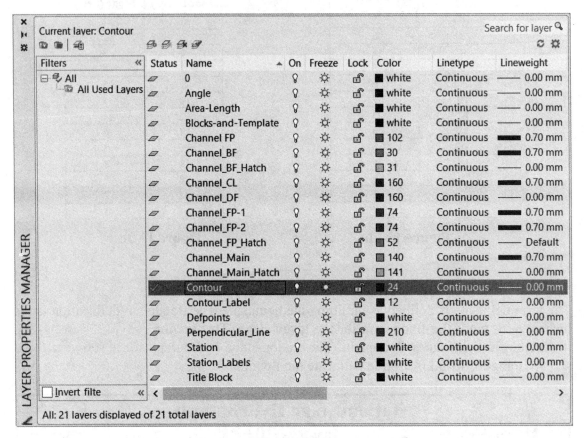

Figure 13-4

3. <u>Contour labels</u>
   - Make the *Contour_Labels* layer to be the current layer.
   - Label the index contour using the *Text*, *Background Mask*, and the *Rotate* commands, Figure 13-5. The text height is 15 feet in the sample contour map.

4. <u>Centerline</u>
   - Make the *Channel_CL* layer to be the current layer.
   - A channel flows from the higher elevation to the lower elevation. From Chapter 10, the contour lines cross the streambed upstream by creating V's with the closed end of the V's pointing upstream.
   - Draw the centerline for the channel, Figure 13-6.
     o Activate the *Polyline* command.
     o Draw a polyline through the closed end of the V's as shown in Figure 13-6.

Figure 13-5

Figure 13-6

5. <u>Direction of the flow</u>
   - Make the *Channel_DF* layer to be the current layer.
   - Show the direction of the flow for the channels using the quick leader. Use the first part of the *qleader* command to draw the arrows, Figure 13-7.
   - The arrowhead size varies from 24ft to 40ft.
   - The direction of flow label's text size is 12 ft.

Figure 13-7

6. <u>Main channel</u>
   - Make the *Channel_Main* layer the current layer.
   - The main channel is 20ft, Figure 13-8.
     - o Activate the *Offset* command.
     - o Set the offset distance to 10ft.
     - o Create an offset on either side of the centerline.
     - o Move the offsets to the *Channel_Main* layer.
     - o If necessary, use *Trim* and *Extend* commands near the ends of the centerline.

Figure 13-8

7. Bankfull
   - Make the *Channel_BF* layer the current layer.
   - The bankfull is 40ft, Figure 13-9.
     - ○ Activate the *Offset* command.
     - ○ Set the offset distance to 20ft.
     - ○ Create an offset on either side of the centerline of the main channel.
     - ○ Move the offsets to the *Channel_BF* layer.
     - ○ If necessary, use *Trim* and *Extend* commands near the ends of the centerline.

Figure 13-9

8. Gauging station
   - Turn *Off* the *Contour*, *Contour_Label*, *Channel_DF*, *Channel_Main*, and *Channel_BF* layers. Only the *Channel_CL* layer should be *On*.
   - Make the *Station* layer the current layer.
   - Add the stations' locations shown in Figure 13-11 as follows.
     - ○ From the *Home* tab and the expanded *Utilities* panel, click on the *Point Style...* tool to open the *Point Style* dialog box, Figure 13-10a.
     - ○ Change the point style and size. In the figure, the point size is set to be 9'. For ANSI units, the *Point Style* dialog box takes input ONLY in inches. So set the size to 108 (**DO NOT TYPE 9'!**); however, it displays it in feet.
     - ○ From the *Home* tab and the expanded *Draw* panel, click on the *Point Measure* (⬚) tool, Figure 13-10b, to activate the point command to draw points at a regular interval. The prompt shown in Figure 13-10c appears.

Figure 13-10a

Figure 13-10b

o Click on the desired polyline. In the current example, click on the left edge of the centerline, Figure 13-10c. The accuracy of the floodplain delineation depends on the accuracy of this point.

o The prompt shown in Figure 13-10d appears.

o Specify the distance between the stations (in the current example the distance is 50ft), and press the *Enter* key. The software assumes that the distance between the stations is constant, Figure 13-10d.

o The points appear on the centerline. The first point is 50' from the beginning of the polyline, Figure 13-10e.

o Draw a point at the beginning of the centerline, Figure 13-10f.

Click at the starting point for the object selection

Select object to measure:

Figure 13-10c

Specify length of segment or   50'

Figure 13-10d

- Make the *Station_Label* layer to be the current layer.
- Label the stations using *Text* and *Background Mask* commands, Figure 13-10f and Figure 13-11.

Figure 13-10e

Figure 13-10f

Figure 13-11

9. Perpendicular lines
    *   Stage-Station hydrograph of Figure 13-13d shows that the stage (water surface elevation) at station P5 is 151ft.
    *   Figure 13-12a shows the perpendicular lines for stations P2 to P9.
    *   Make the *Perpendicular_Line* layer to be the current layer.
    *   Draw a line originating at station P5 and ending at the nearest contour (148ft).
    *   Rotate the line at 90 degrees; use the end of the line at P5 as the base point for the rotation. The line will be perpendicular to the centerline, Figure 13-12a.
    *   Since the stage at P5 is 151ft; extend the perpendicular line at P5 to the 151ft contour.

Figure 13-12a

*   Refer to the Station-Stage hydrograph shown in Figure 13-3d and repeat the process for all the stations.
*   Figure 13-12b shows the perpendicular lines for all of the stations.

Figure 13-12b

- Make the *Angle* layer to be the current layer.
- Add the angular dimensions to the perpendicular lines, Figure 13-12c.

Figure 13-12c

10. <u>Delineate the floodplain</u>
- Make the *Channel_FP-1* layer to be the current layer.
- Draw a polyline passing through the upper end point of the perpendicular lines.
- Make the *Channel_FP-2* layer the current layer.

- Draw a polyline passing through the lower end point of the perpendicular lines.
- These polylines represent the floodplain for the 100 year flood, Figure 13-13.

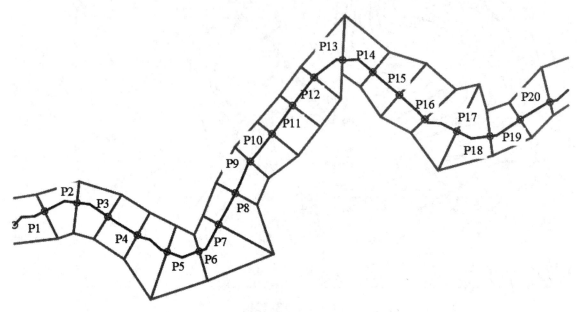

Figure 13-13

11. <u>Display the channel, bankfull, and floodplains</u>
    - Turn on the *Channel_Main*, *Channel_BF*, *Channel_FP-1*, and *Channel_FP-2* layers, Figure 13-14. Turn *Off* the other layers.
    - Extend the floodplain lines to the edge of the contour map, Figure 13-14.
    - Draw polylines at the end to create a closed boundary for the hatch, Figure 13-14.

Figure 13-14

12. Hatch
- Make the *Channel_Main_Hatch* layer to be the current layer.
- Activate the *Hatch* command and hatch the main channel. Use *MUDST* and 200 for the hatch pattern and the scale, respectively, Figure 13-15.
- Make the *Channel_BF_Hatch* layer to be the current layer.
- Activate the *Hatch* command and hatch the bankfull channel. Use *GRAVEL* and 150 for the hatch pattern and the scale, respectively, Figure 13-15.
- Make the *Channel_ FP_Hatch* layer to be the current layer.
- Label the floodplains as shown in Figure 13-15.
- Activate the *Hatch* command and hatch the floodplains. For hatching, click on one of the floodplains. Use *GRASS* and 40 for the hatch pattern and the scale, respectively, Figure 13-15. Repeat the process for the other floodplain. Hatching the floodplain independently helps in finding the area of the floodplains.

Figure 13-15

13. Channel length
- Make the *Area-Length* layer the current layer.
- Set the drawing units to engineering as follows. (i) Type *Units* on the command line and press the *Enter* key. This opens the *Drawing Units* dialog box. (ii) In the *Drawing Units* dialog box, under the *Length* panel, select the *Engineering* units, Figure 13-16a.

Figure 13-16a

- Find the length of the channel in feet (length of the channel's centerline). The length of the channel in feet can be obtained using one of the following two techniques.

    (a) Using the *Property* palette
    - o The easiest and the fastest method is the property palette.
    - o Select the centerline of the channel and open its property palette, Figure 13-16b.
    - o The last entry in the *Geometry* panel is the length of the channel.

Figure 13-16b

    (b) Using the *Inquiry* command
    - o Lengthy method!
    - o From the *Home* tab and *Utilities* panel, expand the *Measure* drop down menu and select the *Distance* ( ) tool.
    - o Follow the prompts.

Floodplains area
- Make the *Area-Length* layer to be the current layer.
- Find the area of the floodplains in acres.
- The area of the floodplains can be obtained using one of the following two techniques.

    (b) Using the *Property* palette
    - o Select the hatch of the floodplain labeled as A and open its property palette, Figure 13-17a.
    - o The second entry in the *Geometry* panel is the area of the floodplain A.
    - o Similarly, find the area of the floodplain labeled as B.

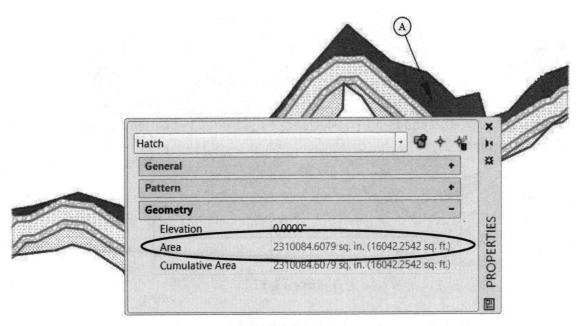

Figure 13-17a

(a) Use the *Inquiry* command.
   o Lengthy method!
   o From the *Home* tab and *Utilities* panel, expand the *Measure* drop down
   menu and select the *Area* (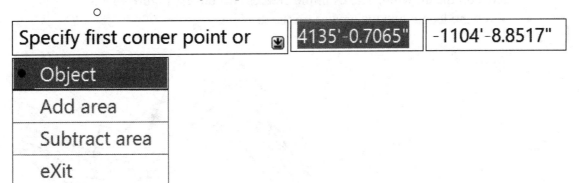) tool.
   o The prompt shown in Figure 11-17b appears. Use the down arrow and
   choose the object option for the polyline.
   o

| Specify first corner point or 🔽 | 4135'-0.7065" | -1104'-8.8517" |

| Object |
| Add area |
| Subtract area |
| eXit |

Figure 13-17b

   o The prompt shown in Figure 11-17c appears.
   o Click on the hatch of the floodplain A. The area information appears on
   the screen, Figure 11-17d.

| Select objects: |

Figure 13-17c

Area = 2310084.6079 square in. (16042.254222 square ft.), Perimeter = 2119'-5.9535"
Enter an option

Distance
Radius
Angle
• ARea

Figure 13-17d

- o Press the *Esc* key to exit the command.
- o The information is available in the command line.
- o Repeat the process with the floodplain B.
- Convert the areas into acres using the conversion factor of 1 Acres = 43560 sq. ft.

14. <u>Display lengths and areas</u>
- Either create three texts boxes to show the length in feet and the areas in acres on the drawing, or create two tables to show the length in feet and the areas in acres on the drawing. The example creates two tables, Figure 13-18.
- Show the length and the area as on the drawing.

HYDROLOGIC LENGTH: 1032 FT
FLOODPLAIN-A AREA: 0.3683 ACRES
FLOODPLAIN-B AREA: 0.5123 ACRES

Figure 13-18

15. <u>Insert Template file</u>
- Finally, insert the landscape layout from the template file labeled as "My_acad_Landscape.dwt."
- Set the viewport scale to 1:1000.
- Lock the viewport.
- Update the Title block.
- The resultant drawing in the layout is shown in Figure 13-19.

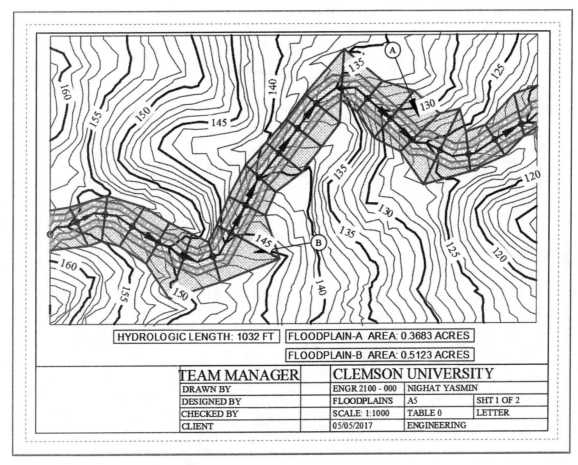

Figure 13-19

<u>Notes:</u>

14. Road Design

14.1. Learning Objectives

After completing this chapter, you will demonstrate competency in the following areas:

- Basics of plan, profile, and cross-section of a road
- Drawing plan, profile, and cross-sections using AutoCAD

14.2.   Introduction

Humans have been using many different modes of transportation on land, from horseback to automobiles (car, bus, truck, etc.). One common feature among these modes is the road. A road can be as simple as a walking trail to several lanes paved road. A road design is a complicated process. It depends on several factors. Some of the factors are listed here: location of the road, types of the vehicles using the road, geometric design, drainage system, and parking facilities. The road location factor is further subdivided into the land topography, soil characteristics, and environmental effects. Once the decision for the road location is made, the area is surveyed and various drawings are prepared. The focus of this chapter is two of the major drawings: (i) the plan and profile and (ii) the cross-sections drawings.

14.3.   Plan And Profile

The plan and profile drawing is commonly known as the PnP drawing. It is a two-view drawing. It is divided into two parts, Figure 14-1. The upper half always displays the plan view (and the contour map), and the lower half displays the profile. The PnP drawing is also an important drawing for most of the civil engineering projects, such as water and sewer pipelines, storm drainage system, curbs, and sidewalk construction.

Figure 14-1

14.3.1. Plan

The plan view represents the area as seen from the top or a birds-eye-view. A plan view contains all the necessary information for the road construction. The upper half of the Figure 14-1 shows the plan of a road.

14.3.2. Profile

The profile is the representation of the natural ground. It is defined as a display of the elevation of a set of equidistant points along a continuous line, for example, the centerline of a road. It is represented as a graph of elevation with respect to the distance along the centerline. The elevation is represented on the y-axis and the distance along the centerline is shown on the x-axis. The lower half of Figure 14-1 shows the profile of the centerline of the road.

14.4.   Draw Road Plan Using AutoCAD

This section provides step-by-step instructions to create a plan of the proposed road.

1. Launch AutoCAD 2018.
2. Create the layers as needed. Assign color, linetype, and lineweight appropriately to each layer, Figure 14-2.

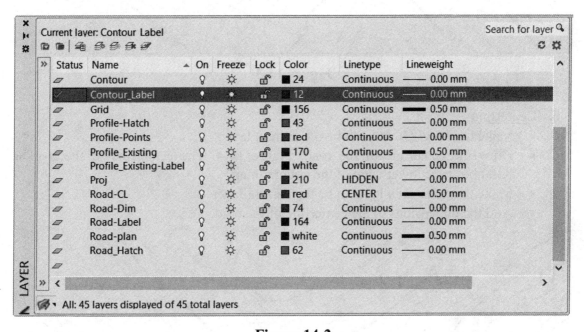

Figure 14-2

3. Turn *On/Off* and freeze the layers as needed.

4. Contour map
    *   Open a previously created or downloaded (RoadDesign-16-Students) contour map, Figure 14-3.

5. Add label to the contour map
    *   Make the *Contour-Label* layer to be the current layer.
    *   Label the index contour using the *Text* and the *Background Mask* commands, Figure 14-3.
    *   Set the height of the text to be 4ft.

Figure 14-3

6. Centerline
   - Make the *Road-CL* layer to be the current layer.
   - Draw the centerline of the road, Figure 14-4. The centerline of the road is 82ft above the lower edge of the counter map.
   - Make the *Road-Dim* layer to be the current layer.
   - Add the dimensions to the centerline of the road.

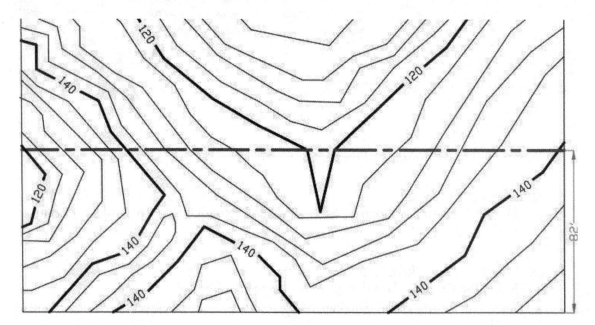

Figure 14-4

7. Road plan
   - Make the *Road-Plan* layer to be the current layer.
   - The road is 26'-8" wide, Figure 14-5a.
     - o Activate the *Offset* command. Set the offset distance to 13'-4".
     - o Create an offset of the centerline on either side of the centerline.
     - o Move the offsets to the road plan's layer.
     - o The road plan is shown in Figure 14-5a.
   - Make the *Road-Label* layer to be the current layer.
   - Add the road label, Figure 14-5a.

Figure 14-5a

   - Make the *Road-Hath* layer to be the current layer.
   - Add the hatch to the plan of the road. Use AR-CONC, 0, and 4 for the hatch pattern, angle, and scale, respectively, Figure 14-5b.

Figure 14-5b

14.5.   Plot The Profile Using AutoCAD

This section provides step-by-step instructions to create a profile of the centerline of the proposed road.

1. Draw the grid
   - Make the *Grid-0* layer to be the current layer. Generally, the grid color is light blue, light green, or light orange.
   - Use the *Array* command to draw the grid.
     (a) Draw two vertical lines 25 feet long as shown in Figure 14-6a. These lines are highlighted by displaying their grip points.
     (b) Draw a horizontal line (the length of the line is equal to the width of the counter map) at the lower end of the lines drawn in step (a), Figure 14-6a.
     (c) Activate the *Array* command and create a rectangular array of the horizontal line. The array contains 11 rows with row spacing of 1 foot and the number of columns is set to 1.
   - Use the *Explode* command to break the array.
   - Change the line weight of every fifth row, Figure 14-6b.
   - Add the labels as shown in Figure 14-6b. The minimum elevation on the grid is less than the minimum elevation of the counter lines intersecting the centerline; and the maximum elevation on the grid is greater than the maximum elevation of the counter lines intersecting the centerline.

Figure 14-6a

Figure 14-6b

2. Draw the projection line
   - Make the *Proj* layer to be the current layer.
   - Draw straight lines originating at the intersection of the centerline and the contour lines and terminating at x-axis of the grid, Figure 14-7.
   - Set the linetype scale of the projection line to 0.4.

Figure 14-7

3. Plot the elevation on the grid
    - From the *Home* tab and expanded *Utilities* tab select the *Point Style...* to open the *Point Style* dialog box, Figure 14-8a.
    - Change point style and size as shown in Figure 14-8a. Although the dialog box shows the point size in feet, the input is always in inches.
    - Make the *Profile-Point* layer to be the current layer.
    - The first projection line originates at 120 feet contour line. On the profile's grid, draw a point on this projection line at the elevation of 120 feet.
    - Repeat the process for the other projection lines, Figure 14-8b and Figure 14-8c.

Figure 14-8a

Figure 14-8b

Figure 14-8c

4. Plot the existing profile
   - Make the *Profile-Existing* layer to be the current layer.
   - To create the profile, activate the *Polyline* command and connect the points, Figure 14-9a. This profile is known as the existing profile or the ground line.

Figure 14-9a

5. Add the label to the existing profile
    •   Make the *Profile-Existing_Label* layer to be the current layer.
    •   Using the *Text*, *background Mask* and *qleader* commands, add label to the profile, Figure 14-10.

Figure 14-10

6. Hatch the existing profile
    •   Turn *Off* the grid and projection layers.
    •   Make the *Profile-Hatch* layer to be the current layer.
    •   Using an *Offset* command, create an offset of the profile with the offset distance of 5ft, Figure 14-11a.
    •   Move the offset to the hatch layer, Figure 14-11b.
    •   Connect the ends of the profile using small lines, Figure 14-11c.
    •   Activate the *Hatch* command.
    •   Add the hatch; set the pattern to *EARTH*, angle to 0, and scale to 200, Figure 14-11d.

Figure 14-11a

Figure 14-11b

Figure 14-11c

Figure 14-11d

7. <u>PnP</u>
   - Finally, insert a layout from the template file labeled "My_acad_Landscape," Figure 14-12.
   - Set the scale of the drawing to 1:400, Figure 14-12.
   - Update the blocks, Figure 14-12.
   - The complete PnP drawing is shown in Figure 14-12.

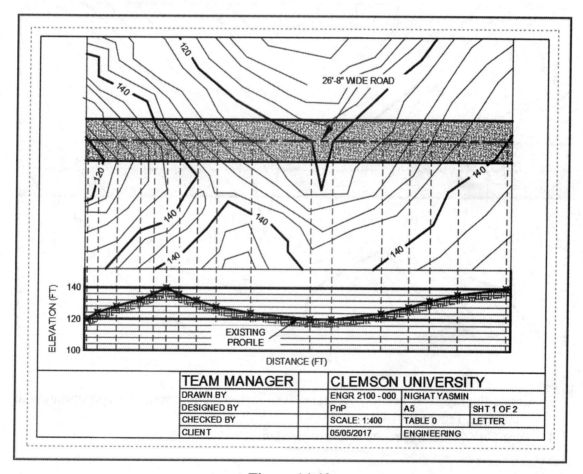

TEAM MANAGER	CLEMSON UNIVERSITY		
DRAWN BY	ENGR 2100 - 000	NIGHAT YASMIN	
DESIGNED BY	PnP	A5	SHT 1 OF 2
CHECKED BY	SCALE: 1:400	TABLE 0	LETTER
CLIENT	05/05/2017	ENGINEERING	

Figure 14-12

8. <u>Save the drawing</u>
   - Save the drawing as *PnP.dwg*.

14.6.   Cross-Section

A cross-section is defined as a display of the elevation of a set of equidistant points along a continuous line that runs perpendicular to the centerline. Usually, the sections are drawn at a regular interval, for example, at every station (and stations are 50' apart). The process for creating cross-sections is the same as for a profile. However, cross-sections are smaller than profiles. Generally, for cross-sections, both the existing and proposed shapes are drawn. For discussion purposes, only the existing shapes are drawn.

14.7.   Draw The Cross-Section Using AutoCAD

1. This section assumes that the user has created the road plan.
2. Open the drawing containing the road plan (*PnP.dwg*). Figure 14-13 show the plan of the road.

Figure 14-13

3. Create the layers as needed. Assign color, linetype, and lineweight appropriately to each layer, Figure 14-14.
4. Turn *On/Off* and freeze the layers as needed.

Status	Name	▲	On	Freeze	Lock	Color	Linetype	Lineweight
▱	Grid-2		♀	☼	⌗	■ 180	Continuous	—— 0.00 mm
▱	Stations		♀	☼	⌗	■ 172	Continuous	—— 0.00 mm
▱	Stations-Dim		♀	☼	⌗	■ 74	Continuous	—— 0.00 mm
▱	Stations-Label		♀	☼	⌗	■ white	Continuous	—— 0.00 mm
▱	XS-Dist		♀	☼	⌗	■ 160	Continuous	—— 0.00 mm
▱	XS-Draw_Hatch		♀	☼	⌗	■ white	Continuous	—— 0.00 mm
▱	XS-Draw_Label		♀	☼	⌗	■ white	Continuous	—— 0.00 mm
▱	XS-Draw_LN		♀	☼	⌗	■ white	Continuous	■■ 0.50 mm
▱	XS-Draw_PT		♀	☼	⌗	■ white	Continuous	—— 0.00 mm
▱	XS-PT		♀	☼	⌗	■ white	Continuous	—— 0.00 mm
▱	XS_DS		♀	☼	⌗	■ white	Continuous	—— 0.00 mm
▱	XS_LN		♀	☼	⌗	■ white	Continuous	■■ 0.50 mm

Current layer: Contour Label

Figure 14-14

5. Draw stations
   - Make the *Stations* layer to be the current layer.
   - Add the stations, Figure 14-15a and Figure 14-15b using *Point* command. The command is performed as follows:
     - From the *Home* tab and expanded *Draw* panel, select the *Point Measure* command.
     - Click on the left end of the centerline.
     - For the prompt "*Specify the length of the segment*," specify 50', and press the *Enter* key.
     - Multiple points 50 feet apart are drawn.
     - If necessary, change the point style and size (*Home* tab and expanded *Utilities* panel, click on *Point Style...* tool and follow the prompts.)

6. Dimension the stations
   - Make the *Station_Dim* layer to be the current layer.
     - Add the dimensions to the station, Figure 14-15a and Figure 14-15b.

7. Label the stations
   - Make the *Station_Label* layer to be the current layer.
     - The left end of the centerline is labeled *00+00*. The first station is 50 feet from the left end, hence labeled 00+50. The remaining stations are 50 feet apart, therefore labeled accordingly, Figure 14-15a and Figure 14-15b.
     - Write the first label using the *Text* command.
     - Rotate the text 90 degrees using the *Rotate* command.
     - Create a copy at each station using the *Copy* command.
     - Update the values to match the station label, Figure 14-15a and Figure 14-15b.

Figure 14-15a

Figure 14-15b

8. <u>Draw the section line perpendicular to the centerline at the selected station.</u>
    - Make the *XS_LN* layer to be the current layer.
    - Turn *Off* the contour and contour labels layers.
    - In the example, the cross-section at station 00 + 50 is created.
    - Turn on the *Perpendicular* option in the object snap setting dialog box.
    - Start a line at the centerline of the station 00 + 50 and move to the outer edge of the road, Figure 14-16a.

Figure 14-16a

- Click at the perpendicular point. A perpendicular line is created from the centerline to the outer edge, Figure 14-16b.
- Repeat the process on the other side of the centerline or use the *Mirror* command. Figure 14-16c shows the perpendicular lines.
- Repeat the process at the other stations or use the *Copy* command.

9. Draw points on the perpendicular lines.
    - Make the *XS_PT* layer to be the current layer.
    - Draw four points, two on each line drawn in step #4 as shown in Figure 14-17a (two at the midpoints and two at the outer edges of the road).
    - Repeat the process at the other stations or use the *Copy* command, Figure 14-17b.

Figure 14-16b   **Figure 14-16c**   **Figure 14-17a**

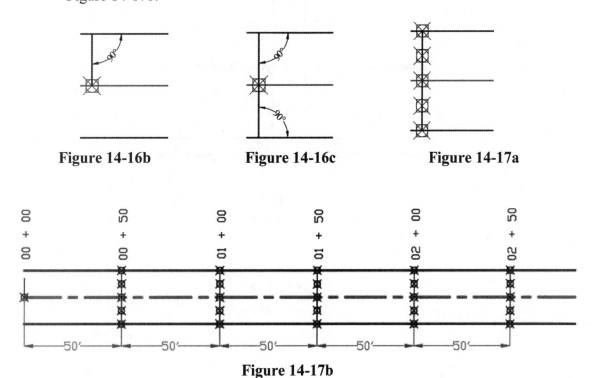

Figure 14-17b

10. <u>Show the distance to the points from the nearest contours.</u>
   - Make the *XS_DS* layer to be the current layer.
   - Change the dimensions to decimal style as follows. (i) Open the *Dimension Style Manger* dialog box. (ii) Click the *Modify* button. (iii) Open the *Modify Dimension Style* dialog box; select the *Primary Units*. (iv) Finally, under the *Linear Dimension* panel and for *Unit Format* select *Decimal*.
   - Use the *Align* dimension command to add the distance to every point from the two contours (one on each side), Figure 14-18a.
   - If necessary, extend the perpendicular line (beyond the edge of the road) to the nearest contour line.
   - Repeat the process for the other stations, Figure 14-18b.
   - The last two stations are left for the user.

Figure 14-18a

Figure 14-18b

11. <u>Find the elevation of the cross-section points using interpolation.</u>

- Interpolation is not needed if a contour line is passing through a station or if a contour line above and below a station has the same value. Hence, skip this step.
- If a contour line is not passing through a station and the point is not enclosed by the same contour then find the elevation of the station using linear interpolation.
- Let **es** be the elevation of a point in question (unknown); **e1** and **e2** are the elevations of the contours above and below the point, respectively; and **d1** and **d2** are the distance as shown in Figure 14-19. Find the elevation of the station (**es**) using the formula: *d1/d2 = (e1 - es) / (e1 – e2)*.
- Similarly, find the elevation of the other stations.

Figure 14-19

12. Cross-section's grid
    • In Figure 14-20, the distance along Y-axis is distorted.
        ○ On X-axis: 1ft on the grid represent 1ft of the road.
        ○ On Y-axis: 2ft on the grid represents 1ft of the road.

    • Make the *Grid* layer to be the current layer and draw the grid as shown in Figure 14-20. In the figure:
        ○ *-13'-4"* represents the upper edge of the road.
        ○ *0* represents the centerline of the road.
        ○ *13'-4"* represents the lower edge of the road.

Figure 14-20

13. Cross-section drawing
    • Make the *XS_Draw_PT* layer to be the current layer.
    • Draw points for the elevation of stations across the centerline, Figure 14-21.
    • Make the *XS_Draw_LN* layer to be the current layer.
    • Draw polylines through the points for the elevation of station, Figure 14-21.

14. Cross-section labels
    • Trim the grid from the cross-sections, Figure 14-22.
    • Make the *XS_Draw_Label* layer to be the current layer.
    • Add the labels to the cross-sections.
    • Add the rectangles around the labels using *Express Tools* tab → *Text* panel → *Enclose in Object* command.

Figure 14-21

Figure 14-22

15. Hatch
   - Make the *XS_Draw_Hatch* layer to be the current layer.
   - Activate the *Hatch* command and hatch the cross-sections.
   - Use *GRAVEL* pattern and 75 for the scale, respectively, Figure 14-23.

16. Insert Template file
   • Finally, insert a layout from the template file labeled "My_acad_Landscape.dwt."
   • Set the scale of the drawing to 1/16" = 1'-0", Figure 14-23.
   • Lock the viewport.
   • Update the Title block.
   • The resultant drawing in the layout is shown in Figure 14-23.

17. Save the drawing
   • Save the drawing as *PnP_XS.dwg*.

Figure 14-23

Notes:

15. Earthwork

15.1. Learning Objectives

After completing this chapter, you will demonstrate competency in the following areas:

- Basics of earthwork in a road design
- Delineate earthwork using AutoCAD

15.2.   Introduction

The earthwork, also known as the cut and fill in road construction terminology refers to the excavation and embankment of the earth. The volume of earthwork plays an important role in the selection of a road location because the cost of the road construction is greatly influenced by the earthwork. The construction cost can be reduced if the volume of cut is equal to the volume of the fill.

15.3.   Earthwork

In the plan and profile drawing, the profile represents the natural ground. After developing the PnP, the proposed profile is added to the drawing. The slope of the proposed profile represents the elevation of the centerline of the proposed road.

15.3.1. Cut

If the existing profile is above the proposed profile, then the extra material between the two profiles represents the volume of excavation or cut, Figure 15-1.

15.3.2. Fill

If the existing profile is below the proposed profile, then the empty space between the two profiles represents the volume of embankment or fills, Figure 15-1.

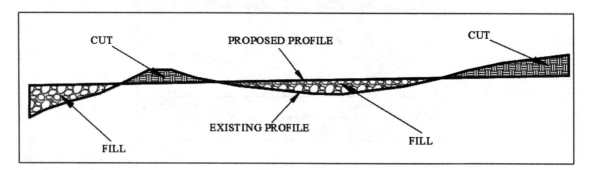

Figure 15-1

15.3.3. Location of a road

The volume of cut and fill greatly affects the cost of a road construction. If the volume of cut is more than the volume of fill, then the extra material must be removed from the site. This increases the cost of the project. If the volume of fill is more than the volume of cut, then the extra material must be brought to the site. This increases the cost of the project, too. Generally, the road is located such that the volume of the cut is equal to the volume of fill. However, this is not possible in every road construction.

15.4.   Slope

A slope of a line is defined as the ratio of change in altitude (ΔV_d) to the change in horizontal distance (ΔH_d). The slope is positive for an upward line (Figure 15-2a), whereas it is negative for a downward line (Figure 15-2b).

Slope can be specified as a percentage or an angle. It can be calculated using one of the following equations.

$$Slope\ (ratio) = (\Delta V_d\ /\ \Delta H_d) * 100$$
$$Slope\ (angle) = tan^{-1}(\Delta V_d\ /\ \Delta H_d)$$

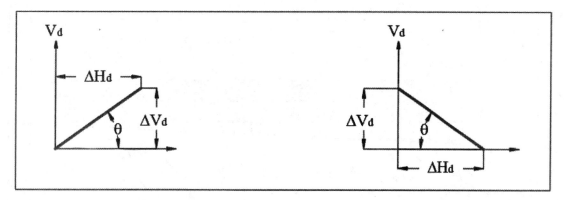

Figure 15-2a   **Figure 15-2b**

15.5.   Angle Of Repose

When a granular material is poured on a horizontal surface, it makes a pile; Figure 15-3 shows a pile of sand. The height of the pile increases as more material is poured. However, when the height of the pile reaches to V_d, pouring of any more material collapses the pile. The angle of the incline surface (Φ) just before the collapse is known as the angle of repose. Some of the factors affecting the angle of repose are density, surface area of the particle, and coefficient of friction of the material.

The angle of repose can be specified as a ratio or an angle. It can be calculated using one of the following equations.

$$\Phi\ (ratio) = H_d : V_d$$
$$\Phi\ (angle) = tan^{-1}(\Delta V_d\ /\ \Delta H_d)$$

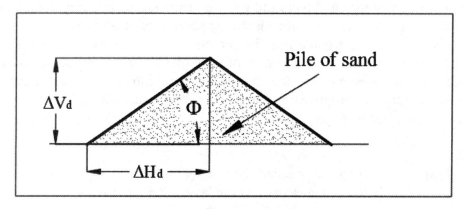

Figure 15-3

15.6.   Plan And Existing Profile Of A Road

Create the plan and profile file following the steps from Chapter 14. This section uses the plan and profile created in Chapter 14 and is shown in Figure 15-4.

Figure 15-4

15.7.   Proposed Profile Of A Road

It is clear from the existing profile of Figure 15-4 that with the current undulation of the road it will not be safe for the drivers and vehicles. Hence, it is very important to provide a safe slope to the road. The new slope is the proposed profile of the road. The proposed profile is also known as the grade line. The proposed profile depends on several factors such as soil condition, vehicle type, budget of the project, environmental issues, etc. This section assumed that the engineers have decided on the slope of the proposed profile. For the current example, the proposed profile has a +2% grade (that is, for every 100 feet horizontal distance, the road goes up by 2ft).

Layers:
- Create the layers as needed and assign color, linetype, and lineweight appropriately to each layer, or add the layer shown in Figure 15-5 to the profile drawing. **Before using a layer, make the desired layer current.**

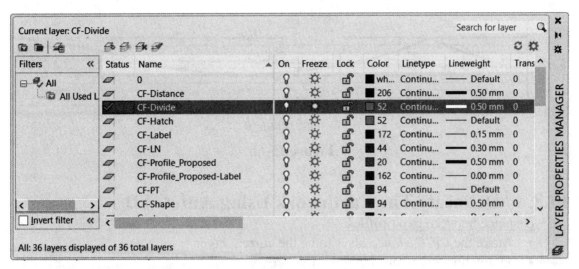

Figure 15-5

Proposed profile:
- For the current example, the proposed profile is +2% grade as shown in Figure 15-6a.
- Make the *CF_Profile-Proposed* layer to be the current layer.
- Draw the proposed profile. The proposed profile is highlighted by displaying its slope, Figure 15-6b.
  - Activate the *Line* or *Polyline* command.
  - Starting at the elevation of 124 feet on the left side of the grid, draw a line with +2% slope.
  - Use the *Extend* command to extend the profile to the right side of the grid.

Figure 15-6a

- Make the *CF_Profile-Proposed-Label* layer to be the current layer.
- Label the proposed profile as shown in Figure 15-6b.

Figure 15-6b

15.8. Delineate The Earthwork Using AutoCAD

1. <u>Distance between two profiles</u>:
   - Make the *CF-Distance* layer to be the current layer.
   - Draw line segments between the proposed and existing profiles. These line segments are highlighted by displaying their grip points, Figure 15-7a and Figure 15-7b.

Figure 15-7a

Figure 15-7b

2. <u>Delineation of cut and fill</u>: The angle of repose for both the cut and fill is 2:1.
   - The example shows the delineation of the (cut or fill) boundary for the 140 feet contour. **Refer to Figure 15-8a**.
   - Assume d140 is the distance between the two profiles. It is measured along the projection line originated at the intersection of the 140 feet contour and the centerline.

- Since the angle of repose is 2:1, multiply d140 by 2.
- Draw line segment *AB* of length 2*d140 from the edge of the road. In AutoCAD, this can be achieved by creating two copies of d140 as follows.

  (i) Turn *On* ORTHO mode from the status bar by clicking the ⬛ button. (ii) Activate the *Copy* command. (iii) Select d140 between the two profiles. (iv) Select the upper end as the base point for the *Copy* command. (v) Place one copy at the intersection of the lower edge of the road and the projection line originated at 140 contour. (vi) Place the second copy at the lower end of the first copy.
- Make the *CF_HL* layer to be the current layer.
- Draw horizontal line segment *BC* starting at the lower end of line *AB* and terminating at the 140 contour (the length of *BC* can be few inches to few feet).
- Make the *CF_Pt* layer to be the current layer.
- Draw a point at C, at the intersection of line *BC* and the 140 contour.

Figure 15-8a

- Repeat the process for the remaining contours, Figure 15-8b (left side of the contour map), and Figure 15-8c (right side of the contour map).

Figure 15-8b

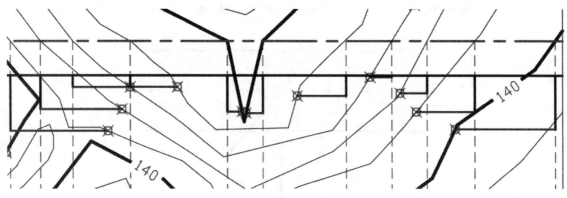

Figure 15-8c

- To repeat the delineation process for the other edge of the road, the first step is to extend the projection lines to the other edge of the road, Figure 15-9.

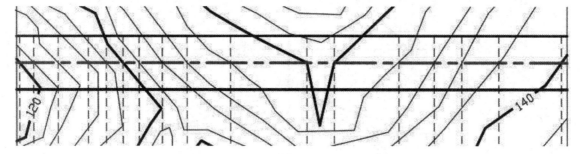

Figure 15-9

- Use the *Mirror* command to mirror the vertical lines (the distance between the two profiles); use the center line of the road plan as the mirror line, Figure 15-10a.

Figure 15-10a

- Make the *CF_HL* layer to be the current layer.
- Draw horizontal line segment, Figure 15-10b.
- Make the *CF_Pt* layer to be the current layer.
- Draw the points, Figure 15-10b.

Figure 15-10b

3. Draw boundary:
   - Make the *CF-Shape* layer to be the current layer.
   - Draw polylines through the points to delineate the boundary, Figure 15-11.
   - If necessary, extend the polylines drawn in the above step to the end of the contour map using the *Extend* command.

Figure 15-11

4. <u>Separate the cut and fill area</u>:
   - Make the *CF-Divide* layer be the current layer.
   - Turn *Off* the layers as shown in Figure 15-12.
   - Draw vertical lines originating from the intersection of the two profiles (in the grid area) to the contour map to separate the cut and fill's boundary, Figure 15-12.

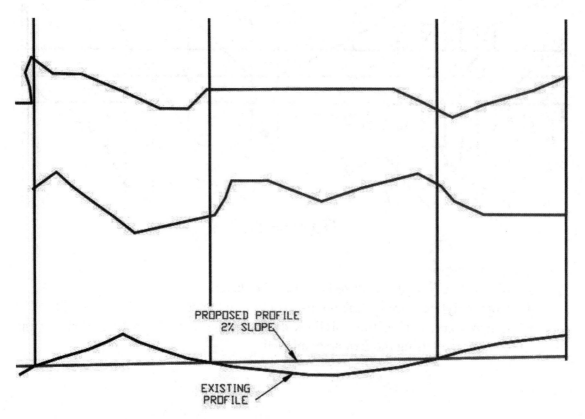

Figure 15-12

5. Label:
    *   Make the *CF-Label* layer the current layer
    *   Add labels to the cut and fill, Figure 15-13. The area above the proposed profile represents the cut, and the area below the proposed profile represents the fill.

6. Hatch:
    *   Make the *CF-Hatch* layer to be the current layer
    *   Draw lines to close the open ends of the cut and fill, Figure 15-13.
    *   Hatch the areas as shown in Figure 15-13. The fill is hatched using the GRAVEL pattern at the scale of 150, and the cut is hatched using the EARTH pattern at the scale of 200.

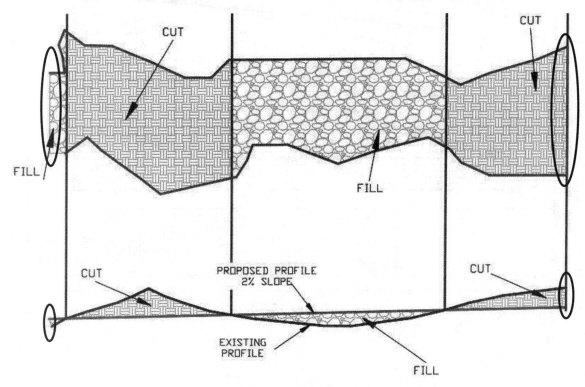

Figure 15-13

7. Insert Template file:
    *   Finally, insert the landscape layout from the template file labeled as "My_acad_Landscape."
    *   Set the scale of the drawing to 1:400, Figure 16-14.
    *   Lock the viewport.
    *   Update the Title block.
    *   The resultant drawing in the layout is shown in Figure 16-14.

8. <u>Save the file</u>:
   - Finally, save the drawing named as *CutFill.dwg*.

Figure 15-14

<u>Notes:</u>

16. Floor Plan

16.1. Learning Objectives

After completing this chapter, you will demonstrate competency in the following areas:

- Design and draw a floor plan
- Create window and door openings
- Insert user created and *Design Center*'s block in the floor plan
- Add dimensions to the floor plan
- Create door and window schedules for the floor plan

16.2.   Introduction

Consider a simple angle bracket shown in Figure 16-1a. The question is how it can be sketched to convey its shape correctly in two dimensions.

- The bracket is three-dimensional and describing it in words is difficult.
- To make the drawing process of a 3D object easier, engineers use a standard system called orthographic projection or orthographic views.
- The orthographic view shows two-dimensional views of three dimensional objects.

Figure 16-1a

The concept of orthographic projection is similar to the reflection of an object in a mirror. Figure 16-1b shows an image of the bracket in a mirror. Parallel rays from the bracket are creating the image on the mirror; the mirror is perpendicular (orthogonal) to the rays. Similarly, in technical drawing the front view is projected on the frontal plane.

If the bracket is looked at from the top, front, and right sides (Figure 16-1a), then its orthographic projections are two dimensional views, Figure 16-1c. Vertical lines are used to project information between top and front views. Horizontal lines are used to project information between front and right-side views. Horizontal and vertical lines are used to project information between front and right-side views using 45° miter line, Figure 16-1c.

Figure 16-1b

TOP VIEW

45°

H

H

L

W

FRONT VIEW   RIGHT SIDE VIEW

Figure 16-1c

The focus of this chapter is the top view of a building, also known as a floor plan. The front and side views (or elevations) are the focus of the next chapter. Consider a simple building shown in Figure 16-1d. The figure shows the southeast isometric view of a building.

Figure 16-1d

The three orthographic views (top, front, and right side view) are shown in Figure 16-1e. Notice the projection of the skylight (the box in the roof), front door, and the gable roof (the triangular roof) in the three orthographic views.

Figure 16-1e

16.3.   Floor Plan

In architecture and building engineering terminology, a version of a top view is called a floor plan. A floor plan is a simple two-dimensional line drawing resulting from looking at a building from above (below the ceiling level). It displays the relationship between rooms, windows, doors, walls, stairs, fireplace, and other features at one level of a building as if seen from the top. The focus of this chapter is designing and drawing a floor plan for a typical residential building with three bedrooms, two bathrooms, and a single car garage.

The floor plan is the most important and detailed dimensioned drawing of a building. Some of the information included in a floor plan of a residential building is the location and thickness of the exterior and interior walls; sizes and location of the doors and windows; details of the kitchen, laundry-, storage-, bed- and bath- rooms; ventilation, plumbing, electrical, and mechanical systems; slopes in the floor; etc. For multistory buildings, stairs are also shown on the floor plan. The scale of the drawing depends on the size of the building and size of the printing paper. Generally, the floor plans are printed at a scale of 1:48 or 1:96.

The floor plan design is an iterative process. Usually, it is the first drawing to be started. On the other hand, it is the last drawing to be completed. It is revised several times to accommodate the decision made in the elevations and sectional views' design.

16.4.   Windows

Windows are an important part of a building. Windows have evolved over time, from an opening in the wall for fresh air to enter and smoke to leave to the modern day sophisticated windows. Windows provide light and ventilation to the residents and architectural enhancement to the building; however, improperly placed windows detract from the house's appearance. Generally, 12% of a wall should be windows and the total glass area of the window should be about 10% of the floor area.

16.4.1. Types of windows

Based on the method of opening a window, the commonly used windows are classified as fixed, casement, sliding, and double-hung.

- Casement: Casement windows provide 100% ventilation and 100% light. These windows are hinged.
  - **Side hinge:** Side hinge windows are hinged at the side, Figure 16-2a. Usually these windows are narrow but can be joined to one another, or to a fixed window to fill wider openings.
  - **Awning or top hinge:** Awning windows are hinged at the top, Figure 16-2b. These windows are wider and shorter. Generally, opened awning windows swing outward.
  - **Hopper or bottom hinge:** Hopper windows are hinged at the bottom, Figure 16-2c. These windows are commonly used in commercial buildings. Generally, opened windows swing inward; otherwise, the rain water comes inside if it opens outward.

Figure 16-2a   **Figure 16-2b**   **Figure 16-2c**

- Sliding: Sliding windows open by gliding window panels on horizontal tracks in pairs, Figure 16-2d. These windows provide 50% ventilation and 100% light.
- Double-hung: Double-hung (also known as vertical-slide) windows open by gliding window panels on vertical tracks, Figure 16-2e. These windows provide 50% ventilation and 100% light. These windows are commonly used in small residential buildings.
- Fixed: Fixed windows are also known as picture windows. These windows do not have any moving parts. Although these windows can provide 100% light, they provide 0% ventilation. These are the cheapest windows.

16.4.2. Window sizes

A window can be of any size. Window companies manufacture windows in various shapes and sizes. Nonetheless, the type and size of the windows depends on the building style and the client's requirements. As a rule of thumb, the width of a window is about half of its height. Typically, the top of a window opening is 6'–8" from the floor. The bottom of the opening depends on the type of room. For example, a bedroom, dining, and a living room window's openings are 3'–10", 2'–10", and 1'– 10" above the floor level, respectively.

Figure 16-2d   **Figure 16-2e**

16.4.3. Window selection

The selection of a window type and its location depends on several factors. The windows should be located to improve the cross ventilation. Also, the hinged window openings in hallways or walkways should be high enough (per se 6 feet) to avoid injuries.

- Site orientation: In the northern hemisphere, the windows should be located in the southern walls, thus allowing sunlight to enter the room during the winter months.
- Insulation: The information regarding thermal performance (how much energy is lost for heating or cooling the building) of a window is very important. Inadequately insulated windows increase the air-conditioning cost, cause discomfort to the residents, and stain and decay the window material due to condensation.
- Operation: The ease of opening, closing, and cleaning a window are important criteria in the selection of the type of window.
- Service: Before making the decision about the style and size of a window, it is important to check the services provided by the manufacturer, such as the warranties, accessibility of spare parts, and availability of representatives at the site.
- Floor level: In two story residential buildings, generally, windows of the first floor are taller than the windows on the second floor.
- Safety: In residential buildings, at least one window should have a clear space big enough for occupants to exit and firefighters to enter the room. The window opening space should be at least 1'–8" wide and 2' high; and its area should be at least six square-feet.
- Security: The windows should be built from break-resistant material.
- Window sill: The window sills should be located below the eye level of a seated person. For example, it should be 1' above the floor level in the living room and 4' in the bedrooms.

16.5. Doors

Doors are also important parts of a building. They provide access to a building from outside and to different parts of a building from inside and outside.

16.5.1. Types of Door

The doors are classified as exterior and interior based on their location; flush, panel, and louvered doors based on their appearance; hinged, folding, sliding, accordion, and overhead based on the method of door opening. French and Dutch doors are the special purpose doors.

- Exterior: As the name suggests, exterior doors are used to enter a building from the outside. The front and rear entrance doors are the exterior doors.

- Interior: Interior doors are used to access different parts of a building. These doors include bedroom, bathroom, kitchen, and laundry room doors.

- Flush: Flush doors have smooth and easy-to-maintain surfaces, Figure 16-3a. These doors are the most commonly used doors due to their low maintenance and construction cost. These doors may be solid- or hollow-cored. The solid-core doors are heavier and denser than the hollow-core doors.

- Panel: Panel doors were developed centuries ago to overcome the dimensional distortions caused by weathering effects because the changes in the moisture content would expand and contract wooden doors. These doors contain built-in panels, which help maintain the door's shape. The panels can be of different shapes and sizes. Figure 16-3b shows a 6-paneled door with two types of panels.

- Louvered: Louvered doors have horizontal stripes placed on the diagonal for the ventilation. These doors are attractive but difficult to maintain (dusting and painting takes a very long time), Figure 16-3c.

Figure 16-3a   **Figure 16-3b**   **Figure 16-3c**

- Hinged: Typically, these doors are hinged at the side; they are also known as swinging doors. These doors may be flush, panel, or louvered. These doors can swing inward or outward for 90° or 180°. These doors can be installed as a double unit or two-leaved, where one is hinged on the left side and the other is hinged on the right side, Figure 16-4a. The minimum space requirement for these doors is the width of one panel of the door.

- Sliding: Sliding doors are used to save floor space (because these doors do not swing) and may be flush or panel. A single leaf sliding door slides into a pocket built in the wall. In case of the two leaves sliding door, one leaf slides in front of the other leaf, Figure 16-4b. The drawback of two leaves sliding doors is that at a given time only half of the doorway space is available.

- <u>Folding</u>: Folding doors are a combination of hinged and sliding doors. The two leaves are hinged together and one of the leaves is also hinged at the side, Figure 16-4c. The advantage of folding doors is that the door can be completely open; thus, all of the doorway space is available. These doors can be single (two leaves as shown in Figure 16-4c) or double units (four leaves).

| **Figure 16-4a** | **Figure 16-4b** | **Figure 16-4c** |

- <u>Accordion</u>: Accordion doors are similar to folding doors but consist of several narrow leaves, Figure 16-4d. The folded retracted door can be exposed or hidden in a pocket in the wall.
- <u>Garage</u>: Garage doors can be sliding, roll-up, hinged, and accordion. The most commonly used type is the overhead type. These doors are bulky; therefore, most are mechanically operated. An overhead door is composed of several hinged sections, Figure 16-4e, that slide up into the ceiling on overhead tracks, and is operated with counterweights or springs on overhead tracks.

Figure 16-4d   **Figure 16-4e**

16.5.2. Door sizes
A door can be of any type and size; companies manufacture doors in various shapes and sizes. Nonetheless, the type and size of the door depends on the building style, room type, and the client's requirements. Typically, a door opening is 3 inches wider and 3 inches longer than the size of the door. As a rule of thumb, the width of a door is about half of its height. The commonly used residential door sizes are listed below.
- Front entrance door 3'-0" X 6'-8" X 1 3/4"
- Bedroom doors 2'-6" or 2'-8" X 6'-8" X 1 3/8"
- Bathroom doors 2'- or 2'-6" X 6'-8" X 1 3/8"
- A garage door is 7 feet high and its width can be 8 feet or 9 feet for single-car garages and 16 feet for a double-car garage.

16.5.3. Door selection
The selection of a door depends on the location of the door. Other factors affecting the door selection process in a typical residential building are listed below.

- Weather- and break-resistances are major factors in selecting the exterior doors.
- Fire- and noise-resistances are major factors in selecting the interior doors.
- Solid-core flush doors are typically used for exterior entrances and hollow-core doors are suitable for interior use.
- Louvered doors are the best candidate for the closet doors.
- Hinge doors are commonly used for main entrances, bedrooms, and bathrooms.
- Swinging doors are commonly used in kitchens and dining areas for easy operation in both directions.
- Sliding doors are selected for the closets and exterior doors (opening in the porch or backyard) from the living area.
- Folding doors are used for closets and laundry rooms.
- Accordion doors are used between dining and living areas.

16.5.4. Door appearance in floor plan
The following list is the plan view of the different types of doors discussed earlier.
- <u>Figure 16-5a</u>: Hinged, single panel, swing inward.
- <u>Figure 16-5b</u>: Hinged, single panel, swing outward.
- <u>Figure 16-5c</u>: Hinged, double panel, swing inward.
- <u>Figure 16-5d</u>: Accordion.
- <u>Figure7-5e</u>: Folding, double panel, 4 leaves.
- <u>Figure 16-5f</u>: Sliding, double panel.

Figure 16-5a

Figure 16-5b

Figure 16-5c

Figure 16-5d   **Figure 16-5e**   **Figure 16-5f**

16.6. Wall

Walls are the structures that demarcate a building from the surrounding buildings or open spaces and divide the building space into rooms and hallways. They support the load of the superstructure (roof, ceiling, and upper level floors) of the building. They provide security against intrusion and shelter from the weather. Generally, power outlets, phone connections, lighting switches, thermostats, and plumbing ducts are placed inside the walls. The walls in a building can be grouped as exterior and interior walls or load bearing and non-load bearing walls.

16.6.1. Exterior

The design of an exterior wall is a crucial part in the architectural design of a building. Some basic features of an exterior wall are listed here.

- Access to the building: The exterior wall should provide a method of entry and exit to the occupants of the building yet keep intruders out. The access is achieved through the doors.
- Vision: The vision from the exterior walls should be unidirectional; that is, the resident could be able to look outside. On the other hand, outsiders should not be able to look inside.
- Surface finish: The exterior surface of an exterior wall is exposed to the weather; therefore, it should be heat, wind, and rain resistant.
- Climate control: The exterior wall should provide for the methods of ventilation, heat transfer, and noise control. These characteristics can be achieved by appropriate placement of windows and by properly insulating doors and windows.
- Fire control: The exterior wall should prevent the spreading of a fire from inside to outside and vice versa.
- Durability: The walls should be durable for the life of the building.

16.6.2. Interior

The interior walls should also satisfy the vision, fire control, durability, and the characteristics mentioned in the exterior walls.

16.6.3. Non-load bearing

The non-load bearing walls should be strong enough to support their dead load; that is, it should be able to support its own load. The non-load bearing interior walls are called partition walls and the non-load bearing exterior walls are called curtain walls.

16.6.4. Load bearing

The load bearing walls not only support the dead load of the structure but also support the load of the roof, ceiling, and upper level floors.

16.6.5. Wall thickness

The wall thickness depends on the construction material. For example, usually wood frame exterior walls are 6 inches thick and solid brick are 9 inches or 12 inches thick.

16.7.   Stair

For multilevel buildings, the inter-level movement (also known as vertical movement) is made possible through the stairs, elevators, ramps, and escalators. This section discusses stairs. The terms stairwell, stairway, staircase, and stairs are often used interchangeably. A stairwell is the space in the building where the stairs are constructed. A staircase is often used for the stairs (steps, railings, landings, etc.). The expression stairway is reserved for the entire stairwell and staircase in combination.

The location of stairs is very important. In case of an emergency, the stairs are used to evacuate the building. In case of tornado, a stairwell can also be used as an area of refuge.

16.7.1. Terminology

Some of the commonly used terms are explained in this section and are illustrated in Figure 16-6.

- Flight: A flight is an uninterrupted series of steps.
- Landing: A landing is the floor area near the top or bottom step of a stair, or a small platform built as part of the stair used to change the flight's direction, or to provide the user a resting place.
- Tread (or going): A tread is the horizontal surface part of each step that is stepped on. The tread length is measured from the outer edge of the step to the riser between two adjacent steps.
- Riser: A riser is the vertical portion of the step between two adjacent steps.
- Rise: A rise is the vertical distance between two adjacent treads.
- Total rise: The total rise represents the total vertical distance traveled by a stair; that is, it is the floor-to-floor distance.
- Total run: Total run is the total horizontal length of the stair (from the first riser to the last riser).
- Handrail: A handrail is the round or decorative member of a railing used for hand holding during ascent or descent. It runs parallel to the imaginary line drawn from the top of the first tread to the top of the last tread.
- Step: A step is the combination of a riser and one of the adjacent treads.
- Nose: A nose is the edge part of the tread that protrudes from the riser underneath.
- Headroom: Headroom is the vertical distance from the top of a tread to the ceiling above it.
- Angle of a flight: The angle of a flight (θ) is the ratio of the total rise and the total run ($\theta = tan^{-1}(Total\ rise\ /\ Total\ run)$).
- Winders: The winders are the triangular steps used to change the direction of the flight, Figure 16-7b.

Figure 16-6

16.7.2. Important points to remember

Following is the list of some of the important points that must be considered when designing a staircase in a residential building.

- <u>Flight</u>: For a long flight, provide a break in the flight using landing(s).
- <u>Riser</u>: For comfortable stairs, a riser should be 7 inches. If the riser is too high then the stairs are very tiring and if it is too low then people will hit their toes against the riser.
- <u>Tread</u>: For comfortable stairs, a tread should be 11 inches. If the tread is too short then the stairs may not be safe and if it is too long then the horizontal space is wasted.
- <u>Headroom</u>: Headroom should be 7 feet - 4 inches or 6 feet - 8 inches for the major stairs, and 6 feet - 6 inches for the minor stairs (to the basement or attic).
- <u>Handrail</u>: For safe stairs, a railing should be always provided on the open side of the stairs. The height of the railing should not be less than 32 inches and not more than 36 inches.
- <u>Angle of a flight</u>: For residential buildings, the angle of a flight (θ) should be in the range of 30° to 33°.

16.7.3. Types of stairs

A stair without any wall on its side is called an open stair and a stair with walls on both sides is called a closed stair.

Based on the availability of the space for the staircase, a designer can choose among different types of stairs. The straight (Figure 16-7a), L-shaped with winders (Figure 16-7b), L-shaped with landing (Figure 16-7c), narrow U (Figure 16-7d), and spiral stairs (Figure 16-7e).

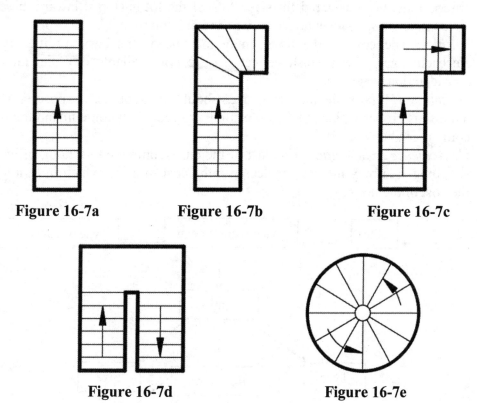

Figure 16-7a	**Figure 16-7b**	**Figure 16-7c**

Figure 16-7d	**Figure 16-7e**

16.8. Basics Of Floor Plan Design

A building's planning is one of the fundamental architectural and engineering design problems. A residential building is smaller in size as compared to a large commercial building, yet it involves various aspects of design and very intricate details. Hence, the focus of this section is a floor plan design for a small residential building. Figure 16-8a shows a simple flow chart of the major steps involved in the design.

- Budget: In designing a house, the monthly and yearly income of the family greatly influences the cost of the house. As a rule of thumb, the price of the house should not be more than three times the yearly income. Also, the cost of the house and the price of the lot should be proportional. On average, the price of the lot should be 15% to 20% of the house cost.

- <u>Site</u>: Some of the important features of the lot that must be considered before designing and creating architectural drawings are listed here.
  - o *Size*: The number and size of the rooms is directly related to the lot size. For the same size and number of rooms, a single story house on a larger plot and multistory house on a smaller plot may be the best options.
  - o *Shape*: The shape of the house depends on the shape of the lot. A house design for a broader lot may not be feasible for a narrow lot.
  - o *Contours*: Contour lines indicate the change in the elevation. Special design criteria must be considered for steep lots. If the lot is sloped inward, based on the contours, a split-level house may be the only option.
  - o *Utilities*: The cost of the house may increase if the basic utilities (water, electricity, gas, sewer, trash collection) are not available near the lot under consideration.
  - o *Orientation*: If possible, the living areas should have southern exposure. Also, if a house is properly planned than the summer breeze can come in and the winter cold air can be kept out.
  - o *Convenience to amenities*: The cost of the daily commute to school, office, and shopping area may increase or decrease the cost of a lot, which in turn affects the cost of the house.

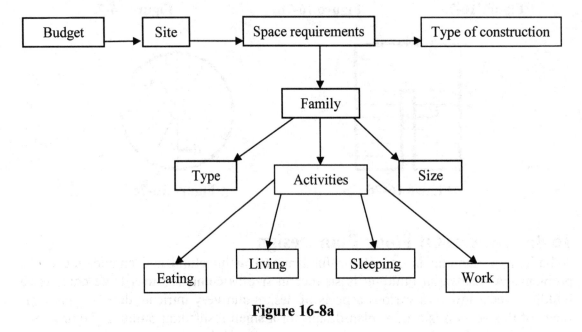

Figure 16-8a

- <u>Space requirements</u>: The space requirement depends on the following factors.
  - o *Family type*: The space requirement depends on the building's occupants. For example, a single story house may the better option for a family with small children and/or a senior citizen.
  - o *Family size*: The number and size of the rooms depends on the number of occupants.
  - o *Family's activities*: The main activities in a residential building can be grouped into eating, sleeping, living/entertainment, and work zones. Figure 16-8b shows

the movement between various zones. The activities zones divide a house into the following rooms.

- Eating: Kitchen, breakfast room, and dining room
- Sleeping: Bedrooms and guest rooms
- Living/entertainment: Living room, exercise room, library, entrance hall
- Work: Kitchen, pantry, laundry, garage, and storage room

- Type of construction: The type of the construction material (for example, wood, brick, steel, etc.) affects the cost of the house.

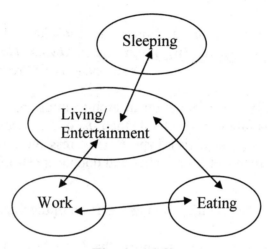

Figure 16-8b

16.9.   Design Technique

The arrangement of the various rooms depends upon the residents. However, appearance, comfort, and convenience are the main factors that must be considered in every building without compromising the cost.

The best method of a floor plan design is called *inside-out*. This technique can be divided into four major sections.

1. Space requirements: Find the space requirement of (i) every occupant, (ii) the family collectively, and (iii) special needs for the guests.
2. Setup: (i) Find the arrangement of the rooms, size of the rooms, and furnishings. (ii) Revise the plan (if necessary) for comfort, convenience, economy, and appearance.
3. Construction type: Find the method of construction: wood, brick, steel, etc.
4. Finance: Find the method to finance the construction project.

16.10.   AutoCAD And Floor Plan

This section provides step-by-step instructions to create a floor plan using AutoCAD 2017.

16.10.1.   New file

New file: Open a new "My_acad_Landscape" file. It is one of the template files created in Chapter 7. Save the file named as *FloorPlan.dwg*.

16.10.2.   The input units

Before starting the floor plan, set the input units or the drawing units and the precision.

16.10.2.1. Architectural

Before starting the floor plan, set the input units to the Architectural units. The user inputs lengths in feet and inches as follows:

(i) Type *Units* in the command line and press the *Enter* key. This opens the *Drawing Units* dialog box, Figure 16-9a. (ii) From the *Drawing Units* dialog box, select *Architectural* from the *Length* panel and *Type* sub-panel. (iii) Press the *OK* button.

Now the user can specify the information in architectural units (feet and inches). The length 5'-6" is entered as follows: (i) activate the *Line* or *Polyline* commands. (ii) Type 5. (iii) Type the apostrophe (') key. (iv) Type 6. (v) Press the *Enter* key. (vi) DO NOT TYPE hyphen (-) to separate feet from inches and double apostrophe to represent inches.

16.10.2.2. Precision

Before starting the floor plan, set the drawing precision of the input units as follows:

(i) Type *Units* in the command line and press the *Enter* key. This opens the *Drawing Units* dialog box. (ii) From the *Drawing Units* dialog box, select the *0'-0 1/4* from the *Length* panel and *Precision* sub-panel Figure 16-9b. (iii) Press the *OK* button.

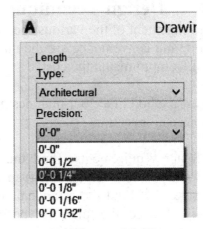

Figure 16-9a   **Figure 16-9b**

16.10.3.   Load linetypes

The floor plan uses solid or visible (known as continuous in AutoCAD), dashed (known as hidden in AutoCAD), and centerlines. Therefore, load *Hidden* and *Center* linetype; *Continuous* is the default linetype. Figure 16-9c shows the loaded linetypes. Refer to Chapter 3 for loading linetypes.

Figure 16-9c

16.10.4. Orthogonal lines

Since most of the lines in a floor plan are either horizontal or vertical, turn *On* the *ORTHO* option by pressing the corresponding button (⊡) on the status bar.

16.10.5. Layers

(i) Create layers as necessary. (ii) Set the layers' colors and lineweights. (iii) Before using a layer, make the layer to be the current layer. (iv) Make sure that the current layer is *on* (not frozen or *off*).

16.10.6. The floor plan

This section provides step-by-step instructions for drawing a floor plan of a typical single story residential building with three bedrooms, two bathrooms, and a single car garage.

- Do not add any dimensions! Dimensions are added later.
- The drawing is printed from the layout! Keep checking the appearance of the linetypes and lineweights in the layouts.

16.10.6.1. Exterior wall

- Create a layer, *Main_Drawing*, and set its lineweight to 0.7mm. This layer is used for the walls, doors, and windows.
- Make the *Main_Drawing* layer to be the current layer.
- Use the *Polyline* command to draw the exterior face of the exterior wall as shown in Figure 16-10a.

- Draw the interior face of the exterior wall as follows:
  1. The exterior wall thickness is 1 foot.
  2. Use the *Offset* command with an offset distance of 1' to create the interior face of the exterior wall. To create the offset, click inside the exterior face of the exterior wall, Figure 16-10b.

Figure 16-10a

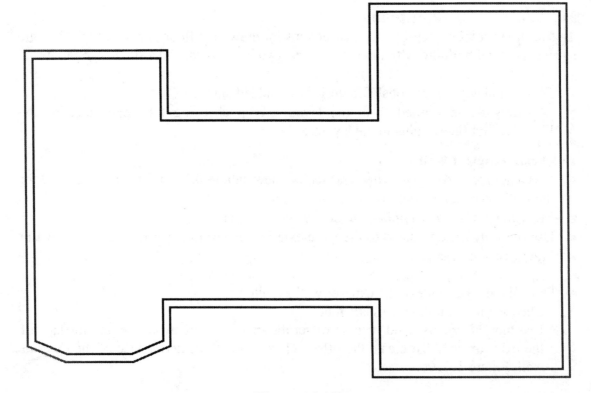

Figure 16-10b

16.10.6.2. Interior walls

The load bearing interior wall thickness is 1 foot, Figure 16-11a; and the non-load bearing interior wall thickness is 9 inches, Figure 16-11b.

- Draw the interior walls as follows:
  1. Make the *Main_Drawing* layer to be the current layer.
  2. Use the *Offset*, *Line*, *Trim*, and *Extend* commands to create the interior walls.

Figure 16-11a

16.10.6.3. Label

- Label the various parts of the house, Figure 16-12.
- Create a layer, *Rm_Label*, for displaying the names of the various rooms.
- Make the *Rm_Label* layer to be the current layer.
- Add the label using the *Text* command.
- The labels' text height is 1'-2".
- In the figure, *BRKFST* is breakfast and *BTHR* is the bathroom.
- Use the four corner's grip points of the text to match the four corners of the room to place the text in the center as shown for the MASTER BEDROOM.

Figure 16-11b

Figure 16-12

16.10.6.4. Doors

The door drawing process can be divided into four major steps: (i) door location, (ii) doors labels, (iii) door opening in the walls, and (iv) drawing the door panels. An architect can draw the doors using the following steps.

- Abbreviation in Figure 16-13
  SSI: Single panel Swing Inward
  DSI: Double panel Swing Inward
  DSO: Double Swing Outward
  ACDN: Accordion
  DDFL: Double panel Double Folding
  DTFL: Double panel Triple Folding
  OH: Overhead

DOOR WIDTH

D1	2'-6"	SSI
D2	2'-8"	SSI
D3	4'-0"	DSI
D4	4'-0"	DSO
D5	3'-6"	ACDN
D6	6'-0"	DDFL
D7	9'-0"	DTFL
D8	10"-0"	OH

Figure 16-13

- Door Location: The architect needs to decide on the door location and the distance from the nearest wall. The door location can be shown by drawing the centerline of the door opening. For the current example, the door location and the distance from the nearest wall are shown in Figure 16-13.
  1. Load the linetype *Center*.
  2. Create a layer, *DoorCL*, for the center of the doors; set linetype as *Center*.
  3. Make the *DoorCL* layer to be the current layer.
  4. Draw 8'-0" long centerlines for the doors' center, Figure 16-13.

- Doors' labels: Figure 16-13.
  1. Create a layer, *DoorLabel*, for the labels of the doors.
  2. Make the *DoorLabel* layer to be the current layer.
  3. Using the *Text* command, label the doors as shown in the Figure 16-13. The door labels' text height is 1'-2".

- Doors' openings: The architect needs to decide on the door width. For the current example, the doors' widths (opening sizes) are shown in Figure 16-13.
- In the sample house, the front door is 4 feet wide. The current door opening creation demonstration creates the door opening for the front door.
  1. Make the *Main_Drawing* layer to be the current layer.
  2. Use the Offset command with the offset distance of 2' (half of the door width) to create a line at a distance of 2', Figure 16-14a. Move this line to the *Main_Drawing* layer, Figure 16-14b.

Figure 16-14a   **Figure 16-14b**

  3. Use the *Mirror* command to create a similar line on the right side, Figure 16-14c.
  4. Use the *Trim* command to trim the lines representing the wall and extra portion of the two parallel lines drawn in the previous steps, Figure 16-14d.
  5. Repeat the process for the other doors, Figure 16-14e. The door widths are shown in the figure, too.

Figure 16-14c   **Figure 16-14d**

DOOR WIDTH

D1	2'-6"	SSI
D2	2'-8"	SSI
D3	4'-0"	DSI
D4	4'-0"	DSO
D5	3'-6"	ACDN
D6	6'-0"	DDFL
D7	9'-0"	DTFL
D8	10"-0"	OH

Figure 16-14e

- Draw the doors: Figure 16-17 shows the different types of doors used in the building.
  1. Make the *Main_Drawing* layer to be the current layer.
  2. ***Single panel swing doors***: Figure 16-15a shows an opening for a single panel swing door. Draw a single panel swing door using the following steps.
     - Draw a circle of radius equal to the door opening and center as shown in Figure 16-15b.
     - Draw the door panel using the *Line* command and the *Intersection* option in object snap setting. Also change the line's lineweight to 1.40mm, Figure 16-15c.
     - Use the *Trim* command to create the desired appearance of the door, Figure 16-15c and Figure 16-15d.

Figure 16-15a   **Figure 16-15b**

Figure 16-15c   **Figure 16-15d**

3. ***Double panel swing doors***: The double panel swing door is created as follows.
   (i) Draw a single panel swing door, Figure 16-16a. (ii) Use the mirror command to
   create the other panel of the door, Figure 16-16b.

Figure 16-16a   **Figure 16-16b**

4. ***Double panel folding doors***: The double panel folding door is created as follows.
   ▪ Draw a leaf for a panel by drawing a line as shown in Figure 16-16c.
   ▪ Use the mirror command to create the other leaf of the panel, Figure 16-16d.
   ▪ Use the mirror command to create the other panel, Figure 16-16e.

Figure 16-16c   **Figure 16-16d**   **Figure 16-16e**

5. ***Triple panel folding door***: The triple panel folding door is created as follows.
   ▪ Draw a leaf for a panel by drawing a line as shown in Figure 16-17a.
   ▪ Use the mirror command to create the second leaf of the panel, Figure 16-17b.
   ▪ Use the mirror command to create the third leaf of the panel, Figure 16-17c.
   ▪ Use the mirror command to create the other panel, Figure 16-17d.

6. ***Accordion door***: The accordion door is created as follows.
   ▪ Draw a straight line.
   ▪ Change the linetype to Zig-Zag.
   ▪ Set the linetype scale, Figure 16-17e.

Figure 16-17a   **Figure 16-17b**

Figure 16-17c   **Figure 16-17d**

Figure 16-17e

7. *Front door*: Two panels with inward swing.
    - Draw a single swing door.
    - Use the mirror command to create the other panel.

8. *Back door*: Two panels with outward swing.
    - Draw a single swing door.
    - Use the mirror command to create the other panel.

9. *Garage door*: The garage door height is 8'; and it is an overhead type door;
    - Draw a polyline and change its linetype.

10. *Other doors*: Use the *Mirror*, *Copy*, and *Move* commands to create the remaining doors.

Figure 16-17f

16.10.6.5. Walls cleanup
Clean the walls. Using trim command, clean the intersection of the walls, Figure 16-18.

16.10.6.6. Windows
The window drawing process can be divided into three major steps: (i) window location, (ii) window labels, (iii) and draw the windows. An architect can draw the windows using the following steps.

- Window location: The architect needs to decide on the window location and the distance from the nearest wall. However, for the current example, the window location and the distance from the nearest wall are shown in Figure 16-18.
  1. Create a layer, *WindowCL*, for the center of the windows; make the linetype as *Center*.
  2. Make the *WindowCL* layer to be the current layer.
  3. Draw the centerlines for the windows of length 8'-0'', Figure 16-18.

- Add the windows label: Figure 16-18.
  1. Create a layer, *WindowLabel*, for the labels of the windows.
  2. Make the *WindowLabel* layer to be the current layer.
  3. Using the *Text* command, label the windows.
  4. The window labels' text height is 1'-2"

5. The windows in Figure 16-19 shows the width of W1, W2, W3, and W4. However, the height of these windows depends on the location in the house. For example, W1 is in the great room and it is 5' tall and 2' above the ground; whereas W3 is in bathroom and it is 3' tall and 4' above the ground. The window schedule (discussed in Section 16-11) shows the height of the windows.

Figure 16-18

- Draw the windows: The detail of the windows labeled as W1, W2, and W3 are shown in Figure 16-19.
1. Make the *Main_Drawing* layer to be the current layer.
2. Draw the windows once.
3. Use the *Mirror*, *Copy*, and *Rotate* commands to create multiple copies of the windows to place them at appropriate locations, Figure 16-20.

Figure 16-19

Figure 16-20

16.10.6.7. Roofline

- Add the roof line, Figure 16-21:
  1. Load the *Hidden* linetype.
  2. Create a layer, *RoofLine*, and make it the current layer; set its linetype to *Hidden*.
  3. Draw the roof line:
     - Draw a polyline over the exterior face of the exterior wall.
     - Offset the polyline from the previous step by 2' outward.
     - If necessary, set the linetype scale from the *Properties* palate.
     - Delete the original polyline.

16.10.6.8. Wall hatch

- Hatch the exterior and interior walls, Figure 16-21:
  1. Create a layer *Wall_Hatch* and make it the current layer.
  2. Activate the *Hatch* command.
  3. Select the *AR-CONC* pattern. The scale factor in the current example is 2.0.
  4. Select the exterior and interior walls to hatch, Figure 16-21.

Figure 16-21

16.10.6.9. Porch

- Draw the front and back porches, Figure 16-22 and Figure 16-23:
  1. Create a layer *Porch* for the front and back porches, and make it the current layer.
  2. The front porch is a covered porch and the back porch is a brick paved patio.

3. (i) Create the front porch on the *Porch* layer; the dimensions are given in Figure 16-23a. (ii) Hatch the steps with *AR-CONC* with a scale factor of 2. (iii) Hatch the porch with *ANSI37* with a scale factor of 75. (iv) Also, create the roofline for the porch.
4. Create the back porch on the *Porch* layer; the dimensions are given in Figure 16-23. Hatch the porch with *AR-HBONE* with a scale factor of 2.0.

Figure 16-22

Figure 16-23

16.10.6.10.Kitchen

- Draw the location of appliances: Draw the location for the various items as follows:
  1. Create a layer (*KitchenAppliances*) for the appliances and make it the current layer.
  2. Using the *Offset* command, create an offset of the inner face of the kitchen wall with an offset distance of 2' as shown in Figure 16-24a, and move the offset to the *KitchenAppliances* layer. Also, draw a lines to connect the offset to the kitchen wall.
  3. Divide the 2' wide strip for the oven, sink, dishwasher, and the counter space, Figure 16-24b.
  4. On the right side wall, draw the location of the refrigerator, Figure 16-24b.

Figure 16-24a

- The kitchen's appliances: Draw the kitchen appliances as follows:
  1. The blocks for the *Range-Oven-Top* (RG), *Refrigerator* (REF), *Sink*, and *Faucet-Kit-Top* are inserted from the *Design Center*. The inserted blocks must be scaled appropriately.
  2. **Note**: Calculate the scale factor as follows:
        Scale factor = Desired size/Size from the Design Center
  3. **Angle: Specified on the screen**. If the user selects this option from the block insertion dialog box then use the following steps; refer to Figure 16-24c. (i) Specify the *Insertion point* and *Scale* values. (ii) Check the *Specify On-screen* option under the *Rotation* panel. (iii) Press the *OK* button of the dialog box. Click for the block insertion location and the prompt for the angle appears. Align the rubber band (the dashed line) with the desired orientation and press the left button of the mouse. The inserted block is rotated. **Alternate method**: Find the angle of the wall using the *Angular* dimension and then specify the angle at step (ii).

4. The blocks are inserted (Figure 16-24d) from the *Design Center → Kitchen.dwg* of AutoCAD 2018. The design center is discussed in detail in Chapter 6. The scale factors of the blocks and the angles are listed here.

- Sink: X-scale = 30/36; Y-scale = 24/21; and angle = 90°, Figure 16-24c.
- Faucet: Keep the scale factors the same as used for the corresponding sink; that is, X-scale = 30/36; Y-scale = 24/21; and angle = 90°.
- Range-Oven: X-scale = 36/30; Y-scale = 1; and angle = 180°.
- Refrigerator: X-scale = 1; Y-scale = 30/27; and angle = -90°.

Figure 16-24b

Figure 16-24c

Figure 16-24d

- Kitchen hatch, Figure 16-25: Hatch the kitchen as follows:
  1. Create a layer *KitchenHatch* and make it the current layer.
  2. Create the boundary of the floor area using *Polyline* command.
  3. Hatch the kitchen floor using *Hatch* command and *Hound* pattern at the scale of 50.
  4. Hatch the counter tops using *Hatch* command and *GRASS* pattern at the scale of 5.

Figure 16-25

16.10.6.11.Master bathroom

- <u>Add bathroom fixture's location.</u>: The step-by-step process for inserting the bathroom fixtures is listed here.
  1. Create a layer for the fixtures' locations and make it the current layer.
  2. Draw the fixtures' locations, Figure 16-26a. For a sink's location, draw ellipses.

- <u>Add bathroom fixture's labels:</u> Figure 16-26a: The step-by-step process for inserting the bathroom fixtures' labels is listed here.
  1. Create a layer for the fixtures' labels and make it the current layer.
  2. Using the Text command, create the labels as shown in Figure 16-26a.

Figure 16-26a

- <u>Add bathroom's fixtures:</u> Figure 16-26b: The step-by-step process for inserting the bathroom fixtures's is listed here.
  1. Create a layer for the fixtures and make it the current layer.
  2. Insert *Toilet top*, *Sink-oval Top*, *Faucet Bathroom Top*, and *Bath tub*'s blocks, Figure 16-26b. The blocks are inserted from the *Design Center* → *House Design.dwg* of AutoCAD 2018
  3. The design center is discussed in detail in Chapter 6. The inserted blocks must be scaled appropriately. **Note**: Calculate the scale factor as follows:
     Scale factor in the x-direction = Desired size/Size from the Design Center
     For scaling, keep the units consistent. (i) If one of the sizes is the combination of feet and inches then convert both sizes to inches. For example, 1'-8" is entered as

20 and not as 1.67'. For example, check the Y-scale of the *Sink* inserted as the drainage of the shower.

- Sink: X-scale = 1.0; Y-scale = 1; and angle = -90°.
- Faucet Bathroom Top (faucet for sink): X-scale = 1.0; Y-scale = 1.0; and angle = -90°.
- Use the mirror command to create the second sink.
- Bath Tub: X-scale = 78/60; Y-scale = 42/36; and angle = -90°.
- Faucet Bathroom Top (faucet for tub): X-scale = 78/60; Y-scale = 42/36; and angle = 0°.
- Toilet: X-scale = 1; Y-scale = 1; and angle = 0°.
- Sink as drainage for shower: X-scale = 8/24; Y-scale = 8/20; and angle = 0°.

Figure 16-26b

- Add bathroom hatch: The step-by-step process for inserting the bathroom hatch is described here, Figure 16-26c and Figure 16-26d.
1. Turn *off* the fixture layer.
2. Turn *off* the fixture's label layer.
3. Create a layer for the bathroom hatch and make it the current layer.
4. Add the hatch to the bathroom floor. Use the *HEX* pattern at the scale of 20.
5. Add the hatch to the counter area. Use the *HEX* pattern at the scale of 9.
6. Turn *on* the fixture layer.

Figure 16-26c

Figure 16-26d

16.10.6.12. North direction

- <u>The North sign</u>: The step-by-step process for inserting the north sign is listed here.
  1. Create a layer for the North sign. Make it the current layer.
  2. Insert *North Arrow* block, Figure 16-27 from the *Design Center* →
     Landscaping.dwg of the AutoCAD 2018. The design center is discussed in detail in
     Chapter 6.
  3. X-scale = 2; Y-scale = 6; and angle = -45°.

16.10.6.13.The complete plan
- Update the title block, Figure 16-27.
- Set the scale of the drawing to 1:108, Figure 16-27.

TEAM MANAGER	CLEMSON UNIVERSITY		
DRAWN BY	ENGR 2100 - 000	NIGHAT YASMIN	
DESIGNED BY	FLOORPLAN	A5	SHT 1 OF 1
CHECKED BY	SCALE: 1:108	TABLE 0	LETTER
CLIENT	05/05/2017	ARCHITECTURAL	

Figure 16-27

16.11. Dimensioning An Architectural Drawing

The major reason for adding dimensions to an architectural drawing is to provide communication between the architect and the builder. Architectural dimensioning depends on the type of construction material brick, concrete, and wood, etc. However, some common rules are listed here.

- Avoid the crossing of extension and dimension lines.
- Avoid crowding the dimensions.
- Omit the obvious dimensions, such as the width of side-by-side identical closets, interior doors at the end of hallways, and interior door at the corner of a room.
- Dimension lines are continuous lines; numbers are placed on top of the dimension lines; and arrows are replaced by the architectural ticks.
- Dimensions greater than 12" should be given in feet and inches. For example, a dimension of 27" should be given as 2'-3".

- For dimensioning tight places, use a dot, triangle, perpendicular line, or diagonal lines instead of arrows.
- Generally, three dimension are used on each wall: (i) dimensions to locate the doors and windows; (ii) dimensions to locate the walls; and (iii) dimensions to show the overall size.
- Display the scale of the drawing in the title block.
- Irrespective of the scale, the dimensions should always indicate the actual length, that is, the dimensions of a particular item that is constructed.

16.11.1. Create Layers

Create the following layers. For each layer choose the *Continuous* linetype, *0.25* for the lineweight. However, choose different colors for each layer.

1. *Dim_Door* for the location of the centerline of the doors.
2. *Dim_Window* for the location of the centerline of the windows.
3. *Dim_WtoW* for the wall to wall distance.
4. *Dim_Overall* for the overall dimension on each side of the building.
5. *Dim_Roomsize* to specify the size of each room.
6. *Dim_Interior* for the sizes of some of the interior walls.
7. *Dim_Porch* for the dimensions of the porch.
8. *Dim_BathRM* for the dimensions of the bathrooms.
9. *Dim_Kitchen* for the dimensions of the kitchen.
10. *Dim_Schedule* for the door and window schedule.

16.11.2. Set Dimension Style dialog box

1. Open the *Dimension Style Manager* dialog box using one of the following methods:
   a. From the *Annotate* tab and *Dimensions* panel, click on the small arrow in the right corner.
   b. From the *Home* tab, expand the *Annotation* tab and click on the ▨ button.
2. Click on the *Modify* button.
3. This opens the *Modify Dimension Style* dialog box.
4. Select the *Symbols and Arrows* tab as shown in Figure 16-28a.
   a. In the *Arrowheads* panel, click on the down arrow under the *First* option and select the *Architectural tick* option.
   b. Make sure that the *Architectural tick* option is also selected for the *Second* arrow.
   c. In the *Arrowheads* panel, set the *Arrowsize* (not shown in the figure).
5. Select the *Primary Units* tab as shown in Figure 16-28b.
   a. In the *Linear dimension* panel, click on the down arrow under the *Unit format* option and select the *Architectural* option.
   b. Set the *Precision* field to 0'-0" (not shown in the figure).

Figure 16-28a   **Figure 16-28b**

6. Select the *Text* tab as shown in Figure 16-28c.
   a. In the *Text appearance* panel, set the *Text height*.
   b. In the *Text placement* panel, click on the down arrow under the *Vertical* option and select the *Above* option.
   c. In the *Text placement* panel, set the *Offset from the dim line*. If the text is too close to the dimension line or too far from the dimension lines then increase or decrease this number.
   d. In the *Text alignment* panel, select the *Aligned with dimension line* option.

Figure 16-28c

16.11.3.   Add dimensions to the floor plan

1. Doors' dimensions:
    a. Turn *On* the door label layer.
    b. Make the *Dim_Door* layer to be the current layer.
    c. Using the *Linear* dimension tool, add the dimensions to the centerline of the doors, Figure 16-29.

Figure 16-29

2. Windows' dimensions:
    a. Turn *On* the windows label layer.
    b. Make the *Dim_Window* layer to be the current layer.
    c. Using the *Linear* dimension tool, add the dimensions for the centerlines of all the windows, Figure 16-30.

Figure 16-30

3. Wall to Wall dimensions:
   a. Make the *Dim_WtoW* layer to be the current layer.
   b. Using the *Linear* dimension tool, add the dimensions for the wall to wall distance, Figure 16-31.

4. Overall dimensions:
   a. Make the *Dim_Overall* layer to be the current layer.
   b. Using the *Linear* dimension tool, add the dimensions for the overall distance, Figure 16-31. Some of the dimensions can be calculated from the other dimensions; the overall dimension of the front side, 72', in Figure 16-31 can be obtained by adding 25', 28', 18', and 1' (wall thickness). However, it is recommended to display the overall dimensions in an architectural drawing and not to omit any useful dimensions.

5. Room size:
   a. Make the **Dim_Roomsize** layer to be the current layer.
   b. Using the *Text* command, create text boxes for the room size. A room size is written as x-dimension times y-dimension, Figure 16-32.
   c. Use the four corner grip points of the text to match the four corners of the room to place the text in the center.

Figure 16-31

Figure 16-32

6. Interior dimensions:
   a. Make the *Dim_Interior* layer to be the current layer.
   b. Using the *Linear* dimension tool, add the dimensions to the interior walls which are not dimensioned in any of the previous steps, Figure 16-33.

Figure 16-33

7. Porch dimension:
   a. Make the **Dim_Porch** layer to be the current layer.
   b. Turn *On* the porch layer.
   c. Using the *Linear* dimension tool, add the dimensions to the front (Figure 16-34a) and back porch (Figure 16-34b).

Figure 16-34a

Figure 16-34b

8. Master bathroom dimension, Figure 16-35:
   a. Make the *Dim_BathRM* layer to be the current layer.
   b. Turn *On* the bathroom's fixtures layer.
   c. Using the *Linear* dimension tool, add the dimensions to the bathroom's fixtures.

9. Kitchen dimension:
   a. Make the Dim_Kitchen layer to be the current layer.
   b. Turn *On* the kitchen fixtures layer.
   c. Using the *Linear* dimension tool, add the dimensions to the kitchen fixtures, Figure 16-36.

Figure 16-35

Figure 16-36

10. <u>All the dimension:</u> Figure 16-39 shows all the dimensions.

Figure 16-37

11. <u>Doors and windows schedules</u>: Complete the dimensioning process by creating the schedule for the doors and window, Figure 16-38a and Figure 16-38b. In architectural terminology, a schedule is a table displaying detailed information about the doors and windows.

   a. Make the *Dim_Schedule* layer the current layer.
   b. Using the *Table* command create the tables as shown in Figure 16-38a and Figure 16-38b.

12. <u>Save the floor plan</u>: Resave the file as *FloorPlan.dwg*.

DOOR SCHEDULE

DOOR	SIZE	QUANTITY	DESCRIPTION	LOCATION
D1	2'-6" x 7'-0"	3	INTERIOR, SINGLE PANEL	WIC, MBTHR, BTHR I
D2	2'-8" x 7'-0"	4	INTERIOR, SINGLE PANEL	MBDR, BDR I, BDR II, GRG
D3	4'-0" x 7'-0"	1	EXTERIOR, DOUBLE PANEL	FOYER
D4	4'-0" x 7'-0"	1	INTERIOR, DOUBLE PANEL	LIVING ROOM
D5	3"-6" x 7'-0"	1	ACCORDION	PANTRY
D6	6'-0" x 7'-0"	1	FOLDING, DOUBLE PANEL, FOUR LEAVES	MECHANICAL
D7	9'-0" x 7'-0"	1	FOLDING, TRIPLE PANEL SIX LEAVES	LAUNDRY
D8	10'-0" x 8'-0"	1	OVERHEAD	GRG

LEGEND: WIC: WALK IN CLOSET; M: MASTER; BTHR: BATH ROOM; BDR: BEDROOM; GRG: GARAGE

Figure 16-38a

WINDOW SCHEDULE

WINDOW	SIZE	QUANTITY	DESCRIPTION	LOCATION
W1	8'-0" x 5'-0"	8	CASEMENT + SLIDING	MBDR, BDR I, BDR II, BREAKFAST, KITCHN
W2	4'-0" x 5'-0"	1	SLIDING	BDR I, LAUNDRY
W3	3'-0" x 2'-0"	3	SLIDING	MBTHR, BTHR I
W4	2'-0" x 5'-0"	7	SLIDING	BDR I, FOYER, LIVING R., GRAGE

LEGEND: M: MASTER, BTHR: BATH ROOM: BDR: BEDROOM, GRG: GARAGE

Figure 16-38b

<u>Notes:</u>

17. Elevations

17.1. Learning Objectives

After completing this chapter, you will demonstrate competency in the following areas:

- Draw simple roofs
- Draw the front and left side elevations
- Project from the floor plan to the front elevation
- Project from the floor plan and the front elevation to create the left side elevation
- Insert blocks (window, door, north, landscaping, …) from the *Design Center*

17.2.   Introduction

The exterior elevations are commonly used for conveying the appearance of a building from the exterior. Figure 17-1b shows the front elevation of the residential building of the floor plan, Figure 17-1a, created in the previous chapter. In architecture and building engineering terminology, elevation is an orthographic projection of a building from a side. The elevations can be used to envision the building's appearance from all four sides; that is, from the front, rear, left, and right sides. Therefore, the architectural drawings of a building include one drawing for each of the front, rear, left, and right sides elevation.

Figure 17-1a

Figure 17-1b

The elevation drawings are simpler than a floor plan. The elevation drawings display the height and appearance of the windows and doors, shape of the roof, floor to floor levels (for multistory buildings), and the exterior walls. A single level building's elevation drawing starts with the ground level. In the drawing, objects below the ground level (foundations and crawl spaces) are shown using dashed (*Hidden*) lines. The next step is the drawing of the floor slab, windows, doors, and walls. Finally, the elevations are finished with the roof. Since the roof is an important part of the elevation design of a building, the next section briefly discusses the basics of roofs.

The focus of this chapter is the front and left side views of a building, also known as the front and left side elevations. Consider a simple building shown in Figure 17-1c. The figure shows the south east isometric view of the building. The three orthographic views (top, front, and right side view) of this building are shown in Figure 17-1d.

Figure 17-1c

Figure 17-1d

Notice the projection of the skylight (the box in the roof), front door, and the gable roof in the three orthographic views. Vertical lines are used to project information between top (floor plan) and front views. Horizontal lines are used to project information between front and left-side views. Horizontal and vertical lines are used to project information between front and left-side views using a 45 degree miter line, Figure 17-1d.

17.3.   Roof

17.3.1. Terminology
Some of the commonly used terms are listed here and are shown in Figure 17-2.

- *Span*: The span of a roof is the horizontal distance covered by the roof.
- *Run*: The run of a roof is half of the span.
- *Rise*: The rise of a roof is the vertical distance covered by the roof.
- *Pitch*: The pitch of a roof is the slope of a roof. The pitch is the ratio of the rise and the run (*Pitch = Rise/Run*). The steepness of a roof increases as the pitch of the roof increases.

Figure 17-2

17.3.2. Types of roof
There are many types of roofs based on the type of the house, such as traditional, dormer, contemporary, etc.

- Gable roof: A gable roof is the most common type of the roof and is shown in Figure 17-3a. It is easy to construct and is pitched for drainage.
- Dormer gable roof: The dormers are used for the light, Figure 17-3b. The use of a dormer enhances the appearance of the roof, but increases the cost of construction and maintenance.
- Hip roof: A hip roof (Figure 17-3c) is more expensive than a gable roof and is commonly used on ranch type houses. It is a low pitch roof. In a hip roof, the chances of leakage increase with an increase in the number of hips.
- Flat roof: A flat roof is shown in Figure 17-3d. Flat roofs are commonly used in commercial buildings. The slope of a flat roof is negligibly small. The slope is used for drainage only.

17.3.3. Important points
The selection of a roof type depends on several factors.
- Low pitched verses high pitched roof: Low pitched roofs are cheaper than high pitched roofs. However, a high pitch roof enhances the appearance of the house.

- <u>Color and material</u>: The color and material of the roof should be selected based on the durability and in accordance with the materials used on the exterior of the building. As a general rule, only two types of material should be used in the exterior finish.

Figure 17-3a   **Figure 17-3b**

Figure 17-3c   **Figure 17-3d**

17.4.   AutoCAD And Roof Plan
The roof plan drawings of a building are closely related to the floor plan. This section provides step-by-step instructions for drawing the roof plan of the floor plan of the three bedroom residential building drawn in the previous chapter.

17.4.1. Open file
<u>Open file</u>: Open the floor plan (*FloorPlan.dwg*) file created in the previous chapter, and save it as the *RoofPlan.dwg* file.

17.4.2. Load linetypes
The roof plan uses continues and dashed (known as *Hidden* in AutoCAD) lines. The hidden linetype is loaded for the floor plan. If it is not loaded, then load *Hidden* linetype; *Continuous* is the default linetype.

17.4.3. Layers
Create the layers as necessary and set the layer colors and lineweights. Before using a layer, make it the current layer and ensure that it is *on* (not frozen or *off*).

17.4.4. The roof plan

In the roof plan and elevations created in this chapter, the right side of the house (*master bedroom, walk-in closet, master bathroom, pantry, laundry, mechanical closet, and garage*) is covered by a 10' high hip roof; the middle of the house (living room, breakfast area, kitchen, and foyer) is covered by 12' high hip roof; and the left side of the house (*bedroom I, bathroom I, and bedroom II*) is covered by 10' high gable roof, Figure 17.4a; This figure does not show the front and back porch roof.

Figure 17-4a

This section provides step-by-step instructions to create the roof plan shown in Figure 17.4 (b, c, and d). Create the roof plan shown in Figure 17.4c as follows.

Figure 17-4b

- Create a layer called *Roofplan* (Linetype: *Continuous*; Lineweight: 0.7).
- Make the *Roofplan* layer to be the current layer.
- (i) Create a copy of the roof line and paste it on top of itself. (ii) Move the copy to the *Roofplan* layer. (iii) Freeze the roof line layer. (iv) Draw the roof plan as shown.
- For the dashed line, change the linetype to hidden. If necessary, change its linetype scale. In the current example, the linetype scale is 0.75.
- Create a layer called *Roofplan-Dim* (Linetype: *Continuous*; Lineweight: 0.0).
- Make the *Roofplan-Dim* to be the current layer.
- Add the dimensions as shown.
- In the current example, the text height is 1'-6" and the tick mark size is 10".

Add the hatch to the roof plan shown in Figure 17.4c as follows.

- Create a layer called *Roofplan-Hatch* (Linetype: *Continuous*; Lineweight: 0.0).
- Make the *Roofplan- Hatch* layer to be the current layer.
- Add the hatch as shown using *Hatch* command with pattern *AR-RSHKE* at the scale value of 2; use the hatch angle as shown in the figure. The user must create hatches independently.
- The figure also displays the hatch angles (HA) of the various hatches used in the roof plan. In AutoCAD, the degree symbol can be created by typing %%d in the text

command. Using *Text* command add the hatch labels. In the current example, the font is Times New Roman and the text height is 1'-2".

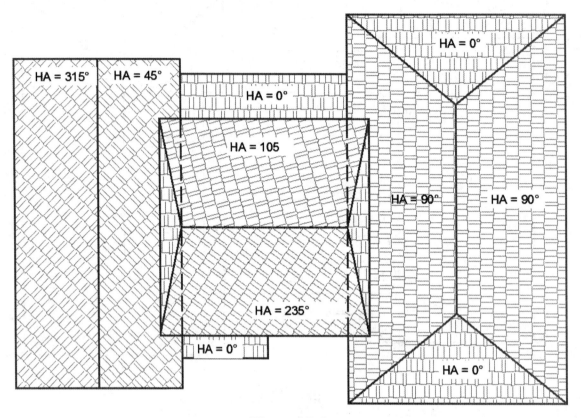

Figure 17-4c

Figure 17-4d shows the location of the ridges, valleys, hip lines, eave, and the slope arrows. In the figure, the arrows adjacent to the ridge labels and near the hip lines indicate the direction of the down slope. Add the labels and arrows as follows.

- Create a layer called *Roofplan-Label* (Linetype: *Continuous*; Lineweight: 0.0).
- Make the *Roofplan-Label* layer to be the current layer.
- Using the *Text* command create one label for ridge, one for valley, and one for hip line. The text height is 1'-2".
- Enclose the text in a rectangle using the *Enclose in Object* command with the offset factor of 0.35; this command is available from *Express Tool* tab and the *Text* panel.
- The arrows are created using the first two clicks of the *qleader* command (press the Esc key after the first two clicks). The arrowhead size is 2'.
- Rotate the labels using the *Rotate* command.
- Create multiple copies of the labels using the *Copy* command.
- Resave the *RoofPlan.dwg* file.

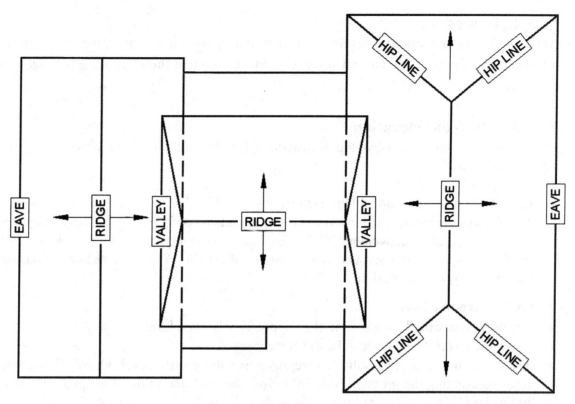

Figure 17-4d

17.5.   AutoCAD And The Front Elevation
The front elevation drawings of a building depend on its floor plan and roof plan. This section provides step-by-step instructions for drawing the front elevation of the floor plan of the three bedrooms residential building drawn in the previous chapter.

17.5.1. Open file
Open file: Open the roof plan file (*RoofPlan.dwg*) created in the previous section, and save it as the *FrontElev.dwg* file.

17.5.2. Load linetypes
The front elevation uses continues and dashed (known as *Hidden* in AutoCAD) lines. The hidden linetype is loaded for the roof plan. If it is not loaded, then load *Hidden* linetype; *Continuous* is the default linetype.

17.5.3. Orthogonal lines
Since most of the lines in the front elevation are either horizontal or vertical, turn *On* the *ORTHO* option by pressing the corresponding button (▣) on the status bar.

17.5.4. Layers

(i) Create layers as necessary. (ii) Set the layers' colors and lineweights. (iii) Before using a layer, make the layer the current layer. (iv) Make sure that the current layer is *on* (not frozen or *off*).

17.5.5. The front elevation

This section provides step-by-step instructions for drawing the front elevation of the given floor plan.

- Do not add any dimensions! Dimensions will be added later.
- The drawing is printed/displayed from the layout! Keep checking the appearance of the linetypes and lineweights in the layouts. The linetype should be clearly and properly visible in the layouts. If necessary, adjust the *Properties* palate →*General* tab → *Linetype Scale* option.

17.5.5.1. Ground level

- Create a layer called *Grade_Line* (Linetype: *Continuous*; Line weight: 0.0).
- Make the *Grade_Line* layer to be the current layer.
- The grade line is a thick solid line representing the ground level. Draw a horizontal line representing the ground level, 38' below the roof line in the floor plan as shown in Figure 17-5a. Change its lineweight scale to 0.50.

Figure 17-5a

- Draw a 2' wide rectangle, Figure 17-5b.
- Change the lineweight of the rectangle to 0.50.
- Hatch the grade line using *Earth* pattern at scale of 100, Figure 17-5c.

Figure 17-5b

Figure 17-5c

17.5.5.2.   Slab level

- Create a layer called *Slab_Line* (Linetype: *Continuous*; Line weight: 0.0).
- Make the *Slab_Line* layer to be the current layer.
- The slab surface is shown as a thick solid line representing the main floor level. Draw a horizontal line representing the main level, 2'-0" above the grade line, as shown in Figure 17-6a. Change its lineweight to 0.50.
- Close the edges by drawing lines.
- Hatch the slab using *AR-CONC* pattern at scale 2, Figure 17-6b.

Figure 17-6a

SLAB

2'

Figure 17-6b

17.5.5.3. Doors

- Draw the projection lines for the doors in the front wall:
  1. Create a layer called *Proj_Door*.
  2. Set its linetype to *Hidden*, lineweight: 0.0, and change its color.
  3. Make the *Proj_Door* layer to be the current layer.
  4. Since the projection lines are perpendicular to the floor plan, turn *On* the *ORTHO* option by pressing the corresponding button ( ) on the status bar.
  5. Draw the projection lines starting at the front door in the floor plan and terminating at the slab line, Figure 17-7a. Use the *Trim* or *Extend* commands as necessary.
  6. Draw the projection lines starting at the grage door in the floor plan and terminating at the slab line, Figure 17-7a. Use the *Trim* or *Extend* commands as necessary.
  7. Using the Properties palate, set the linetype scale to 0.5.

- Draw the front entrance door: The front entrance door is 7'-0" high.
  1. Make the *Elevation* layer to be the current layer.
  2. Open the blocks folder of the *House Design.dwg* from the *Design Center* (*View* tab and *Palette* panel).
  3. Insert the *Door-Fancy 36 inch* block, Figure 17-7b.
     - Front door: X-scale = 2/3; Y-scale = 1; Z-scale = 1; and angle = 0°.
  4. Use the *Mirror* command to add the second panel, Figure 17-10c.

- Draw the garage door: The garage door is 10'-0" high.
  1. Make the *Elevation* layer to be the current layer.
  2. Open the blocks folder of the *House Design.dwg* from the *Design Center* (*View* tab and *Palette* panel).
  3. Insert the *Garage Door Paneled 10 ft* block, Figure 17-7d.
     - Garage door: X-scale = 1; Y-scale = 10/7; Z-scale = 1; and angle = 0°.

Figure 17-7a

Figure 17-7b   **Figure 17-7c**

Figure 17-7d

17.5.5.4. Windows

- <u>Draw the projection lines for the windows in the front wall:</u>
  1. Turn *Off* the *Proj_Door* layer.
  2. Create a layer called *Proj_Window*.
  3. Set its linetype to *Hidden*, lineweight: 0.0, and change its color.
  4. Make the *Proj_Window* the current layer.
  5. Turn *On* the *ORTHO* option by pressing the corresponding button on the status bar.
  6. Draw the projection lines starting at the windows, Figure 17-8, in the floor plan and terminating at the slab line. Use the *Trim* or *Extend* commands as necessary.
  7. The windows in the front wall are 5' tall and their base is 2' above the ground level; therefore, draw a horizontal line 7' and 2' above the slab level.
  8. The horizontal lines make the block insertion and copying process faster. These lines are deleted after inserting all the windows.

- <u>Draw the windows in the front wall:</u>
  1. Make the *Elevation* layer to be the current layer.
  2. In the front elevation three types of windows are used, Figure 17-8: W1 in the kitchen, W2 in Bedroom I, and W4 in Bedroom I, Foyer, and garage. The draftsman can increase the productivity and reduce the drawing creation time, if the multiple occurrences of the windows are created using the *Copy* command. This section creates W1, W2, one occurrence of W4 in the garage (use copy command for Foyer), and one occurrence of W4 in Bedroom I (use mirror command for the other window).

Figure 17-8

3. **Keep the units consistent when inserting blocks for scaling purposes.** (i) If one of the dimensions of the block to be inserted (in the *Design Center* or in the actual drawing) is the combination of feet and inches, then convert both sizes to inches. That is, 2'-6" is entered as 30" and not as 1.5'. For example, check the X-scale of *W2-1* below. (ii) If both of the sizes are in feet then conversion is not necessary. For example, check the X-scale of *front door*, Figure 17-7b.

4. **Create W1 window:**
   - Divide the space for W1 in the compartments as shown in Figure 17-9a.
   - The *Scale factor = Desired size / Size from the Design Center*
   - Using the 2' line as a guide line, insert the following scaled window blocks from the *Design Center* → *House Designer.dwg*:
   - For all three blocks: Z-Scale: 1
   - W1-1: *Window Wood Frame 36X36*; X-Scale: 30/36; Y-Scale: 42/36
   - W1-2: *Window Wood Frame 36X36*; X-Scale: 1; Y-Scale: 42/36
   - W1-3: *Window Half-circle 36 in*; X-Scale: 1; Y-Scale: 1

Figure 17-9a

Figure 17-9b

5. **Create W1 side panel**:
   - Using the projection lines and the height of the window as guidelines, draw rectangles on either side of the windows, Figure 17-9c. The rectangles are shown by their grip points.
   - Activate the *Hatch* command.
   - Select *ANS131* pattern, set *Angle* to 135° and *Scale* to 20.
   - Now, hatch the rectangles on both sides of the windows, Figure 17-9c.
   - Use copy command for the other windows.

Figure 17-9c

6. **Create W4 window for Garage**:
   - The front elevation of W4 is shown in Figure 17-9d. This window is created with one block and two side panels.
   - Insert the following block from the *Design Center* → *House Design.dwg* as follows:
   - *Window Wood Frame 36X36*; X-Scale: 2/3; Y-Scale: 5/3; Z-Scale: 1
   - Side panel: repeat the W1's side panel process.

Figure 17-9d

7. **Create W4 window for Bedroom I**:
    - Since the window is in the slanted wall, therefore it appears distorted in the front elevation.
    - The front elevation of W4 is shown in Figure 17-9e. This window is created with one block and two side panels.
    - Insert the following block from the *Design Center* → *House Design.dwg* as follows:
    - *Window Wood Frame 36X36*; X-Scale: 22/36; Y-Scale: 5/3; Z-Scale: 1
    - Side panel: repeat the W1's side panel process.
    - Use mirror command for the other window.

Figure 17-9e

- Figure 17-9f shows all the windows in the front wall.

Figure 17-9f

17.5.5.5. Front wall

- Draw the projection lines for the wall:
  1. Create a layer called *Proj_Wall*.
  2. Set its linetype to *Hidden*, lineweight: 0.0, and change its color.
  3. Make the *Proj_Wall* layer to be the current layer.
  4. Turn *On* the *ORTHO* option by pressing the corresponding button on the status bar.
  5. Draw the projection lines, Figure 17-10a, starting at the corners of the wall (that are visible from the outside) in the floor plan and the roof line and terminating at the slab line. Use the *Trim* or *Extend* commands as necessary.

- Add the exterior face of the front wall:
  1. Make the *Elevation* layer to be the current layer.
  2. The walls are 12'-0" high.
  3. Draw the exterior face of the exterior wall, Figure 17-10a.

Figure 17-10a

Figure 17-10b

- Add the hatch to the wall:
  1. Make the *Elevation* layer to be the current layer.
  2. Turn *On* the *Proj_Window* and *Proj_Door* layers, Figure 17-10b.
  3. **Do not create the hatch for the front wall with the door and window's projection lines *Off*. It takes a very long time and the hatch enters inside the doors and window blocks.**
  4. Activate the *Hatch* command.
  5. Select *AR-B816* (brick) pattern, set *Angle* to 0° and *Scale* to 0.
  6. Now, hatch the rectangles created by the doors and window's projection lines, Figure 17-10c.
  7. Zoom into the window to check that the hatch did not enter inside the windows.
  8. Change the color of the hatched area and set the lineweight to 0.0.

Figure 17-10c

17.5.5.6. Roof

- Draw the projection lines for the roof:
  1. Turn *On* the layer of the roof plan.
  2. Turn *Off* the layers of the floor plan.
  3. Create a layer called *Proj_roof*.
  4. Set its linetype to *Hidden*, lineweight: 0.0, and change its color.
  5. Make the *Proj_roof* layer to be the current layer.
  6. Turn *On* the *ORTHO* option by pressing the corresponding button on the status bar.
  7. Draw the projection lines starting at the roof in the roof plan and terminating at the wall height, Figure 17-11. Use the *Trim* or *Extend* commands as necessary.

Figure 17-11

- <u>Add the main house roof</u>: The right side of the house (*master bedroom, walk-in closet, master bathroom, pantry, laundry, mechanical closet, and garage*) is covered by a 10' high hip roof; the middle of the house (living room, breakfast area, kitchen, and foyer) is covered by 12' high hip roof; and the left side of the house (*bedroom I, bathroom I, and bedroom II*) is covered by 10' high gable roof. Figure 17.4a.

1. Make the *Elevation* layer to be the current layer.
2. Create the lines as shown in Figure 17-12a.
3. Use a combination of the *Offset* (set *Offset* distance = 6"), *Extend*, and *Trim* commands to create the lines shown in Figure 17-12a.

- <u>Add the hatch to the roof</u>.
1. Turn *Off* the *Projection Line*'s layer.
2. Make the *Elevation* layer to be the current layer.
3. Use the *Hatch* command to hatch the roof, select *AR-B816* and *AR-RSHKE* patterns. Set the hatch scale as follows, Figure 17-12b.

   - *AR-RSHKE*: Scale = 1.25, angle = 0°, and color =By Layer.
   - *AR-B816*: Scale = 1.0, angle = 0°, and color =204.

ALL OFFSETS = 6"

Figure 17-12a

Figure 17-12b

17.5.5.7. Front porch

- Draw the projection lines for the front porch:
  1. Create a layer called *Proj_Porch*.
  2. Set its linetype to *Hidden*, lineweight: 0.0, and change its color.
  3. Make the *Proj_Porch* the current layer.
  4. Turn *Off* the roof plan, wall hatch, doors and window projection layers.
  5. Turn *On* the floor plan layer.
  6. Turn *On* the *ORTHO* option by pressing the corresponding button on the status bar.
  7. Draw the projection lines starting at the front porch, Figure 17-13a, in the floor plan and terminating at the slab line. Use the *Trim* or *Extend* commands as necessary.

- Draw the front porch, Figure 17-13a and Figure 17-13b:
  1. Make the *Elevation* layer to be the current layer.
  2. Draw the columns and create the hatch.
  3. Hatch the columns using *SOLID* pattern for the columns
  4. Draw the posts between the column using straight line with LWT of 0.8mm.
  5. Draw the step (riser = 7") and create the hatch, Figure 17-13a and Figure 17-13b.

Figure 17-13a

Figure 17-13b

- Draw the projection lines for the front porch's roof:
  1. Make the *Proj_Porch* the current layer.
  2. Turn *On* the roof plan layer.
  3. Turn *On* the floor plan layer.
  4. Turn *On* the *ORTHO* option by pressing the corresponding button on the status bar.
  5. Draw the projection lines starting at the front porch's, Figure 17-13c, in the floor plan and terminating at the slab line. Use the *Trim* or *Extend* commands as necessary.

- Draw the front porch's roof: Figure 17-13c and Figure 17-13d:
  1. Make the *Elevation* layer to be the current layer.
  2. Draw the roof and create the hatch.

Figure 17-13c

Figure 17-13d

17.5.5.8. Landscaping

- Add the landscaping features:
    1. Create a layer called *Landscaping*. Make the *Landscaping* layer the current layer.
    2. Insert the blocks for the trees, bushes, and street lights from the *Design Center → House Landscaping.dwg*, Figure 17-14.

Figure 17-14

17.5.5.9. Template file

- Add template file:
  1. Insert an appropriate layout from one of the template files, Figure 17-15.
  2. Set the scale of the drawing to 1:124, Figure 17-15.
  3. Update the blocks, Figure 17-15.
  4. The complete front elevation is shown in Figure 17-15.
  5. Save the *FrontElev.dwg* drawing file.

TEAM MANAGER		CLEMSON UNIVERSITY		
DRAWN BY		ENGR 2100 - 000	NIGHAT YASMIN	
DESIGNED BY		FRONT ELEV	A6	SHT 1 OF 1
CHECKED BY		SCALE: 1:124	TABLE 0	LETTER
CLIENT		05/05/2017	ARCHITECTURAL	

Figure 17-15

17.6.   AutoCAD And The Left Side Elevation

The left side elevation not only depends upon the floor plan; it also depends on the front elevation. The process of drawing the doors and windows appearing only in the left side wall is the same as the process for the front elevation. However, the process of creating the height of the left side wall, the roof appearance, and the doors and windows appearing in both the front and left side elevation is different and is discussed in detail.

The left side elevation is created by projecting the information from the floor plane using horizontal lines and by projecting the information from the front elevation to the left side elevation using horizontal, vertical, and 45° miter lines, Figure 17-16.

17.6.1. Open file

<u>Open file</u>: Open the front elevation file (*FrontElev.dwg*) created in the previous section, and save it as the *LeftElev.dwg* file.

17.6.2. Load linetypes

The left elevation uses solid or visible (known as continuous in AutoCAD), dashed (known as hidden in AutoCAD), and center lines. These linetypes are loaded for the floor plan. If not, then load these linetypes; the *Continuous* is the default linetype.

Figure 17-16

17.6.3. Orthogonal lines

Since most of the lines in the left elevation are either horizontal or vertical, turn *On* the *ORTHO* option by pressing the corresponding button (⬚) on the status bar.

17.6.4. Layers

*   <u>Create layers</u>:
    1. Create four layers and name them *Proj_45*, *Proj_45_GL_Slab*, *Proj_45_Roof*, and *Proj_45_Wall*.
    2. Set their linetype to *Hidden*, lineweight to 0.0, and change their color.
    3. Turn *On* and *Off* these and previously created layers as necessary.

17.6.5. The left side elevation

This section provides step-by-step instructions for drawing the left side elevation of the given floor plan.

- Do not add any dimensions! Dimensions are added later.
- The drawing is printed from the layout! Keep checking the appearance of the linetypes and lineweights in the layouts.

17.6.5.1. Miter line

- Draw 45 degrees miter line:
  1. Refer to Figure 17-17.
  2. Draw a rectangle using upper and lower right corners of the roof line.
  3. At the lower left corner of the rectangle, draw a 55' long line at 45°. This line will be used to project information from the front elevation to the left side elevation.

Figure 17-17

17.6.5.2. Ground and slab level

- Draw ground and slab level:
  1. Refer to Figure 17-18.
  2. Turn on the *Grade_Line* and *Slab_Line* layers.
  3. Make the *Proj_45_GL_Slab* layer to be the current layer.
  4. Since the slab is drawn in the front elevation, its height is projected from the front elevation. From the front elevation, draw horizontal lines starting at the left end of the grade and slab lines and terminating at the 45° miter line.
  5. Draw vertical lines starting at the 45° miter line (where lines of step #4 terminated) and terminating beyond the floor plan. If necessary, use *Trim* and *Extend* commands.
  6. Now complete the ground and slab level as discussed in the front elevation.

17.6.5.3.   Windows

- For the windows in the left side elevation refer to Figure 17-19a and Figure 17-19b.
  1. Since Bedroom I and II (W1) and Bathroom (W3) windows do not appear in the front elevations, therefore, follow the procedure from the front elevation to insert these windows. Keep W1, 2' above the ground and W3, 4' above the ground.
  2. Since, one of W4 window of Bedroom I appears in both elevations, therefore, use the horizontal, vertical, and miter line appropriately.

Figure 17-18

Figure 17-19a

Figure 17-19b

17.6.5.4. Wall

- For the wall in the left side elevation refer to Figure 17-20.
- Since the wall is drawn in the front elevation, its height is projected from the front elevation.
  1. Project the length of the wall in left side elevation; draw horizontal lines starting from the left side of the floor plan and terminating at the slab level.
  2. From the front elevation, draw horizontal lines starting at the top and bottom ends of the wall and terminating at the 45° miter line.
  3. Draw vertical lines starting at the 45° miter line (where lines of step #2 terminate) and terminating beyond the floorplan. If necessary, use *Trim* and *Extend* commands.
  4. Now complete the wall as discussed in the front elevation.
  5. Hatch with *AR-B816* (brick) pattern, set *Angle* to 90° and *Scale* to 0.

Figure 17-20

17.6.5.5. Roof

- The roof drawing in the left side elevation is a complicated process. Therefore, each roof is drawn independently.

- For demonstration purposes, the projection lines of an individual component of the roofs are shown. In the left elevation, the user should hatch the roof after the completion of the left side elevation.

The gable roof for the left side of the house

- The left side of the house (*bedroom I, bathroom I, and bedroom II*) is covered by 10' high gable roof
- Refer to Figure 17-21.
- Since the roof is drawn in the front elevation, its height is projected from the front elevation.
  1. Draw horizontal lines starting from the roof plan towards the left elevation.
  2. From the front elevation, draw horizontal lines starting at the top and bottom ends of the roof and terminating at the 45° miter line.
  3. Draw vertical lines starting at the 45° miter line (where lines of step 2 terminate) and terminating at the horizontal line drawn from step #1. If necessary, use the *Trim* and *Extend* commands.
  4. The gables of these roofs are on the back of the house
- Draw the outline of the roof as it appears in the left side elevation.

Figure 17-21

The hip roof for the middle of the house

- The middle of the house (living room, breakfast area, kitchen, and foyer) is covered by 12' high hip roof.
- Refer to Figure 17-22.
- Draw the roof as follows:
  1. Draw horizontal lines starting from the roof plan towards the left elevation.
  2. From the front elevation, draw horizontal lines starting at the top and bottom ends of the roof and terminating at the 45° miter line.
  3. Draw vertical lines starting at the 45° miter line (where lines of step 2 terminate) and terminating at the horizontal line drawn from step #1. If necessary, use the *Trim* and *Extend* commands.
- Draw the outline of the roof as it appears in the left side elevation.
- Note: Most of this roof is behind the left side's gable roof.

Figure 17-22

The hip roof for the right side of the house

- The right side of the house (*master bedroom, walk-in closet, master bathroom, pantry, laundry, mechanical closet, and garage*) is covered by a 10' high hip roof.
- Refer to Figure 17-23.

- Draw the roof as follows:
  1. Draw horizontal lines starting from the roof plan towards the left elevation.
  2. From the front elevation, draw horizontal lines starting at the top and bottom ends of the roof and terminating at the 45° miter line.
  3. Draw vertical lines starting at the 45° miter line (where lines of step 2 terminate) and terminating at the horizontal line drawn from step #1. If necessary, use the *Trim* and *Extend* commands.
- Draw the outline of the roof as it appears in the left side elevation. The grip points of this roof are shown in the figure.
- Note: Most of this roof is behind the left side's gable roof.

Figure 17-23

Complete roof

- Hatch the roof, Figure 17-24 shows the three components of the complete roof.

Figure 17-24

17.6.5.6. Porch
- Both the front and back porches are hidden from the left side of the house.

Landscaping:
- Repeat the process from the front elevation.

Complete elevation
The complete elevation is shown in Figure 17-25.

Figure 17-25

The floor plan, the front elevation, and the left side elevations are shown in Figure 17-26. The bake and the right side elevations are left for the readers.

TEAM MANAGER		CLEMSON UNIVERSITY		
DRAWN BY		ENGR 2100 - 000	NIGHAT YASMIN	
DESIGNED BY		FP + 2 ELEV	A7	SHT 1 OF 1
CHECKED BY		SCALE: 1:180	TABLE 0	LETTER
CLIENT		05/05/2017	ARCHITECTURAL	

Figure 17-26

Notes:

18. Site Plan

18.1.   Learning Objectives

After completing this chapter, you will demonstrate competency in the following areas:

- Basics of a site plan
- Draw a site plan using AutoCAD

18.2.   Introduction

The map of an individual construction site is known as a site plan, plat, or plot. The site plan not only displays the location of the project, but it also exhibits other key features. A site plan of a typical building shows an outline of the building, utilities (sewer line, water supply, power lines, gas supply, etc.), driveways, walkways, adjacent roads, adjoining building (if any), etc.

18.3.   Terminology

- Property line: A property line is the legal boundary of a parcel of land. It is described as a closed traverse using lengths and bearing (or azimuth) of each course. The boundary is set using one of the survey methods discussed in Chapter 10.
- Easement: An easement is defined as a right of way or privilege offered by the property owner to a general public or selected users.
- Setback: A setback is the distance from the property line to any structure on the property (site). Setbacks guarantee that sufficient sunlight would reach the street and lower levels of the adjacent buildings. Generally, setbacks are provided on the front and rear, and left and right side of a building. The front setback is typically measured from one foot away from the sidewalk bordering the property. If there is no sidewalk then the City still owns the area where it normally would be placed. Each street is a different width, so the Department of Public Works must be contacted for detailed information

18.4.   Components of a site plan

The information represented by a site plan may vary from state to state. However, a typical site plan for a residential building contains the following information.

1. Property description, including township, range, section and tax lot number, and property address if available.
2. North arrow.
3. Property line.
4. Dimensions (length and angle) of all the property lines.
5. Direction and percent of the slope.
6. Distance (setbacks) from all structures to the property lines.
7. Names and locations of all the roads adjacent to the property.
8. Names (or labels) and locations of all other properties adjacent to the property in question.
9. Location, size, and intended use of all structures, existing and proposed.
10. Location of driveways, walkways, or any other roads on the property, existing and proposed.
11. Location of any public utility.
12. Location of all major features (e.g., canals, irrigation ditches, or rock ledges).
13. Location of well or water sources on the property under consideration and adjacent properties.

14. Location of test holes used for the site evaluation during the feasibility process.
15. Height from grade to all shade producing points of roof lines for solar calculation. NOTE: in some cases, plat plans for parcels over 2 acres may need to be scaled for solar purposes.
16. For new septic construction, three elevation shots on each leach line for both the initial and reserve leach field area.
17. Location of proposed septic tank, drain field, and replacement field, showing dimensions and spacing of leach lines. Furthermore, the distance from the septic tank and system to the property lines should be included. NOTE: In some cases, a sanitarian may require the system to be drawn to scale.

18.5.   AutoCAD and site plan

This section creates a site plan for the residential building designed in the previous two chapters (Floor plan and Elevation) using the lot 16 from the lots and blocks drawing created in the Chapter 10.

18.5.1. Open file

Launch AutoCAD 2018 and open a file to create the site plan using one of the two methods.

8. Open a new file (the landscape template file for the ANSI units) and work through all the steps listed in this section.
9. Open the lots and blocks drawing, Figure 18-1a, draw a closed polyline as shown in Figure 18-1b (grip points are shown), and use the *Trim*, *Delete*, and *Move* commands to modify the drawing as shown in Figure 18-1c. The user may skip a step or perform the step partially. For example, the user can skip *Units* step; for the property line, create a layer and move the boundary of Lot 16 to the layer.

THE WHITE OAK SUBDIVISION

Figure 18-1a

THE WHITE OAK SUBDIVISION

Figure 18-1b

Figure 18-1c

18.5.2. Layers

(i) Create layers as necessary. (ii) Set the layers' colors and lineweights. (iii) Before using a layer, make the layer the current layer. (iv) Make sure that the current layer is *On* (not frozen or *Off*).

18.5.3. Units

(i) Type *Units* on the command line and press the *Enter* key. This opens the *Units* dialog box. (ii) From the Units dialog box, expand the *Length* option and select the *Engineering* option, Figure 18-2a; (iii) expand the *Precision* option and select the *0'-0.0000"* option, Figure 18-2b. (iv) Press the *OK* button to close the dialog box.

Figure 18-2a

Figure 18-2b

18.5.4. Load linetypes

Load the linetypes shown in Figure 18-3. For details refer to Chapter 3.

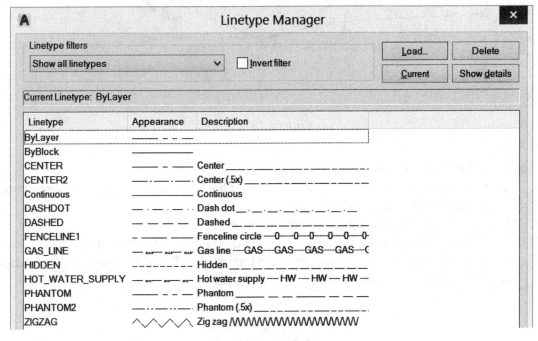

Figure 18-3

18.5.5. Property line

• Create the property line as follows.

1. Create a layer and name it *Property_Line*. Set its *linetype* to *Phantom*, *lineweight* to *0.7*, and change its color.

2. Make the *Property_Line* layer to be the current layer.

3. Draw the property's boundary as a closed traverse or trace over the Lot 4 of the lots and blocks drawing. Make sure that the linetype is clearly visible; if necessary, set the linetype scale, Figure 18-4.

Figure 18-4

• Add the dimension to the property line as follows.

1. Create a layer and name it *Property_Line_Dim*. Set its *linetype* to *Continuous*, *lineweight* to *0.0*, and change its color.

2. Make the *Property_Line_Dim* layer to be the current layer.

3. Show the dimensions following a closed traverse dimensioning techniques, Figure 18-4. The angles are represented as azimuths. The dimension and extension lines are turned *Off* for the length of each course.

- Create the property label as follows.
  1. Create a layer and name it *Property_ Label*. Set its *linetype* to *Continuous*, *lineweight* to *0.0*, and change its color.
  2. Make the *Property_Label* layer to be the current layer.
  3. Show the label using the *Text* and *Rotation* commands and arrow using the *qleader* command, Figure 18-4.

18.5.6. North

- The step-by-step process for inserting the north sign is listed here.
  1. Create a layer for the North sign and name it as *North*. Set its *linetype* to *Continuous*, *lineweight* to *0.0*, and change its color.
  2. Make the *North* layer the current layer.
  3. Insert the *North Arrow* block (Figure 18-5) from the *Design Center* → *Landscaping.dwg* of the AutoCAD 2018. The design center is discussed in detail in Chapter 6.
  4. Scale the block as: X-scale = 5 and Y-scale = 10.

18.5.7. Ground slope

- Create the ground slope as follows.
  1. Create a layer and name it *Slope*. Set its *linetype* to *Continuous*, *lineweight* to *0.5*, and change its color.
  2. Make the *Slope* layer to be the current layer.
  3. Draw points using the *Point* command, Figure 18-5. In this example, points are drawn where the property line changes its direction. Change the point style and size using the *Point Style* dialog box from the *Home* tab and the *Utilities* panel.
  4. Using the *Text* command, label the elevation as shown in Figure 18-5.
  5. Using the *Text* and *qleader* commands show the direction of slope. (Activate *qleader* command three times to draw three arrows or use *Add Leader* command.)

18.5.8. Setbacks

- Create the setbacks as follows.
  1. Create a layer and name it as *Setback*. Set its *linetype* to *Dashdot*, *lineweight* to *0.5*, and change its color.
  2. Make the *Setback* layer to be the current layer.
  3. Draw the setbacks from the property lines as shown in Figure 18-6. In this example, the front setback is 20', the rear and the side setbacks is 10'. (i) Create two offsets (offset distance 20' and 10') of the property line. (ii) Move the offsets to the *Setback* layer. (iii) Use *Trim* and extend commands to create the setback. Make sure the linetype is clearly visible; if necessary, change the linetype scale. (iv) Use the *Join* command to join the parts of the setbacks.

- Add the setbacks' dimension as follows.
  1. Create a layer and name it *Setback_Dim*. Set its *linetype* to *Continuous*, *lineweight* to *0.0*, and change its color.
  2. Make the *Setback_Dim* layer to be the current layer.
  3. Show the dimensions, Figure 18-6.

Figure 18-5

Figure 18-6

- Create the setbacks' label as follows.
  1. Create a layer and name it *Setback_Label*. Set its *linetype* to *Continuous*, *lineweight* to *0.0*, and change its color.
  2. Make the *Setback_Label* layer the current layer.
  3. Add the label using the *Text* and *Rotation* commands, Figure 18-6.

18.5.9. Road

- Create the roads as follows.
  1. Create a layer and name it *Road*. Set its *linetype* to *Continuous*, *lineweight* to *0.5*, and change its color.
  2. Make the *Road* layer to be the current layer.
  3. Draw the roads. The width of the road is shown in the Figure 18-7 or trace over the road drawn in the lots and blocks drawing.

- Add the roads' dimension as follows.
  1. Create a layer and name it *Road_Dim*. Set its *linetype* to *Continuous*, *lineweight* to *0.0*, and change its color.
  2. Make the *Road_Dim* layer the current layer.
  3. Show the dimensions, Figure 18-7.

Figure 18-7

- Create the roads' centerline as follows.
   1. Create a layer and name it *Road_CL*. Set its *linetype* to *Center*, *lineweight* to *0.5*, and change its color.
   2. Make the *Road_CL* layer to be the current layer.
   3. Add the centerline. Make sure the linetype is clearly visible, Figure 18-7.

- Create the roads' labels as follows.
   1. Create a layer and name it *Road_Label*. Set its *linetype* to *Continuous*, *lineweight* to *0.0*, and change its color.
   2. Make the *Road_Label* layer to be the current layer.
   3. Add the names of the roads using the *Text* command, Figure 18-7. Remember to use the *Mask Background* option (for further details, check for Chapter #3).
   4. Add the centerline symbol (Figure 18-7) using the *Text* command as follows: (i) Activate the *Text* command. (ii) Change the font to "gdt." (iii) Type "q". (iv) Set the font size.

18.5.10.   Adjacent properties
- Create the adjacent properties as follows.
   1. Create a layer and name it *AP*. Set its *linetype* to *Zigzag*, *lineweight* to *0.5*, and change its color.
   2. Make the *AP* layer the current layer.
   3. Draw the adjacent properties or trace over the lots and blocks drawing. Make sure the linetype is clearly visible, Figure 18-8.

- Create the adjacent properties' labels as follows.
   1. Create a layer and name it *AP_Label*. Set its *linetype* to *Continuous*, *lineweight* to *0.0*, and change its color.
   2. Make the *AP_Label* layer the current layer.
   3. Add the names of the adjacent properties using the *Text* and *Circle* commands or transfer to the current layer from the lots and blocks drawing, Figure 18-8.

18.5.11.   Building
- Create the structure as follows.
   1. Create a layer and name it *Building*. Set its *linetype* to *Continuous*, *lineweight* to *0.0*, and change its color.
   2. Make the *Building* layer to be the current layer.
   3. Draw the location and size of all the structures. Copy the exterior face of the exterior wall and the roofline of the residential building created in the floor plan chapter and paste it in the current file. Note that the roof line is drawn inside the setbacks, Figure 18-9.
   4. Garage and front door, and front and back porches are shown in Figure 18-9. This part of the building is used to place the driveway and walkways.

Figure 18-8

Figure 18-9

- Add the dimensions as follows.
  1. Create a layer and name it *Building_Dim*. Set its *linetype* to *Continuous*, *lineweight* to *0.0*, and change its color.
  2. Make the *Building_Dim* layer to be the current layer.
  3. Add the dimensions of the building and its location, Figure 18-9.

- Create the structure's label as follow.
  1. Create a layer and name it as *Building_Label*. Set its *linetype* to *Continuous*, *lineweight* to *0.0*, and change its color.
  2. Make the *Building_Label* layer to be the current layer.
  3. Add the label using the *Text* command. The label is: PROPOSED BUILDING, 3 BEDROOMS HOME, EL MAIN FLOOR 101', Figure 18-9.

- Create the structure's hatch as follows.
  1. Create a laycr and name it *Building_Hatch*. Set its *linetype* to *Continuous*, *lineweight* to *0.0*, and change its color.
  2. Make the *Building_Hatch* layer to be the current layer.
  3. Add the hatch using the *Hatch* command. Set the pattern: *GRASS*, *Angle*: 0, and *Scale*: 25, Figure 18-9.

18.5.12.   Driveway

- The step-by-step process for creating the driveway is listed here.
  1. Create a layer and name it *Driveway*. Set its *linetype* to *Continuous*, *lineweight* to *0.0*, and change its color.
  2. Make the *Driveway* layer to be the current layer.
  3. Draw the driveway as follows, Figure 18-10.
     - Driveway is parallel to the garage door.
     - Use the *Offset* command to create an offset on both sides of the garage door, offset distance = 2'.
     - Move the offset to the *Driveway* layer.
     - Extend the offset lines to Cherry Dr..

- Create the driveway's label as follows.
  1. Create a layer and name it *Driveway_Label*. Set its *linetype* to *Continuous*, *lineweight* to *0.0*, and change its color.
  2. Make the *Driveway_Label* layer to be the current layer.
  3. Add the label, Figure 18-10, using the *Text* command and arrow using *qleader* command.

- Create the driveway's dimensions as follows.
  1. Create a layer and name it *Driveway_Dim*. Set its *linetype* to *Continuous*, *lineweight* to *0.0*, and change its color.
  2. Make the *Driveway_Dim* layer to be the current layer.
  3. Show the dimensions.

- Create the driveway's hatch as follows.
  1. Create a layer and name it *Driveway_Hatch*. Set its *linetype* to *Continuous*, *lineweight* to *0.0*, and change its color.
  2. Make the *Driveway_Hatch* layer to be the current layer.
  3. Add the hatch using the *Hatch* command, Figure 18-10. Set the pattern: *AR-HBONE*, *Angle*: 0, and *Scale*: 10.

Figure 18-10

18.5.13.   Walkway

- The step-by-step process for creating the walkway is listed here, Figure 18-11a.
  1. Create a layer and name it *Walkway*. Set its *linetype* to *Continuous*, *lineweight* to *0.0*, and change its color.
  2. Make the *Walkway* layer to be the current layer.
  3. Draw the walkway as follows.
     - The first part of the walkway is parallel to the sides of the step (at front door).
     - Draw a polyline with segments length of 5' and 18'.
     - Use the *Offset* command to create the other side of the walkway with the offset distance = 6'.
     - Move the offset to the *Walkway* layer.
     - Trim/Extend the offset as needed.

Figure 18-11a

- Create the walkway's label as follows.
  1. Create a layer and name it *Walkway_Label*. Set its *linetype* to *Continuous*, *lineweight* to *0.0*, and change its color.
  2. Make the *Walkway_Label* layer to be the current layer.
  3. Add the label, using the *Text* command and arrow using the *qleader* command.

- Create the walkway's hatch as follows.
  1. Create a layer and name it *Walkway_Hatch*. Set its *linetype* to *Continuous*, *lineweight* to *0.0*, and change its color.
  2. Make the *Walkway_Hatch* layer to be the current layer.
  3. Add the hatch using the *Hatch* command. Set the pattern: *AR-HBONE*, *Angle*: 0, and *Scale*: 10.

- Add the walkway's dimension as follows.
  1. Create a layer and name it *Walkway_Dim*. Set its *linetype* to *Continuous*, *lineweight* to *0.0*, and change its color.
  2. Make the *Walkway_Dim* layer to be the current layer.
  3. Show the dimensions.

- Figure 18-11b shows the driveway and the walkway.

Figure 18-11b

18.5.14.   Swimming pool

- The step-by-step process for creating the swimming pool is listed here.

  1. Create a layer and name it *Swimming_pool*. Set its *linetype* to *Continuous*, *lineweight* to *0.5*, and change its color.
  2. Make the *Swimming_pool* layer to be the current layer.
  3. Draw the swimming pool. The swimming pool dig is inside the setback. Its location is shown in Figure 18-12a. Draw the swimming pool as follows:
     o Draw the swimming pool boundary as shown in Figure 18-12a.
     o Using the *Fillet* command (radius option), create a fillet of the specified radius, Figure 18-12b.
     o For the finished pool, make an offset of 2' inside, Figure 18-12c.
     o Create circular steps at the upper left corner. The inner circles are created at an offset distance of 2', Figure 18-12d.

Figure 18-12a

Figure 18-12b

Figure 18-12c   Figure 18-12d

- Create the swimming pool's label as follows.
  1. Create a layer and name it *Swimming_pool_Label*. Set its *linetype* to *Continuous*, *lineweight* to *0.0*, and change its color.
  2. Make the *Swimming_pool_Label* layer to be the current layer.
  3. Add the label, using the *Text* command and arrow using *qleader* command.

- Create the swimming pool's dimensions as follows.
  1. Create a layer and name it *Swimming_pool_Dim*. Set its *linetype* to *Continuous*, *lineweight* to *0.0*, and change its color.
  2. Make the *Swimming_pool_Dim* layer to be the current layer.
  3. Show the dimensions.

- Create the swimming pool's hatch as follows.
  1. Create a layer and name it *Swimming_pool_Hatch*. Set its *linetype* to *Continuous*, *lineweight* to *0.0*, and change its color.
  2. Refer to Figure 18-13.
  3. Make the *Swimming_pool_Hatch* layer to be the current layer.
  4. For the finished pool, add the hatch using the *Hatch* command. Set the pattern: *MUDST*, Angle: 125, and Scale: 100.
  5. For the sides of the pool, add the hatch using the *Hatch* command. Set the pattern: *AR-HBONE*, Angle: 125, and Scale: 5.

- Create the swimming pool's walkway as follows.
  1. Create a layer and name it *Swimming_pool_walkway*. Set its *linetype* to *Continuous* and change its color.
  2. Make the *Swimming_ pool_walkway* layer to be the current layer.
  4. Draw the walkway as follows.
     - Draw 11' long vertical lines and a horizontal line terminating at the swimming pool, Figure 18-13.

- ▪ Draw 15' long vertical lines and a horizontal line terminating at the swimming pool, Figure 18-13.

Figure 18-13

- Create the swimming pool's walkway label as follows.
  1. Create a layer and name it *Swimming_pool_walkway_Label*. Set its *linetype* to *Continuous*, *lineweight* to *0.0*, and change its color.
  2. Make the *Swimming_pool_walkway_Label* layer to be the current layer.
  3. Add the label, Figure 18-13, using the *Text* command and the arrow using the *qleader* command.

- Create the swimming pool's walkway hatch as follows.
  1. Create a layer and name it *Swimming_pool_walkway_Hatch*. Set its *linetype* to *Continuous*, *lineweight* to *0.0*, and change its color.
  2. Make the *Swimming_pool_walkway_Hatch* layer to be the current layer.
  3. For the finished walkway, add the hatch using the *Hatch* command. Set the pattern: *AR-HBONE*, Angle: 0, and Scale: 5, Figure 18-13.

- Add the swimming pool's walkway dimensions as follows.
  1. Create a layer and name it *Swimming_pool_walkway_Dim*. Set its *linetype* to *Continuous*, *lineweight* to *0.0*, and change its color.
  2. Make the *Swimming_pool_walkway_Dim* layer to be the current layer.
  3. Show the dimensions.

Figure 18-14

18.5.15.   Utilities

- The step-by-step process for creating the utilities is listed here, Figure 18-15.
  1. Create a layer and name it *Utilities*. Set *lineweight* to *0.0*, and change its color. In this case, *linetype* is set independently for each utility.
  2. Make the *Utilities* layer to be the current layer.
  3. Change linetype to *Fenceline1* and draw the sewer line.
  4. Change linetype to *Gas_Line* and draw the gas supply line.
  5. Change linetype to *Hot_Water_Supply* and draw the water supply line.

- Create the utilities labels as follows.
  1. Create a layer and name it *Utilities*. Set *lineweight* to *0.0*, and change its color. In this case, *linetype* will be set independently for each utility.
  2. Create a layer and name it *Utilities_Label*. Set its *linetype* to *Continuous*, *lineweight* to *0.0*, and change its color.
  3. Make the *Utilities_Label* layer to be the current layer.
  4. Add the labels using the *Text* command and arrows using the *qleader* command.

- Add the utilities dimensions as follows.
  1. Create a layer and name it *Utilities_Dim*. Set its *linetype* to *Continuous* and change its color.
  2. Make the *Utilities_Dim* layer the current layer.
  3. Show the dimensions.

Figure 18-15

18.5.16.   Template file

- The step-by-step process for inserting an appropriate layout from one of the template files is listed here, Figure 18-16.
    1. Insert an appropriate layout from one of the template files, Figure 18-16.
    2. Set the scale of the drawing to 1: 800, Figure 18-16.
    3. Update the blocks, Figure 18-16.
    4. The complete site plan is shown in Figure 18-16.

LOT 4 OF BLOCK 8 OF
THE WHITE OAK SUBDIVISION,
SECTION 15-T4S-R4E,
CITY OF CLEMSON,
PICKENS COUNTY, SC

PROPERTY LINE

TEAM MANAGER		CLEMSON UNIVERSITY		
DRAWN BY		ENGR 2100 - 000	NIGHAT YASMIN	
DESIGNED BY		SITEPLAN	A8	SHT 1 OF 1
CHECKED BY		SCL: 1/64" = 1'-0"	TABLE 0	LETTER
CLIENT		05/05/2017	ENGINEERING	

Figure 18-16

Notes:

19. Construction Drawings

19.1. Learning Objectives

After completing this chapter, you will demonstrate competency in the following areas:

- Family of drawings

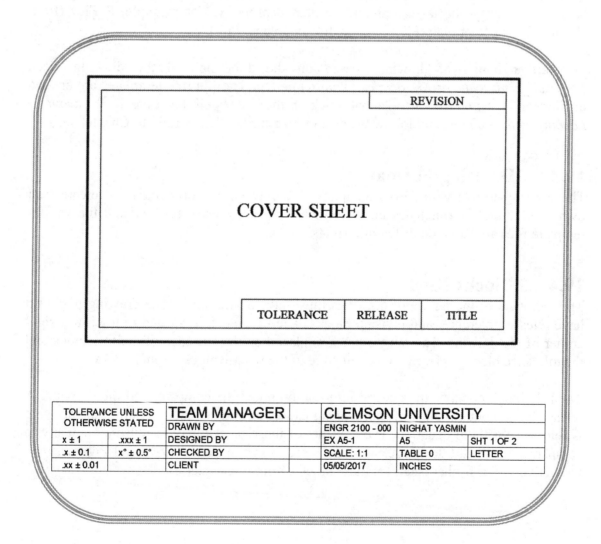

TOLERANCE UNLESS OTHERWISE STATED		TEAM MANAGER		CLEMSON UNIVERSITY		
		DRAWN BY		ENGR 2100 - 000	NIGHAT YASMIN	
x ± 1	.xxx ± 1	DESIGNED BY		EX A5-1	A5	SHT 1 OF 2
.x ± 0.1	x° ± 0.5°	CHECKED BY		SCALE: 1:1	TABLE 0	LETTER
.xx ± 0.01		CLIENT		05/05/2017	INCHES	

19.2.   Introduction

Construction drawings are the collection of several drawings that are used to complete a project. The development of a working drawing is the last step of the design process. The next step is the construction of the project!

Generally, the arrangement and number of the drawings depend on the client's requirement, company, and project type and size. Some of the commonly used drawings are shown in Figure 19-2. For most of the projects at least one of these sheets is created, and for larger projects, there can be more than one of the same types of drawings. For example, for a single story building, there can be only one floor plan. On the other hands, for a multilevel building there can be as many floor plans as the number of levels. For both of the single and multilevel buildings there can be four exterior elevation drawings (north-, south-, east-, and west-side elevations).

This chapter uses layouts to create different types of the drawing. Hence, to navigate the layouts efficiently, the layouts should be named properly. For example, F_Elev (front elevation), first floor plan (FF_Plan), profile and plane (PnP), etc.

To start a family of drawings based on the dimension of the drawing, open *My_acad_Landscape* or *My_acadiso_Landscape* template file (the templates are created in Chapter 7). To create a new layout, click on the *Insert* pull down menu → *Layout* → *Layouts from Template* and follow the prompt (for further details refer to Chapter 7).

19.3.   Drawing Format

The drawing format varies from company to company, and draftsmen can create their own style. AutoCAD includes many formats known as template files, and the various template files are based on different formats.

19.4.   Blocks Used

The members of the family of drawings must have a title block. The drawing may also have release, tolerance, and revision blocks. The title block is located in the lower right corner of the drawing. The release block is placed on the left edge of the title block and the tolerance block is placed on the left edge of the release block, Figure 19-1a.

The title block contains the general information about the company and the drawing. A release block contains a list of approval signatures or initials required before the drawing is released for the production. The contents of these blocks may vary from company to company. A typical title and release blocks are shown in Figure 19-1b and Figure 19-1c, respectively. For further details of these blocks, refer to Chapter 6.

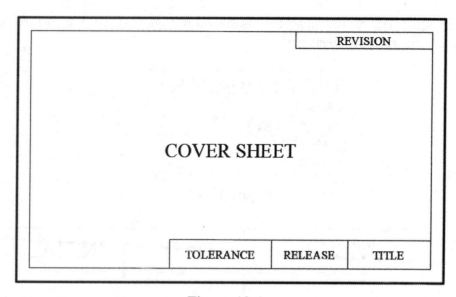

Figure 19-1a

CLEMSON UNIVERSITY		
ENGR 2100 - 000	NIGHAT YASMIN	
EX A5-1	A5	SHT 1 OF 2
SCALE: 1:1	TABLE 0	LETTER
05/05/2017	INCHES	

Figure 19-1b

TEAM MANAGER	
DRAWN BY	
DESIGNED BY	
CHECKED BY	
CLIENT	

Figure 19-1c

The tolerance block is used to list the standard tolerances. The block is created using line and text commands. In AutoCAD, the plus-minus symbol is created by typing %%p in a text object. The contents of this block may vary from company to company. The tolerance block is placed on the left edge of the release block. A typical tolerance block is shown in Figure 19-1d. The tolerance of "*X plus-minus 1*" implies that if the basic or theoretical dimension of an object is 15 then 16 and 14 are acceptable, too. For further details of blocks in general, refer to Chapter #9.

A revision block is used to show the name of the modification made to the drawing, initial or signature of the person responsible for the revision, and the date of the revision. The block is created using line and text commands. The contents of this block may vary from company to company. A revision block is generally located in the upper right corner of the drawing. A typical revision block is shown in Figure 19-1e. For further details of blocks in general, refer to Chapter 6.

TEAM MANAGER	
DRAWN BY	
DESIGNED BY	
CHECKED BY	
CLIENT	

Figure 19-1d

REVISION	DATE	INITIAL

Figure 19-1e

19.5. Family Of Construction Drawing

This section briefly describes the drawings shown in Figure 19-2.

19.5.1. Cover sheet

As the name suggests, the cover sheet is the title page for the set of the drawings. It is always the first sheet. A cover sheet includes the project's title, number, location map, name of the owner, names and signature and stamps of the designers, index of sheets, legend, survey data, perspective drawing, etc.

19.5.2. General information

The general information sheets are also known as G sheets. These sheets include the site data, location map, abbreviations, index to the other drawings, and building code data. In some projects, the cover and general information sheets are merged into one cover sheet.

19.5.3. Quantity sheet

The quantity sheet represents the estimate of the quantities (sod, concrete, lumber, paint, glass, etc.) and the cost of the activities (clearing, digging, hauling, etc.). That is, it represents the estimated cost of the projects. It includes the cost of everything used in the project, ranging from the cost of buying a pepper clip to renting heavy machinery.

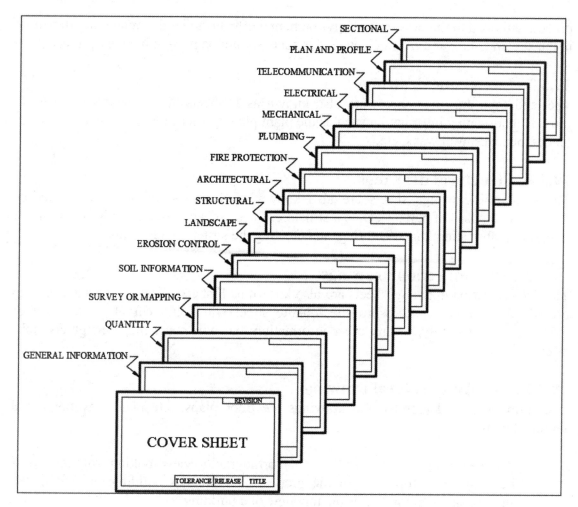

Figure 19-2

19.5.4. Survey or mapping

The survey or mapping sheets are also known as V sheets. The cover and/or general information sheets include brief data. On the other hand, survey sheets represent the detail information. These sheets are used to represent the real estate information and the vicinity information. These sheets are developed by professionals; however, the data is provided by the owner. The cost of the survey may or may not be included in the estimated cost of the project.

19.5.5. Soil information

The soil information sheets are also known as G sheets. These sheets are used to provide the geotechnical characteristic of the land used for the construction.

19.5.6. Erosion control

The erosion control sheets provide the information on the methods and techniques used in the erosion control of the project site. For example, the first step in the construction process is the clearing of the site (cutting the trees and removal of the top soil). This process will lead to the erosion and environmental effect (the eroded material will end up in the stream, lakes, and rivers). Hence, this sheet should be present in every project.

19.5.7. Landscape drawings

The landscape drawings sheets are also known as L sheets. These sheets are used to provide landscaping information such as the plant plan, types of plants, irrigation system, fences, benches, walkways, etc.

19.5.8. Structural drawings

The structural drawings sheets are also known as S sheets. In heavy construction, anything composed of parts is called a structure. These sheets provide the information for designing, fabricating, manufacturing, and erecting the structural elements.

19.5.9. Fire protection drawings

The fire protection drawings sheets are also known as F sheets. These sheets are used to provide the fire code, access to site, on-site street width and curvature, location of hydrants, power supply, or any other information that will make the fire fighters' jobs effective.

19.5.10.   Architectural drawings

The commonly used architectural drawings are floor plans, site plan, elevations, and sectional views.

- *Plan views*: A plan view is a horizontal orthographic view looking from the top. A site plan is the top view of the proposed or existing building situated in the building site. A floor plan is the top view of a building.
- *Elevation views*: An elevation is a vertical orthographic view looking from the side. For example, they include the front, rear, left, and right side elevations for a building.
- *Sectional views*: Sectional views represent the internal details of the project. As a rule of thumb, the sectional views should be drawn at the same scale as the plan and elevations. In a building, generally the sectional views of the foundations, beams, column, joints, doors and windows jams, etc. are used to display the internal detail.

19.5.11.   Plumbing drawings

The plumbing drawings sheets are also known as P sheets. These sheets are used to provide the drain waste, hot and cold water supply, and fixtures information for the site as well as for the proposed structure.

19.5.12.   Mechanical drawings

The mechanical drawings sheets are also known as M sheets. These sheets are used to provide the information regarding the location, size, and type of the units used for distributing, filtering, humidifying/dehumidifying, and cooling and heating air.

19.5.13.   Electrical drawings

The electrical drawings sheets are also known as E sheets. These sheets are used to provide the information regarding the electrical services (wiring, metering, main switch), distribution (panel boards and switches), branch work (circuitry), and devices used during the construction and of the proposed project.

19.5.14.   Telecommunication drawings

The telecommunication drawings sheets are also known as T sheets. These sheets are used to provide the information regarding how to use computer technology on the site.

19.5.15.   Plan and profile drawings

The plan and profiles drawings sheets are also known as PnP sheets. These sheets are used for the water and sewer pipelines, storm drainage system, curbs, sidewalk, and road construction.

- *Plan*: A plan view is a horizontal orthographic view looking from the top.
- *Profile*: A profile is a vertical orthographic view looking from the side.

Notes:

20. Plotting from AutoCAD 2018

20.1. Learning Objectives

After completing this chapter, you will demonstrate competency in the following areas:

- Plot the drawing from model space
- Plot a scaled drawing from layouts
- Send a drawing file as an attachment
- Create a pdf

20.2.   Introduction

Printing a drawing on a paper or electronic medium is an important part of AutoCAD users. The focus of this chapter is printing from the model space and paperspace (layouts) on paper, creation of portable document format (pdf) files, and launching email with a drawing file as an attachment from AutoCAD.

20.3.   Print

The *Print or Plot* command is used to output a drawing file. The output can be sent to a printer/plotter or written to a file for use with another application. The *Plot* command is activated using one of the following procedures.

1. Menu method: Select the *Application* pull-down menu, Figure 20-1a, and select the *Print* option.

Figure 20-1a

2. Toolbar method: Select the plot drawing tool ( ), Figure 20-1b, in the quick access toolbar. It is located on the upper left corner of the dialog box.

Figure 20-1b

3. Panel method: Select the *Output* tab, from the *Print* panel, select the *Plot* option ( ) to print, Figure 20-1c.
4. Command line method: Type "plot," "Plot" or "PLOT" or "print," "Print" or "PRINT" in the command line and press the *Enter* key.
5. Keyboard method: Hold down the control "Ctrl" key and type "p" or "P".

Figure 20-1c

- The activation of the command opens the *Plot* dialog box, Figure 20-2a. If the *Plot* command is activated from the model space then it is called *Plot-Model* (Figure 20-2a) and if it is activated from a layout then it is called *Plot – Layout Name*.

Figure 20-2a

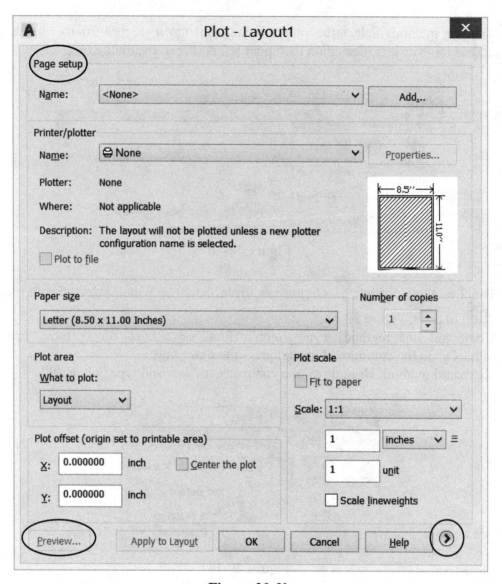

Figure 20-2b

20.3.1. Plot dialog box

The activation of the command opens the *Plot* dialog box, Figure 20-2a and Figure 20-2b. Click on the arrow in the lower right corner of the *Plot* dialog box to display the hidden features of the dialog box, Figure 20-2c.

The main features of the *Plot* dialog box are briefly discussed here. The greyed options of the *Plot* dialog box depend on the other options of the dialog box and are discussed in their respective sections.

The properties of some of the options available from the *Plot* dialog box can be changed from the Options dialog box. The Options dialog box is discussed later in this chapter.

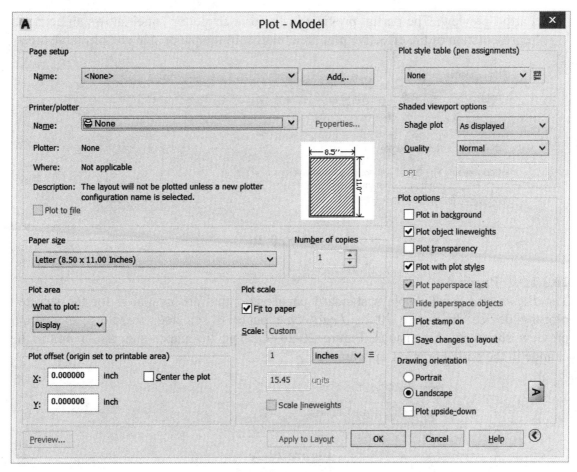

Figure 20-2c

20.3.1.1. Page setup

The *Page setup* panel displays the name of the current page setup. If a user plots drawings in a specific style (certain combination of the options from the *Plot* dialog box) then the user can increase the productivity by saving and reusing those plot styles. Page setup or plot styles are attached to the layouts; therefore, creating and saving a page setup is discussed later in this chapter.

20.3.1.2. Printer/plotter

The *Printer/plotter* panel provides the options for the selection of a configured plotting device to use when plotting or publishing from model space, layouts, or sheets, Figure 20-2d.

- <u>Name</u>: Lists the available PC3 files or system printers. Press the down arrow (▾) to display the available printers. If a printer is selected then the *Preview* button (lower left corner of Figure 20-2b) is activated.
- <u>Plot to file</u>: If the *Plot to file box* is checked then the output is saved as a file. This option is discussed in detail later in this chapter under *Portable document format file* and *Option dialog box* sections.

- Partial preview: The partial preview in the printer/plotter panel shows an accurate representation of the effective plot area relative to the paper size and printable area.

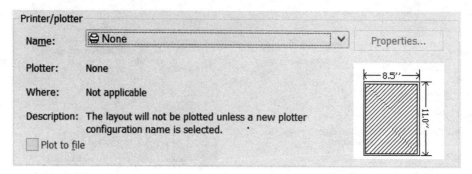

Figure 20-2d

20.3.1.3. Paper size

The *Paper size* panel displays standard paper sizes that are available for the selected plotting device. In Figure 20-2e, *Legal* type paper is selected; therefore, the partial preview shows its dimensions, Figure 20-2d. Change the paper size and monitor the change in the partial preview appearance.

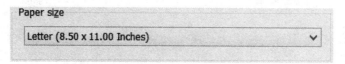

Figure 20-2e

20.3.1.4. Plot area

The *Plot area* panel specifies the area of the drawing to be plotted. The list under *What to Plot* is based on the location (model space or layout) of the activation of the *Plot* command. If the *Plot* command is activated from the model space then the options shown in Figure 20-2f are available. On the other hand, if the *Plot* command is activated from the layout, then the options shown in Figure 20-2g are available.

Figure 20-2f

Figure 20-2g

- Display: The *Display* option plots the view in the current viewport in the *Model* tab or in the current paper space view in a layout tab. That is, the drawing is plotted as it appears in the drawing area. Figure 20-3a shows a drawing in the model space. Figure 20-3b shows the same drawing in the preview window with the selection of the *Display* option in the *Plot* command. Note that the drawing objects are in the lower right corner of the drawing area; and printed in lower right corner of the drawing sheet.

Figure 20-3a

Figure 20-3b

- Limits: When the Plot command is activated from the model space, this option prints every object in the drawing area, even if it is not in the viewport. Figure 20-3a shows two pipe cutters. However, Figure 20-3c shows the three pipe cutters. Note that the grid is not appearing in the preview window because it is not printed.

Figure 20-3c

- <u>Window</u>: This option allows the user to plot any portion of the drawing that the user specifies. (i) When this option is selected, then the *Plot* dialog box closes temporarily and the prompt shown in Figure 20-4a appears on the screen. (ii) Click at slightly above and to the left of the upper left corner of the drawing. (iii) This creates a rectangle starting at the point clicked in the previous step, Figure 20-4b. Also, the prompt shown in Figure 20-4b appears on the screen. (iv) Click slightly below and to the right of the lower right corner of the drawing, Figure 20-4c. (v) Try to keep the window border above and below the same, and the left and right border should be the same, too. (Note: the borders are uneven) As soon as the second corner is selected, the *Plot* dialog box reappears. Also, the *Window* button appear in the plot area, Figure 20-4d. (vi) If necessary to change the window then click on the *Window* button and repeat the process. Figure 20-4e shows the drawing of Figure 20.4a in the preview window with the selection of the *Window* option in the *Plot* command.

| Specify first corner: | 442.6499 | 203.539 |

Figure 20-4a

| Specify opposite corner: | 155.7576 | 74.5564 |

Figure 20-4b

Specify opposite corner: | 262.7571 | 25.7702

Figure 20-4c

Figure 20-4d

Figure 20-4e

- Extents:
  a) If the *Plot* command is activated from the model space and *Extent* option is selected then every object in the current drawing is printed; even if the object is not visible in the drawing window. Figure 20-5 shows the sample drawing in the preview window with the selection of the *Extent* option in the *Plot* command. However, if this command is activated from a layout then the visible objects are plotted.
  b) *Layout*: This option is available only if the *Plot* command is activated from the *Layout* tab. When plotting a *Layout*, everything within the printable area of the specified paper size is plotted, with the origin calculated from (0, 0) in the layout.

Figure 20-5

- <u>Layout</u>: This option is available only if the *Plot* command is activated from the *Layout* tab. When this option is selected, then the following two options are not available. (i) Under the *Plot offset*, the *Center the plot* option is not available. (ii) Under the *Plot scale*, the *Fit to paper* option is not available.

20.3.1.5. Plot offset

This option specifies an offset of the plot area relative to the lower-left corner of the printable area or from the edge of the paper. The printable area of a drawing sheet is defined by the selected output device and is represented by a dashed line in a layout.

- <u>X and Y</u>: The X and Y values offset the geometry on the paper by entering a positive or negative value in the respective boxes, Figure 20-6a. The partial preview shows the accurate representation of the effective plot area relative to the paper size, printable area and plot offsets, Figure 20-6b.
- <u>Center the plot</u>: Automatically calculates the X and Y offset values to center the plot on the paper. This option is available only if the *Plot* command is activated from the model space, Figure 20-6a.
- Repeat the previous examples with *Center the plot* option and observe the difference in the plot preview.

Figure 20-6a

Figure 20-6b

20.3.1.6.   Plot scale
This panel controls the relative size of the drawing units to the plotted units. The default setting is *Fit to paper* when the *Plot* command is activated from the *Model* tab, Figure 20-6a. The default scale setting is 1:1 when the *Plot* command is activated from the *Layout* tab, Figure 20-1b.

- Fit to paper: If this box is checked (Figure 20-7a), then the plot is scaled to fit within the selected paper size and the rest of the options in the plot scale window are inactive.
- Scale: The scale list defines the exact scale for the plot. A custom scale can be created by entering the number of inches (or millimeters) equal to the number of drawing units.
- inches = mm =: Specifies the number of inches or millimeters equal to the specified number of units. Pixel is available only when a raster output is selected.
- Units: Specifies the number of units equal to the specified number of inches, millimeters, or pixels, Figure 20-7b.
- Scale lineweights: This option is available only if the plot command is activated from the *Layout* tab. It scales the lineweights in proportion to the plot scale. Lineweights normally specify the line width of the plotted objects and are plotted with the line width size, regardless of the plot scale.

| Figure 20-7a | Figure 20-7b |

20.3.1.7.   Shaded viewport options
This panel specifies how shaded and rendered 3D viewports are plotted and determines their resolution levels and dots per inch (dpi).

- Shade plot: These options specify how views are plotted. These options are available only for 3D objects and if the *Plot* command is activated from the *Model* space, Figure 20-8a. For the *Model* tab, select from the following options: (i) *As Displayed*: Plots objects the way they are displayed on the screen. (ii) *Wireframe*: Plots objects in wireframe regardless of the way they are displayed on the screen. (iii) *Hidden*: Plots objects with hidden lines removed regardless of the way they are displayed on the screen. (iv) *Rendered*: Plots objects as rendered regardless of the way they are displayed on the screen.

- Quality: These options specify the resolution at which shaded and rendered viewports are plotted, Figure 20-8b. Select one of the following options. (i) *Draft*: Sets rendered and shaded model space views to be plotted as wireframe. (ii) *Preview*: Sets rendered and shaded model space views to be plotted at one quarter of the current device resolution, to a maximum of 150 dpi. (iii) *Normal*: Sets rendered and shaded model space views to be plotted at one half of the current device resolution, to a maximum of 300 dpi. (iv) *Presentation*: Sets rendered and shaded model space views to be plotted at the current device resolution, to a maximum of 600 dpi. (v) *Maximum*: Sets rendered and shaded model space views to be plotted at the current device resolution with no maximum. (vi) *Custom*: Sets rendered and shaded model space views to be plotted at the resolution setting that the user specifies in the DPI box, up to the current device resolution.
- DPI: Specifies the dots per inch for shaded and rendered views, up to the maximum resolution of the current plotting device. This option is unavailable for most of the options under *Shade plot* and *Quality* boxes.

Figure 20-8a

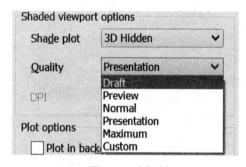

Figure 20-8b

20.3.1.8.   Plot options
Plot options specifies the options for lineweights, plot styles, shaded plots, and the order in which objects are plotted, Figure 20-9a. The inactive field in the option list becomes active if the *Plot* command is activated from a layout. Plotting from a layout is discussed in detail later in this chapter.

- Plot in background: The selection of this option allows the user to work in AutoCAD while plotting is processed in background. In some situations, selection of this option makes the computer slow.
- Plot object lineweights: Specifies whether lineweights assigned to objects and layers are plotted.

- <u>Plot with plot styles</u>: Specifies whether plot styles applied to objects and layers are plotted. When the user selects this option, *Plot Object Lineweights* is selected automatically.
- <u>Plot paperspace Last</u>: Plots model space geometry first. Paper space geometry is usually plotted before model space geometry.
- <u>Hide paperspace Objects</u>: Specifies whether the HIDE operation applies to objects in the paper space viewport. This option is available only from a layout tab. The effect of this setting is reflected in the plot preview, but not in the layout.
- <u>Plot stamp on</u>: Selection of this option allows the plotter to place a stamp with specified information at a specified location on every plot. In addition, a stamp button appears. Click the stamp button () to open the *Plot Stamp* dialog box, Figure 20-9b; if necessary, change the information.

Figure 20-9a

Figure 20-9b

- <u>Save changes to layout</u>: If the *Plot* command is activated from a layout, and the user selects the option for plotting then those selections can be saved by checking this box. The selections are attached to the layout initiating the plot command.

20.3.1.9. Drawing orientation

Specifies the orientation of the drawing on the paper for plotters that support landscape or portrait orientation, Figure 20-10.

- <u>Portrait</u>: Orients and plots the drawing so that the short edge of the paper represents the top of the page.
- <u>Landscape</u>: Orients and plots the drawing so that the long edge of the paper represents the top of the page.
- <u>Plot upside-down</u>: Orients and plots the drawing upside-down.

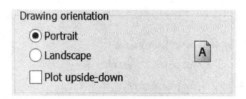

Figure 20-10

20.3.1.10. Preview

The preview command displays the drawing as it appears when plotted on paper. The user must preview the drawing file before clicking the *OK* button! This option is available only if under the *Printer/plotter* panel and *Name* field, a printer is selected. The plot *Preview* button is located in the lower right corner of the *Plot* dialog box. In Figure 20-11, this option is not available. To exit the print preview and return to the *Plot* dialog box, press the *Esc* or the *Enter* key or click on ⊗ button in the preview window.

Figure 20-11a

If the preview window is open then to exit the print preview and return to the *Plot* dialog box, press the *Esc* or the *Enter* key or click on ⊗ button on the preview window.

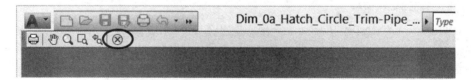

Figure 20-11b

20.3.1.11. Plot to layout

This option is available only if the *Plot* command is activated from a layout and the user had made changes to the *Plot* dialog box. In Figure 20-11, this option is available.

20.3.1.12. OK and cancel

As the name suggests, click the *OK* button to make changes effective, close the *Plot* dialog box, and click the *Cancel* button to ignore changes and close the *Plot* dialog box, Figure 20-11.

20.4. Plot from Layouts

The *Print* and *Plot* commands are used to plot a drawing file. When plotting a *Layout*, everything within the printable area of the specified paper size is plotted. Layers and layouts are discussed in detail in Chapter #5 and Chapter #7 and are used heavily in the application part of the textbook.

The process of plotting from a layout is summarized in the following steps.
1. Click on the desired layout.
2. Double click INSIDE the viewport (WCS appears) and center the drawing using the scroll bars or pan command.
3. Freeze the unnecessary layers.
4. If necessary, set the linetype scale.
5. Double click OUTSIDE the viewport (WCS disappears).
6. From the *Properties* sheet, set the viewport scale and lock the scale.
7. Update the *Title* block by modifying the block attributes to the desired value.
8. Activate and complete the *Plot* command.
9. On the printout, initial by hand the *Release* block entries.

Figure 20-12 shows the settings of the *Plot* dialog box when the *Plot* command is activated from a layout.

- The *Plot* command is activated from the layout named as TestPrint; and the software named the dialog box as *Plot-TestPrint*.
- In the *Plot area* panel under *What to Plot*, the *Layout* is the default option.
- In the *Plot offset* panel, the *Center the plot* option is inactive.
- In the *Plot Scale* panel, the *Fit to paper* option is inactive; and the *Scale* option is full scale. However, the user can change the scale.
- In the *Shaded viewport options* panel, the *Shade plot* and *DPI* options are inactive.
- In the *Plot options* panel, every option is available.

- In the *Orientation* panel, AutoCAD selects the *Landscape* option because the TestPrint layout is in landscape format, Figure 20-13a. The longest dimension of the pipe cutter in Figure 20-13a is not parallel to the longer side of the paper. Hence, this drawing should be printed in portrait form. Select the *Portrait* option from the *Plot* dialog box and preview the drawing before printing, Figure 20-13b. The pipe cutter is vertical but the viewport is distorted (it cannot be fixed here).

This issue can be fixed by changing the orientation of the layout before activating the *Plot* command.

Figure 20-12

Figure 20-13a

Figure 20-13b

20.5. Change Layout's Orientation

A user can change the layout orientation using one of the following two methods. (i) Insert a layout from an appropriate template file (refer to Chapter 7), or (ii) change the orientation using the page setup manager.

A user can change the layout orientation using page setup manager as follows.

- Bring the cursor on a layout tab.
- Press the right button of the mouse and the option panel appears, Figure 20-14a.

Figure 20-14a

- Move the cursor to the *Page Setup Manager* option and press the left button of the mouse. The *Page Setup Manager* dialog box shown in Figure 20-14b appears.
- On the *Page Setup Manager* dialog box, click on the *Modify* button. The *Page Setup – TestPrint* dialog box shown in Figure 20-14c appears.
- Select the *Portrait* option and press the *OK* button.
- Click on the *Close* button from the *Page Setup Manager*.
- The layout is changed to portrait form, Figure 20-14d.

- The viewport is still distorted; however, it can be fixed.
- Click on the upper right corner of the viewport and move it to the left, Figure 20-14d. Center the viewport and print!

Figure 20-14b

Figure 20-14c

Figure 20-14d

Figure 20-14e

20.6.   Page Setup From Layouts

A plot style can be defined as certain combination of the options from the *Plot* dialog box. If a user plots drawings in a specific style, then the user can increase the productivity by saving and reusing those plot styles. Page setup or plot styles are attached to the layouts; therefore, creating and saving a page setup is the topic of this section.

A user can create a new page setup as follows.

- Bring the cursor on a layout tab.
- Press the right button of the mouse and the option panel appears, Figure 20-15a.

- Move the cursor to the *Page Setup Manager* option and press the left button of the mouse. The *Page Setup Manager* dialog box shown in Figure 20-15b appears.
- On the *Page Setup Manager* dialog box, Figure 20-15b, click on the *New* button. The *New Page Setup* dialog box shown in Figure 20-15c will appear.

Figure 20-15a

Figure 20-15b

Figure 20-15c

- Specify the name of the page setup and press the *OK* button. This closes the *New Page Setup* dialog box and opens the *Plot* dialog box, Figure 20-15d.
- Figure 20-15d shows the settings of the *Plot* dialog box for the new page setup.
  - o Note that, in the *Page setup* panel the name is *My Setup*, the newly created page setup's name.
  - o In the *Plotter/printer* panel under *Name*, the default printer's name is selected.
  - o In the *paper size* panel, the *Letter* is the default option.
  - o In the *Plot area* panel under *What to Plot*, the *Display* is the default option.
  - o In the *Plot offset* panel, the *Center the plot* option is selected.
  - o In the *Plot Scale* panel, the *Fit to paper* option is selected.
  - o In the *Plot options* panel, three options are selected.
  - o In the *Drawing orientation* panel, the *Portrait* option is selected.
  - o Click the *OK* button of the dialog box. This will close the dialog box and create the new page setup.
  - o Activate the *Plot* command and select the *My Setup* option, Figure 20-15e. Check the available options on the *Page Setup* dialog box.

Figure 20-15d

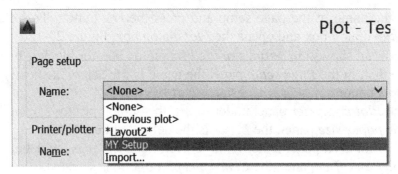

Figure 20-15e

20.7.   Layout Plotting: FAQ

Sometimes the user relates the problem associated with layers with plotting from layouts. The most commonly occurring problem is that the user *can see the objects but cannot plot them*. Generally, there are two reasons for this situation: either the objects in question are drawn in the *defpoints* layer or the layer's plot option is *off* (⬛). This problem can be solved as follows.

1. If the objects are drawn on the *defpoints* layer, then move them to their respective layers and the drafter will be able to plot the objects.
2. If the objects are NOT drawn on the *defpoints* layer, then perform the following steps. (i) Open the *Layer Properties Manager* palette. (ii) If the layer's (containing the objects in question) plot option is *off*, that is, the layer's printer icon shows the no entry sign (⬛) then just click on the printer icon. The no entry sign disappears (⬛) and the drafter is able to plot the objects on the layer in question.

20.8.   Portable Document Format (PDF)

Suppose an architect has created drawings and needs to electronically communicate with the client. The architect can send the drawing file as an email attachment from AutoCAD following the path shown in Figure 20-16.

However, if the client does not have access to AutoCAD then it is not possible to view an AutoCAD file. The solution to this problem is to convert AutoCAD files to portable document format (pdf) file. A user can create pdf files either using the Plot dialog box or the file menu.

*   Plot dialog box method: From the *Plot* dialog box, the user can select the appropriate pdf format. This conversion will create the pdf file only for the first layout.

*   File menu method: Open the pdf option following the path shown in Figure 2-17b. This opens the *Save As PDF* dialog box, Figure 2-17c. Follow the prompts. One key

advantage of this method is that the user can create one pdf file for a drawing with multiple layouts using *All layouts* under the *Export* option.

Figure 20-16

Figure 20-17a

Figure 20-17b

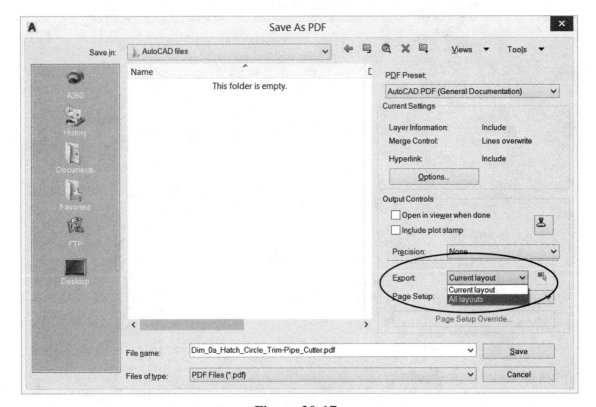

Figure 20-17c

20.9. Option dialog box

The properties of some of the options available from the *Plot* dialog box can be changed from the *Plot and Publish* tab of the *Options* dialog box, Figure 20-18. The user should explore the capabilities provided by this dialog box.

Figure 20-18

Notes:

21. Suggested In-Class Activities

21.1. Introduction

This chapter provides in-class activities (or ICAs). Every ICA begins with its objectives. The next is the hints section that refers to the corresponding sections in the text followed by the ICA description. Finally, the ICA describes the submission method. The ICAs are submitted using one of the following three methods.

- Students show (on screen) the complete drawing in class.
- Students submit the online/printout from the model space making sure that the linetypes and lineweights are clearly visible.
- Students submit the online/printout from the layout making sure that the layers are frozen appropriately, linetypes and lineweights are clearly visible, and the drawings are properly scaled to the given scale factor in the layouts.

For some of the initial ICAs, step-by-step instructions to complete the drawing are also provided. If an ICA uses a drawing created in one of the previous ICAs or a figure from the text, then a thumbnail (a small size image where dimensions and text may not be clearly visible) is shown at the end of the ICA in question. Therefore, students should check the corresponding chapter for details.

** The students should save the drawing at various stages (10-15 minutes intervals) of the development process.

General Information

- Based on the topic of the ICA, follow the instructions from the corresponding chapter of the book.
- Use the *Erase* command or *Delete* button on the keyboard.
- If drawing horizontal or vertical lines is necessary, then turn *On* the ORTHO option from the status bar.
- If necessary, turn *On/Off* object snap.
- If necessary, show/hide lineweight option.
- If necessary, create layers and manipulate layers in model space and layouts.
- The draftsman may need to change the linetype scale from the *Properties* palette. **Linetype scale depends on the size of the drawing, zoom factor, drawing environment (model space or layout), and lineweight.**
- The lineweight of 0.3mm creates a reasonably thick line in the model space. However, in a layout, the same effect may be created by the lineweight of 0.5mm.

21.2. Download AutoCAD 2018

Objectives
- Learn to download AutoCAD 2018
- Get familiar with AutoCAD 2018
- General information about ICAs

Hints
- Refer to Chapter 2 for help

ICA Description
1. Download AutoCAD 2018.
2. Start AutoCAD 2018.
3. If you have provided the license numbers correctly, you should be able to perform step 2, otherwise, take the necessary steps to fix the problem.

ICA Submission
1. Launch AutoCAD 2018 in class.
2. Show the default workspace in class to the instructor or TA.

21.3. Customize a Workspace

Objectives
- Learn to customize and save a workspace.

Hints
- Refer to Chapter 2 (ribbon interface), especially Figure 2-58c, for help.

ICA Description
1. AutoCAD ribbon: Create and save the workspace shown in Figure 21-3.
   a. Create a tab called MyTab.
   b. Create a panel called MyPanel.
   c. Add the command shown in the figure.
   d. Display the information on the status bar as shown in the figure.
   e. Save the workspace.
2. Do not add text boxes or arrows.

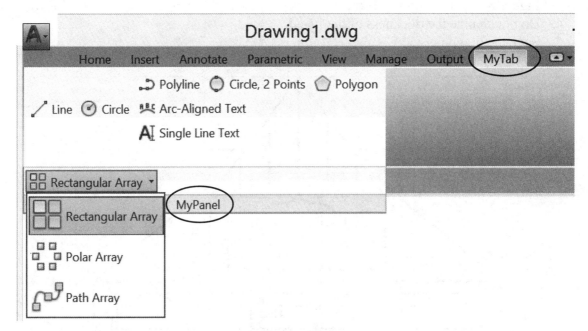

Figure 21-3

ICA Submission
1. Show the workspace in class (on or before the due date) to the instructor or TA.

21.4. Grid and Snap Capabilities

Objectives
- How to set and use grid and snap capabilities.

Hints
- Refer to Chapter 2 for help.

ICA Description
1. Drawing units: Millimeters
2. Create a grid.
   a. Input format: Decimal units
   b. Drawing limits: 420, 430
   c. Grid: 10
   d. Snap: 5
3. Use the grid created above to draw the line diagram of a cottage shown in Figure 21-4a and Figure 21-4b.
4. Do not change the thickness of the lines.
5. Save the drawings.

Figure 21-4a

Figure 21-4b

ICA Submission

1. Show the drawings in class (on or before the due date) to the instructor or TA.

21.5. Erase, Line, Polyline and Polyline Edit

Objectives
- Learn to use *Erase*, *Line*, *Polyline*, *Polyline Edit*, and ORTHO commands.

Hints
- Refer to Chapter 3 and Chapter 4 for help.

ICA Description
1. Drawing units: Inches
2. Create and save the drawing shown in Figure 21-5 using *ORTHO*, *Line* and *Polyline* commands and polar coordinates.
3. Do not add dimensions.
4. Save the drawing.

Figure 21-5

ICA Submission
1. Show the drawings in class (on or before the due date) to the instructor or TA.

21.6. Point, Circle, Polygon, Offset, Move, Trim, Extend, and Zoom

Objectives
- Learn to use *Point, Circle (radius and ttr), Polygon, Offset, Move,* and *Trim* commands.
- Learn to use *Zoom* capabilities.

Hints
- Refer to Chapter 3 and Chapter 4 for help.

ICA Description - Part 1
1. Create the light bulb arrangement shown in Figure 21-6a using *Line* and *Point* commands.
2. Open the drawing created in ICA 5 and save it as ICA 6.
3. Add the points (Point size = 1), and *Set size in absolute units*.
4. Save the drawing.
5. Do not add dimension.

Figure 21-6a

ICA Description - Part 2
1. Drawing units: Inches
2. Create and save the drawing shown in Figure 21-6b using *Line, Polyline, Polygon, Circle, Offset,* and *Trim* commands.
3. Save the drawing.
4. Do not add dimension.
5. Follow the step-by-step instructions.

Figure 21-6b

Step-by-Step instructions for Figure 21-6b
1. In the following figures, ϕ is the symbol of 'diameter' and the figures correspond to the step number.

2. Create a new acad file, that is, open an *acad* template file.
3. (i) Draw a horizontal line of length 5.0. (ii) Draw two circles of diameter 1.5. (iii) Draw the circle of diameter 5.0 using the TTR option. (iv) Using the center of diameter 5.0, draw another circle of diameter 12.0. (v) Draw two points of size 0.5 in absolute units.

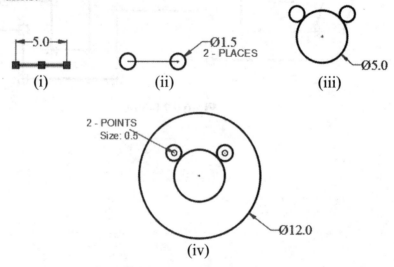

4. (i) Draw two circles of diameter 6.9 and 3.7 with center at the lower quadrant of circle $\phi5.0$. The new circle in the figures is selected to display the grip points. These grip points help in locating the center of a circle. (ii) Draw two more circles of $\phi6.9$.

(i) (ii)

5. Use the *Trim* command to create the shape shown below.

6. Draw a polygon. (i) The center of the polygon is the center of the 12" diameter circle. Select the *Circumscribed about circle* option. (ii) Use the *Offset* command for the outer polygons. Set offset distance to 0.5 inches.

(i) (ii)

7. Use the *Line* command to draw the outline of the base.

8. Use the *Offset* command for the inside of the base.

9. Draw ONE closed, non-overlapping, and non-intersecting polyline of the base. The line command or several polylines will make the next step difficult.

10. Use the *Offset* command (offset distance 0.5) to complete the drawing.

ICA Submission
1. Show the drawings in class (on or before the due date) to the instructor or TA.

21.7. Color, Linetype, Lineweight, Mirror, Copy, Scale, and, Hatch

Objectives
- Learn to use *Circle (ttr)*, *linetype*, *lineweight*, *Mirror*, *Copy*, *Scale*, and *Hatch* commands.

Hints
- Refer to Chapter 3 and Chapter 4 for help.

ICA Description - Part 1
1. Drawing units: Inches
2. Draw the lines and circle as shown in Figure 21-7a.
   Hints: *Mirror* command, Figure 21-7aa, Figure 21-7ab, Figure 21-7ac.
3. Save the drawing.
4. Do not add the dimension or center lines of the circle.
5. Set the lineweight and linetype as shown in the figure.

Figure 21-7a

Figure 21-7aa

Figure 21-7ab

Figure 21-7ac

ICA Description - Part 2

1. Drawing units: Inches:
2. Use *Line, offset, Mirror, Copy,* and *Scale* commands to create the objects shown in Figure 21-7b.
3. The smaller barn is 60% of the larger barn.
4. Save the drawing.
5. Do not add dimension or center lines of the circle.
6. Show the complete drawings on one screen.
7. The step-by-step instructions start on the next page.

Figure 21-7b

Step-by-Step by instructions for Figure 21-7b

1. Open an *acad* template file.
2. Draw the lines as shown in Figure 21-7ba.
3. Using the *Offset* command with the offset distance of 0.5,
    a. Create rectangles outside the windows (two top rectangles).
    b. Create rectangle inside the door (bottom rectangle).
    c. A line below the roof line, Figure 21-7bb.

Figure 21-7ba

4. Use the *Mirror* command to create the other side of the barn, Figure 21-7bc.

Figure 21-7bb   **Figure 21-7bc**

5. Use the *Trim* and Extend command as needed on top of the barn, Figure 21-7bd.
6. Use the *Hatch* command to hatch the barn, Figure 21-7be.

Figure 21-7bd

PATTERN: CORK   PATTERN: STEEL
ANGLE: 0°, SCALE: 4   ANGLE: 0°, SCALE: 4

Figure 21-7be

7. Use the *Copy* command to create the second barn, Figure 21-7bf.
8. Scale the barn: (i) Activate the *Scale* command, (ii) select the copy created in step 7, (iii) select the lower left corner as the base point, (iv) for the scale factor, type the value 0.60, and (v) press the *Enter* key, Figure 21-7bg.

Figure 21-7bf

Figure 21-7bg

ICA Submission
1. Show the drawings in class (on or before the due date) to the instructor or TA.

21.8. Array, Text, Hatch, Ellipse, qleader, and Draw Order

Objectives
- Learn to use *Array Rectangular, Text, Hatch, Ellipse, Mirror*, and *qleader* commands.
- Learn to use *Draw Order* capabilities.

Hints
- Refer to Chapter 3 and Chapter 4 for help.

ICA Description
1. Drawing units: Inches:
2. Draw the bridge shown in Figure 21-8b using *Array, Text, Hatch, Ellipse*, and *qleader* commands.
   a. Figure 21-8a shows the details of the columns used in Figure 21-8b.
   b. The bridge is symmetrical in the center.
   c. Assume reasonable value for the missing dimensions, if any.
3. Add the text boxes and arrows.
4. Save the drawing.
5. Do not add dimensions or center lines of the circle.

Basic steps
1. Draw the right column as shown in Figure 21-8a.
2. Draw an ellipse with the major axis 40.0" and the minor axis 10" for the central cable of the bridge, Figure 21-8b.
3. Draw the cable on the right side of the bridge.
4. Draw the right side gravity wall.
5. Use the *Mirror* command to draw the left side of the bridge.
6. Complete the bridge.

ICA Submission
1. Show the drawings in class (on or before the due date) to the instructor or TA.

Figure 21-8a

Figure 21-8b

21.9. Layers

Objectives
- Learn to create *Layers* commands.
- Learn to use *Linetype*, *Linetype Scale*, and *Mirror* commands.

Hints
- Refer to Chapter 5 for help.

ICA Description - Part 1
1. Drawing units: Inches
2. Draw the object shown in Figure 21-9a using *Line*, *Circle*, and *Mirror* commands
3. Create appropriate layers.
4. Set the lineweight and linetype shown in the figure.
5. Set linetype scale (not shown in the figure).
6. Use a reasonable value for *linetype scale* in *Properties* palette.
7. Save the drawing.
8. Do not add dimension or center lines of the circle.
9. The step-by-step instructions are given.

Figure 21-9a

Step-by-Step instructions for Figure 21-9a:
a. Create two layers and name them *Circle* and *Rectangle*. Set the properties of the layers as shown in Figure 21-9ab.

Figure 21-9ab

b. Make the *Circle* layer the current layer and draw the circles.
c. Make the *Rectangle* layer the current layer and draw the rectangles.
d. Turn *Off* the *Circle* layer; only rectangles are displayed.
e. Turn *Off* the *Rectangle* layer; only circles are displayed.

ICA Description - Part 2

1. Drawing units: Millimeters
2. Draw the object shown in Figure 21-9b using *Line* and *Circle* commands.
3. Create appropriate layers.
4. Set the lineweight and linetype shown in the figure.
5. Set linetype scale (not shown in the figure).
6. Use a reasonable value for the *linetype scale* in the *Properties* palette.
7. Save the drawing.
8. Do not add dimension or center lines of the circle.
9. The step-by-step instructions are given.

Step-by-Step instructions for Figure 21-9b:

a. Create two layers and name them *Flower* and *Tracks*. Set the properties of the layers as shown in Figure 21-9ba.
b. Make the *Flower* layer to be the current layer and draw the circles.
c. Make the *Tracks* layer to be the current layer and draw the circles.
d. Select the *Tracks* layer and draw the lines.
e. Turn *Off* the *Flower* layer; only tracks will be displayed.
f. Turn *On* the *Flower* layer; both tracks and flower will be displayed.
g. Turn *Off* the *Tracks* layer; only circles will be displayed.

Figure 21-9b

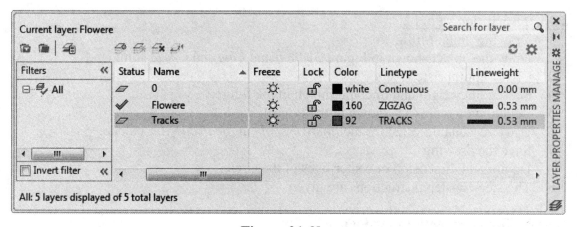

Figure 21-9ba

ICA Submission

1. Show the drawings in class (on or before the due date) to the instructor or TA.

21.10.   Make & Insert Block, Layouts, and Template Files

Objectives
- Learn to use *Block Attribute*, *Make Block* and *Insert Block* commands.
- Learn to create and use *Block and Template* files.
- Learn to create *Layout* command.
- Learn to rename a layout and freeze layers in layouts.

Hints
- Refer to Chapter 5, Chapter 6, and Chapter 7 for help.

ICA Description – Part 1
1. Download the two template files or create the template file from Chapter 6 and Chapter 7.

ICA Description – Part 2
1. Open the drawing created in ICA 9-Part 1 (shown on the next page).
    a. Insert layout from the appropriate template file in the drawing.
    b. Create three layouts and rename them as shown in Figure 21-10a.
    c. In each layout, use a reasonable value for the *linetype scale* in *Properties* palette.
    d. Switch to the *ShowAll* layout to show circles and rectangles.
    e. Switch to the *Circle* layout and show only circles by freezing the *Rectangle* layer as follows: (i) Double click inside the viewport; the viewport becomes bold and WCS appears in the viewport. (ii) Now freeze the unnecessary layers.
    f. Switch to the *Rectangle* layout and show only rectangles by freezing the *Circle* layer as follows: (i) Double click inside the viewport; the viewport becomes bold and WCS appears in the viewport. (ii) Now freeze the unnecessary layers.
    g. Update the title block.

Figure 21-10a

ICA Description – Part 13
1. Open the drawing created in ICA 9-Part 2 (shown on the next page).
    a. Insert layout from the appropriate portrait template file in the drawing.
    b. Create three layouts and rename them as shown in Figure 21-10b.
    c. In each layout, use a reasonable value for the *linetype scale* in *Properties* palette.
    d. Switch to the *ShowAll* layout to show flowers and tracks.

e. Switch to the *Flower* layout to show only the flowers by freezing the *Tracks* layer as follows: (i) Double click inside the viewport; the viewport becomes bold and WCS appears in the viewport. (ii) Now freeze the unnecessary layers.

f. Switch to the *Tracks* layout to show only the tracks by freezing the *Flower* layer as follows: (i) Double click inside the viewport; the viewport becomes bold and WCS appears in the viewport. (ii) Now freeze the unnecessary layers.

g. Update the title block.

Figure 21-10b

ICA Submission

1. Show the drawing in the viewport and the updated Title block in class (on or before the due date) to the instructor or TA.

21.11.   Dimension

Objectives
- Learn to add *dimensions* to a drawing.

Hints
- Refer to Chapter 8 for help.

ICA Description - Part 1
1. Open the drawing shown in Figure 21-5 (ICA 5).
   a. Create a layer for the dimension and make it the current layer.
   b. Add the dimensions to the drawing.
   c. Insert layout from the appropriate template file.
   d. Set the drawing scale appropriately.
   e. Lock the viewport.
   f. Update the title block.
   g. Initialize the entries on the printout in the release block by hand (do not type).

Figure 21-5

ICA Description - Part 2
1. Open the drawing shown in Figure 21-6b (ICA 6).
   a. Repeat the above process.

Figure 21-6b

ICA Submission
1. Show the drawing in the viewport and the updated Title block in class (on or before the due date) to the instructor or TA.

21.12.   Azimuths, Bearing, and Closed Travers

Objectives
- Learn to convert an azimuth into a bearing and vice versa.
- Learn to draw closed traverses using azimuths and bearings.

Hints
- Refer to Chapter 10 for details and help.

ICA Description - Part 1
1. Drawing units: Millimeters
2. Draw the closed traverse shown in Figure 10-4e of the textbook.
    a. Create appropriate layers.
    b. Add the dimensions as shown in the figure.
    c. Find the length and bearing labeled as **?**.
    d. Save the drawing.

ICA Description - Part 2
1. Drawing units: Millimeters
2. Draw the closed traverse shown in Figure 10-5 of the textbook.
    a. Create appropriate layers.
    b. Add the dimensions as shown in the figure.
    c. Find the length and azimuth labeled as **?**.
    d. Save the drawing.

ICA Description - Part 3

1. <u>Convert bearing to azimuths</u>: **Answers must be in degree, minutes, and seconds format.** Hand written solutions are accepted.
   a. N43°32"W
   b. S23°5'E
   c. N15°E
   d. S75°W

ICA Description - Part 4

1. <u>Convert azimuths to bearing</u>: **Answers must be in degree, minutes, and seconds format.** Hand written solutions are accepted
   a. 123°12'32"
   b. 19°47'56"
   c. 258°08'01"
   d. 349°15'21"

ICA Submission

1. Show the drawings (Figure 21-12a and Figure 21-12b) in class (on or before the due date) to the instructor or TA.
2. Submit the solution to bearing-azimuth conversion. Hand written solutions are acceptable.

21.13.   RSS, Lots and Blocks

Objectives

- Learn to label subdivisions using RSS.
- Learn to draw lots and blocks (Textbook: Figure 10-20).

Hints

- Refer to Chapter 10 for details and help.

ICA Description - Part 1

1. Range and township:
   a. Take the printout of the following figure.
   b. Find SECTION31-T4S-R5E using the Rectangular system.

Figure 21-13a

ICA Description - Part 2
1. RSS:
    a. Take the printout of the following figure.
    b. Label the various subdivisions using the Rectangular system.

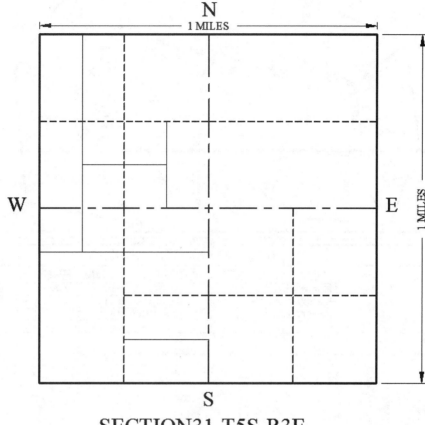

SECTION31-T5S-R3E

Figure 21-13b

ICA Description - Part 3
2. Lots and Blocks:
    a. Draw the parcel of land and divide it into lots, Figure 10-17c of the textbook.
    b. Find the area of each lot and display it on the drawing.
    c. Add the dimensions
    d. Insert the layout from the appropriate template file.
    e. Set the drawing scale to 1/128":1'-0".
    f. Set the drawing units to ENGINEERING.
    g. Update the title block.
    h. Initialize the entries on the printout in the release block by hand (do not type).

THE WHITE OAK SUBDIVISION

TEAM MANAGER		CLEMSON UNIVERSITY		
DRAWN BY		ENGR 2100 - 000	NIGHAT YASMIN	
DESIGNED BY		LOTS_BLOCKS	A5	SHT 1 OF 1
CHECKED BY		SCL: 1/128" = 1'-0"	TABLE 0	LETTER
CLIENT		05/05/2017	ENGINEERING	

Figure 21-13c

ICA Submission
1. Submit the solution of Part 1 and Part 2.
2. Submit the print of the Lot and Block created in Part 3.

21.14.   Rotate, Text, Background Mask, & Table Command and Contour map

Objectives
- Learn to label a *Contour* map.
- Learn to use the *Table* command.

Hints
- Refer to Chapter 3 and Chapter 12 for details and help.

ICA Description
1. Drawing units: Engineering
2. Download the contour map file from the course website.
3. Download the contour file.
4. For the contour map: Label each index contour at three different places using the *Text* and *Background Mask* commands.
5. Contour Interval = 1ft.
6. If the elevation of the first index contour is H1 and the elevation of the next index contour is H2 then H2 = H1 + 5* Contour Interval.
7. If the elevation of the first index contour is 160, then the elevation of the next index contour is: 160 - 5*1 = 155ft.
8. In the contour map file, insert the layout from the appropriate template file.
9. Set the viewport Scale to 1:1000.
10. Set the drawing units to ENGINEERING.
11. Update the title block.
12. Save the drawing.

ICA Submission
1. Show the drawings in class (on or before the due date) to the instructor or TA.
2. Show the contour map with every layer on.

21.15.   Drainage Basin Delineation

Objectives
- Learn to delineate a drainage basin of a channel.

Hints
- Refer to Chapter 3 and Chapter 12 for details and help.

ICA Description
1. Drawing units: Engineering
2. Download the contour file.
3. The index contours are labeled.
4. Draw the centerline of the channel.
5. Show the direction of the flow in the channel.
6. Display the outlet point of the watershed.
7. Delineate the watershed (drainage basin) boundary; (Hint: Connect ridges).
8. Hatch the watersheds.
9. Find the length of the channel in feet.
10. Find the drainage areas in acres.
11. Display the area of the watershed and length of the channel appropriately.
12. Insert an appropriate layout from one of the template files.
13. Set the viewport scale to 1:1000.
14. Set the drawing units to ENGINEERING.
15. Update the blocks.

ICA Submission
1. Show the drawing in class (on or before the due date) to the instructor or TA.
2. Submit the printout.

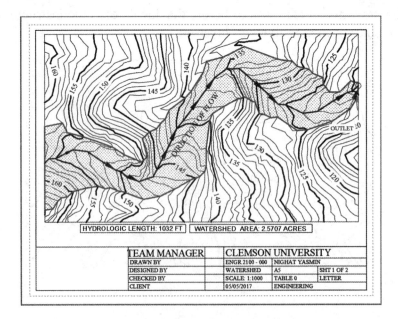

21.16.   Floodplain Delineation

Objectives

- Learn to delineate the floodplain of a channel.

Hints

- Refer to Chapter 3 and Chapter 13 for details and help.

ICA Description

1. Drawing units: Engineering
2. Download the contour file.
3. The index contours are labeled.
4. Draw the centerline of the channel.
5. Show the direction of the flow in the channel.
6. Mark the gauging stations at a distance of 50' intervals.
7. Display the main channel using the *Offset* command; offset distance is 10'.
8. Display the bankfull using the *Offset* command; offset distance is 20'.
9. Draw the perpendicular lines to the direction of flow.
10. Draw a polyline to delineate the floodplains.
11. Hatch the main channel, bankfull, and the floodplains.
12. Find the length of the channel in feet.
13. Find the floodplain areas in acres.
14. Display the area of the floodplain and length of the channel appropriately.
15. Insert an appropriate layout from one of the template files.
16. Set the viewport scale to 1:1000.
17. Set the drawing units to ENGINEERING.
18. Update the blocks.

ICA Submission

1. Show the drawing in class (on or before the due date) to the instructor or TA.
2. Submit the printout.

21.17.   Road Design: Plan and Profile

Objectives
- Learn to draw a plan and profile of a road.

Hints
- Refer to Chapter 14 for details and help.

ICA Description
1. <u>Drawing units</u>: Engineering
2. Download the contour file from the course management system.
3. Use the layers created in the drawing.
4. Draw the centerline of the road 23'-3" above the lower edge of the contour map.
5. Draw the road plan; the road is 9' wide.
6. Hatch the road plan.
7. Draw and label the grid.
8. Draw the projection lines.
9. Draw the points on the grid.
10. Draw the profile through the points.
11. Hatch the profile.
12. Label the profile.
13. Insert an appropriate layout from one of the template files.
14. Set the scale of the drawing to 1:1000.
15. Set the drawing units to ENGINEERING.
16. Update the blocks.

ICA Submission
1. Show the drawing in class (on or before the due date) to the instructor or TA.
2. Submit the printout.

21.18.   Road Design: Cross-Section

Objectives
- Learn to draw cross-sections of a road.

Hints
- Refer to Chapter 14 for details and help.

ICA Description
1. Open the PnP drawing created in ICA 17 and save it as ICA 18.
2. <u>Drawing units</u>: Engineering
3. Download the contour file.
4. For the given plan of a road, draw and label the stations.
5. At each station, draw the cross-section lines.
6. Mark the point on the cross-section lines.
7. Find the distance (for the points of step 5) from the nearest contours.
8. Find the elevation for the points of step 5 (using the distance of step 6 and elevation from the contour map) by interpolation.
9. Draw the grid for the cross-section.
10. Draw cross-sections.
11. Label the cross-sections.
12. Hatch the cross-sections.
13. Insert an appropriate layout from one of the template files.
14. Set the scale of the drawing to 1/16" = 1'-0".
15. Set the drawing units to ENGINEERING.
16. Update the blocks.

ICA Submission
1. Show the drawing in class (on or before the due date) to the instructor or TA.
2. Submit the printout.

21.19.   Road Design: Earthwork

Objectives
- Learn to delineate the cut and fill boundaries

Hints
- Refer to Chapter 15 for details and help.

ICA Description
1. Open the PnP drawing created in ICA 18 and save it as ICA 19.
2. Draw the proposed profile. Refer to the textbook for details.
3. Delineate the earthwork.
   a. Draw vertical lines between two profiles.
   b. Delineate cut and fill on the lower side of the road
   c. Extend the projection lines to the other edge of the road.
   d. Repeat the delineation process for the other edge of the road.
   e. Hatch and label the cut and fill.
4. Insert an appropriate layout from one of the template files.
5. Set the scale of the viewport of the drawing as 1:400.
6. Set the drawing units to ENGINEERING.
7. Update the blocks.

ICA Submission
1. Show the drawing in class (on or before the due date) to the instructor or TA.
2. Submit the printout.

21.20. Floor plan

Objectives
- Learn to draw a floor plan of a residential building

Hints
- Refer to Chapter 16 for details and help.

ICA Description
1. Drawing units: Architectural:
2. Open your "*My_acad_Landscape*" template file.
3. Create an entry "1:108" in the scale list.
   a. Set the drawing scale to 1:108.
   b. Set the drawing units to ARCHITECTURAL.
4. Update the Title block.
5. If necessary, create a new layer at each step.
6. Assume a reasonable value for a missing dimension.
7. Now draw the floor plan shown in Figure 16-12 of the textbook.
8. Do not add dimension.
9. Set the scale appropriately.
10. Update the blocks.

ICA Submission
1. Show the drawing in class (on or before the due date) to the instructor or TA.
2. Submit the printout.

21.21.   Floor plan (Cont.)

Objectives
- Learn to draw a floor plan of a residential building

Hints
- Refer to Chapter 16 for details and help.

ICA Description
1. Open the floor plan drawing created in ICA 20 and save it as ICA 21, and update to the floor plan shown in Figure 16-17 and Figure 16-20 of the textbook. That is, add doors and windows to the floor plan.
2. If necessary, create a new layer at each step.
3. Assume a reasonable value for a missing dimension.
4. Do not add dimension.
5. Set the scale appropriately.
6. Update the blocks.

ICA Submission
1. Show the drawing in class (on or before the due date) to the instructor or TA.
2. Submit the printout.

21.22.   Floor plan (Cont.)

Objectives
- Learn to draw a floor plan of a residential building

Hints
- Refer to Chapter 16 for details and help.

ICA Description
1. Open the floor plan drawing created in ICA 21 and save it as ICA 22.
2. If necessary, create a new layer at each step.
3. Assume a reasonable value for a missing dimension.
4. Complete the floor plan (Figure 16-27 of the textbook).
   a. Add the kitchen and bathroom fixtures.
   b. Hatch the kitchen and bathroom.
   c. Add the roofline.
   d. Add the front porch.
   e. Hatch the walls
5. Set the scale appropriately.
6. Update the blocks.

ICA Submission
1. Show the drawing in class (on or before the due date) to the instructor or TA.
2. Submit the printout.

21.23.   Dimensions (Architectural drawing)

Objectives
- Learn to add the dimensions to the floor plan.

Hints
- Refer to Chapter 16 for details and help.

ICA Description
1. Drawing units: Architectural
2. Open the floor plan drawing created in ICA 22 and save it as ICA 23.
3. Create the layers, as necessary.
4. Add dimensions to the floorplan; schedules are part of the dimensions.

ICA Submission
1. Submit the following four prints.
2. Set the scale appropriately.
3. Update the blocks.
   a. Floor plan with the dimensions, labels and room sizes Scale: 1:148.
   b. Dimensioned and labeled MBR, Scale: 1:40.
   c. Dimensioned and labeled Kitchen, Scale: 1:40.
   d. Doors' and windows' schedule, any scale is acceptable.

DOOR SCHEDULE				
DOOR	*SIZE*	*QUANTITY*	*DESCRIPTION*	*LOCATION*
D1	2'-6" x 7'-0"	3	INTERIOR, SINGLE PANEL	WIC, MBTHR, BTHR I
D2	2'-8" x 7'-0"	4	INTERIOR, SINGLE PANEL	MBDR, BDR I, BDR II, GRG
D3	4'-0" x 7'-0"	1	EXTERIOR, DOUBLE PANEL	FOYER
D4	4'-0" x 7'-0"	1	INTERIOR, DOUBLE PANEL	LIVING ROOM
D5	3"-6" x 7'-0"	1	ACCORDION	PANTRY
D6	6'-0" x 7'-0"	1	FOLDING, DOUBLE PANEL FOUR LEAVES	MECHANICAL
D7	9'-0" x 7'-0"	1	FOLDING, TRIPLE PANEL SIX LEAVES	LAUNDRY
D8	10'-0" x 8'-0"	1	OVERHEAD	GRG
LEGEND: WIC: WALK IN CLOSET; M: MASTER; BTHR: BATH ROOM; BDR: BEDROOM; GRG: GARAGE				

21.24.   Roof Plan

Objectives
- Learn to develop a roof plan for the given floor plan.

Hints
- Refer to Chapter 17 for details and help.

ICA Description
1. Drawing units: Architectural
2. Create the layers as necessary.
3. Open the floor plan drawing created in ICA 23 and save it as ICA 24.
4. Create the roof plan shown in Figure 17-4b, Figure 17-4c, and Figure 17-4d of the textbook.
5. Set the scale to 1:124.
6. Update the blocks.

ICA Submission
1. Submit the print of the roof plan.

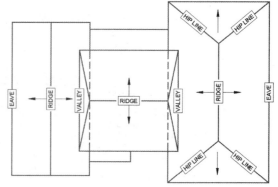

21.25.   Front Elevation

Objectives
- Learn to insert a block from the *Design Center*.
- Learn to develop front elevation for the given floor and roof plans.

Hints
- Refer to Chapter 17 for details and help.

ICA Description
1. Drawing units: Architectural:
2. Create the layers, as necessary.
3. Open the drawing created in ICA 24 and save it as ICA 25 (both the floor plan and roof plan in the same file).
4. Create the front elevation shown in Figure 17-15 of the textbook.
5. Do not add dimension.
6. Landscaping is optional
7. Set the scale to 1:124.
8. Update the blocks.

ICA Submission
1. Submit the print of the front elevation.

TEAM MANAGER	CLEMSON UNIVERSITY		
DRAWN BY	ENGR 2100 - 000	NIGHAT YASMIN	
DESIGNED BY	FRONT ELEV	A6	SHT 1 OF 1
CHECKED BY	SCALE: 1:124	TABLE 0	LETTER
CLIENT	05/05/2017	ARCHITECTURAL	

21.26.   Left Elevation

Objectives
- Learn to insert blocks from the *Design Center*.
- Learn to develop a front elevation for the given floor and roof plans.

Hints
- Refer to Chapter 17 for details and help.

ICA Description
1. <u>Drawing units</u>: Architectural
2. Create the layers, as necessary.
3. Open the drawing created in ICA 25 and save it as ICA 26 (the floor plan, roof plan, and front elevation in the same file).
4. Create the front elevation shown in Figure 17-29 and Figure 17-30 of the textbook.
5. Do not add dimensions.
6. Landscaping is optional.
7. Set the scale (Figure 17-29 -- 1:148 and Figure 17-30 -- 1:240).
8. Update the blocks.

ICA Submission
1. Submit the print of the left elevation.
2. Submit the print of the front plan and front and left elevations.

21.27.   Site Plan

Objectives
- Learn to develop a site plan (Textbook: Figure 18-16)

Hints
- Refer to Chapter 17 for details and help

ICA Description
1. Drawing units: Engineering: Draw the site plan shown in Figure 18-16 of the textbook.
2. Add the labels.
3. Add the dimensions.

ICA Submission
1. Submit the print of the site plan, Figure 18-5, Figure 18-6, and Figure 18-16 at the Scale: 1:800.

TEAM MANAGER		CLEMSON UNIVERSITY		
DRAWN BY		ENGR 2100 - 000	NIGHAT YASMIN	
DESIGNED BY		SITEPLAN	A8	SHT 1 OF 1
CHECKED BY		SCL: 1/64" = 1'-0"	TABLE 0	LETTER
CLIENT		05/05/2017	ENGINEERING	

Notes:

22. Homework Drawings

22.1.   Grid-1 (Units: Inches)

22.2.   Grid -2 (Units: Millimeters)

22.3. Light Signal (Units: Inches)

ABSOLUTE COORDINATES (INCHES)			
A	(0, 0)	I	(4.5, 9.5)
B	(0, 30)	J	(7.5, 12.5)
C	(22, 5)	K	(7.5, 20.5)
D	(22, 29)	L	(4.5, 17.5)
E	(6, 20)	M	(14.5, 11.5)
F	(16, 22)	N	(17.5, 14.5)
G	(6, 19)	O	(17.5, 22.5)
H	(16, 21)	P	(14.5, 19.5)
CIRCLES (INCHES)			
DIAMETER = 2.0			
1	(6, 17.5)	4	(16, 19.5)
2	(6, 15.0)	5	(16, 17.0)
3	(6, 12.5)	6	(16, 14.5)

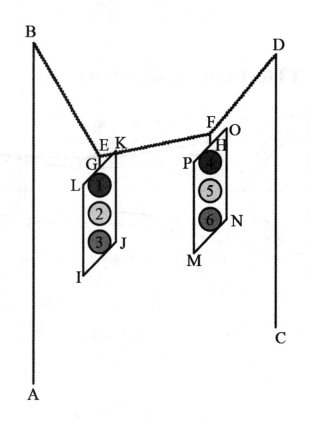

22.4.   Plate with holes (Units: Inches)

22.5.   Circle-TTR (Units: Millimeters)

22.6.   Pier (Units: Millimeters)

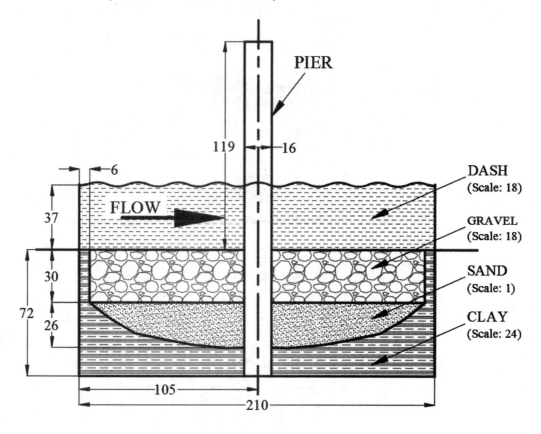

22.7.   Simple shape (Units: Inches)

22.8.   Pipe Cutter (Units: Millimeters)

22.9.   Rectangular Array (Units: Inches)

22.10.   Zoom Polar Array (Units: Inches)

22.11.   Mirror, Copy, and Scale (Units: Inches)

1. Use the TTR option of the *Circle* (TTR), *Mirror, Copy,* and *Scale* commands to create the objects shown in Figure 22-11.
    a. Save the drawing.
    b. Do not add dimensions or center lines of the circle.
    c. The smaller object is 60% of the bigger object.
    d. Show the complete drawing on one screen.

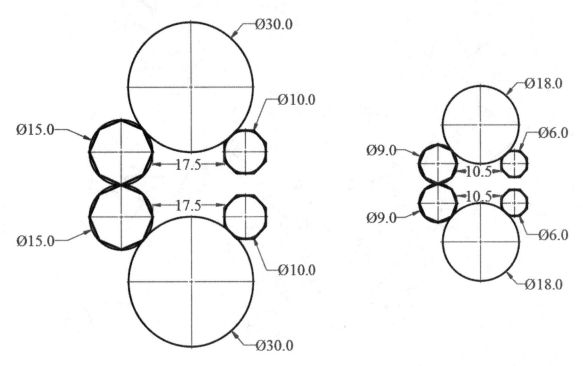

Figure 22-11

Step-by-Step by instructions for Figure 22-11
1. Open an *acad* template file.
2. Draw the circles (ϕ is the symbol of 'diameter'), Figure 22-11a.

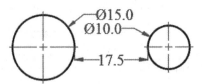

Figure 22-11a

3. Draw the bigger circles (diameter = 30) using the TTR option of the circle command, Figure 22-11b.
4. Draw the polygons, Figure 22-11c. (15-inch circle: *Inscribed* option and 10-inch circle: *Circumscribed* option), Figure 22-11c.

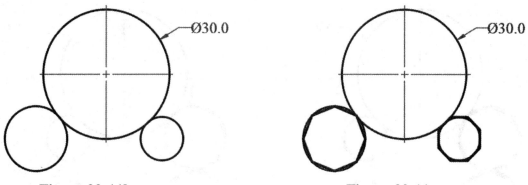

Figure 22-11b   **Figure 22-11c**

5. (i) Turn *On* the ORTHO option. (ii) Activate the *Mirror* command. (iii) Use the lower quadrant of the circle of diameter = 15 as the basc point and complete the *Mirror* command, Figure 22-11d.

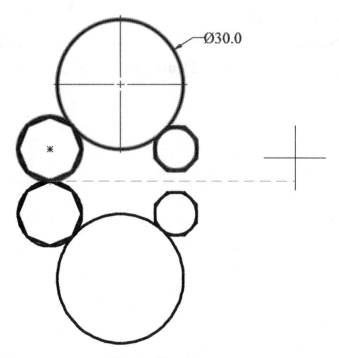

Figure 22-11d

6. Use the *Copy* command to create the second object, Figure 22-11e.
7. Scale the object: (i) Activate the *Scale* command, (ii) select the copy created in step 6, (iii) select the center of one of the large circles as the base point, (iv) for the scale factor, type the value 0.60, and (v) press the *Enter* key, Figure 22-11.

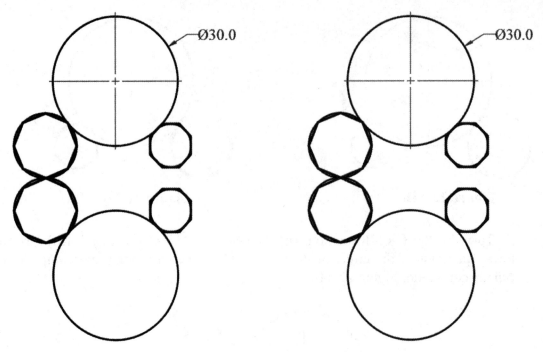

Figure 22-11e

22.12.   Spiral of Archimedes (Units: Millimeters)

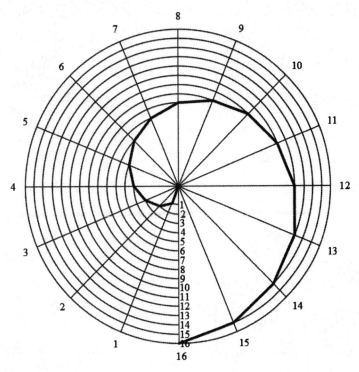

Figure 22-12

Step-by-step instructions for the spiral of Archimedes

1. Draw a circle of the given diameter, Figure 22-12a.

Figure 22-12a

2. Create 16 concentric circles with offset distance = 20mm, Figure 22-12b.
3. Draw a straight line starting at the center of the circles and terminating at the right quadrant of the outermost circle, Figure 22-12c.
4. Create 16 straight lines using *Arraypolar* command, Figure 22-12d.
5. Label the lines created in step 4 as shown in Figure 22-12.
6. Figure 22-12e: (i) Activate the polyline command. (ii) Click at the center of the circle. (iii) Click at the intersection of the first circle and the first line. (iv) Click at the intersection of the second circle and second line. (v) Repeat the process for the remaining circles and lines.
7. The Figure 22-12f shows the spiral of Archimedes.
8. Finally, trim the part of the circles as shown in Figure 22-12.

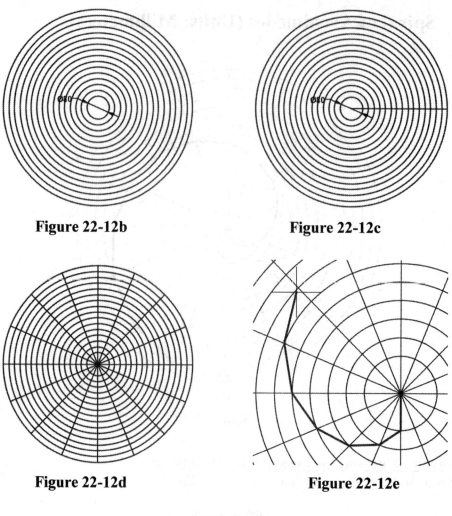

Figure 22-12b   Figure 22-12c

Figure 22-12d   Figure 22-12e

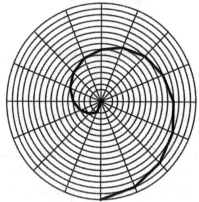

Figure 22-11f

22.13.   Elevator system (Units: Millimeters)

Figure 22-13

Step-by-step instructions for the elevator

First sheave

1. Draw the concentric circles of the given dimensions, Figure 22-13-1.

Figure 22-13-1

2. Draw a line of an arbitrary length starting at the top quadrant, Figure 22-13-2a.
3. Use the *Offset* command to create one line on either side, Figure 22-13-2b.

| **Figure 22-13-2a** | **Figure 22-13-2b** |

4. Use the extend command to extend the lines drawn in step 3, Figure 22-13-3.

Figure 22-13-3

5. Delete the line drawn in step 2, Figure 22-13-4a.
6. Use the trim command to trim the (two parallel) lines to create the desired shape, Figure 22-13-4b.
7. Use the *Arraypolar* command to create the polar array, Figure 22-13-4c.
8. Use the trim command to trim the part of the circle (diameter 90.0) between the two parallel lines to create the desired shape, Figure 22-13-4d

Figure 22-13-4a   **Figure 22-13-4b**   **Figure 22-13-4c**   **Figure 22-13-4d**

Cable
1. Draw the cable by drawing a line of length 150.0 units starting at the right quadrant, Figure 22-13-5a.
2. Change the linetype of the line drawn in the above step to the "Zig-Zag," Figure 22-13-5b.

3. Change the Linetype scale (using the properties palette) of the line to 0.1, Figure 22-13-5c.
4. Use the *Copy* command to create the copy of the modified line at the left quadrant, Figure 22-13-5d.

Figure 22-13-5a   **Figure 22-13-5b**   **Figure 22-13-5c**   **Figure 22-13-5d**

Second sheave

1. Use the Mirror command to create the mirror image (second sheave), Figure 22-13.6.

Figure 22-13-6   **Figure 22-13-7a**

Elevator

1. Draw front half of the elevator by drawing the lines, Figure 22-13-7a and Figure 22-13-7b.
2. Use the *Mirror* command to complete the elevator, Figure 22-13-7c.
3. Use the *Trim* command to remove the part of the cable from the central part of the elevator, Figure 22-13-7d.

Figure 22-13-7b   **Figure 22-13-7c**   **Figure 22-13-7d**

Counter weight

1. Draw a small square by drawing the lines, Figure 22-13-8a.
2. Use the array command to create the rectangular array, Figure 22-13-8b.

Figure 22-13-8a   **Figure 22-13-8b**

Complete system

1. The complete system is shown in Figure 22-13.

22.14. Ferris wheel (Units: Millimeters)

Figure 22-14

Wheel

1. Draw the concentric circles of the given dimensions, Figure 22-14-1.

Figure 21-14-1

Spoke

1. Draw a straight line originating at the center of the circles and terminating at the right quadrant of the outermost circle, Figure 22-14.
2. Draw a 0.34mm long horizontal line originating at the intersection of the horizontal line drawn in step 1 and the 20mm diameter circle, Figure 22-14-2a.
3. Draw a vertical line originating at the left end of the horizontal line drawn in step 2 and terminating at the 20mm diameter circle, Figure 22-14-2a. Label the intersection of the vertical line and the circle as A.

Figure 22-14-2a

4. Draw a straight line originating at point A and terminating beyond the 200mm diameter circle, Figure 22-14-2b.

Figure 22-14-2b

5. Trim the line drawn in step 4 with respect to the outer most circle, Figure 22-14-2c.
6. Use the *Mirror* command to create a line below the horizontal line, Figure 22-14-2c.

Figure 22-14-2c

7. Use the *ArrayPolar* command to complete the spokes, Figure 22-14-2c.

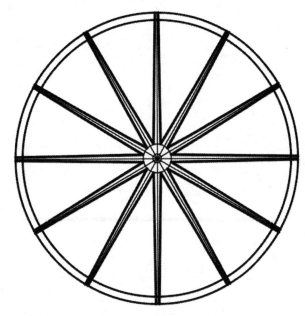

Figure 22-14-2d

Seats
1. Draw a seat of the given dimensions on the vertical spoke, Figure 22-14-3.
2. Use the *ArrayPolar* command to complete the seats, Figure 22-14.

Figure 22-14-3

3. The complete system is shown in Figure 22-14.

Notes:

23. Bibliography

Edward Allen and Joseph Iano, *"Fundamental of Building Construction: materials and methods,"* John Wiley and Sons, Inc, 4th ed., 2004.

James Ambrose, *"Building Construction and Design,"* Van Nostrand Reinhold, 1992.

AutoCAD 2008, Help Documentations.

AutoCAD 2010, Help Documentations.

Gerald Baker, *"Civil Drafting for the Engineering Technician,"* Thomson Delmar Learning, 2006.

Gary R. Bertoline and Eric N. Wiebe, *"Fundamentals of Graphics Communication,"* McGrawHill, 5th ed., 2005.

James D. Bethune, *"Engineering Graphics with AutoCAD 2006,"* Prentice Hall, Pearson Education, 6th ed., 2006.

Wilfried Brutsaert, *"Hydrology: An Introduction,"* Cambridge University Press, 2005.

David A. Chin, *"Water Resources Engineering,"* Prentice Hall, 2nd ed., 1988.

Ven Te Chow, David R. Maidment, and Larry W. Mays, *"Applied Hydrology,"* McGraw-Hill Book Company, 3rd ed., 1988.

Mackenzie L. Davis and David A. Cornwell, *"Introduction to Environmental Engineering,"* McGraw-Hill, 3rd ed., 1998.

Raymond E. Davis, Francis S. Foote, and Joe W. Kelley, *"Surveying: Theory and Practice,"* McGraw-Hill Inc., 5th ed., 1966.

Raymond E. Davis and Joe. W. Kelley, *"Elementary Plane Surveying,"* McGraw-Hill Book Company, 4th ed., 1967.

James H. Earle, *"Fundamentals of Graphics Communication,"* Prentice Hall, Pearson Education, 6th ed., 2002.

Stephen V. Estopinal, *"A Guide to Understanding Land Survey,"* John Wiley and Sons, Inc, 2nd ed., 1993.

David Frey, "*AutoCAD 2002,*" SYBEX, 2002.

Nicholas J. Garber and Lester A. Hoel, "*Traffic and Highway Engineering,*" University of Virginia, Cengage Learning, Toronto, Canada, 4th ed., 2009.

Frederick E. Giesecke, Alva Mitchell, Henry C. Spencer, Ivan L. Hill, and John T. Dygdon, "*Technical Drawing,*" Macmillan Publishing Company and Collier, 8th ed., 1986.

Frederick E. Giesecke, Alva Mitchell, Henry C. Spencer, Ivan L. Hill, John T. Dygdon, and Shawna Lockhart "*Technical Drawing,*" Published by Pearson – Prentice Hall , 13th ed., 2009.

David L. Goetsch, "Structural, Civil, and Pipe Drafting for CAD Technicians," Thomson Delmar Learning, 2003.

David L. Goetsch, "*Technical Drawing,*" Macmillian Publishing Company, 8th ed., 2003.

Randolph P. Hoelscher and Clifford H. Springer, "*Engineering Drawing and Geometry,*" John Wiley & Sons, INC. New York, 1955.

William J. Hornung, "*Architectural Drafting,*" Prentice Hall, 3rd ed., 1960.

Mark Huth, "*Basic Principles for Construction,*" Thomson Delmar Learning, 2004.

Barry F. Kavanagh, "*Surveying Principles and Applications,*" McGraw Hill Inc., Prentice Hall, 6nd ed., 2003.

Philip Kissam, "*Surveying for Civil Engineers,*" McGraw Hill Inc., 2nd ed., 1981.

Philip Kissam and Jerry A. Nathanson, "*Surveying Practice,*" McGraw Hill Inc., 4nd ed., 1987.

A. S. Levens, "*Graphics in Engineering and Science,*" John Wiley & Sons, INC. New York, 2nd Printing, 1957.

Warren J. Luzadder, "*Fundamental of Engineering Drawing for Design, Communication, and Numerical Control,*" Prentice Hall, 6rd ed., 1971.

David A. Madsen and Terence M. Shumaker, "*Civil Drafting Technology,*" Prentice Hall, 3rd ed., 1998.

David A. Madsen and Terence M. Shumaker, "*Civil Drafting Technology,*" Prentice Hall, 6th ed., 2007.

Jack C. McCormac, "*Surveying Fundamentals,*" Prentice Hall, 2nd ed., 1991.

Jack C. McCormac, *"Surveying,"* Prentice Hall, 4nd ed., 1991.

Richard H. McCuen, *"Hydrologic Analysis and Design,"* Prentice Hall, 3rd ed., 2004.

John G. McEntyre, *"Land Survey System,"* John Wiley and Sons, Inc, 1978

Edward J. Muller, James G. Fausett, and Philip A. Grau III, *"Architectural Drawing and Light construction,"* Prentice Hall, 6th ed., 2002.

Jerry A. Nathanson and Philip Kissam, *"Surveying Practice,"* McGraw-Hill Book Company, 4th ed., 1988.

Ralph W. Liebing and Mimi Ford Paul, *"Architectural Working Drawings,"* John Wiley and Sons, 2nd ed., 1983.

William J. O'Connell, *"Graphic Communications in Architecture,"* Stripes Publishing Company, 1972.

Dave Rosgen, *"Applied River Morpohology,"* Wildland Hydrology, Pagosa Springs, Colorodo, 1996.

Harry Rubey, George Edward, and Marion Wesley Todd, *"Engineering Surveys: Elementary and Applied,"* The Macmillan Company, 2nd ed., 1950.

George K. Stegman and Harry J. Stegman, *"Architectural Drafting,"* American Technical Society, 2nd ed., 1974.

Warren Viessman, Jr. and Gary L. Lewis, *"Introduction to Hydrology,"* Prentice Hall, 5th ed., 2003.

Harvey W. Waffle, *"Architectural Drawing,"* The Bruce Publishing Company, Revised edition, 1962.

Ernest R. Weidhaas, *"Architectural Drafting and Design,"* Allyn and Bacon, 6th ed., 1989.

"Webster's New Collegiate Dictionary," G. & S. Merriam Co., Publishers, Springfield. MASS, U.S.A.

<u>Notes:</u>

24. Index

U

V

W

Z